PENGUIN BOOKS

THE WESTERN

George N. Fenin was born in Russia in 1916, fled to Turkey with his family at the time of the Revolution, and eventually emigrated to Italy. He began writing about films in 1937, and in 1939 he earned his doctorate in law at the University of Naples. During the war he fought with Italian patriots against Nazi and Fascist troops, and he was subsequently awarded the War Merit Cross by the Italian government. Since 1948 he has lived in the United States, where, owing to his fluency in five languages, he has served as cultural correspondent for Italian, French, Spanish, and Central European publications.

William K. Everson was born in England in 1929. During World War II he cut short his education to enter the film industry, becoming, at the age of fourteen, Publicity Director of Renown Pictures Corporation. After service with the British army in Germany, he worked as Publicity Manager for Monseigneur News Theatres, in London, and from 1951 to 1955 as Foreign Publicity Manager of Allied Artists Pictures in New York. Since then he has continued to live in the United States, teaching courses in cinema and frequently contributing articles and reviews to film journals.

Revised Edition

George N. Fenin and

William K. Everson

The Western

from silents to the seventies

Penguin Books

Penguin Books Ltd, Harmondsworth,
Middlesex, England
Penguin Books, 625 Madison Avenue,
New York, New York 10022, U.S.A.
Penguin Books Australia Ltd, Ringwood,
Victoria, Australia
Penguin Books Canada Ltd, 2801 John Street,
Markham, Ontario, Canada L3R 1B4
Penguin Books (N.Z.) Ltd, 182–190 Wairau Road,
Auckland 10, New Zealand

First published in the United States of America
by The Orion Press 1962
Revised edition published by Grossman Publishers 1973
Published in Penguin Books 1977

LIBRARY OF CONGRESS CATALOGING IN PUBLICATION DATA
Fenin, George N.
  The Western, from silents to the seventies.
  Reprint of the 1973 ed. published by Grossman,
New York.
  Includes index.
  1. Western films—History and criticism.
I. Everson, William K., joint author.   II. Title.
[PN1995.9.w4f4 1977]   791.43′5   76-54996
ISBN 0 14 00.4416 7 (pbk.)

Printed in the United States of America
by Halliday Lithograph, West Hanover, Massachusetts
Set in Baskerville

Foreword

For many years the Western film has been strangely and unfairly neglected. Although many articles and essays have appeared in general and specialized periodicals all over the world, substantially organic books dealing exclusively with the Western are very rare indeed. And of all this material, the majority has been disguised publicity, or at best essays which refused to take the Western seriously, the work of writers who knew little or nothing of Westerns, writers who glibly referred to the cliché of the hero always kissing his horse instead of the girl, leaving it at that.

There have been innumerable histories of the cinema, more specialized histories dealing with the cinema in various countries, and books devoted to individual directors, producers, executives, and stars. But if the general history of the movies has been told, only three books of any stature have been devoted specifically to the Western, all of foreign origin: *Il Film Western,* by Italian critic Antonio Chiattone; *Il Western Maggiorenne,* a symposium of essays by various Italian critics, edited by Tullio Kezich; and *Le Western,* by French critic Jean-Louis Rieupeyrout. Of these, the first is a serious but necessarily incomplete and at times rather arbitrary study of the aesthetics of the Western; the second is most useful as a ground-breaking instrument for a systematic treatise, although it is necessarily fragmentary as a symposium; and the third is a less than thorough attempt to both narrate the historical background of the West and to describe the growth of the Western film, the coverage of this second aspect being characterized by numerous errors of a nature almost unavoidable when one is working so far from the bulk of the source material.

We felt, therefore, that there was not only room, but a need, for a detailed history of the Western, a book which would represent not only a useful study of the industrial and aesthetic growth of a popular movie genre, but a critical analysis of it, as well. For the most part, we have adopted a strictly chronological approach, but, in the parlance of the film, it has sometimes been necessary to use "flash-forwards and cut-backs" and even a form of *montage,* in order to follow a thesis through to its logical conclusion.

We hope that our efforts may clarify past misunderstandings and mis-conceptions regarding the Western film, contributing at the same time to a fuller appreciation of the real essence of what is considered by many to be the most representative form of the American cinema.

New York, 1962

George N. Fenin
William K. Everson

Foreword to the Second Edition

Since the first publication of this book a decade ago, the Western has been the subject of several new books. Of particular importance are *La Grande Aventure du Western* (Paris, 1964) by French critic Jean-Louis Rieupeyrout, *Le Western* by AA.VV. (Paris, 1966), a *John Ford* by American critic and director Peter Bogdanovich (London, 1967) and another by French critic Philippe Haudiquet (Paris, 1966). A remarkable contribution to the esthetics in the genre is represented indeed by *Western—Problemi di Tipologia Narrativa* (University of Parma, 1970) by Italian writer and critic Roberto Campari. The new material in this edition—chapters 19 and 20— is my own work, not that of Mr. Everson, and any faults in it are, of course, mine.

I earnestly hope that the growing enthusiasm of young scholars toward the Western will materialize in the near future, with even more substantial contributions, thus linking the old and the new, the tradition with the controversy, for the sake of the only genuinely American trend in cinema.

Emerson, New Jersey, 1973

George N. Fenin

TO WILLIAM S. HART

the finest Western star and director of them all, and the best friend the West ever had, this book is reverently and sincerely dedicated.

ACKNOWLEDGMENTS

The authors wish to thank Mr. Jonas Mekas of Film Culture *(New York) for his permission to reprint material by Mr. Fenin published in that magazine, Mr. F. Maurice Speed of* The Western Film Annual *(London) and Mr. Henry Hart of* Films in Review *(New York) for their permission to reprint material by Mr. Everson which appeared in those publications between 1951 and 1957, and also Mr. John Adams of the Museum of Modern Art (New York) and Mr. James Card of the George Eastman House (Rochester) for their co-operation in screening prints of certain rare Westerns in order that re-evaluations might be made. Further grateful acknowledgment is made to Major George J. Mitchell, United States Army, for his valuable assistance, particularly in the research on the life and career of William S. Hart. A sincere vote of thanks to Italian theoretician Guido Aristarco and critics Giovanni Grazzini and Morando Morandini for their suggestions on the production of the Italian Westerns, and to Japanese critic Tadao Sato for his information and assistance on the Japanese Westerns. George Geltzer's* Index to American Silent Serials (1913–1930) *was most helpful, and we are grateful to him.*

Contents

Illustrations

The illustrations for this volume have been chosen for both documentary and decorative purposes. A list of captioned, documentary illustrations follows.

xvii

ILLUSTRATIONS

"I don't know how much the Western film means to Europe; but to this country it means the very essence of national life. I am referring now to the later frontier—the frontier of the range and the mining camp, with all its youthful follies and heartbreaks and braveries that we know and love best. It is but a generation or so since virtually all this country was frontier. Consequently its spirit is bound up in American citizenship."

William S. Hart, 1916

the Western

"I've labored long and hard for bread
For honor and for riches
But on my corns too long you've tred
You fine-haired sons of bitches . . ."

BLACK BART, THE PO-8
(alias for Charles E. Bolton, poet
and outlaw, who may have died
in Nevada with his boots on.)

Western history and

the Hollywood version

1

Birth of a state of mind

During the American Revolution, the no man's land that lay between the American regular forces in the North and the New York encampment of the British in the South was known as neutral ground. It was devastated country in which two opposing partisan groups sought for and battled each other in bloody skirmishes. The guerrillas fighting for Washington's cause were called "skinners." Those operating with the support of King George III's British dragoons and Hessian mercenaries were known as "cowboys," this name deriving from the English farm lads who cared for the cattle in the Surrey and Essex countrysides.

It was, in fact, not until several decades after the establishment of the Colonies' independence that the cowboy became an American. In a few years, he achieved the required status of maturity, graduated with honor into folklore and legend, and stood from then on as a living symbol of the Wild West, of the truly original American frontier period. The transformation in the meaning of the word cowboy within a geographical cycle was complete. From the bucolic atmosphere of the British farms to the horrors of partisan warfare in the American East to the conquest of untamed land in the West, the term *cowboy* finally came to synthetize the *Grandeur et Servitude* of one of the most amazing events in history. For the swiftness and proportion of the "Westward Ho!" march of colonization can only be matched by the Russian conquest of Siberia, begun by the great Yermak in 1579 and highlighted in 1638 by the founding of Okhotsk, thus bringing the Slavs to the shores of the Pacific, after they had crossed an entire continent.

The American trek west to the Pacific was the fundamental background for the rise of the cowboy, a background which began to materialize in the fifty years following 1770. When the great Anglo-Saxon immigration of substantially Scotch and Welsh descent stopped, there came German political refugees, discontented Englishmen, starving Irish and Italians, adventurous Russians and Poles, all of whom looked to the new land with hope. They were the advance patrols, the battalions and, later on, the brigades of an international army of thirty-five million immigrants that was to land on the American shore in the nineteenth century, filling the eastern cities deserted by those who had migrated to virgin lands, or simply following others in the wake of the march to the West.

Thus, in an incredibly short time, the colonists and farmers of the Oregon and Overland Trails learned the cattle trade from the Mexican *vaqueros* in California, and the Santa Fe *routiers* tasted the acrid and exciting sense of competition with the Russians and the British in their development of the Fur Trade Empire. With the subsequent discovery of gold, farmers and merchants became adventurers; with the advance of railroads, they became buffalo hunters; with the establishment of property (land and cattle) they wore guns and fought on opposite sides of the barbed-wire fence—the era's symbol of revolutionary changes.

The shrinkage of the wide-open spaces brought about the rapid and progressive destruction of what, with wistful euphemism, the United States government had labeled the "Permanent Indian Frontier," and in a few years the American Indian and the American bison were forced to relinquish their prairies. Shortly after the turn of the nineteenth century, this explosive expansion came to a halt. Public opinion had not forgotten, indeed, the 1871 speech of Carl Schurz, outlining the dangers of prolonged territorial expansion, warning that the United States could extend its institutions on rigid isothermic lines only, and that, should the penetration reach the tropics, those same institutions would wither and disintegrate, causing also the ultimate ruin of the Union.

This expansion had already created a substantial amount of hostility south of the Rio Grande. Lucas Alamán, the Mexican patriarch of Latin America's great concern over foreign imperialism, has passionately analyzed the great era of North American territorial expansion.

"The United States of the North in less than fifty years have succeeded in making themselves masters of extensive colonies belonging to various European powers,

The glory of virgin forests. A scene from Hiawatha *(1952).*

and of districts, still more extensive, formerly in the possession of Indian tribes which have disappeared from the face of the earth; proceeding in these transactions not with the noisy pomp of conquest, but with such silence, such constancy, and such uniformity, that they have always succeeded in accomplishing their goals. Instead of armies, battles, and invasions, which raise such an uproar, and generally prove abortive, they use means which, considered separately, seem slow, ineffectual, and sometimes palpably absurd, but which unite, and in the course of time, are certain and irresistible.

They commence by introducing themselves into the territory which they covet, upon the pretense of commercial negotiations, or of the establishment of foreign colonies with or without the assent of the government to which the territory belongs. These colonies grow, multiply, become the predominant party in the population and, as soon as a support is found in this manner, they begin to set up rights which are impossible to sustain in a serious discussion, and to bring forward ridiculous pretensions founded upon historical facts which are admitted by no one.

Their machinations in the country they wish to acquire are then brought to light by the appearance of pioneers, some of whom settle on the soil, alleging that their presence does not effect the question of the right of sovereignty or possession of the land. These men excite, by degrees, movements which disturb the political state of the country in dispute. When things have come to this pass, diplomatic management commences; the inquietude excited in the territory in dispute, the interests of the colonists therein established, the insurrection of adventurers and savages instigated by them, and the pertinacity with which the opinion is set up as to the colonists' right of possession, become the subjects of notes, full of expressions of justice and moderation, until, with the aid of other incidents—never wanting in the course of diplomatic relations—the desired end is attained by concluding an arrangement as onerous for one party as it is advantageous to the other."

But if the Louisiana Purchase, the Seminole War, the $7,200,000 paid to the Czar of All Russias for Alaska were but some of the examples characterizing the conscious development of a political phenomenon, the conquest of the Great Plains and of California, for instance, represented rather the product of a powerfully articulated, but genuinely unconscious—on a political plan—migration. The dynamic imperialism manifested by the pioneers was based on racial arrogance towards the Mexican and Indian natives, and economic realism, but also on a deep idealism. For the pioneers the conquest of the frontier represented the colonization of enormous tracts of land for the establishment of all those free laws, regulations, and moral principles which guide self-qualified men of destiny. This gigantic task kept the pioneers occupied for several decades, thus allowing the dynamic urge for further American penetration to crystallize.

The Rio Grande frontier represented the *ne plus ultra* limit of this penetration, and the principle of existence and development of a civilization on isothermic lines was effectively carried on. Thus the frontier came to an end and tradition began.

The impact of this tradition on successive decades of American life and progress has amply proved the frontier's existence in the hearts and minds of Americans as something much more appealing than a splendid historical period. The frontier is, in fact, the only mythological tissue available to this young nation. Gods and demigods, passions and ideals, the fatality of events, the sadness and glory of death, the struggle of good and evil—all these themes of the Western myth constitute an ideal ground for a liaison and re-elaboration of the Olympian world, a refreshing symbiotic relationship of Hellenic thought and Yankee dynamism.

The cowboy on horseback shapes into the fabulous Centaurus, guardian of a newly acquired legend; the woman—whose presence is biologically sought in the frontier town—becomes a sort of Minerva, dispensing wisdom, often moral principles, warm comfort, and unrelenting excitement and incitement; Marshal Wyatt Earp's exploits come strikingly close to the labors of Hercules, while William Frederick Cody's (Buffalo Bill) and Wild Bill Hickok's struggles with Indians and "badmen" are often recognized as the modern versions of the classic heroes. The massacre of the Seventh Cavalry at Little Big Horn carries the seed of fatality bearing down upon Oedipus, and the "Remember the Alamo!" reminds us of Thermopylae.

Above this epic looms the pathos of the fight between good and evil so dear to Anglo-Saxon hearts, a theme that finds its highest literary expression in Herman Melville's *Moby Dick*. An epoch such as this, representing the joint effort of a great heterogeneous people, sparked with the manifestations of a striking individualism, appealed to both the individualist and the collectivist. The conquest of nature and the law of the gun must have appealed to the first; the collectivist had his work cut out for him in the tremendous amount of organized effort needed to plow the earth, raise cattle, mine, create towns, counties, and cities. A state of mind evolved and it was accepted with enthusiasm in the eastern states. The literature it spawned must indicate this: from the *Western Journal* by Irving, followed by *Astoria, The Adventures of Captain Bonneville, U. S. A.* and *Tour of Prairies* to *Roughing It* by Twain, *The Luck of Roaring Camp* and *The Outcasts of Poker Flat* by Harte, *The Virginian* by Wister, and *Heart of the West* by O. Henry, *The Westerners* by White, *The Big Sky* by Guthrie, *Wyatt Earp* by Lake, *The Oregon Trail* by Parkman, *Crazy Horse* by Sandoz, *The Ox-Bow Incident* by Clark, and many others.

In the course of years, such literature increased continuously, and the names of authors like Ernest Haycox, Luke Short, Max Brand, Will Ermine, Charles W. Webber, Emerson Hough, E. C. Mann and Zane Grey characterize a specific Western narrative in the form of novels, short stories, and essays which did not exert a substantial influence on the entire American culture, but which, nevertheless, gave body and form to a legend. We should also mention Clarence E. Mulford and William Colt MacDonald, above-average writers of standard Western novels, and writers much drawn upon by the movies. Mulford was first used by Tom Mix in the twenties, became more familiar later when his novels were filmed in the Hopalong Cassidy series. W. C. MacDonald's *3 Mesquiteer* Western novels inspired a few one-shot Western films, such as *Powder-smoke Range* (1935) and *Law of the 45's* (1935–6) and later a whole series at Republic Studios from 1937 to 1945. The term *mesquiteer* was obviously derived from the French *mousquetaire;* and *mesquite* is a form of prairie shrubbery.

The American legend was subsequently transformed, from the craftsmanlike effort of the previous writers, into the smoothly organized, slickly presented assembly line product flooding America even today with books by the hundred, magazine stories and novelettes by the thousand. They have become an almost unbearable weight on the intellectual faced in most cases with tons of pulp publications of no value whatsoever. They cannot in any way aid in exactly evaluating the American western epic but the sociologist finds, in the specialized western essays and short stories, an effective ground for the study of their influence on the American public and its mores.

American western literature would have remained confined to the limited domains of folklore and a narrow literary genre or, at best, to the specialized field of history if the birth of motion pictures had not exerted the stupendous verdict of their own possibilities.

This new art, based among other things on movement, found in the Western theme its ideal expression, and made of it the American cinema *par excellence*. In the words of André Bazin, the noted French film critic:

"The history of cinema has known but one other cinema, and this is also historical cinema. . . . As with the conquest of the West, so the Soviet Revolution is a compound of historical events marking the birth of an order and of a civilization. One and the other have given birth to the myths necessary to a confirmation of history; both were also obliged to rediscover the morale, rediscover at their living source, before their mixing or their pollution, the principles of the law which will put order in the chaos, will separate the sky from the earth. But it is possible that the cinema was the only language capable not only of expressing this, but above all of giving it the true aesthetic dimension. Without the cinema, the conquest of the West would have made of the 'Western stories' but one minor literature; and it is not with its painting nor with its best novels that Soviet art has given the world the image of its greatness. That is why the cinema is already the specific art of epic."

At the beginning of the twentieth century, the United States was still a land of opportunity where private enterprise bordered often on unscrupulous and illegal practices, and adventure appealed to hardy individuals. The California Gold Rush and the Great Cattle Depression of 1886–87, among many events, made outlaws and gunfighters of many cowboys; though they were already part of a colorful past, banditry had not disappeared.

On August 29, 1900, a few minutes after 8 P.M., train no. 3 of the Union Pacific Railroad Company, after having passed the station at Tipton, Wyoming, began to slow down as it approached Table Rock. Four men emerged from the darkness, forced the conductor, E. J. Kerrigan, to uncouple the passenger cars while the express and mail cars were pulled a mile distant and subsequently robbed. The thieves were some of the Wild Bunch boys: Butch Cassidy, Deaf Charlie Hanks, Bill Carver, Harvey Logan. The raid netted a little more than five thousand dollars in cash and a few hundred dollars' worth of watch movements, and reconfirmed their fame as "the largest, toughest and most colorful of all Western outlaw gangs . . . the first such aggregation to have an orderly organization," as stated by James D. Horan and Paul Sann in their

Pictorial History of the Wild West. In a special article that appeared three years later, when the Pinkerton detectives had already killed or arrested the majority of the gang's members, the *Denver Daily News* revealed that the Wild Bunch outlaws had caused Governor Wells of Utah to contact the governors of Colorado and Wyoming in order to create a concerted plan of action to combat the menace.

Such exploits vividly aroused popular fantasy, and the traditional sympathy of the American masses for the underdog, fanned by sensational newspaper reports, provided ideal ground for the emergence of the myth of the outlaw. They provided ground, too, for the physical expression of those stark puritanical values implicit in the struggle between good and evil, which have so affected the American unconscious as revealed in the country's folkways and mores. Even if the Koster and Bial Music Hall's first showing of "moving pictures" on April 23, 1896, brought to the American public visions of sea waves breaking upon the shores, as well as some comic vaudeville items, and even if factual events continued to attract attention, the growing demand for theatrical films became hard to dent. This phenomenon, stimulated as well by the urge to contemplate something more realistic and dramatic, materialized ultimately and, after many attempts at cinematic storytelling, in 1903 Edwin S. Porter made his *The Great Train Robbery.* Lewis Jacobs in his *The Rise of the American Film* said the film "has since represented the Bible of the film-makers." Actually this somewhat exaggerates its personal value, but until 1909 it did have a very great deal of influence.

From then on, the Western was a genre of the American cinema. It also was the vehicle through which motion pictures and the public consorted in a remarkable symbiotic relationship. The fact that the motion picture, this "flower and crown of the twentieth century," could express in indisputably effective terms the magnitude of the recent American saga, an essential force still permeating the lives and the philosophy of life of great masses of the people, was accepted with enthusiasm by a public anxious to learn quickly of its pioneer heritage, in order to acquire fundamental principles for its destiny.

Thus, from that year which represented the birth of film Westerns, that year which saw the headlines of the nation's dailies echo the most recent exploit of the Wild Bunch, the film-makers began a long and exciting march, the milestones of which were represented—after an adolescence—by an epic school, the sound era, color, wide screen . . . right up to the present film, a Western very different from the one imagined by Edwin S. Porter. The Western of today seems to be choosing some rather offbeat paths, and the psychological, sophisticated, "adult" tale of the West is proof of this evolution. In these more than fifty years we have seen one of the most amazing cases of a deliberate manipulation of a nation's history in the hands of a powerful group of film-makers.

The drab and grim frontier, with its people struggling for existence as ranchers, farmers and merchants was depicted to movie audiences in an often entirely different fashion. All of the West's mushrooming communities—many of them peaceful and monotonous, heroic only in their dedication to the building of a new empire—became compressed into a stock formula town, the prototypes of Tombstone and Dodge City, with rustlers, desperadoes, and outlaws roaming the streets, or engaged in bloody saloon fights.

The great cattle empire, the gold and silver rushes, and the covered wagon treks were some of the phases of the West's history which the movies implied were a "permanent" part of the Western scene; actually, these phases were all of fairly short duration. Life in the old West was certainly a lawless one in many communities, but the generalized concept of the shooting down of endless villains and ranchers without so much as a second glance at the corpses is very much at odds with fact. A killing was as serious a matter in the West as it was in the East, although admittedly the justice meted out was a less standardized one. The laws of mob and vigilante groups were not inclined to temper justice with mercy and understanding, and in territories where the forces of crime and corruption outweighed those of law and order, an open and acknowledged felony might go unpunished. But regardless of the varying degrees of justice, even taking into account a "kill-or-be-killed" attitude among men who made their living outside the law, the taking of a human life was still not regarded lightly. The Westerns of William S. Hart recognized this principle; there was no casual extermination of badmen in the Hart-Ince pictures and among recent Westerns, Lesley Selander's *Stampede* (1949) was one of very few films which treated killing seriously.

In the glamorization of the outlaw, Hollywood has contradicted itself on many occasions, in addition to contradicting history. In *Badmen's Territory* (1946) the outlaw Sam Bass is played as a villain, in completely evil fashion by fat, swarthy Nestor Paiva. When Universal-International later made *Calamity Jane and Sam Bass* (1949)—inventing a quite fictional romance between the two—Bass was portrayed as the misunderstood hero played by clean-cut Howard Duff.

Reconstruction of historical events was and still is changed to suit the script; sympathetic or unsympathetic portrayals of events are often dependent on the importance of an historical character in a specific script.

In *They Died With Their Boots On* (1941), Errol Flynn plays General Custer, depicted as a brilliant soldier, sympathetic to the Indians, whose command was ruthlessly massacred in a battle brought on by political chicanery. In *Sitting Bull* (1954) the story was told primarily from the Indian viewpoint: Sitting Bull was literally forced into battle by the stupidity and double-dealing of Custer, played in bullheaded fashion by Douglas Kennedy. Custer was an Indian-hater opposed to the efforts of hero Dale Robertson to effect a peace treaty. Another Indian-oriented work, *Chief Crazy Horse* (1955), gave that sachem, instead, the credit for the Little Big Horn battle, putting Sitting Bull in the position of a casual supervisor. The Warner film, *Santa Fe Trail* (1940) showed Custer, a lesser character in the film, graduating from West Point in the accustomed manner. Yet in *They Died With Their Boots On,* in which Custer was the main figure, a film made by the same studio only a year later, the audience saw General Sheridan commissioning Custer before his graduation and dispatching him forthwith to Washington where Union forces, expecting a Confederate attack momentarily, were desperately short of manpower. Here we have a clear-cut example of historical incident being manipulated to suit script requirements.

Historical events apart, neither film presented a very realistic picture of Custer the man. In *Santa Fe Trail,* played by Ronald Reagan, he was a quiet, sincere, and dedicated soldier; as written for Errol Flynn, he became the embodiment of the daredevil soldier, contemptuous of orders,

Douglas Kennedy as one of the later, unsympathetically treated General Custers. From Sitting Bull *(1954).*

more concerned with a fight for its own sake than for its underlying causes. Later, of course, according to this particular script, he became something of an idealist. In actuality, brilliant soldier or not, Custer had a mass of neurotic complexes—an aspect of him that no motion picture has yet presented, although there were good hints of it in the distinctly and deliberately critical and unpleasant Custer portrait presented in *Sitting Bull.*

One wonders now whether or not movie traditions sometimes have a more lasting effect than the authentic traditions they copy. For example, Custer's famed Seventh Cavalry, wiped out at the Little Big Horn, was subsequently reformed as a cavalry unit and retained as a permanent force in the United States Army. The Seventh Cavalry is still in action today and, like Custer himself, it utilizes flamboyant accessories to glamorize a regulation uniform—including cavalry boots, a western-style neckerchief and, among the officers, cavalry sabres. From several first-hand accounts, it seems that these "descendants" of Custer adopt a swaggering behavior more than casually related to, although somewhat enlarged upon, the behavior of the cavalry officers in a John Ford super-Western.

Hollywood's portrayal of Geronimo created the false impression that the Apaches were the most warlike Indians of all. Actually, although savage fighters, they were comparatively few in number, and far less troublesome than many lesser-known tribes. The capture of Geronimo, too, has been fictionalized in diverse ways, especially in the film *Geronimo* (1939), in which he is captured attempting to kill a white

In the modern Western, airplanes, helicopters, and even atomic missiles became standard props. From Roy Rogers' Bells of Coronado (*1950*).

trader in a cavalry encampment. Another Western, *I Killed Geronimo* (1950), had him killed off in a last-reel fist fight. Universal's *Walk the Proud Land* (1956) finally told the true and comparatively straightforward account of how the warrior was induced to surrender. The serious approach of William S. Hart, the singular—although romanticized— interpretation of John Ford, the wholly or partially rigorous renditions of David W. Griffith, Thomas Ince, James Cruze and other film-makers concerning the true atmosphere of the old West are drowned in a sea of distorted, standardized clichés. The American public, in part at least, recognized these clichés for the counterfeits they were. It is this same public, largely the Eastern audience, which has lately indicated its approval and acceptance of a more realistic and historically accurate treatment.

A new cycle has thus emerged in the contemporary cinema. In the past, Hollywood frequently used the Western as a proving ground for directors many of whom later achieved fame in other genres (e.g. Edward Dmytryk, William Wyler) and planned its Western output a.most on the basis of calculated laboratory formula. Now, without new inspiration, Hollywood found itself regarding its perennial bread-and-butter in a new light. The renewed success and popularity of the Western, stimulated by the dumping of literally hundreds of "B" Westerns on television, has led to a gradual revamping of policies, toward a recognition of the need to present the West in more realistic terms. This has taken place in the midst of a competitive situation in which Hollywood has had to produce fewer films, of better quality.

The ultra-streamlined Westerns of Autry and Rogers brought together, in weird fashion, the standard ingredients of the old-time Westerns (chases, cattle stampedes, gunslinging, saloon fights) with contemporary elements (night clubs, radio, television, chorus girls, high-powered cars, jet-rockets, uranium deposits). Even when Autry and Rogers stopped making theatrical Westerns, they often incorporated these innovations— admittedly to a much lesser degree than before—into their television Westerns. And, of course, their late theatrical Westerns do still occasionally play in American theatres and more frequently on television. They are still regularly seen in Europe, always slower to absorb the huge quantities of "B" Westerns. Thus, old and new Westerns are available side by side, to further cloud the already confusing issues.

Today, the main street of Dodge City is a drab and rather unattractive artery, without the slightest resemblance to the picturesque terminal of the western trail. Tombstone jealously preserves its Crystal Palace Saloon, the old headquarters of Wyatt Earp's enemies. Deadwood survives as a little city in South Dakota, earning its money from the gold industry and the exhibition of an assortment of fake Wild Bill Hickok relics, including Wild Bill's "death chair," complete with bullet holes and painted bloodstains. A series of towns tries to perpetuate the tradition of the old West to attract tourist business; Covered Wagon Day, Pioneer's Day, Frontier Days, Old Times are some of the celebrations periodically organized, with a shrewd commercial instinct, in cities and towns like Prescott, Fort Worth, Cheyenne, Dodge City, and Gallup. The last laugh in the adulteration of the Wild West is represented by Las Vegas, a small Mormon center founded in 1855, and maintained by that religious body for more than fifty years as a devout community refusing to consider itself a part of the generally lawless era in which it lived. Today gambling and easy divorce bring masses of Americans to the modern part of the city, and while the old section continues its calm and uneventful existence, the fabulous gambling halls of the new city (where floor shows can afford to pay a well-shaped chorus girl two hundred dollars a week plus, and hire famous show-business entertainers) aim for an ever larger business running into millions of dollars. The Las Vegas "cowboys" today are not the grim and unshaven gunfighters of old, but "plain folk" from all parts of the Union, dressed in gaudy outfits. The Las Vegas cowboys are the products created by Hollywood, and the grotesque masquerade in only one way connects up with the open towns of another time: if Las Vegas is more or less open today, it is because the underworld has really gone underground in respectable clothing.

Ironically, one of the few authentic traditions of the West is displayed annually in—among other cities, of course—New York. That tradition and heritage is the rodeo, once the cowboys' way of letting off steam, of competing among themselves, and of displaying the skills of their trade by riding wild horses and steers, bulldogging cattle, roping, etc. Since the excitement and danger of the rodeo is authentic, and cannot be streamlined (there is no way of informing a wild Brahma bull that he must behave according to the 1973 concepts of 1895 life) the rodeo remains a genuine and thrilling experience. Of course, it has been both commercialized and vulgarized: big name attractions, usually children's idols from television (Roy Rogers, Gene Autry, The Lone Ranger, Rin Tin Tin and others), are brought in as stars, and perform their somewhat tame specialties like songs and roping tricks to the delight of the youngsters, and to the disgust, no doubt, of the seasoned rodeo riders risking their necks for a fraction of the star's salary. The sale of Roy Rogers buttons, cowboy outfits, guns, and other staple star accessories is a lucrative business permeating every aspect of the modern rodeo. But when rider and wild horse are alone in the arena for an unrehearsed contest, in which the animal is often the winner, the commercial gimmicks must take a back seat and the spectator may share the rodeo rider's agony as John Huston's direction of *The Misfits* (1961) demonstrated. This is one unchanging and elementary part of the West that was. It is an aspect that is relatively unknown outside the United States, since the cost of transporting the vast amount of livestock around the world would be prohibitive. In many countries—notably England—permits may not be issued for such exhibitions, on the ground that rodeos violate regulations concerning cruelty shown to animals. This is unfair, for the animals undergo no

Montgomery Clift and Clark Gable roping wild horses in a scene from The Misfits *(1961).*

harsher treatment than they do, or did, in the course of a spring roundup.

It is not surprising to note, therefore, that the alleged "Wild West" shows put on in England by such Western stars as Gene Autry and Tex Ritter have been extremely tame, and with their emphasis on musical and low comedy elements they have represented a grave disappointment to juvenile audiences expecting fast Western action. Australia, on the other hand, with its outdoor heritage and history not dissimilar to America's, does, however, reflect this heritage in its own rodeos, all staged on traditional cowboy lines. The Western being the most American of all cinematic genres and representing—as stated by Italian critic Giulio Cesare Castello—"a common patrimony because among all themes it is perhaps, in its primitiveness, the most universal one," had a mythological, human, social, and dramatic appeal which the subsequent trend towards assembly-line, studio production ignored, with only a few exceptions. But the adulterated "grade B" Western, necessarily shot on location, saved the day for Hollywood, as we shall see.

Ernest Callenbach affirms that "in a sense, therefore, the Westerns provided a link of continuity from the earliest years of the cinema to the later work of the documentary school: in their unassuming simplicity they supplied evidence that the real world could furnish abundant drama for the camera."

The monotonous Hollywood carousel of battles against badmen and Indians continued for many years, a gross distortion of historical fact and the pioneering spirit.[1]

The cataclysm of World War II, the rapid advance in the movies' technology, the appalling world-wide decay in moral and intellectual values, were the concomitant factors in the appearance of a truly remarkable film, which presented the frontier in proper proportion, a film which pioneered the new Western. William Wellman's *The Ox-Bow Incident* (1943) was a successful experiment in social comment, striking out at, in the name of authenticity, the dignity of and America's respect for the agony of a breed of pioneers, the whole false picture which the horse opera had presented to Americans. The frontier as a day-by-day chronicle of grim, gray, dedicated humanity, all its passions realistically exposed, was now seen for the first time. The psychological and social trend, this trend toward the truth at last, was followed in *The Gunfighter* (1950) and *High Noon* (1952), while John Ford attempted a personal interpretation of Custer's Last Stand in *Fort Apache* (1948), although Ford did not refer in every case to history.

[1] It is therefore not surprising to read that in a study conducted in 1942 by the Motion Picture Research Bureau with two thousand respondents in forty-five towns, the percentage reserved to the influence of the Western as a selective criterion for attending the showing of motion pictures in theatres indicated that 6.9% men liked the genre, but 7.4% disliked it; this feeling was even more antagonistic among women, since 1.5% came out in favor of it, while 14.4% expressed themselves against it. The rest of the overall percentage was represented by the influences derived from other genres: drama, comedy, gangster pictures, musicals, et cetera.

James Stewart proposes marriage to Debra Paget in a scene from Broken Arrow (*1950*).

Town marshal Gary Cooper has to shoot it out alone in a scene from High Noon (*1952*).

The rehabilitation of the Indian was a must, but Delmer Daves' *Broken Arrow* (1950) tended to go too far in the opposite direction, and several later films have had whites in the villains' roles. Although failures from a serious historical and sociological point of view, films like *Sitting Bull* (1954) and *Broken Arrow* nevertheless displayed an attitude in the desire to approach the real frontier from a radically different point of view. The Indian is finally achieving his important place in the Western saga just as the Negro in Southern literature is becoming, in the words of Callenbach, "a moral problem and a symbol."

Definite progress can be noted in the sympathetic and realistic depiction of the American Indian when one compares *Broken Arrow* with the similar *Run of the Arrow* (1957), directed by Samuel Fuller some seven years later. Although *Run of the Arrow* is a lesser film, far too sensational and unnecessarily brutal, far too little given to the gentle poetry that so distinguished Delmer Daves' earlier film, it is nevertheless a basically honest picture. Both deal with a white man who comes to the Indians as a sympathetic stranger, learns their ways, and lives as one of them. In *Broken Arrow,* the hero's first meeting with the Apaches comes just after he has seen the mutilated bodies of two whites, tortured to death by the Indians. Thus the cliché image of Indians as brutal savages is initially sustained, although there will be no more such brutality in the film. Once the hero and the Apache chief, Cochise, have gradually formed a firm friendship, the worthwhile point is made that the Indians are also human beings, with a code of behavior worth respecting. But that code is made to resemble the white man's code; it is a "civilized" code because it is a reasoning one, devoid of barbarity. The earlier episode of callous torture is ignored, and it is hoped that the audience will not recall it. *Run of the Arrow* likewise introduces its hero to the Indians—in this case the Sioux—in a savage episode of torture emphasizing the barbaric nature of the Indians. By the time white man and Indian finally make friends, the film has established that grounds exist for compromise, a mutual respect for bravery and basically similar religious beliefs. The climax comes in a shocking scene in which the Sioux, in accordance with their tribal laws, put to death a captured white man, slowly skinning him alive. It is this act which finally forces the hero to the conclusion that he can no longer live as a Sioux; he acknowledges that the Sioux have a perfect right to live, unmolested, by their codes, but he is also forced to the reluctant admission that their codes can never be his. He then returns to his people, taking with him his Indian wife and adopted Indian child. The solution is more mature than the one presented in *Broken Arrow.* In Daves' film, the hero, after having lost his Indian wife

—killed in a contrived skirmish—rides through the wilderness alone, condemned to a lonely life in a no man's land somewhere between the world of the whites, which would not accept him because of his friendship with the Indians and his past marriage to an Indian girl, and the world of the Indians, which he could not entirely accept, being a white man. In proportion, and for its year (1950), *Broken Arrow* was the more outspoken film, since its ideas were then less certain of sympathetic acceptance than the more advanced ideas expressed years later in *Run of the Arrow*.

Moral issues symbolically presented are appearing in an increasing number of films. The Western theme is no more being exploited merely as a commercial product. True, even today the mass of Westerns are, of course, mostly commercial, but the knowledge that the Western "has come of age" has not failed to impress some creative men. George Stevens has already recognized the mythological potential of the frontier sage with his *Shane* (1953), as has Fred Zinnemann with his *High Noon*.

André Bazin in *Cahiers du Cinema* (Christmas, 1955 issue) insisted on the recent vein of the *"Sur-Western,"* stressing the *romanisation* of frontier themes, using a very happy expression in our opinion. It is exactly the

Brandon De Wilde bids farewell to his idol, the gunfighter Shane, played by Alan Ladd. A scene from Shane *(1953).*

"Sur-Western" of today that is the basis for a truly remarkable series of experiments made by Mann, Ray, Dmytryk, Aldrich, Brando, and other directors in order to achieve in due time, and with sensitivity, cultural research, and a genuine enthusiasm a new approach in the *"Discours sur la Méthode du Western."* The difficulties in rehabilitating the frontier spirit in the cinema are many and relevant. Let us not forget the pulp and

trash magazines, the comic strips, the easy merry-go-round routine of sheriffs and rustlers, still impressing the minds of both the young and adult. Let us remember Gene Autry's "Ten Commandments of the Cowboy," which gained the approval of the motion picture industry, distributors, church groups, and grateful parents. Under this code, the cowboy becomes a sort of adult Boy Scout. He must not take unfair advantage, even when facing an enemy. He must never go back on his word, or on the trust confided in him. He must always tell the truth, be gentle with children, elderly people, and animals. He must not advocate or possess racially or religiously intolerant ideas. Moreover, he must help people in distress, be a good worker, keep himself clean in thought, speech, action, and personal habits. He must respect women, parents, and his nation's laws. He must neither drink nor smoke. And finally, the cowboy is a patriot.

Let us keep in mind the hostility of many producers toward social themes. It is easier to let French sociologists write about the Western hero as a frustrated man, who finds needed satisfaction, the "safety valve," in releasing the charges of his gun, a typical phallic symbol. Yes, the Westerner was puritanically inhibited, but he did not sublimate his desires with his pistol. And yet Hollywood, horrified, has not explained this particularly vital situation to the audiences. However, a few years ago, a marvelous sequence in Robert Wise's *Tribute to a Bad Man* (1956) gave us a clue. In this Western film depicting the adventures of a rancher who lays down his own law of necessity in a wild country, the camera focuses on a group of cowboys resting in their bunks; overhead, on the next floor, the rancher's woman plays the piano. Finally the music stops. In the silence the men look at each other and so express their thoughts. Upstairs, a man and a woman have begun to make love, while they, the cowboys, are left to their physical and psychical loneliness. This is an example of cinematic and sound treatment which is still worth the hope of those—and there are many—who want a true description of the frontier.

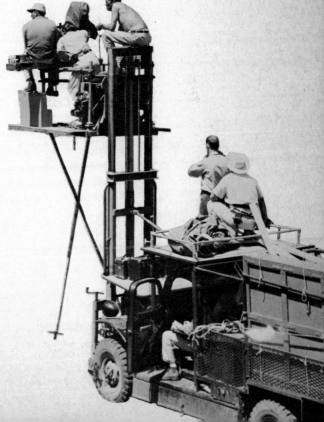

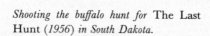
Shooting the buffalo hunt for The Last Hunt *(1956) in South Dakota.*

But many worthy projects are ruined. In *The Last Hunt* (1956) the director, Richard Brooks, could have achieved a truly great Western in this story of the buffalo hunters, the men who destroyed in less than thirty years a fantastic patrimony of sixty million beasts. But the paranoic instinct presented by Robert Taylor as a killer and the saccharine love story hopelessly drained the most vital content of the film. Still, this was an interesting experiment, and the documentary sequences of the shooting of some of the surviving three thousand buffaloes in the reservation—in order to keep down their biological reproduction—provided an unforgettable vision of earlier times, lived by a different breed of men. Worth noting for its stark impact in visual, dramatic terms is the death of the neurotic villain, Taylor, in the film's closing reel. He has cornered his more sympathetic partner (Stewart Granger) and the Indian girl (Debra Paget), who had been his own unwilling mistress before turning to Granger for protection, in a cave. The two men vow to duel to the death in the morning, and Taylor wraps himself outside in a buffalo hide as shelter from a blizzard. In the morning, as Granger comes to shoot it out with his former associate, now his deadly enemy, he is greeted with the grim sight of Taylor frozen to death in the buffalo hide, during the fury of the night's blizzard. Director Brooks spares nothing in this sequence, putting it over for shock effect with a sudden close-up and a thunderous musical score. In itself an unimportant plot element, it is interesting to note, however, that this is one of the few examples of death on the range presented horribly. In depicting death in ugly and realistic terms, Brooks made a minor, but positive contribution to the growing school of serious artists and students of the Western genre.

A somewhat romantic old-timer remembered that the cowboys "were dressed differently; they had their own language, code and costume. They lived by the gun and died by the gun. There were seldom any cowards among them. They loved best the open range, the sky, the mountains, and the breathless expanse of their wild, untamed land . . ." But they were also human beings, who only recently have arrived from a conformist shell to be presented realistically with their universal values intact.

If the present trend continues, the Western film of today may constitute a rocky surface on which talented and sensitive men of the new schools of thought, more at one with our own day, will finally be able to dedicate their efforts to the frontier as part of the American heritage. They will truly present the unparalleled phenomenon of the West in the nation's history; they will give cultural expression to a significant mythology which knows no geographical or human limits, spreading the word on the authentic "homo americanus."

Only then, will the vehement verses of Black Bart, the PO-8, no longer be applicable to dishonest manipulators of the true Western theme; these men will be in eclipse. This history to follow of the Western film will reflect our respect for truly creative achievements based on the real Western theme, our uncompromising criticism towards that mediocrity which, according to José Ortega y Gasset, has the gall to try to impose its rights everywhere.

Contents and

The stereotype villain of the Thirties: a Mexican, oily, ugly, gross, over-dressed. This is Richard Cramer who was so villainous that he was actually much better as a burlesqued heavy in Laurel and Hardy comedies.

moral influence of the Western

The hero

The Western theme, based on the triplex system of the hero, the adventure, and the law, has at all times been fascinating to movie audiences. In the long, sometimes straightforward, but often tortuous road towards development, the motion pictures have presented the theme with different approaches and results. But in its more than fifty years of existence, the Western film has completed, from at least a moral point of view, a first cycle.

The early Westerns, approached in a quasi-documentary fashion, were characterized by sincerity of sentiment and a poetic spirit. Later, the attention of film-makers to the genre jeopardized its freshness, and only William S. Hart's undeniable contributions to realism stressed the morality inherent in the West's history. This was true in the sense that an authentic depiction of this history made the spectator feel he was witnessing not merely casual entertainment but, rather, a serious and dignified visual discussion of an era which had already passed into the nation's heritage.

The epic, which enlarged the Western for audiences with the depths of its research and the advantages of a gradual aesthetic and commercial development in movies, further enhanced the genre's prospects. But studio policies, guided by the public's clamor for more modern, lighter, "escapist" Westerns—the fast, showy vehicles of Ken Maynard and Hoot Gibson, for example—brought about the first fundamental change

2

in the contents and morals of the Western. From now on, the cowboy was not necessarily the successor to the pioneer; he was no longer just the man who toiled hard raising cattle or defending the land barons' privileges, the man whom the Great Cattle Depression of 1886–87 forced to roam the West looking for ways and means of supporting himself. An idealized, whitewashed hero emerged, his character influenced by the various codes of associations, clubs, and groups. This new "hero" reached his zenith the closer he followed Gene Autry's "Ten Commandments of the Cowboy," listed in the previous chapter. All promulgated codes of morality are inevitably influenced by current moral trends; and the perfectly acceptable behavior of the Western hero in the Twenties might be considered by some today as the ultimate in un-Americanism. We have a perfect example of this in a mild and quite unimportant Western of 1925 entitled *Shooting Square*. In it, the hero and heroine are to be married, and while they celebrate with a party at the ranch, a cowhand is sent to bring the preacher. The preacher, it turns out, is black. Although he is presented likably, certain aspects of the traditional image of the comic Negro persist. His clothes are ill-fitting and he speaks—subtitles, of course—in traditionally stereotyped fashion. "I'se de preacher," is his first line upon greeting the distinctly shocked gathering. The result is astounding. The heroine almost faints and, indignantly returning the hero's ring, asks him: "How can you treat me like this?" The heroine's outraged father appears to be in a lynching mood, and

Saloon girl Louise Glaum, villain Robert McKim, and reformed outlaw William S. Hart in The Return of Draw Egan (*1916*).

he orders the black man from the ranch. The little preacher is bustled out as quickly as possible.

Later, however, the hero (Jack Perrin) restores himself to the heroine's favor, by assuring her that he meant no harm. The line that clinches the reconciliation is: "I didn't know he was *black*." All this is treated casually; the incident is not used to incite racial hatred. Jack Perrin's hero is otherwise absurdly virtuous, possessed in abundance of the nine other commandments.

Today, of course, if such a sequence were included in a film, wholesale picketing would automatically result, and possibly even violence. Later in the film, hero and heroine seek out a white minister, and are then "married" by an apparent preacher, actually an outlaw in disguise; the heroine's discovery that her marriage is illegal provokes a much less concerned reaction from her than did her encounter with the authentic, but black, minister!

The cowboy-hero, this bulwark of physical and moral strength, was the backbone in the boom of the "B" Westerns in the Thirties. But his influence was felt in the epics that were then being made (*Jesse James, The Oklahoma Kid, Union Pacific, Stagecoach*—all in 1939), and this influence generally continued to be felt in the philosophy and policies of movie producers right through World War II.

It is no surprise, therefore, to notice that right after the end of the War, the ferment of new times began to exert its influence toward a revision of the cowboy cliché. There was a marked move to make the hero a less idealized character; his aims might continue to be those of the chivalrous knight, but he was too much of a realist to achieve those aims chivalrously. The war had destroyed too many illusions.

Bill Elliott was perhaps the foremost exponent of this new "realism" in a series of Westerns made for Monogram and Allied Artists. The Elliott Western saw a number of remarkable changes in the makeup and behavior of the Western hero. In *Bitter Creek*, the hero needs information from a villain and, wasting no time playing the gentleman, Elliott proceeds to beat the information out of him, all the time keeping him covered with a gun. The villain protests: "You wouldn't get away with this if you'd put that gun down!" In the old films, of course, such a taunt would have led to the hero's dropping both gun and belt and proving that right must always win by beating the tar out of his opponent in a fair fist fight. Elliott is not taken in, however; he replies: "But I'm *not* going to put it down," and proceeds to slug away until the "heavy" gives in and makes his confession.

In *Kansas Territory* (1952) Elliott also resorts to brutal methods to run

Bill Elliott, who emulated William S. Hart in his Westerns of the Forties and Fifties. A scene from Waco (*1952*).

down the man responsible for the death of his brother, and in at least two films in the series, *Waco* (1952) and *Topeka* (1953), he plays an outlaw for most of the film—*not* a lawman posing as an outlaw in the time-honored tradition.

Topeka bears a particularly close relationship to William S. Hart's *The Return of Draw Egan* (1916). In both films, the ultimate reformation is brought about not by genuine remorse over a life of crime, but rather through a more sentimental expedient: the love of a good woman. In both films, the hero turns on his former cronies, still hoping to turn the situation to his own advantage, and he "reforms" only late in the game. Elliott had the integrity not to weaken his reformation by a complete transformation. His reformation still works to his own advantage: through services to the community, he is pardoned; he gets the girl, and he keeps any stolen wealth he may have accumulated.

A character even more obviously a product of the war was the near-mystical leader, quite recognizably patterned on Nazi types; however, he did not appear on the screen until the Nazi evil had been effectively minimized for the public due to the cold war. One has good examples of the leader-hero in such films as *Arrow in the Dust* (1954) with Sterling Hayden and *The Last Wagon* (1956) with Richard Widmark. The hero is an outlaw or an Army deserter, frequently a killer. He is reconciled to the fact that he is being hounded, and he is not unduly bitter about it. Given to contemplation, he is convinced his crime was perfectly justified; but unconsciously placing himself apart from other men, he does not overly concern himself with proving his case.

However, fate places him in the position of guiding the destiny of a group of men—in the Western, obviously, the wagon train to be guided through hostile Indian country is the perfect answer. He must maintain perfect discipline, to the point of extreme arrogance, brutality, and ruthlessness; the lives of the group are more important than the life of an individual; the end always justifies the means. Before the adventure is over, the leader-hero has not only proven himself to the group under his command, but has made almost unnecessary and irrelevant any proof concerning his earlier crime. Injurious effects the pioneer leader and the brutal, pragmatic cowboy may have had on youthful audiences were probably nullified by the completely whitewashed Western heroes galloping then on television. Now, however, that television has swung to greater realism, there may well be a far from salutary effect on American youth. Few films, fortunately, went quite as far as did *Jack Slade* in extolling the courage of a killer, demanding sympathy and understanding, if not approval, for his acts. Slade was a colorful

Mark Stevens and Barton MacLane in a scene from Jack Slade (*1953*).

historical character of the post-Civil War West, a trouble-shooter for the stagecoach lines, and his very ruthlessness with outlaws brought with it a measure of law and order. Finally, however, killing became an obsession, an obsession fanned by alcohol, to the point that he became a menace to the law he was paid to uphold, and he was finally lynched by vigilantes. In the film version, this bitter end was averted, and he died, almost seeking death in a form of self-atonement, in a fairly fought gun battle. Mark Stevens acted in and co-directed this interesting and powerful film, but in such an overwrought fashion that it was reminiscent of the German film dramas of the Twenties, such as *Warning Shadows* (1922) and that it failed to become the honest portrait of a man and an era that it might have been. It always seemed somewhat confusing in its demand for sympathy for a man whose very actions, including the crippling of a child, made such sympathy impossible.

Generally, the war years left the scars of cynicism and bitterness on heroes, and it was with no surprise that we saw in *The Rawhide Years* (1956), a well-constructed and exciting Western by Rudolph Mate, a hero who is a cardshark, and a heroine who willingly becomes the villain's mistress. These matters are so much taken for granted that the main issue of the film becomes not the regeneration of the hero and heroine, but the elimination of the villain so that the love affair between hero and heroine, presumably now to be sanctioned by marriage, may resume!

The hero has been presented as an archangel without wings, a superman whose main interest on this earth is to redress wrongs. This saccharine formula was based on the hero's rescuing a girl or a widow, left alone to administer a farm or a ranch, from the crafty scheming of the mortgage holder. The hero had to rely entirely upon his rather elementary wits—after all, the situation did not involve too much thinking—and, above all, on his physical prowess, substantiated by a very accurate gun, two powerful fists, and a fast horse.

It was to his horse that the hero perennially returned, after he had disposed of the villain whose intentions concerning the girl were either dishonest or immoral or both. Occasionally, particularly in the older Westerns, the hero would ride off on his horse alone, the essence of Western *camaraderie;* but a romance of which there had been no sign throughout the action would frequently blossom in time for the fadeout. Under such circumstances, it became somewhat of a cliché for the horse to give its blessing to the union in one bit of "business" or another. The most common of these little routines was for the understanding horse to nudge his very bashful master, and in so doing force him into the arms of the girl. Ken Maynard and his beautiful palomino, Tarzan, made a speciality out of this sort of thing.

Despite endless writings to the contrary—usually by critics who haven't seen enough "B" Westerns—it is by no means unheard of for the hero to kiss the heroine. True, such displays of emotion hold little appeal for the juvenile audience, and thus are usually employed, if at all, only at the end. Nevertheless, irresponsible writing has created the impression that a kiss in a "B" Western is one of the "Thou Shalt Nots," and that is far from the case. Although his work can hardly be discussed along with "B" Western clichés, William S. Hart, sentimentalist that he was, frequently injected prolonged embraces into his Westerns. Certainly Buck Jones, William Boyd, Ken Maynard, and all the others have, too, although admittedly Gene Autry, zealous upholder of the cowboy's "Commandments," has kept such scenes out of almost all of his films.

But he would frequently add some spice for the adults. On the few occasions when he did "clinch" right in front of the camera, Autry emerged a trifle shamefaced afterwards, but all this was usually handled in a light vein. As the "clinch" approached, the camera would pan to Champion, Autry's horse, who would react with surprise (stressed more by comic music than by his own "expression") as the audience heard the off-camera kiss. Then the camera would swing back to a hot-and-bothered Autry, wiping off lipstick, and "The End" would fade on before any further exploitation of the situation was possible.

Hero versus badman

Occupying prime position in the Western genre is the group that we may loosely term "Hero versus Badman." In these films, the hero battles outlaws (bank robbers, cattle rustlers, stagecoach bandits) simply because good must fight evil—and triumph. Motivation for both sides is simple and clear-cut. Some strength is added to these Westerns when the hero is a U. S. marshal or some other form of law enforcement officer; in this way a measure of historical authenticity is added, and the fairy-tale-like conception of the hero as a knight seeking to right wrongs is minimized.

The outline of the "Hero versus Badman" group was soon exhausted in stereotypes, and a number of sub-conflicts were added to the basic theme. A frequently used twist was for the hero himself to be a reformed outlaw, creating a moral tension (he was turning on his former friends) and a physical tension (he was distrusted by both sides). Because the hero's crimes were usually innocuous enough to permit a happy ending, the use of this theme had only indifferent success except in the hands of William S. Hart. Hart had no qualms about making himself a completely ruthless, although never despicable, outlaw. Only his mood and his sense of the film dictated whether his endings were to be happy or sad, completely disregarding the so-called "moral considerations" of those pre-code days.

Another twist in the formula might be the adding of an extra incentive for the hero to pursue the villain. The villain was often the actual culprit in a crime for which the hero, or his father, had been wrongly convicted. A stronger motive was for the villain to have killed or seduced the hero's sister. In the years right after World War II, this theme was expanded and made even more personal: the hero's wife, and sometimes his entire family, had been wiped out by the villain. This particular motif was comparatively rare in the silent era, for although the movies were freer then of censorship restrictions and had less fear of controversial material, they did naturally reflect current moral trends. Divorce and remarriage were far less acceptable socially, and less prevalent, than they are today, and for the hero to be a widower raised the problem of the acceptability of a new love story and his ultimate marriage to the heroine. This is not to suggest that such themes were never utilized in silent Westerns, but they were certainly not used as widely, or as casually, as they were in such post-World War II films as *Tomahawk* and *Distant Drums,* both made in 1951.

Another variation was the hero's masquerade as an outlaw. He would join the gang in order to bring the outlaws to justice, thus adding the tension of potential discovery to the standard action. This theme was adopted by the non-Westerns in subsequent years; in the Thirties, gangsters, in the Forties, Nazis, and in the Fifties, Communists, were all rounded up and brought to book by this enterprising method.

Perhaps the last of many small changes in the general outline saw the hero framed on a murder or robbery charge. He would break out of jail and remain thereafter only one jump ahead of the sheriff and one jump behind the villains. Finally, he would manage to prove his innocence by subduing the leading villain. This plot itself had an alternate version in that, apart from being pursued by both sheriff and outlaws, the hero was also plagued by the knowledge that the heroine believed him to be guilty. This motif reached heights of absurdity, becoming virtually unwitting satire in a group of "B" Westerns manufactured like sausages by Columbia in the Forties. Each one had an almost identical plot and cast, and with monotonous regularity Iris Meredith would turn on fiancé Charles Starrett for the murder of her father, Edward Le Saint, while the real miscreant—Dick Curtis—surveyed the scene with a sardonic smile from a safe distance.

A classic cliché-scene from almost any Columbia "B" of the late Thirties or Forties, in this case The Stranger from Texas (1939). *Left to right, in the roles they always played: Edward Le Saint, the heroine's murdered father; Charles Starrett, the hero, unjustly accused; villain Dick Curtis, the real killer; weak brother Richard Fiske, who redeems himself at the end; sheriff Jack Rockwell, honest but stupid; Alan Bridge, the murdered man's competitor and an innocent suspect; and Lorna Gray, the orphaned daughter.*

The killer (Jack Palance) prepares to gun down the farmer (Elisha Cook, Jr.) in a scene from Shane *(1953)*.

The villain

The crimes of the badman were always prompted by a recognizable human emotion—greed, either for wealth or power. That greed was expressed by robbery and murder in the more elementary Westerns, and in the legal manipulations which brought about the " theft" or control of towns and even territories, in the more elaborately plotted Westerns. Such immoral practices were still products of understandable minds. In many cases, the hero was depicted as a patient and understanding man who hoped, by reason, to bring about a change in the behavior of the villain, before swinging into physical action to affirm and enforce the fundamental values.

The badman, although a brute in most cases, still represented something that the audience could understand and possibly justify, although never condone, in view of the rigidly upheld code of ethics the hero represented. "Crime does not pay," was the ubiquitous moral these Westerns taught, but the audience was still able to indulge vicariously in the various manifestations of lust and crime the screen badmen presented.

There was subtlety in subplots which presented conflicts in the outlaws' methodology. Many of the villains' get-rich-quick schemes were essentially legal: the crimes were moral rather than legal in that the vil-

Douglas Fowley, a stock villain in gangster films, occasionally made a convincing Western heavy too. A scene from Santa Fe Trail *(1940).*

lains usually tried to cheat homesteaders out of potential wealth of which the latter themselves were not aware. One of the most reliable plots was for the villain to know in advance that "the railroad is coming through." Such an event meant, of course, that the land which the railroad would have to buy would become extremely valuable to its owners, and one can readily understand the villain's sharp business sense in trying to acquire all the available land in advance of the event.

Since such practices are, of course, quite legal, it was necessary to put the "heavy" in an unsympathetic light—in other words, he must achieve legal ends by illegal means. The ranchers must be subjected to a reign of terror. Their cattle must be stolen to prevent their paying off notes on their lands held by the banks. (One of the movies' oldest clichés was for the town banker, outwardly the territory's most respected citizen, to be the brains behind the outlaw activities.) This basic idea was applied in other ways, too; the need for land by the cattle barons, or hidden gold located on the property, unknown to the owners. Manipulation of land away from Mexicans living in California, by voiding their old Spanish land grants, brought a minor racial issue into the chicanery at times, but this was never fully developed.

A formidable trio of villains from Dawn on the Great Divide *(1942): Harry Woods, Roy Barcroft, and Robert Frazer.*

Villains of the Thirties and Forties: Edmund Cobb (a Western hero in the Twenties), Roy Barcroft, and Bud Osborne.

The building of a town in Cimarron *(1931).*

Town scene from The Iron Horse *(1924).*

The most disturbing aspect of these legal crooks was the reaction they provoked in the townspeople. For the most part, the citizens were all for taking the law into their own hands, and having it out with their tormentors in blazing gun battles. It is interesting to note that the villains were usually assisted in their machinations by a crooked sheriff who used legal loopholes to achieve dishonest results, and that the hero's staunchest ally was the newspaper editor. Often this editor was the heroine, bravely carrying on after her father had been killed by the villains, and who was, herself, defying threats from the outlaws. Perhaps in an unconscious way, these two clichés reflect the American people's casual acceptance of corruption in politics, and their exaggerated enthusiasm for the value and power of a free press. (This, of course, is not to decry the democratic principles behind a free press, but rather to suggest that in America, abuse of that freedom, beyond the bounds of both good sense and good taste, is sadly permitted.)

Generally speaking, law and order is presented as somewhat ineffectual and not extraordinarily clever, but it is the unusual stupidity of the villains which brings about their downfall!

The use of American history in the average horse opera has been mainly a matter of adaptation, the exploitation of a formula rather than the careful reconstruction of a period. Such films as *The Covered Wagon* and *The Iron Horse* apart, great events in American history have successfully been reduced to a stale pattern. The coming of the Pony Express has been depicted faithfully occasionally; far more commonly it has been used merely as motivation: the villains oppose it because it threatens their own livelihood (a monopoly on stagelines, with a government mail-carrying contract). The villains rouse the Indians to waylay riders and generally to destroy faith in the Express' mounts. The Express accepted, more motivation was provided with the introduction of wild horses, culminating in an unlikely and irrelevant race between the two opposing parties. Such a cross-country race, with the villains pulling every trick in the book to put their opponents out of the running, created a rousing climax to many a Western. These endings provided countless opportunities for stunt men and trick riders to display their odd talents.

Range wars were very much a part of the American scene, but aside from the factually accurate staging of the Lincoln County Wars in King Vidor's *Billy The Kid* (1930), they have been barely touched on in their true perspective by the Hollywood Western. The natural and understandable enmity between sheepmen and cattlemen, the hatred of barbed wire, the control of water rights—all these elements which provoked open warfare between basically honest men have usually been presented not for their own sake, but as instruments which the villains might manipulate for their own ends. *The Rangers Step In* (1937), *Fargo* (1952), *Barbed Wire* (1952) were all films in this category.

Except in *Cimarron* and *Tumbleweeds,* the land rush had never been presented as a moment in a nation's progress, but as a fairly common occurrence (which it wasn't) which inevitably had one result—land grabbers would set up a minor western crime empire. *The Oklahoma Kid* (1939) was a film in this category.

Similarly, the conditions which produced such outlaws as Jesse James and the Dalton gang have been presented in so many different lights on the screen that the outsider, knowing nothing of the real facts, must be totally confused. This question is discussed in greater detail elsewhere in the book; suffice it to say here that, according to the movies, most of the West's outlaws were latter-day Robin Hoods, forced into banditry by the sordid schemes of crooked politicians and the social upheaval of the post-Civil War period, much as James Cagney and his brethren were so often forced into gangsterism after World War I, in *The Roaring Twenties* (1939), *Public Enemy* (1931), and other films.

The Indian

If most films dealt with heroes rescuing girls from villains, a large portion of the remaining ones manipulated the American Indian into the role of a red-skinned menace. Except for the first phase in the history of the Western, and the contemporary phase, the Indian's existence in the United States has been dealt with by the movies in a stereotyped manner. The tragedy of the Indian tribes, pushed backwards and backwards again in violation of treaties and agreements, their confinement on reservations where unscrupulous Indian agents exploited them shamelessly, the disintegration of their fighting spirit and their traditional desire to live in peace with the white man—all these were aspects of Indian life which American audiences were seldom able to witness, evaluate, and reflect upon on the screen.

"The only good Indian is a dead Indian." This belief, which was strictly held and put into practice in many parts of the West, represented an inviolate pillar of thought for the creators of screen formulae. The most that the Indian could expect in Hollywood's hands was a presentation as the white man's equal; but this only so that he could be killed, coldbloodedly, under the same "justice" that dispatched badmen who were white. But the Indian was usually not even granted those human failings and influences which motivated the crimes of whites. Despite the writings of James Fenimore Cooper and Germany's Karl Mai, whose many books had as much success in Germany as did the works of Zane Grey in America, the Indian proved to be a far less useful character to film-makers than the cowboy, the Texas Ranger, or even the infrequently seen Canadian mountie. Initially, at least, the Indian was seen as a hero almost as frequently as the white man, but already there was a difference. He seemed more of a symbol, less of an individual, than the cowboy, and he was presented in a more poetic, and often more tragic, light. But after 1910 he was not really presented as an individual at all, not until the racial cycle of the late Forties. In the interim, he was an unmotivated enemy; villains might be presented as individuals, but the Indians were always shown *en masse*. There were very few Westerns with Indians as the only heavies, for the simple reason that without motive there could be no plot. Maynard's *Red Raiders* of 1927 is one of the few exceptions in that it has no white villains, and depends on Indian aggression for its sole action. While admitting that Indians can be human enough to want peace, it still dealt with them as warlike children, and never as believable human beings. Few Westerns have emulated *Red Raiders'* example of eliminating white villains entirely. Ford's *Stagecoach,* in which the menace is provided by the pursuit of Geronimo's Apaches, found it necessary to tack on a climactic (or *anti*-climactic) duel between the hero (John Wayne) and an outlaw (Tom Tyler).

This is not to say that the Indians have always been depicted as villainous savages; but in the bulk of the "B" Westerns their function was primarily to provide formula action by taking to the warpath in opposition to the heroes. In films like *Prairie Thunder* (1937) they were spurred on by white renegades; in *The Law Rides Again* (1943) and countless others, they took to the warpath because of fancied grievances against the whites (a crooked white Indian agent had been stealing supplies promised them by the government); and in *Fort Osage* (1952) their warlike actions were deliberately provoked by white renegades who hoped that an Indian war would cover their own depredations. In such Westerns, the Indian was alternately villainous and misunderstood, but he rarely emerged as a human being.

This changed to a very great degree after the advent of *Broken Arrow* (1950). Once Hollywood made up its mind to make up to the Indian for past misrepresentation, the pendulum swung completely to the other side. From now on it was to be the Indian who sought peace, and the white man who was the agitating aggressor. But the pendulum was not to swing so far as to dehumanize the white man as had once been done

to the Indian. There were always to be individual motives attributed to the white villain which made him atypical of his race, e.g. the villainous trader who knows that peace with the Indians will mean an end to his illicit traffic (Grant Withers in Ford's *Rio Grande*), and most common of all, the martinet military commander who hates Indians with a blind passion (Jeff Chandler in *Two Flags West*, Henry Fonda in *Fort Apache*) and is opposed to any means which will bring about a cessation of hostilities short of total defeat of the Indians. Since such men are almost always presented as complete or near-complete neurotics, they stand midway between guilt and innocence, and they are made to appear very much the exception rather than the rule. The Indian is presented in this case in a more realistic fashion; he is the victim rather than the aggressor, but the question of blame, which should rightly be placed on the governmental policies of that time, is neatly side-stepped.

The authentic motives for Indian hostility were seldom, if ever, explained; the main function of these Americans consisted in providing a convenient mass enemy, and a series of spectacular moving targets. Once the cliché was accepted, explanations of motivation were in any case no longer necessary. The very word *Indian* became synonymous with savagery and villainy, just as the words *German*, *Japanese*, *Nazi*, or

Cochise (Jeff Chandler) comforts his white man friend (James Stewart) when renegades kill his Indian bride (Debra Paget). From Broken Arrow *(1950).*

Ruth Roland,
Queen of the Western serials.

Communist in themselves later became not merely descriptive nouns, but adjectives of automatic infamy in many areas of world and cinematic affairs.

The woman

The cult of the super-hero fighting the good fight in a confused and largely hostile world populated by white outlaws and Indian savages, was further developed by the role of the woman.

Originally she was shown as the full-fledged companion of the pioneer, certainly his equal, and occasionally possessed of an inner strength that made her his superior. Later, her image deteriorated into that of a frail creature, forever at the mercy of the lawless element, forever dependent for protection and her livelihood upon the hero. In other words, she ceased to become a plot participant and became a plot motivator; defense of her honor and rights became as important in themselves as the battle between law and lawlessness. Later still, towards the end of the Thirties, she became more self-reliant, increasingly athletic, and conscious of her sex appeal. In the post-war period, this sex appeal became an exasperating and exasperated *leitmotif,* which found its justification in two fundamental exigencies of the motion picture industry: the reaction to the puritanism of the Production Code, exerting an archaic censorship over a depiction of true passion and other legitimate emotions, and the need to stimulate sagging box office returns. Thus the cycle is complete even in this important aspect of the Western: the image of the western woman, as rendered by Hollywood, stands confused, between the sentimental and mythological conception of the pure but weak and defenseless female, without any personality of her own, essentially dependent on the hero, and the titillatingly sexual and aggressive heroine.

Adventure and the law

With the revision of the cowboy image, the demands of the public required the revision of the concepts of adventure and law, two other coefficients in the Western formula. Such a process continues today with different, mixed results, but the first cycle of the Western is complete. In fifty years, the realistic approach has been greatly adulterated and only recently are the real moral issues of the old West again being discussed.

In the meantime, world audiences have had a chance to appraise the Western era as a totally lawless one, and the isolated examples of films in which a true evaluation of this historical period was possible, left only slight marks on audiences. Prolific grade "B" Western production (made probably for U. S. and British consumption and exported elsewhere only in a limited way) has offered an appalling series of clichés which has dominated American thinking concerning the West for decades.

Adventure and the law are linked with the hero as complementing essentials in the visual presentation of the story. Adventure in Westerns has of the three most retained its classic presentation. It has always focused on the Great Plains as the *outdoors* (epitomized by grandiose perspectives, such as those obtained by Ford with his location shooting in Monument Valley for *Stagecoach* and other films) and on the saloon *indoors*. The stories played out against these natural or man-made back-

A typical program Western from Triangle: William Desmond and Luella Maxam in Deuce Duncan *(1918).*

drops have stuck with traditional incidents; chases, barroom brawls, and gun duels are necessary ingredients, basic actions that perennially recur in the evolution of the story. But the concept of the law has changed considerably indeed. The rough sketch of the sheriff of old has recently been undergoing changes in a psychological process, the result of which is a general humanization of the character. The extreme in this modern revaluation has tended to identify the lawman with the type of hero played by Gary Cooper in Fred Zinnemann's *High Noon*. This is an important metamorphosis, which may well be coupled with the parallel revaluation of the Indian in Delmer Daves' *Broken Arrow,* the film that rediscovered the obvious humanity of a conquered but still proud race, and that, in the words of critic Guido Aristarco, "breaks an arrow in favor of the Indians, who enter, in this way, the cinema as adults."

Plot versus action?

The discovery of a "social conscience" in the Western—and this applies not only to films with Indian themes, but also to films like *High Noon* and *At Gunpoint!* which dealt with the responsibility of the individual to the community—had one very definite effect on Westerns. This effect was felt on all films, but it was most noticeable in the Western. It slowed them down, badly, not only in their narration, but in their over-all pacing. In the older Westerns, men acted; for better or for worse, wisely or stupidly, they acted. They didn't ponder, debate, subject their tortured souls to self-examination. And there is no reason to suppose that the pioneers of the old West acted in this pseudo-literary fashion either. If they did, they could hardly have survived and opened up the frontier as they did, even though frontier existence required, and received, mature thought and deliberation as well as determined action.

Plots of "B" Westerns were rarely afflicted with these problems; the "B" of 1950 was little different in plot from the "B" of 1915. Such differences as there were, were in details rather than essentials. In keeping pace with the times, the Westerns introduced gangster methods into the villainy, and also stressed it in their titles. (*Racketeers of the Range, Enemies of the Law, Gangsters of the Frontier, Gangster's Enemy No. 1,* etc.)

With the war in Europe brewing, standard plots were topically revamped. In a John Wayne vehicle for Republic, *Pals of the Saddle,* enemy agents illegally mined tungsten and sold it to a "foreign power" in violation of the U. S. Neutrality Act. In George O'Brien's *Border G-Man,* wild horses are being rounded up and sold, not to the Pony Express, but to that same unnamed foreign power. With America's entry into the war, Nazi agents somewhat improbably supplanted cattle rustlers in films like *Cowboy Commandos, Texas to Bataan* and *Valley of Hunted Men*. With the war over, uranium became a more valid plot-motivating factor than gold or silver—and science-fiction put in some strange appearances, too. On one memorable occasion, Roy Rogers and Trigger galloped not after a runaway stagecoach, but after a runaway jet rocket!

The first real glimpse of a change of morals on the screen came with *The Outlaw*. Its revamping of the Western on an erotic level did not fail to stir up the self-righteous indignation of both those who believed in the preservation of the old order in Westerns, and those pressure groups who sought and still seek to censor and stifle Hollywood on the slightest provocation. With the approach of postwar problems of both national and international significance, problems that had arisen with the cessation of hostilities, and at a time when new values were being introduced into a confused climate even before the old values had been entirely discarded, the Western underwent severe changes. It was, of course, in the Western that the old values were primarily reflected, in a cinematic sense, and in a real sense for America, too; and because of this the Western had to be the principal victim in a critical dissection, the results of which saw traditional concepts of plot and action in the Western overhauled. In the Thirties Aldous Huxley lamented over the exhibition of violent Western films to Asiatic audiences, feeling that they presented a completely erroneous version of life in America on the frontier; in more recent times the trend has gone to the opposite extreme, in the open discussion of moral and racial problems, and in the utilization of psychological and literary themes. Lately, Westerns have given us a hero as extroverted or introverted as a character in Gide or Kafka; his action is presented in a far more complex and measured fashion than was ever possible within the bounds of the cliché of the fast gunman. Greater realism in the actions of individuals, projected against the background of, or submerged within the collectivity of western merchants, farmers, and ranch hands, has begun to materialize.

The honest and dignified mien now allowed the Indian, the shifting of emphasis back to the real pioneer, the re-emphasis of the woman's important and equal role in the opening up of the West, the consideration of the human qualities, the failings as well as the heroism of the law enforcer . . . all these changes have taken root in the new era of Westerns, and even the least important, and least ambitious films aesthetically, show unmistakable signs of these changes. Certainly far too many of these films are little more than maladroit and pretentious essays in sociology and psychology; the action has slowed down drastically, but the mere existence of these Westerns provides a welcome, if no longer refreshing, note.

There is a certain moral dimension to the modernization of the Western, modern not in the sense of *streamlined,* but in the sense of mature in our time. This moral dimension is expressed in the effort made by producers and directors to find inspiration in original sources, and in so doing abandoning stale clichés. But these undertakings, or at least the successful ones, are still relatively isolated instances, and praiseworthy as it is to clean house of old clichés, it is regrettable to see, even now, a great many new ones coming into being. But at least this signals evolution and, hopefully, progress. It is certainly not stagnation. A healthier, more realistic influence is being brought to bear on those movie audiences—still large—that love the Western. Instinctively, the audience realizes that it has been deprived for a long time of the true and unvarnished depiction of one of the most essential and interesting periods in American history. The Western no longer represents an innocuous adventure story, supplemented at home by children playing "Cowboys and Indians." Before World War II, the United States audience and the international public were confronted with great numbers of "entertainment commodity" Westerns: some attracted top playing time in metropolitan centers; others—a majority—were cheaply made five-reelers designed for more general consumption in small towns and rural areas.

The oleographic conceptions of story presentation, and the archaic formulae, largely devoid of any creativity or artistry, did not lead to a general protest over the so-called moral values presented, for the simple reason that patent immorality did not manifest itself on the screen. The games of chase and fight, of crime and retribution, had become so conventional that the public looked at them without having to think on the subject, and certainly without being deeply moved by it. In the postwar years, this began to change, and the pressing requirement for firmly established plot lines in conjunction with fast action is generally recognized now, even among the most emphatic supporters of the "psychological Western," since an effective, interdependent, and mutually beneficial relationship between plot and action is a prime requirement for successful—that is, honest—Westerns.

Necessity for a living legend

The new moral strength of the Hollywood Western lies in its statement to audiences that life in the old West, notwithstanding the falsely glamorized and savage portrait that Hollywood painted in the past, was hard, monotonous, but also heroic . . . a life that had neither gods nor devils; Hollywood has begun to inform the public that the West was peopled with simple human beings with all their strengths and weaknesses, a folk not very different from those in the audience.

In due time, and with proper care, such a tradition should acquire all the necessary attributes of a living legend, a myth whose authentic example will be accepted by the American nation in its true perspective. Non-American, and specifically European audiences have always approached the Western in an enthusiastic manner, granting even the poorer examples some poetic and realistic foundations which are often baseless. This enthusiastic attitude is often not shared by American audiences who regard the Western naturally, without the emotional enthusiasm for the "foreign" and the "exotic," which is what the Western signifies for the European. These non-American audiences then, kindly disposed towards the Western in any event, have been even quicker to accept and approve the mature changes in the Western format than have their American counterparts.

The combined effects of public taste, the reflections of modern times and the need—now a commercial as well as an aesthetic need—to present the Western in a more adult framework, are all causing Hollywood to take into consideration, both directly and indirectly, the moral influence of their Western product in artistic, social, and human terms. Some of the more dynamic producers of this new school may well know that the vital requirement in their efforts is progression instead of the tested but untrue status quo. The American cinema, on the basis of its past achievements, has the key to a splendid future in developing the fine resources of its epic past. And if the gangster film, the Civil War film, and other branches of adventure in the motion picture, all find their roots in the Western, there is all the more reason to perfect the purest and most original genre of the American cinema.

Such a challenging ideal might in itself bring about a true renaissance in the American cinema, and with it renewed support from the movie audiences of the United States and abroad.

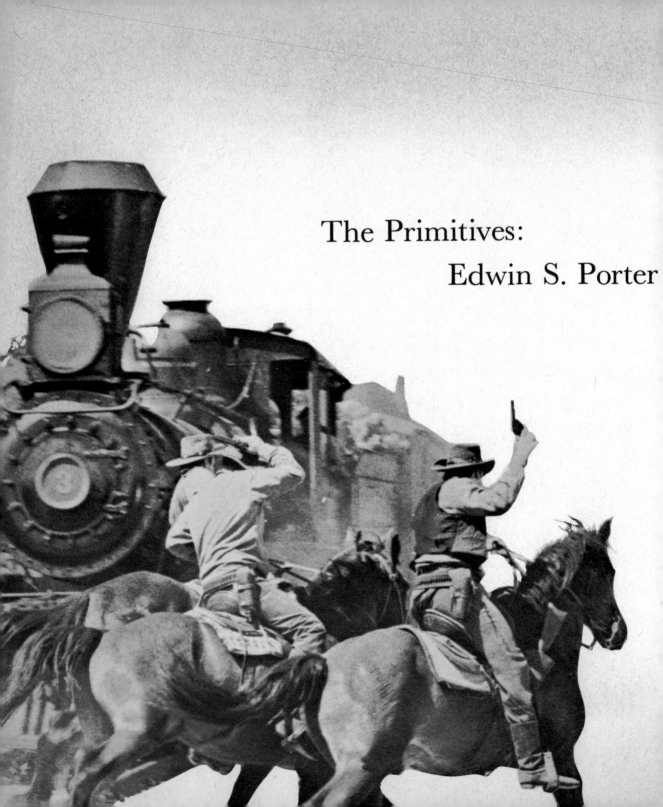

The Primitives:

Edwin S. Porter

and Broncho Billy Anderson

The Great Train Robbery

The Great Train Robbery, made in 1903, has often been erroneously described as "the first story film," "the film that introduced narrative to the screen," "the first Western" and the "film with the first close-up." It was actually *none* of these things, but it was the first dramatically creative American film, which was also to set the pattern—of crime, pursuit, and retribution—for the Western film as a genre.

The Edison company had played with Western material for several years prior to *The Great Train Robbery. Cripple Creek Barroom* of 1898 was a brief vignette of Western life. Buffalo Bill Cody had been filmed, and so had some of the simple action "acts" (Indians scalping white men) that had proved so popular at Koster and Bial's Music Hall. But *The Great Train Robbery* was no mere vignette. Almost a reel in length, it was a remarkably polished film for 1903; it told a dramatic story *visually,* and without subtitles; it cut between interiors and exteriors with fluidity; it utilized good visual compositions; and it built its tension astonishingly well, considering that editing for dramatic effect was then unknown and director Porter had no precedents to which he could refer.

The film was largely shot on a track of the Delaware and Lackawanna Railroad near Dover, New Jersey. Its locale was, of course, supposed to be the Far West, where train holdups were still by no means uncommon.

The Great Train Robbery opens with a se-

3

quence in the interior of a railroad telegraph office; a typical early movie set, photographed in typically static long-shot fashion. However, there is an unusual effect: the arrival of the train shown through a window. Certain historians have claimed that this was achieved by constructing the set immediately adjacent to the railway track, but in actual fact a good, if occasionally unsteady, superimposition was the *modus operandi.*

The bandits bind the telegraph operator; then, a cut to an exterior. As the train pauses by the railroad's water tower outside, the bandits board it. From the New Jersey exterior locale, Porter then cuts to a studio interior set of the express car. This, of course, is elementary movie-making, but was not so in 1903, when films (other than the fantasies of Méliès) were usually limited to single sets and single timespans, in order to avoid confusing the audience. Porter then switches to another exterior, his camera placed on the rear of the tender, photographing the train in motion. The villains approach, and overpower the drivers. There is a well-staged scrap, and in a particularly deft piece of stop-motion work, dummies are substitued for the actors before they are thrown from the moving train. The callous treatment of the drivers seems to have been a deliberate attempt by Porter to emphasize that he

A scene from The Great Train Robbery (*1903*).

Very possibly the first Western of any kind, W. K. L. Dickson's Cripple Creek Barroom *was made by the Edison Company in 1898.*

was not glamorizing outlaws undeserving of sympathy. This is further emphasized when the train stops and an incredible horde of passengers—presumably the entire population of Dover—descends. One of them makes a break for freedom, and is shot down in cold blood.

Their loot secured, the bandits escape in the train, bring it to a halt some distance up the track, and in a long and smoothly executed panning shot, retreat into the woods. The crime established, the development now cuts abruptly to the forces of law and order. At the telegraph office, the operator's little daughter discovers the plight. The film cuts again, this time to the dance hall—a simple set, with painted backdrops, but with so much activity going on that its synthetic quality is not too stridently apparent. With an energetic quadrille in progress, a tenderfoot is forced to dance, the Westerners shooting at his heels to spur him on. This sequence not only presented an interesting slice of Americana to early movie audiences, but it was also a singular attempt at greater conviction in rounding out the story with background material. In addition, it was a method of increasing suspense; the audience *knew* that the telegraph operator would arrive momentarily to seek the aid of the cowboys, and that knowledge kept interest at a high level. The final section of the film—the chase, the robbers thinking they are safe dividing the spoils, and then being surprised and bested in a gun battle—is, of course, a typical Western finish. It is the least successful part of the film *only* because Porter's actors were not experienced riders or stuntmen; the chase is slow and listless, and the falls unconvincing. However, since one must judge *The Great Train Robbery* not so much as a Western, but as a *blueprint* for *all* Westerns, criticism on the score of badly staged physical action is perhaps not justified. The film *has* a certain emotional feeling, the basic factor in cinematic narration.

On the strength of *The Great Train Robbery*, Edwin S. Porter—who wrote, directed, and photographed it—might well have become the "father" of the American cinema. (In fact, on the basis of this one eight-hundred foot film, many historians believe that he is already entitled to be considered just that.) But Porter's case is a curious and perhaps, for him, a frustrating and tragic one. Porter came to Edison in 1896, a mechanic with a rare enthusiasm for experimentation. Attaching himself to the inventor's motion picture company as an all-around man, he worked with films for seventeen years; yet only a handful of films—*The Great Train Robbery, The Life of an American Cowboy,* (together with "lives" of policemen and firemen), *The Kleptomaniac* and *Rescued from an Eagle's Nest* can be said to have any real or lasting value, and of these, only *The Great Train Robbery* had genuinely *creative* cinematic content. Porter's genius seems to have been one of *dramatic* construction, rather than of genuine cinema sense. It could well be accidental that in the case of *The Great Train Robbery* these two elements fused so well. *The Great Train Robbery* may be notable for its use of a close-up, but that close-up was so meaningless and ambiguous that the Edison publicity at the time informed exhibitors that they could use it at either the beginning or the end of the film. Porter realized that the scene—a full close-up of George Barnes, one of the outlaws, pointing his gun at the audience—had both dramatic and shock effect, but he seemed to flounder when deciding what to do with it.

Just how many of Porter's limitations were inherent in the man, and how many were inflicted by Edison, is a matter for conjecture. Edison was not an easy man to get along with, a man who disliked his assistants' branching out too much on their own. An inventor and a craftsman, not an artist, he expected his associates to be likewise. What aesthetic contents the Edison films had were usually ones that found their base in mechanics, e.g., the lighting and camerawork were often well above average. In any event, despite the fact that Porter made other films, none showed any progression from *The Great Train Robbery,* and indeed many of them, including full-length features ten years later, exhibited a distinct step backward. Certainly, however, the 1903 film was a tremendous success. Its title alone was more dramatic, glamorous, and promising of excitement, than any American movie title had been up to that time. Its success inspired a number of sequels, imitations, and outright plagiarisms. Sigmund Lubin even made a film with the same title which duplicated the sets and action of Porter's original exactly, the only difference being the addition of a local bank's calendar to the interior of the telegraph operator's office—presumably for suitable remuneration! Other obviously derivative titles included *The Great Bank Robbery, The Bold Bank Robbery, The Little Train Robbery,* and Biograph's *The Hold-up of the Rocky Mountain Express.* The Edison studios remained quite faithful to the format of *The Great Train Robbery* for a number of years. Even a film as late as *Across the Great Divide* (1913), dealing in its entirety with a train robbery, had advanced from the original only sufficiently to lend greater motivation to the proceedings, and to establish individual characters more clearly. Actually it was a much duller and slower film than Porter's original.

The title retained its magic through the years; by repeated presentation in theatrical shorts of the "Flicker Flashback" type, *The Great Train Robbery* remained one of the most famous movie titles of all. It was used again in 1941, as the title of a Bob Steele melodrama for Republic; a third version was planned in the Sixties, but never appeared.

With all his limitations, Porter was nevertheless the most creative single force in motion pictures between 1901 (when he was among the foremost of the "industry's" reputed total of six motion picture cameramen) and 1907, when D. W. Griffith joined Biograph. It was Porter who, in one of his last notable films, *Rescued from an Eagle's Nest,* introduced Griffith to the screen. Using the name Lawrence Griffith, D. W. had tried to sell the Edison studios a script he had written. The studios weren't interested, but they did offer him the lead in *Rescued from an Eagle's Nest* and, in need of money, he accepted. *Rescued from an Eagle's Nest* is inferior to *The Great Train Robbery,* although admittedly it was a difficult subject to do well in those early days.

The kidnaping of a baby by the eagle, and the pursuit by the father (Griffith) to the eagle's nest, high on a mountain ledge, was a thrilling enough plot premise and, in fact, it did thrill audiences in 1908. However, the cutting between studio scenes, with their painted backdrops, to actual exteriors, filmed in New Jersey, merely emphasized the lack of authenticity of the studio exteriors.

None of the exteriors in *The Great Train Robbery* had been anything but the real thing, only the interiors of telegraph office, saloon, and baggage car being studio reconstructions. The obvious painted flats of rocky mountains and high ledges did not match up too well with New Jersey's wooded slopes. The cutting was somewhat slipshod, and often overlapped badly. At one point Griffith is lowered over a ledge and climbs laboriously downwards; after a few feet of film, Porter cuts to a different angle, with Griffith again only just beginning the descent.

The final fight between Griffith and the stuffed eagle was particularly ineptly photographed; the struggle took place at the extreme left of the camera set-up, yet no attempt was made to move the camera even slightly to catch all of the action, with the result that at least half of the fight is out of the frame, and the rest is overshadowed by the big expanse of black painted backdrop that dominated nine-tenths of the frame. The result was a fight hard to follow and devoid of dramatic realism. Apparently Porter and Edison never made retakes, although it is curious that such a patently bad—yet important—sequence should be accepted in such a state.

Like *The Great Train Robbery* though, *Rescued from an Eagle's Nest* provided some interesting commentaries on life in the early West. Pioneers are shown working in an organized communal fashion in the clearing of land and the felling of trees, and when danger threatens, all recognize their individual responsibility to the group and aid the father in rescuing his child from the eagle.

Perhaps, had Porter like Griffith joined Biograph following *Rescued*

Looking nothing like one of the first directors of Westerns, nor even like a pioneer cameraman (both of which he was), Edwin S. Porter looks more like a highly successful businessman (which he certainly wasn't).

from an Eagle's Nest, he might have realized his full potential as a motion picture director. Instead he chose to stay with Edison, stagnated, and slowly passed into obscurity. When he died on April 30, 1941, in his seventies, he had been so much forgotten that the general reaction was one of surprise that this pioneer had been living until such a late date.

The first Western star

Another Edwin Porter graduate was G. M. Anderson, later better known as "Broncho Billy" and the first real Western star. Anderson stumbled into a role in *The Great Train Robbery* almost by accident. Assuring Porter that he could ride like a Texas Ranger, he was cast in the minor role of one of the bandits and he soon showed that he couldn't even get on a horse, let alone *stay* on it. He was in short order made an "extra" for the rest of the picture, but excited by the possibilities of the films— possibilities which he certainly doubted until he saw the tumultuous reception afforded *The Great Train Robbery* at its initial showing—Anderson told himself that this was the business for him, and went to work for Vitagraph as an actor and general production assistant. He directed a version of *Raffles, The Amateur Cracksman,* in 1905 for that company, moving to Chicago two years later. Chicago was then a

Broncho Billy Anderson, dressed in the Easterner's conception of the Western costume, derived largely from dime novels.

minor movie metropolis with Colonel William Selig, George Kleine, and George K. Spoor busily engaged in the production of one-reelers. Anderson went to work for Selig. Selig never was a very enterprising outfit, and Anderson, remembering the acclaim of *The Great Train Robbery,* thought of going off to Colorado with a cameraman, recruiting a cast out there, and shooting some Western adventures on location.

The films had only indifferent success and, because Selig seemed apathetic to Anderson's work, Anderson looked up his old friend, George K. Spoor. They decided to go into business together, not realizing that the company they were forming, the Essanay Company (based on the initials, S and A, of its founders), was to become one of the most honored of all the early movie studios. Located in Chicago, it was later the headquarters for many of the early Charlie Chaplin, Francis X. Bushman and Henry B. Walthall subjects, and Gloria Swanson's early proving ground.

After having directed comedies, using Ben Turpin, Anderson moved in late 1908 to Niles, California, and launched a West Coast studio for the company. He had time to think now, and he sought the reasons for the failure of his Selig Westerns. His conclusions were that they had tried too hard to repeat the formula of *The Great Train Robbery;* there had been no central character on which the audience could focus its attention. He now decided to build a cowboy hero, a tremendous idea in the days before the star system. He was literally creating the Western star, and laying the groundwork for cowboy heroes yet unborn.

The difficulty, however, was to find such a star. Stage players were still, as a whole, reluctant to risk films. California, in any case, not being an entertainment center, was hardly well stocked with stage players, or even out-of-work actors of any description. After protracted efforts, and out of sheer desperation, Anderson decided to play the lead himself. He had once posed for a cowboy cover on the *Saturday Evening Post*; that, and his undistinguished roles in *The Great Train Robbery,* were his sole connections with the West. He could ride a little better now, but still not like a Texas Ranger. No longer young, he was big and beefy, with striking, but decidedly not handsome features. However, he could not worry about breaking precedents; he was making them. It was a tremendous leap, both for him and for the Westerns. His first film was adapted from a Peter B. Kyne story. It was titled *Broncho Billy and the Baby,* a sentimental tale with Billy playing a "good badman" who is ultimately reformed by love. It was an enormous success, and convinced Billy not only that he should stick with Westerns, but that he should use Broncho Billy as a continuing character—treating each story individ-

A scene from Broncho Billy's
Oath (*1913*).

ually, however, so that it would not matter how often Billy married,
reformed, or was killed off.

Over the next few years, Billy made close to five hundred short
Westerns, one-reelers at first, and then two-reelers. They were the first
real "series" Westerns, the first with an established star, and the films
that really established Westerns as a genre. They were simple in plot
(Billy, not being of the West himself, had to fall back on pulp magazines
and dime novels for inspiration) and had none of the starkness or the
documentary quality that William S. Hart was later to introduce. But
they were often surprisingly strong and vigorous in their action content,
with elaborately constructed and absolutely convincing Western town
sets. The camera work was good, and Anderson, being a husky and well-
built individual, was more than up to the action. A trifle dour in the
later Hart tradition, he presented a reasonably realistic and not too
glamorized portrait of the frontier's manhood.

After a seven-year period, Anderson moved into features, but by this
time William S. Hart had taken over the field, together with Tom Mix,
and the veteran realized that he had missed out. He returned to
comedies, and in the early Twenties produced a good series of Stan
Laurel comedies for Metro release. However, like many another since,
Billy felt that he was being treated unfairly by Louis B. Mayer. Unable
to improve the situation, he said goodbye to films and retired. Thirty-
five years later, in 1958, he told television audiences of his part in the
moulding of Hollywood's cowboy formula, in the course of a ninety-
minute show on NBC. He appeared with John Ford, John Wayne, Gene
Autry, Gary Cooper, and others. He lived well into his eighties alert, vital,
and always eager to talk about the old days of the Western. He died in
January, 1971.

It is a pity that few of the hundreds of Broncho Billy Anderson pictures have survived, which complicates any accurate appraisal of his qualities as a director. But there is certainly no denying the tremendous popularity of his films, or their influence on Western production generally.

We wish to quote at this point, and in its entirety, a typical unsigned review of one of the Anderson Westerns, as published in *The Moving Picture World*, a trade paper, in its May 15, 1909, issue in order to stress the action and solidity of those primitive works:

A MEXICAN'S GRATITUDE

"An Essanay film which had some thrilling scenes and is certain to please the average audience wherever it is shown. There is life and action without bloodshed and the melodramatic features are made attractive rather than repulsive. The story is that a Mexican is saved from being hanged as a horsethief by the sheriff. He writes the word 'Gratitude' on a card, tears it in two and gives one half to the sheriff and keeps the other half himself. Years afterward this same sheriff falls in love with a girl of the West. She is wanted by a cowboy and he contrives to bring the sheriff and another girl together, and gets the girl the sheriff loves there just in time to see him in the scheming girl's embrace. Explanations are impossible and he sees the girl he wants walk away with the false cowboy. The sheriff has a fight with him and forces him to confess his treachery. The cowboy goes to a Mexican's hut and secures the services of two greasers to do his bidding. The three lie in wait for the sheriff and his sweetheart, overpower them and drag them away to the Mexican's hut where the cowboy tantalizes the sheriff for a time and then forces the girl into another room. The Mexican wants some tobacco and sees a sack projecting from the sheriff's pocket. In pulling it out, he pulls out also the half of the card with the word 'Gratitude' upon it. When the cowboy returns to the room he is comparing the card. He then asks the sheriff if that was given him by a man whom he saved from lynching a few years before. The sheriff replies that it was. Whereupon the Mexican immediately loosens the sheriff's bonds, and a fight between the sheriff and the cowboy ensues. The sheriff has him across a table choking him into insensibility when the girl appears and begs him to stop and they go away together.

It is impossible to invest this story in telling with the life that is in the picture. It seems almost as though the characters were going to speak, they do their parts so naturally, while the staging is remarkably good. The film was heartily applauded in two theatres where it was seen the past week, and everyone who attends motion picture shows knows that applause is somewhat rare."

Complete reliability cannot be placed on these early reviews since, of course, film criticism was not yet clearly defined. There were few precedents for comparisons, and many of the terms to describe film grammar and construction had not yet been devised; indeed, film grammar itself was still in the formulative stage. Since trade papers tried to help both exhibitors and distributors, they were probably prone to be lenient with really bad films, and possibly excessively generous to the good ones. But, the reviews as such seem to be honest. There are definite signs of the awareness of dramatic and photographic merit, and appropriate if mild criticism for the lack of those qualities. "Bought" reviews were unlikely; if they existed, they did so far more subtly than their counterparts today.

Hollywood makes more Westerns

As a result of the great success of Anderson's Westerns, there was immediately an increase in the number of Westerns made from 1909 on, and the big vogue of one-reeler classics such as *The Merchant of Venice, Julius Caesar, Romeo and Juliet* declined. 1909, incidentally, was distinguished not only by the upswing in the production of Westerns in the U. S., but also by the increased importing of European films, which also included a fair proportion of Westerns.

Denmark's Great Northern Film Company was particularly adept at imitating American melodramas and Westerns. Their *Texas Tex* was about as thoroughly Western a title as it is possible to conceive.

Selig was among the most prolific of Westerns manufacturers in the United States at this time. His *In Old Arizona* was rated one of his most ambitious subjects to date, and was recommended as being of sufficient merit for repeat bookings in first-class halls, although it was criticized to some extent for its inaccurate military detail. But it was certainly full of action, with a big Indian battle in the desert; the cavalry arrived in the nick of time in response to a call for help, sent via carrier pigeon by the enterprising villain! This was the era of the swarthy Mexican villain, and so it was here—although he had a treacherous Indian as his henchman. However, the Indian was by no means a stock villain in Selig Westerns. In *An Indian's Gratitude,* the hero was an Indian who had been taught the Fifth Commandment. When the villain is captured by the Indian tribe, and is about to be hanged, not without some justification, the Indian hero intercedes, persuading his brothers to follow the white man's moral law. The film prompted a critic of the time to remark: "The Selig trademark has come to mean a film of unusual quality."

Other interesting Selig Westerns of 1909 included *Boots and Saddles,* with the young heroine saving the cavalryman-hero from death at the

A scene from Broncho Billy and the Redskin. *In costuming, plot, and characterization, the Anderson Westerns matured rapidly.*

stake; *In the Badlands,* a bizarre picture in which the villain perished freezing to death in the snow; a film however that was criticized for the painted backdrops it used, and also for the inaccuracy of its costuming; *Stampede,* praised for its accurate depiction of Western ranch life, *Pet of the Big Horn Ranch, Custer's Last Stand, On the Border, Pine Ridge Feud,* and countless others. Despite his obvious reliance on Westerns as his bread and butter, Selig could still afford to kid them occasionally. His *The Tenderfoot* was but one of many satires on Westerns made in 1909 by several companies, Edison among them, who derived a considerable portion of their revenue from Westerns. Pathé's *Misadventures of a Sheriff* seemed amusing, and was probably a forerunner of the hilarious Western satires that Mack Swain made some years later. By 1909 the Western was sufficiently established as a genre for film critics to be harsher with it than they were with other types of motion picture. Because of the often spontaneous nature of the shooting, there were unavoidable anachronisms and inaccuracies in *all* types of pictures, but the critics seemed to single out the Western—and its near relations—for the most pointed barbs. One critic was particularly upset because an Eskimo baby in *A Cry from the Wilderness* was seen to be wearing white underwear beneath his crude skins. And Edison's *The Corporal's Daughter* had its cavalry gallop out of its frontier fort on to a paved road, with a conspicuous sewer. Moving the camera just a foot or two away would have avoided such a boner.

There were other signs that the motion picture was gradually, but surely, being taken more and more seriously. Then, as now, there were protests from British production groups that their product was being boycotted in the U. S. There were cries of despair from pressure groups at the "garbage masquerading as art" that was being imported from France. And already box office polls had been taken to ascertain which areas responded most readily to certain types of film. The Midwest, usually regarded as an area which liked blood and thunder, strangely enough preferred comedy. In Mexico it was found that only thirty-five percent of the overall movie audience would turn out for *Othello,* but one hundred percent would storm the theatres for murder, bullfights, and other strong meat.

Already there was concern over the Western's possible influence on the young, in that it often seemed to glamorize outlawry. Some advertising posters for a Western plugging *Jesse James* (1911) were heavily censured, and a writer, displaying his astonishing racism in print, commented that "an Indian will walk miles to see bloodshed," and that films and advertising which catered to dormant sadism of this type should not be encouraged. At almost the same time, an Indian named I. Lee, a resident of Rochester, New York, voiced strong criticism in the trade papers of the continued depiction of Indians on the screen as bloodthirsty savages.

There was surprisingly little shape and form to the Western field prior to the advent of Griffith and Ince. Companies like Selig, Centaur, Edison, Essanay, Vitagraph, Kalem, Biograph, Lubin, Powhatan Films (a company that had an enormous Indian head as its trademark), Bison, World, Phoenix, Tiger, Carson, and others were all turning out Westerns on an almost assembly-line basis. From the point of view of film history, this was a fascinating period. The birth, growth, life, and death of these little companies, offer ample material for a whole book devoted to just these few years.

From the standpoint of Western film history, few distinguishable trends emerge. One that did was the coexistence of two approaches to the Indian. The one held the Indian to be a senseless, bloodthirsty savage. The other veered to the opposite extreme by depicting the Indian with dignity as the original American. Neither of these two approaches is surprising or unique in itself; what is notable is that the two contrasting cycles should coexist, a state of affairs that has never been repeated since. If anything, the sympathetic approach to the Indian was the one that then dominated. Many of the films with Indian heroes were built around legend and near mysticism, and had a fascinating sort of primitive poetry to them. The Indian's plight was not seen through rose-colored glasses; the majority of these films were tragedies, in which the Indian deliberately went to his death to avoid dishonor, or committed suicide as a gesture of defiance against the unwanted civilization that was being brought by the white man. Many of these films were strong meat indeed. *The Bride of Tabaiva* was replete with all the neuroses of a postwar *film-noir*. Kalem did an interesting series dealing with the Florida Seminole Indians. Vitagraph's *Red Wing's Gratitude* used authentic Indians in the principal roles, and titles like *The Red Man's View, An Indian Wife's Devotion, A True Indian's Heart,* tell their own story.

Films concentrating on the white man's participation in the building of the West included an early adaptation of O. Henry's "Cisco Kid" stories which, in contrast to later filmed adventures, finished with the hanging of the "Kid." Others were *On the Warpath,* with a traditional last-minute cavalry rescue; *The Road Agents,* an Essanay Western praised for its "unusual realism in staging"; *The Skeptical Cowboy,* a really macabre Western from Centaur, in which visions of his dead victim and of his own execution drive a killer to pray for forgiveness; *The Gold Pros-*

pectors, in which an Indian chief is killed by a little child; *Why the Mail Was Late,* a Lubin Western with more visions, in this case of an angel who appears to the dead pony rider; and *Davy Crockett in Hearts United.*

In synopsis form, many of the early Westerns we have mentioned in passing were truly inventive. Certainly their plots were nothing if not imaginative and often courageously stark. But translating the vivid written word into an equally vivid film was another matter. Few of the early pre-Griffith and Ince Westerns are available to us for reappraisal, but of those that are (particularly the films of Bison and Edison) *none* have sufficiently competent direction for the basically good plot material. The Broncho Billy Westerns were certainly the liveliest of these, making up in vigor what they lacked in unusual plot elements.

It is dangerous to generalize in this 1903–1909 period. But from the surviving Westerns, the indication is that they needed both a consistency of purpose and directors who understood the Western per se, directors who were also aware of the genre's tremendous scope and potential. That they did not achieve that consistency, and did not begin to fulfill that potential, until the advent of Griffith and Ince, is definitely not to say that some excellent Westerns were not made prior to 1910. Undoubtedly many were, and, some talented and advanced directors may be unknown to us simply because so little of their material is available today.

In a sense, much of the pre-1910, even pre-1900 material does exist, since negatives have been preserved. But the printing is very expensive and one must gamble on items that, from titles and original reviews, seem promising. Even then, for every worthwhile discovery, there are three or four films of limited quality and interest. More and more of this material is being recovered, but it is a race against time because it is highly probable that the chemically unstable materials may begin to decompose.

But if one cannot avoid uncertainty over the status of Westerns which immediately followed *The Great Train Robbery,* then one can, with unequivocal certainty, sustain the view that the Western was guided into firmer, more creative, and certainly more influential channels when D. W. Griffith and T. H. Ince brought their considerable talents to bear in the next years.

David W

Thomas H. Ince

D. W. Griffith (left) with his cameraman, G. W. Bitzer.

Griffith and
1909 – 1913

D. W. Griffith

The pioneer work of Edwin S. Porter and
Broncho Billy Anderson having already established standard Western plots and basic
elements of technique, it remained for David
W. Griffith and Thomas H. Ince to provide
the momentum. When they began their
work in the genre, the Western film was regarded as outdated, and *Variety,* in fact, in
its reviews of the Westerns of the 1908–09
period, frequently concluded that the films
were competently made, but added: "It has
all been done so often before, and usually
better."

So much has been written about Griffith
as an innovator of film technique and as the
foremost genius of the American screen, that
his extremely valuable contribution to the
early Western in particular is often overlooked. And yet, between 1908 and 1913, he
turned out some of the finest one-reel Westerns ever made, quite outstanding in their
scale, scope and imagination.

We saw in the previous chapter how
Kentucky-born Griffith, an actor and a playwright of seemingly competent but unre-
markable ability, had entered the industry
as an actor in Edison's *Rescued from an Eagle's
Nest* (1907), directed by Porter. Shortly afterwards, he joined the Biograph company in
New York as a writer-actor, subsequently
directing in 1908 his first film, *The Adventures
of Dollie,* an unsubtle but fast-moving melodrama which had immediate success. He
was greatly encouraged at this time by cameraman G. W. "Billy" Bitzer.

4

For a beginning salary of fifty dollars per week, he turned out at least eight films for Biograph every month and, during this period, he was continually experimenting with new forms of film expression and grammar, and especially in the possibilities of building tension through editing. While some techniques, like the close-up, had been introduced by others, they were perfected by Griffith, who in turn created and developed other aspects of film narration.

Chief among these was the cross-cutting technique, developed to add tension and maximum excitement to melodramas. Although the basic idea of cross-cutting seems elementary today in any kind of dramatic movie construction, its introduction in those days was a daring move. Cross-cutting involves the manipulation of time and space. Settlers fighting off Indians are besieged in a cabin. We see a long shot of the Indians circling. A closer shot of the pioneers fighting back. A large close-up, perhaps of a child cowering in fright. Then we cut to a troop of cavalry perhaps twenty miles away. They have learned of the situation and are preparing to rescue the threatened settlers. Back to the fight. Ammunition is low. The settlers can't hold out long. Cut to the Indians preparing for a final assault. Cut to the cavalry racing across the prairie. Depending upon the creative ability of the director and editor, this kind of material can be built and expanded indefinitely; mathematical patterns can be introduced. Long shot can cut to long shot; close-up to close-up. As suspense builds, the shots can get shorter and shorter. Cross-cutting is taken for granted today, but initially it was not. *Because* it "created" excitement instead of just showing it, it was considered (a) dishonest and (b) confusing, just as originally the close-up was regarded with suspicion. A close-up? It's not real! Who ever saw a woman's face alone, or a pair of feet? So it was with regard to cross-cutting, or indeed advanced editing of any kind. Most early Westerns detailed the fight admirably, and left it there. The cavalry arrived in the nick of time (without built-up suspense via cutting), and the matter ended there.

Griffith loved Westerns for the sweep and spectacle they offered, and for the opportunities they provided for a development of his editing theories in terms of essentially visual action. He was, of course, busy in other fields—melodrama, social criticism, adaptations of literary classics, and even semi-propagandistic political melodrama—so that Westerns occupied an important, but not dominant part of his schedule.

His Westerns were filmed both in New Jersey and in California. Until 1913 in his Biograph period, his studios were located in New York, but from October, 1910, he regularly took a troupe to California to escape the dreary New York winters so unsuitable for the cameras, and to arrange for, in the interest of authenticity, his filming of the bulk of his Westerns on the West Coast. Almost all of the Biograph members of Griffith's great stock company—Lillian and Dorothy Gish, Owen Moore, Mae Marsh, Mary Pickford, Robert Harron, Harry Carey, Lionel Barrymore, Charles West, Alfred Paget, Henry B. Walthall, Wilfrid Lucas, Dorothy Bernard, Blanche Sweet—went on to subsequent stardom. Some of the directors who learned their trade under him were Erich von Stroheim, Raoul Walsh, Chester and Sidney Franklin, Lloyd Ingraham, Donald Crisp, Joseph Henabery, Mack Sennett, Dell Henderson, Elmer Clifton, Christy Cabanne, John Emerson, Lowell Sherman, George Siegmann, Jack Conway, and many others; of course, many other top directors, from John Ford to King Vidor, were considerably influenced by Griffith's work.

Griffith was more interested in situations, and his treatment of them, than in plots *per se,* and it is significant that the more plot his Western film had, the less effective it was. For example, *Broken Ways* (1912), a Biograph two-reeler, concerned a frontier wife with a worthless husband, with a suitor in the person of an honest sheriff. The film ran smoothly, with good exterior scenes and generally fine acting. The plot was simple, although the plot details which had to be followed seemed to get in Griffith's way. At this particular phase in his career, he was more interested in dynamic *style,* rather than in dramatic plot *material.*

More successful was *The Wanderer,* with Harry Carey in the lead, this time in the Chaplinesque role of a vagabond who saves the day for two settlers, leaving them to a happy future, unaware that it was he who helped them. The villains, incidentally, were not brought to justice; Griffith frequently allowed his "heavies" to escape unpunished, and in many cases even invested them with likable characteristics which enlisted audience sympathy. It was not Griffith's policy to allow crime to go unpunished, but when the dramatic needs of his films required departure from convention, he had no compunction about letting the villains off, in complete contrast to the ultra-moral films of Ince, in which the guilty always paid a heavy price.

Despite their short running time and the de-emphasis on plots, no two Griffith Westerns were alike; *The Goddess of Sagebrush Gulch* was as distinct from *A Temporary Truce* as it was from *The Squaw's Love,* in striking contrast to the assembly-line products of the late Forties and Fifties, when it was difficult to tell one Roy Rogers or Charles Starrett Western from another.

Three Griffith Westerns are especially noteworthy: *The Last Drop of Water* (1911), *Fighting Blood* (1911), and *The Battle at Elderbush Gulch*

(1913). *The Last Drop of Water* (1911), was the precursor of *The Covered Wagon* (1923). Both had much the same sense of poetry. *The Covered Wagon*—which we shall discuss in much greater detail in a later chapter—disposed of its action as soon as that action had served its purpose, without integrating it into the whole. Griffith's film appeared in many ways more exciting, because the action was part of a total effect, and that effect was accentuated by cross-cutting, providing far more energy and excitement than anything in James Cruze's later film.

The Last Drop of Water is interesting also for the fact that it was one of the few Griffith Westerns in which plot and action assumed equal importance. It was colorful stuff, with heroine Blanche Sweet in love with weak-willed Joseph Graybill, whose fondness for liquor had escaped her notice. Blanche marries Graybill, while another suitor (Charles West) wishes her well, standing gallantly aside. A year later, struggling along in a marriage made increasingly difficult, Blanche and Graybill trek westward with a wagon train, joined by West who is on hand to protect the girl he loves. Water is low when the Indians attack. West, who has volunteered to reach the closest waterhole, does not return. Graybill slips through the Indian lines into the desert, where he finds West dying. At first, he jeers at the sight of his old rival, and then, overcome by compassion, offers him the last swallow of precious water from his canteen. Exhausted, Graybill dies, but West, revived by the water, is able to struggle on, to find water, and to return with a supply to the beleaguered wagon train. A detachment of cavalry finally routs the Indians in a pitched battle and, leaving the grave of Graybill behind as a tribute to the courage of the early pioneers, the wagon train, with Sweet and West now united, rolls on towards distant California. A slow, effective fadeout with the grave starkly in the foreground, shows the wagon train slowly disappearing over the distant horizon.

Richard Barthelmess (in a role originally intended for Rudolph Valentino) and Carol Dempster in a scene from Scarlet Days, *a Griffith Western of 1919.*

Even better, however, and one of the classics of the pre-1913 cinema, although strangely unrecognized as such, was *Fighting Blood* (1911), a triumphant application of treatment over subject matter. The plot is simple: a grizzled, old Civil War veteran and his family are settled on the Dakota frontier during the uneasy interim between the organization of the Dakotas as territories and their admission to the Union as states in 1889. Father and son quarrel, and the boy leaves. Up in the hills, he witnesses a Sioux attack against some pioneers. He warns his sweetheart, takes her to his father's cabin, hotly pursued by the Indians. He races away for troops, while the settlers come to add strength to the small party fighting against overwhelming odds. The battle between the settlers and the Indians, and the hero's ride for help, occupy two-thirds of the film, utilizing an extremely simple, but tremendously exciting—in visual terms—formula which John Ford still employs today. Griffith increased tension by showing children in danger, cowering in a corner or under a bed, threatened with death either from the enemy or even from their parents, to prevent their capture by the Indians. Even in the midst of the action, Griffith found time to insert strikingly original compositions. One long shot showed the long line of cavalry riding across the screen in the distance. This scene had barely been established when the riders at the head of the column suddenly appeared in close-up on the right side of the screen, suggesting an enormous number of riders were present between the long column at the back of the screen and the riders now galloping into the foreground. When the cavalry finally entered the battlefield surrounding the log cabin where the settlers were putting up their defense against the Indians, Griffith gave the rescue dramatic effect by shooting the final battle scenes in massive panoramic shots, photographed from the tops of overlooking hills.

Two years after *Fighting Blood,* he made *The Battle at Elderbush Gulch,* one of his last, and certainly one of his very best two-reel films for Biograph. It had major similarities with *Fighting Blood;* the plot was equally simple, and merely served as the basis for spectacular scenes. Lillian Gish and Mae Marsh played two Eastern girls who came to live in the West (their roles here foreshadowed in some ways the roles they were to play in *The Birth of a Nation*). Mae's dog runs away and is caught by Indians who plan to eat it. Mae, confronting them, is about to be scalped when the settlers rescue her. The Indians then go on the warpath, while Robert Harron, in the manner of *Fighting Blood,* escapes through enemy lines to bring the troops.

Griffith's "child in danger" motif was employed here in two-fold fashion: a baby, abandoned in the open, is rescued by Mae Marsh, while

Indians on the rampage in the Cherry Valley. Panoramic action from Griffith's America *(1924).*

children, cowering in a cabin under attack, are threatened with death. The film had more character development than *Fighting Blood*, greater and even more creative use of the panoramic shot, and far more savagery in the battle scenes, although Griffith was never sadistic, but rather always managed to *suggest* extreme brutality with astounding conviction.

Perhaps the only finesse really lacking from *Fighting Blood* and *The Battle at Elderbush Gulch* was the running insert, or riding close-up, a device he was to develop to perfection with the ride of the Klansmen in *The Birth of a Nation*.

It has always been a source of some regret that, apart from two good program films made between 1916 and 1919 (*Scarlet Days*, a Griffith personal production and *The Martyrs of the Alamo*, a Griffith supervised production), Griffith never made a full-length Western epic. But if he turned his back on the Western as such, he never forgot the lessons he learned from his early horse operas, and the development he pioneered and perfected he used with striking success in other genres.

In his last big historical epic of the silent era, *America* (1924), one saw familiar scenes: the American colonists besieged in their little fort by hordes of redskins, Neil Hamilton racing to the rescue with a band of cavalrymen, individual scenes of children huddled in a corner, riders soon to be seen in a close-up as the leaders complete an off-screen semi-circle to gallop back into the frame. All this can and must be traced back to scenes in *Fighting Blood*.

Thomas H. Ince

Thomas H. Ince, like Griffith a former actor, arrived in Hollywood in 1911, following a year of film-making in New York and Cuba. He was employed by the New York Motion Picture Company to concentrate primarily on Westerns. He soon became bored with the simply plotted and cheaply budgeted horse operas of the period and finally persuaded his bosses to permit him to make a deal with the entire Miller Brothers' 101 Ranch Wild West Show, an outfit with a huge entourage of cowboys, horses, wagons, buffaloes, and other accessories. With this equipment, he filmed a two-reel spectacle in 1911 entitled *War on the Plains,* which was praised not only for its accuracy from a historical viewpoint, but for its considerable artistry. *Moving Picture World* of January 27, 1912, wrote: "... the impression that it all leaves is that here we have looked upon a presentation of Western life that is real and that is true to life, and that we would like to see it again and again so as to observe more of the details."

Unlike Griffith, who was only just beginning to experiment, Ince with *War on the Plains,* his subsequent *Custer's Last Fight,* and *The Battle of Gettysburg* was already at the zenith of the purely creative phase of his career; in fact, it was the only personally creative phase, since he thereafter assumed the role of production supervisor, individual directors working under him. Apart from W. S. Hart's pictures, none of Ince's post-1914 pictures had the authenticity and conviction enjoyed by such earlier films as *War on the Plains.* Ince was first and foremost a showman and a business man. He knew how to organize, and his greatest contribution to the history and art of the cinema is represented by the efficient shooting methods he developed. He placed great stress on the importance of the detailed shooting script, and his strict supervision of scripts, many of which he partially rewrote, injected a measure of "Ince influence" into all pictures produced under his organizations. Forethought in these scripts was astounding, the shooting worked out meticulously down to the last detail. Reading Ince's revised scenario of William Clifford's *The Iconoclast,* for example, one is amazed at the detailed information prepared in advance: a dialogue for all characters, a full description of the furnishings, the décor, the desired facial expressions, the tints to be used, a listing of all different sets, together with the scene numbers identified with each particular set. These time-saving devices are, of course, taken for granted today, but it was Ince who recognized their value, developing to the full the potential in the script method of filming.

While developing the detailed film script, Ince was also making the role of the production supervisor essential, a comparatively rare executive position in the early days of motion pictures, a time when most of the men with money remained very much on their side of the fence, leaving to the director the entire business of making films. In some ways this older system benefited the films produced; today, certainly, the financiers exert a predominant influence over the creative aspects of the cinema— of which they know absolutely nothing. No longer personally directing, and apparently not content with being merely a unique combination of producer and efficiency expert, Ince nurtured the impression that he was a creative craftsman, too. A publicity campaign which he created himself was stepped up between 1915 and 1917. In this period, Ince joined D. W. Griffith and Mack Sennett in the Triangle Corporation. It was his practice to assume director's credit on any film under his over-all production if he considered the film important in any way. Thus *Civilization,* a weak anti-war spectacle, although actually directed by Raymond West, was released with Ince assuming full directorial title, and West getting an "Assisted by . . ." credit. This procedure created an aura of greatness around Ince which many European critics and historians believed, since they were too far from the scene to ferret out the truth. Thus, ironically, some of Ince's fame in France is based on his least creative period, often on the basis of inferior films over which he had comparatively little to say, anyway.

The Westerns of Griffith and Ince made in the 1909–1913 period display the essential differences between the two men in their approach to the same material. Ince was a showman, a routine director, and a mediocre editor. He did not know how to build excitement as Griffith did. Ince's stories were strong, full of drama and complications; Griffith's were really little more than situations. To the casual observer, it might seem that Ince's stories had more maturity than did those of Griffith. But in his effort to be different, Ince went overboard for the morbid.

An incredible number of Ince's Westerns (and Civil War stories, too) had unnecessarily tragic endings. *Past Redemption,* for instance, presents Ann Little as an outlaw girl who, together with her father, sells whiskey to Indians. A new minister spurs a reform movement in town. Prohibition is voted, but the outlaws continue their traffic. A detachment of cavalry engages them in their hideout and Ann's father is killed. The girl escapes after having killed an Indian, first making sure it would seem the cavalry was responsible. This provokes an all-out battle in which many are slain. The girl then goes to the minister's home seeking revenge. She tries to kill him and is caught. Somewhat illogically, she is paroled into the minister's custody. Gradually becoming repentant, she falls in love with the minister, but when the townspeople see scandal in this union, she wanders off alone into the desert to die.

The tragic ending here, in view of Ann Little's violent past, seems to be justified, but this hardly applies to *The Woman* (1913), dealing with a successful opera singer who, in order to save her husband suffering from tuberculosis, moves to the dry climate of Arizona. She takes part in a gigantic land rush in an effort to make a new home for themselves, but she is injured falling from her horse during the rush. Recovered, she goes to work in a saloon where she is molested by drunken cowhands. Driven to desperation by the need for money to help her invalid husband, she marries a wealthy gambler. Some months later, word reaches her that her real husband is dead. That night, when the gambler returns home, he finds the woman dead, a suicide note in her hand, thanking him for all his kindness and begging his forgiveness for the wrong she has done him.

Plot was given far more prominence than the action, the really spectacular land-rush footage employed merely as background incident, not as the film's highlight. Then, too, its moral values are somewhat questionable; not only is the gambler presented idealistically, in comparison with the generally drunken reprehensible behavior of the honest cowhands and miners, but bigamy and suicide are quite casually condoned.

Ince's Civil War films had a similar tendency toward strong meat. One of the best was *The Drummer of the Eighth,* which tells the touching story of a boy who runs away from home to join the Northern forces. He is captured in battle, learns of plans for a big Southern advance, and manages to return to his own lines with the news, although he is seriously wounded. Because of his information, the North is able to win a battle. Lying in a hospital tent, the youth writes to his mother saying he will be home soon. On the day of his return, a big feast is prepared and the household joyously awaits him. At the railroad depot, the returning soldiers detrain, but the boy's sister cannot find him. Then, two soldiers take a simple coffin from the train. The boy is coming home.

Individually, each of these films was powerful and well made, but collectively, they seem to be too much part of a pattern, geared to an off-beat plot and a shock effect. However, not all of Ince's Westerns had tragic endings, nor were all his tragedies contrived. Some of his short Westerns were exciting in the best sense, although they, too, relied more on dramatic situations than on physical action.

One of the best of his "tragedies" was a very moving and beautifully photographed two-reeler, *The Heart of an Indian*, a rather strange film which presented both white man and Indian in a basically sympathetic light. It opened with scenes of everyday life in an Indian village, presided over by J. Barney Sherry, playing the chief, with the Indian actor, William Eagleshirt, as his second in command. The chief's daughter is mourning the death of her child. The film cuts then to the life of the pioneers, tilling the soil, hunting buffalo. Both races are established as equals in the wresting of a livelihood from the land, and in their rights to such livelihood.

Then, an Indian raid is precipitated when a white shoots "Indian" buffalo; from one blazing cabin, the Indian chief rescues a baby girl to give to his daughter for adoption. The real mother, distraught, staggers into the Indian camp, and tries to claim her baby. The Indian girl taunts her, but then, allowing mother and child a temporary embrace, she relents, and in a touching little scene, realizes the universality of motherhood, and, indirectly, of all men. She restores the child to its real mother, escorting them both to safety. But the white men of the settlement, bent on revenge, have taken to the trail and even the sight of the mother and child, both quite safe, does not lessen their hatred. They creep up on the Indian camp and cold-bloodedly massacre its inhabitants. The final scene of the film is an exquisite silhouette, at dusk on the crest of a hill, of the now doubly bereaved Indian girl "commun-

Thomas H. Ince with his first Indian star, William Eagleshirt.

ing with the spirit of her dead child," as she prays for the tiny body wrapped in blankets and placed atop a flimsy wooden framework.

A recurring theme in Ince's frontier dramas is the symbolic struggle between good and evil made simple by having the heroes allied with the church, and the villains with the saloon. In some cases the entire motivation was based on the church's determination to stamp out drinking, and the villains' equally strong determination that it should continue. The implication is inevitably that good can survive only when the temptation to evil (namely, the saloon) is obliterated—not indicative of very pronounced moral stamina on the part of Ince's Christian pioneers.

However, another recurring theme in Ince's pictures made it difficult to determine just where he stood regarding the church, since one of his favorite characters seemed to be the weak-willed minister seduced by a saloon girl, or the devil-may-care cowboy who stood, to be sure, for law and order, but who was usually given a scene in which he ridiculed either the minister or the church, a sort of "Last Stand" to show that he owed no more allegiance to God than anyone else!

If the Westerns of Griffith and Ince had anything at all in common, it was the complete realism of their background, due, of course, to the locations they used, for the California foothills of then-young Hollywood were a living part of the old West, untouched by man or commerce in any way. Ince built his studio, "Inceville," and his Western streets and ranches in an area at the mouth of the Santa Ynez canyon, having in front of him the Pacific Ocean and miles of sandy beaches. Behind him were miles of picturesque virgin wilderness. Its value as a Western backdrop has been lost today, since it takes only one hotel or mansion to turn a Western mountain into a Hollywood hill overlooking the Pacific. Ince's old stamping ground is still a beautiful area, but Hollywood homes have transformed it radically.

One other element in the realism of Griffith-Ince Westerns was the dust. A minor thing, perhaps, but a telling one. Dust was everywhere in the old West—behind men as they walked down streets, behind horses and coaches, in the air itself, wherever the wind blew. The constant visual presence of dust, whether in clouds kicked up, or in layers on the clothes men wore, was a perpetual reminder of the rugged and uncomfortable conditions under which the West was built and won, almost a symbol in itself of a land to be tamed. Because it was there, Griffith and Ince ignored the dust and let it play its own role in their films. Later, Western movie makers learned the neat trick of wetting down the ground before the day's shooting, so that the soil was moist and able to absorb the surface dust. Westerns soon became less dusty—and less convincing.

By 1912, despite ever-stronger plots from Ince, and the increasing technical virtuosity of Griffith, Westerns were losing ground again at the box office. The criticism of tired uniformity that had been flung at them five years earlier, and which was to be reiterated at regular intervals, became particularly sharp. Griffith and Ince then cut down on their Western output, increasing the number of Civil War films they brought to the screen. By that time, however, these two men had already made their major contributions, each in his own way, to the Western film. Ford, Cruze, and several others were now to take over and to enlarge upon these beginnings. But, with the sole exception of William S. Hart, no others were to contribute more to the Western film than had David W. Griffith and Thomas H. Ince.

William Surrey Hart

and realism

5

The man who, single-handed, rescued the Western film from the rut of mediocrity into which it had fallen was William S. Hart, in a career that spanned slightly more than ten years. As an actor, director, and to a lesser degree as a writer, he brought to the Western both realism and a rugged poetry. His films, the motion picture equivalents of the paintings of Frederic Remington and the drawings of Charles M. Russell, represent the very heart and core of that which is so casually referred to as Hollywood's "Western tradition."

Although the third important Western star, arriving on the film scene after Broncho Billy Anderson and Tom Mix, and retiring while Mix was still in his prime, his contributions to Westerns were original, and their influence was of greater importance than those of Anderson and Mix.

William S. Hart was born December 6, 1870, in Newburgh, New York. The "S" stood, not as is often erroneously stated, for Shakespeare, but for Surrey. His family, the father being a traveling miller, led a nomadic existence, wandering across the country in search of water for power, eventually settling near a Sioux reservation in the Dakotas. As a youngster, William played with Sioux of his age, learning their language and customs, and a respect for them that he never lost.

His experiences in the West were rich and varied. He worked as a trail-herd cowboy in Kansas, and once he was caught in the crossfire of a sheriff and two gunmen on

Sioux City's main street. The death of William's baby brother during the family's Dakota residence is movingly described in Hart's book, *My Life East and West.* The baby was buried near the headwaters of the Mississippi by the father, William, and a younger sister; the descriptive passage of that harsh reality, and the unbearable grief of those days is one of the most poignant passages in the book.

His mother's illness took the family back East when William was still only fifteen. He held an assortment of odd jobs, including singing in the Trinity Church choir, to round out the family's income. Participating in athletics, at nineteen he accompanied the famous track star, Lon Myers, to London, and set a record for the three-and-a-half mile walk.

His two ambitions in this period were to become an actor and to go to West Point. The latter was impossible, due to an inadequate academic background. Later in his career, he noted: "The stage idea just came, and always remained, and will be with me when the final curtain is rung down." He had the good fortune to befriend F. F. Markey, one of the most accomplished actors and an excellent teacher of the art. Daniel E. Bandemann, a prominent actor-manager, provided him with his first role on the professional stage, in *Romeo and Juliet,* which coincidentally opened in his native Newburgh. For the next twenty years, Hart's stature as an actor rose. He had a fine speaking voice, even as late as 1939, when he spoke the prologue for the reissue of his silent film, *Tumbleweeds.*

The role of Messala in the original company of *Ben Hur* (1899) brought him his first real critical acclaim, but after a number of successful seasons with the show, his career went into a decline. During this period he lived in the Hotel Harrington, on Broadway and Forty-fourth Street in New York City, and shared his room with another struggling young actor, Thomas H. Ince. Then, things took a turn for the better, with his sudden introduction to Western roles and, as Cash Hawkins in *The Squaw Man,* he had instantaneous success, followed by the starring role in the road company of *The Virginian.*

His success in these plays, and an event which took place in Cleveland, while he was on tour there, determined him on a course that was to succeed far beyond his wildest expectations. In Cleveland, Hart saw his first Western film and, knowing the West well and loving it, he was depressed by the picture's gross inaccuracies. "I was an actor, and I knew the West," he wrote later. "The opportunity that I had been waiting for years to come was knocking at my door . . . rise or fall, sink or swim, I had to bend every endeavour to get a chance to make Western pictures." For the remainder of the season, he saw as many Westerns as he could,

William S. Hart in The Primal Lure (*1916*).

studying and committing them to memory. Later, upon reaching California, on tour with *The Trail of the Lonesome Pine,* he learned that his old friend, Tom Ince, was in charge of the New York Motion Picture Company studios. When he told Ince he wanted Western parts, Ince was apathetic, pointing out that every film company was making them, and that even the best films were having a difficult time. He agreed, however, to give Hart a chance, and as soon as he finished his theater tour, Hart returned to California. It was now the summer of 1914.

Ince's studios were located at the mouth of the Santa Ynez canyon, and consisted of several open-air stages, sets of Western towns, a ranch, a fishing village, and similar buildings. The films were released through Mutual, headed by Roy and Harry Aitken, and John Freuler. The Aitkens were the first financiers to interest New York bankers in motion picture investments; using Reliance as their key production company, they sold stock to influential buyers, and helped finance the New York Motion Picture Company, with studios in Hollywood. Ince had been in charge since September, 1912, of the eighteen-thousand-acre location called "Inceville," while Mack Sennett was located in studios at 1700 Alessandro Street. In late 1913, David W. Griffith joined the outfit.

Profits were considerable for the expanding New York Motion Picture Company; two films were turned out every day, and Griffith, Ince and Sennett—representing the three top film makers and money makers—were installed, if not in the same studio, at least under the collective roof of one busy concern.

It was to this optimistic, energetic, and expanding organization that William S. Hart came. His first two film appearances were in two-reelers that starred, and were directed by, Tom Chatterton. Hart was the villain in both, but he felt very much disappointed and expressed his thoughts to Ince, who then put him into two feature films. The first was *The Bargain,* a five-reel Western written by Hart himself in collaboration with C. Gardner Sullivan, a fine screen writer and later a top production executive. Reginald Barker directed Hart in this five-reel Western; no sooner was the shooting completed on August 6, 1914, than Ince rushed Hart into another Western, *On the Night Stage* (later known also as *The Bandit and the Preacher*). Again directed by Barker, written by Sullivan, and photographed by Robert S. Newhard, it was strong, powerful stuff, the sort of material that could be considered a blueprint for the Hart films still to come. As "Texas" the badman, he opposed "the sky pilot" (Robert Edeson), until reformed by heroine Rhea Mitchell.

Hart was pleased with these works, but it seemed unlikely that they would create much of a stir. With four Westerns under his belt, he assumed demand for his services was over, and parted company with Ince, returning to New York.

Then something unexpected took place. *The Bargain* proved to be such a hit that it was decided not to release it through Mutual, where its full potential might not be realized; Famous Players were very much impressed, and bought the film for distribution. Ince, recognizing now that he had a star in Hart, decided not to release *On the Night Stage* either, but to hold it until Famous Players, with *The Bargain,* had made Hart's name known nation-wide.

Ince sent for Hart immediately and offered him a contract as a director-actor at $125 a week. Unaware of what was going on behind the scenes, or of the anticipated success of his two unreleased pictures, Hart accepted with alacrity. His salary was actually extremely low compared with the fees paid others working for Ince—usually only in *one* capacity —and had Hart known this, he could have secured a much better arrangement. This was the first of a series of events which strained the relationship between Hart and Ince.

From the very beginning, Hart directed all his own films, and only very occasionally did another director—Cliff Smith or Charles Swickard —work on his pictures. Even then, the director credit was largely nominal, for Hart's films were made the way he wanted them to be made. Although there was no secret made at the time of the fact that Hart was directing as well as acting, the fact seems to have become obscured over the years. Ince's high-pressure publicity created the impression that he was the creative mind behind the Hart films, but the facts are quite to the contrary. Not only did Ince never direct Hart in a single foot of film, but after the first few productions he had little to do even with their supervision, despite the large screen credit he took on each film. Ince does rate some credit though for having recognized in Hart the potential artist he was, for having allowed Hart to make his own films without interference. And Hart acquired a great deal of basic technique from a study of the earlier Ince films. Thus, in the face of Hart's rapidly spiraling success, and revenues, Ince's attitude was as shrewd as it was considerate.

Hart's first film as a director-star was *The Passing of Two Gun Hicks;* still learning the trade as a director, he limited himself to two-reelers, but from the very start he revealed himself as a man who thoroughly understood the film medium, despite years of a stage background. *The Scourge of the Desert* followed, and then *Mr. "Silent" Haskins.* Stressing physical action predominantly, the former was an interesting little film in which a Western gambler appoints himself protector of the helpless heroine, newly arrived from the East, finally marrying her. There was some particularly fine camera work of bawdy saloon life, and some good individual compositions. One shot became something of a Hart trademark: a slow pan from the villain's face, in full close-up, across to Hart's grim and defiant face, also in close-up. In this instance, the pan continued past Hart's face to take in a rifle hanging on the wall, panning down to the anxious face of the heroine, desperately afraid, but trusting in Hart to protect her. The symbolism of the scene was obvious, simple, and doubly effective because of it.

The Sheriff's Streak of Yellow, which followed, was a film in the *High Noon* mold, but without any kind of feminine interest or any sentimentality. Hart made this fine two-reeler for only $1,122.36, including his own salary. That he knew his way now was seen in *The Taking of Luke McVane* (also, *The Fugitive*). Enid Markey was his leading lady, and Cliff Smith co-directed while also playing a featured part. This film marked the real beginning of Hart's sentimentality, and it was also one of his few films which ended unhappily. For some reason the erroneous impression was created over the years that Hart's films were usually semi-tragedies, that he either died at the end, or rode away into the desert, leaving behind the girl he loved. Quite the opposite is true. Despite a life of outlawry, Hart's hero usually came to a happy, not a "sticky" end. In *The Taking of Luke McVane* Hart played a gambler who falls in love with a saloon dancer after protecting her from the unwanted advances of drunken Mexicans. In gratitude, she presents him with a rose. Forced to shoot a man in self-defense in a card-game brawl, Hart flees, pursued by the sheriff. They shoot it out in the desert, and Hart wounds the sheriff. Genuinely remorseful of his life of crime, he cares for the sheriff in his cabin. Then, knowing that it means the end of his own freedom, he decides to take the sheriff back to town for medical care. But on the ride back across the desert, the two men are attacked by Indians. A fierce battle ensues. The next morning, the sheriff's posse finds both men dead—Hart smiling, with the dancer's rose in his hand.

The sentimental streak in Hart's films was manifested in many different ways: the reformation of the badman by the love of the heroine, or the admiration of a child (used in the mid-Forties by Wallace Beery in *Bad Bascomb*); the cowboy's love for his horse; and, in many cases, a cowboy's devoted affection for his sister. (This last bit of sentimentality was pure Hart. He was deeply attached to his sister, Mary, and quite obviously, in giving his movie character a sister to be cherished and protected, he was reflecting his own feelings on the screen.)

On May 31, 1915, Hart's first feature as a director was released: *The Darkening Trail.* In *The Ruse,* his next, he played "Bat" Peters, with much of the action taking place in the city. Hart has been lured there by the villians; suspecting that the heroine was unfaithful to him, he settles things in a mighty hand-to-hand battle with the villain. Then, assured of the heroine's affections, he takes her back west. Hart was very fond of the plot of the Westerner coming east, overcoming the smooth chicanery of city crooks by using common sense and Western brawn, and then returning home. The subtitle, "I'm goin' back to the country where I belong" was repeated verbatim, or with little variation, in all the Hart films with plots on this order.

Next came two more two-reelers, *Cash Parrish's Pal* and *The Conversion of Frosty Blake.* When Triangle took over the New York Motion Picture Company, *The Conversion of Frosty Blake* was re-edited and made into a five-reeler. Hart did not appear until the third reel in the new version, and Gilbert Hamilton, incredibly, received credit as the director. To further add to the confusion, the new five-reeler was re-edited once more to two reels, with a fresh title, *The Gentleman from Blue Gulch.* Thus this one film circulated in several different versions, with several different titles! Almost all of Hart's films were later reissued in this fashion.

With these strong, little Westerns, Hart reached tremendous heights of popularity. Having made twenty Westerns, he had only a few more two-reelers to make before he switched to features permanently.

The last of Hart's two-reelers were *Grit* and *Keno Bates, Liar.* The

latter, written by Ince and J. G.
Hawks, and photographed by
Joseph August, was another fine
Western, although a further demonstration of Hart's growing tendency
to sentimentalize. Its story was very
similar to that of *The Taking of Luke
McVane,* complete even to the flower
motif. However, the climax of *Keno
Bates, Liar* sees the heroine emptying
a gun into the reformed gambler,
unaware that he is the man who
saved her. Logic would dictate that
the hero will now die—and there
are indications that possibly such an
ending was originally planned. But
the closing scenes find the gambler
miraculously recovered, reunited
with the girl who now realizes his
true worth.

A new phase in Hart's career soon
began, for there had been dissension

William S. Hart in The Tiger Man (*1918*).

at Mutual for some time. Harry Aitken had invested considerable amounts of Mutual's money into the financing of D. W. Griffith's *The Birth of a Nation,* and the Freuler group had disagreed. The American Film Company, also involved, was annoyed because Aitken considered certain of their pictures to be inferior, refusing to sell them as "Mutual Masterpieces." The crisis exploded with the removal of Aitken as president of Mutual, by Freuler.

Following meetings with the financiers in New York, Harry Aitken called Griffith, Ince, and Sennett to a conference in La Junta, Colorado, where plans for a new company were formulated. Thus, Triangle Pictures was born, represented by Griffith, Ince, and Sennett, with Aitken as president. Triangle was ambitious, and in order to finance their better-quality pictures, they needed increased revenue. This was to be partially achieved by the opening of Triangle's own theaters in key cities, with an advance over prices from the then prevailing fifteen cents to twenty-five cents.

In New York, the Knickerbocker Theatre was leased and refurbished, with a special carriage entrance to cater to the elite. The plan was to present four Triangle films each week, one each from Griffith and Ince, and two from Sennett. The theater opened on September 23, 1915, with prices ranging as high as two and three dollars for loge seats. It was a gala opening, with showmen Samuel Rothapfel (Roxy) in charge of the whole affair, and Hugo Riesenfeld directing the orchestra: Paderewski, William Randolph Hearst, James Montgomery Flagg, Rupert Hughes, and many other notables were there to witness the first program, which consisted of *The Lamb* (Griffith) with Douglas Fairbanks and Seena Owen, *The Iron Strain* (Ince) with Enid Markey and Dustin Farnum, and *My Valet* (Sennett) with Mabel Normand.

Hart's *The Disciple* was the second Triangle feature to play the theater, and the film was his most elaborate vehicle to date. A five-reeler, it cost eight thousand dollars. Dorothy Dalton, the leading lady, was paid forty dollars per week, and assistant director Cliff Smith got thirty dollars. Seventy-five dollars was paid for the story; Robert McKim, the villain, received twenty-five dollars per week, and extras earned five dollars a week and board. Their foreman received ten dollars. Hart, as star and director, was still earning only one hundred and twenty-five dollars a week.

Hell's Hinges

Considering the number of films Hart made, and the regularity with which he turned them out, he sustained a remarkably high standard on his Triangle releases. None of them had the assembly-line stamp, all were competent, and some were outstanding. *Hell's Hinges* (1916) was not only one of his very best subjects, but remains one of the classic Westerns. Sullivan, Smith, and August were again associated with Hart; Louise Glaum was the vamp, Clara Williams the heroine, Alfred Hollingsworth the villain, Jack Standing a weak-willed minister, and Robert Kortman one of the villain's henchmen. *Hell's Hinges* was also John Gilbert's first film—he featured prominently in crowd scenes—and Jean Hersholt, too, could be seen in several crowd scenes. The story of *Hell's Hinges* is an example of C. Gardner Sullivan's really strong screenplays. In later years, *Hell's Hinges* would have been classified as a "psychological" Western; in 1916, all the red meat was there, free of any murky undertones. The film gets under way in the East, where the recently ordained Reverend Robert Henley is preaching a sermon in a slum mission. The initial subtitles in themselves set the stage so neatly that we can do no better than repeat them verbatim:

(To introduce the minister): THE VICTIM OF A GREAT MISTAKE. A WEAK AND SELFISH YOUTH, UTTERLY UNFIT FOR THE CALLING THAT A LOVE-BLINDED MOTHER HAS PERSUADED HIM TO FOLLOW.

Then: HIS MOTHER: RADIANTLY HAPPY IN THE REALIZATION OF HER LIFE'S DREAM, AND BLISSFULLY UNCONSCIOUS OF THE INJUSTICE SHE HAS DONE HER SON AND THE CHURCH.

Back to the minister again: UNTOUCHED BY THE HOLY WORD HE IS CONVEYING, BUT TAKING AN ACTOR'S DELIGHT IN SWAYING HIS AUDIENCE.

The minister's superiors sense that he is too weak to combat the temptations of city life. They present him with a solution: an opportunity to take charge of the establishment of a church in the West. With a superimposed flash-forward, Henley's imagination sees his new parish as a glamorous one filled with romantic señoritas in need of his spiritual guidance. Excited at the prospect, he agrees, and his sister Faith decides to accompany him. Three weeks later, their stagecoach approached Hell's Hinges. Then, some fast-moving scenes, and some vividly written subtitles, each in the atmosphere of the town itself. First the subtitle:

THE REALITY. THE TOWN KNOWN ON THE GOVERNMENT SURVEYOR'S MAPS AS PLACER CENTRE, BUT THROUGHOUT THE LENGTH AND BREADTH OF THE SUN-BAKED TERRITORY AS JUST PLAIN *Hell's Hinges*, AND A GOOD PLACE TO "RIDE WIDE OF."

Hell's Hinges

Just plain Hell's Hinges, and a good place to "ride wide of."

Silk Miller: mingling the oily craftiness of a Mexican with the deadly treachery of a rattler, no man's open enemy, and no man's friend.

The pitifully uneven struggle, when the face of God seemed turned away.

Not until the place is an inferno of flames does he relax and allow his captives to make their escape.

Systematically she breaks him down, and ultimately seduces him on the evening of the opening of the new church.

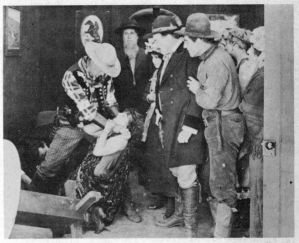

Besides himself with rage, Tracey manhandles Dolly and throws her to the floor.

Hell's Crown.

Blaze Tracey finds Faith, and the body of her brother.

Quick, dramatic shots of crowds watching a vicious gun duel in the dusty main street are followed by a further subtitle:

A GUN-FIGHTING, MAN-KILLING, DEVIL'S DEN OF INIQUITY THAT SCORCHED EVEN THE SUN-PARCHED SOIL ON WHICH IT STOOD.

The villain (Alfred Hollingsworth) is introduced with the subtitle:

SILK MILLER: MINGLING THE OILY CRAFTINESS OF A MEXICAN WITH THE DEADLY TREACHERY OF A RATTLER, NO MAN'S OPEN ENEMY, AND NO MAN'S FRIEND.

One of Miller's henchmen tells him that the minister sent for by the "petticoat brigade" is due at any moment. "The petticoat brigade," of course, is the town's decent element—referred to by a subtitle as:

THE SCANT HANDFUL OF RESPECTABLE PEOPLE IN A SIN-RIDDEN TOWN . . . A DROP OF WATER IN A BARREL OF RUM.

Miller has engaged Blaze Tracey (Hart) to run the minister out of town—or worse. Hart's introductory subtitle is typical:

BLAZE TRACEY. THE EMBODIMENT OF THE BEST AND WORST OF THE EARLY WEST. A MAN-KILLER WHOSE PHILOSOPHY OF LIFE IS SUMMED UP IN THE CREED shoot first and do your disputin' afterwards.

But when the stage arrives, Tracey pushes his way through the mocking crowd to send the minister on his way; he is stopped short by the sight of the girl. As she smiles at him, a subtitle relates:

A DIFFERENT KIND OF SMILE, SWEET, HONEST AND TRUSTFUL, AND SEEMING TO SAY "HOW DO YOU DO, FRIEND?"

Hart stops, unable to carry through the course of action he had planned, while a follow-up subtitle explains:

ONE WHO IS EVIL, LOOKING FOR THE FIRST TIME ON THAT WHICH IS GOOD.

Hart's sudden changes of heart when confronted with the heroine for the first time gave full reign to his sentimental streak, and were always played in the same way, with a maximum of close-up work on Hart's face, suffering pangs of remorse and self-doubt. Individually, they were often tremendously effective, but collectively their effect is weakened, because they constitute the only real cliché in all the Hart films. In *Hell's Hinges,* the sequence is not even particularly legitimate, for audiences knew the Hart character too well to believe him to be evil, while the heroine (Clara Williams) was so excessively homely and unattractive that it is difficult to believe that she could have instilled such feelings in any man, and certainly not on first acquaintance.

Moved, confused, Tracey leaves the minister and his sister to the ribald mocking of the mob, and takes no stand either for or against them. The next Sunday, Henley and his sister hold their first service. In the saloon, Dolly (Louise Glaum), Miller's mistress, and the town's lawless element decide to stop religion in Hell's Hinges before it gets started. In a group, they invade the barn, upset the service, and by carousing, shooting, and cursing, attempt to terrify the worshippers into retreating.

Determined to enjoy the fun, Tracey heads for the barn himself. Inside, the weak minister has given up in despair; but Faith has taken a stand, and is singing a hymn, oblivious to the drunken cowboys, hoping to shame them into silence. A close-up of Tracey dissolves into a close-up of Faith, which in turn dissolves into a shot of a crucifix rising out of the water along a seashore. Then, a subtitle:

THE ETERNAL, UNCONQUERABLE WHITE FLAME THAT SHONE OVER THE BLOOD-DRENCHED ROMAN ARENA, AND ABOVE THE RACKS OF THE INQUISITION.

Tracey bursts into the barn just as one of the drunken cowboys attempts to dance with Faith. Knocking him to the ground, Tracey draws both guns and, crouched low behind them (a typical Hart pose) defies the mob, telling them:

I'M ANNOUNCIN' HERE AND NOW THAT THERE AIN'T GOIN' TO BE NO MORE PICKIN' ON THE PARSON'S HERD SO LONG AS THEY MIND THEIR OWN BUSINESS.

As the turmoil subsides, Tracey sits down to hear the finish of the minister's sermon. But he is unmoved, sensing the insincerity of this man of God. Faith, however, speaks so fervently that Tracey is completely convinced. The subtitle in which he tells her of his conversion reads:

I RECKON GOD AIN'T WANTIN' ME MUCH, MA'AM, BUT WHEN I LOOK AT YOU I FEEL I'VE BEEN RIDIN' THE WRONG TRAIL.

Tracey openly switches his allegiance to the cause of the church, at the same time developing a strong romantic interest in Faith. At this point, Hart injects an interesting note of realism when Tracey reads the Bible for the first time; he is moved and impressed by what he reads, but the old ways are by no means behind him! He smokes as he reads, and a bottle of whiskey stands on the table next to the Bible.

Realizing that he has failed to scare the minister out of town, Silk Miller tries other tactics. Playing on Henley's weak will, he sends Dolly to him. Systematically she breaks him down, and ultimately seduces him on the evening of the opening of the new church. The next morning, Miller's followers ridicule the churchgoers as they vainly wait for their minister to join them, shouting that he is down in Silk's saloon. Tracey leads the way into the saloon, and finds both Dolly and Henley, dead drunk, lying together on Dolly's bed. Beside himself with rage, Tracey manhandles Dolly and throws her to the floor; Miller is jubilant:

HE'S LIKE ALL THE REST OF 'EM, BLAZE—A LOW-DOWN HYPOCRITE AND LIAR. THERE AIN'T NO SUCH THING AS REAL RELIGION.

But Tracey's new-found faith is unshakable:

WHEN WOMEN LIKE HER SAY THERE'S A GOD, THERE *is* ONE, AND HE SURE MUST BE WORTH TRAILIN' WITH!

Tracey takes the disgraced minister home, leaving Hell's Hinges still in the hands of Silk Miller.

Three reels have been devoted to this development. There has been little physical action in the accustomed Western sense, but the suspense has been building up steadily to an inevitable explosion. Dramatically, the film has presented an unusual and effective juxtaposition: Tracey's conversion running parallel with the moral decay of the minister. Having set his stage, Hart is now ready for his cataclysmic finale, in which evil and decadence are wiped away, only the good to survive.

The next morning, Tracey rides to the nearest town to find a doctor for the drunken and delirious minister who, in the meantime, fights his way out of his sister's care to join the cowhands in Miller's saloon, with the decent citizens looking on sorrowfully. Suddenly, one of the cowhands shouts:

TO HELL WITH THE CHURCH! LET'S BURN HER DOWN!

The minister gleefully agrees to be the first to put the torch to his church, while outside "the petticoat brigade" waits with grim determination:

BOYS, THE LORD'S DEPENDIN' ON US TO STAND BY HIM. BEFORE THEY BURN DOWN THAT CHURCH, THEY'VE GOT TO FIGHT.

Then, in superbly organized and directed mob scenes, the saloon gang marches on the church. There is a short, vicious battle outside, but the church's defenders are too few. They are routed and the church set aflame, but the minister is shot and killed in the battle. As the townsmen retreat, a subtitle notes:

THE PITIFULLY UNEVEN STRUGGLE, WHEN THE FACE OF GOD SEEMED TURNED AWAY.

In great, high-angle panoramic shots, the burning church, standing far apart from the rest of the town, the retreating townspeople, and the drunken roistering of their persecutors, are vividly and dramatically filmed. On a full close-up of the burning church, a subtitle is injected:

STANDING LIKE A MARTYR OF OLD, WITH THE SYMBOL OF ITS FAITH PROUDLY UPLIFTED TO THE CRIMSONING SKY.

Then the shot is completed—a slow pan up the burning church and steeple, to the flaming cross silhouetted against the sky.

In stark, dramatic shots, the townspeople flee into the desert. The tempo increases. A shot of Tracey, riding back to town, is intercut with shots of the refugees, and scenes of the wild celebrations in town. He meets the first of the fleeing townspeople, hears their story, leaps into the saddle, gallops hell-for-leather into the town, falls down a steep incline, remounts, and is off again. By the side of the still-burning but now nearly collapsed church (all of the fire scenes were printed on red stock, to tremendously dramatic effect), Blaze Tracey finds Faith, and the body of her brother.

Convulsed with rage, he decides to clean up Hell's Hinges once and for all, and strides into town. Miller's men line up inside the saloon, determined to shoot Tracey down the moment he appears. But Tracey outsmarts them, kicks open the swinging doors, shoots Miller before he can make a move, and holds the rest at bay, allowing only the terrified saloon girls to escape.

Tracey tells the cowering men:

HELL NEEDS THIS TOWN, AND IT'S GOIN' BACK, AND GOIN' DAMN QUICK!

He begins to shoot down the oil lamps; within a matter of moments the wooden saloon is afire. Not until the place is an inferno of flames does he relax and allow his captives to make their escape. Soon all of Hell's Hinges is flame and, like the Sodom of old, it is completely obliterated. On the subtitle:

HELL'S CROWN.

And its subsequent shot of the raging inferno at its peak, the scene fades out, and into another subtitle:

AND THEN FROM THE MOTHERING SKY CAME THE BABY DAWN, SINGING AS IT WREATHED THE GRAY HORNS OF THE MOUNTAINS WITH RIBBONS OF ROSE AND GOLD.

Faith is prostrate with grief; Tracey attempts to lead her away from her brother's grave, but she throws herself upon it. He returns to the now more composed girl, and together they walk to the mountains:

WHATEVER THE FUTURE, THEIRS TO SHARE TOGETHER . . .

Hell's Hinges was, understandably, a tremendous success, but already there were signs that the rigidity of Hart's screen character was being noticed by the critics. After praising the film, and referring to "the genius of direction," the *Moving Picture World* of February 19, 1916, goes on to criticize Hart:

Good enough actor not to require a perpetual repetition of the Western badman reformed through the sweet and humanizing influence of a pure-minded girl, Hart should try himself out in some other role . . . [he] fails to win with a large percentage of the modern audience. Hart is a fine type, and capable of picturing imperfect man as he really is, and long has been, a composite being, 'the riddle of the world.'

Hart, of course, took no notice of the Easterners who were trying to tell him how to make his Westerns. Ten years later, those same criticisms leveled at *Tumbleweeds* on which he had again refused to compromise, finally put him out of business. But what a grand old actor and film-maker he had been—with 12 years of the most personal and vigorous films any one man ever made to his credit!

To regard *Hell's Hinges* as merely a Western is a mistake, for it more resembles *The Atonement of Gosta Berling* than it does *Riders of the Purple Sage*. It was one of Hart's best films, and in its way a prototype, but at the same time it had excesses that were not quite so evident in his later films. The religious angle was never again so pronounced; Hart frequently cast himself as a near-evangelistic Westerner, but his motives arose more from codes of honor and behavior than from religious roots. And the subtitles of *Hell's Hinges,* wonderful examples of the colorful language of the silent screen, a language that understandably seems unduly flowery to those with only a casual knowledge of the silent film, were unusually flamboyant for Hart, who frequently let himself go in injecting Western vernacular into dialogue subtitles, but who was not normally prone to lengthy and poetic descriptive titles.

Hart has many times been accused of being too sentimental a director, and at times he undoubtedly was, but it is astounding that his tremendous talent as a director has gone unrecognized for so long. He is regarded as a "personality," along with Fairbanks, Valentino, and Pickford, and almost never as a creative craftsman in his own right. *Hell's Hinges* is living proof of what an accomplished director he was. The camera placement, the simple yet effective symbolism, and the flair for spectacle, plus the real "feel" for the dusty, unglamorized West, should have earned Hart a reputation as one of the great directors. The staging of the burning of the town is beautifully done, the sheer spectacle never eclipsing the odd moment of individual action, such as when Hart, holstering his guns, walks out of the inferno, apparently oblivious to it all, a sudden burst of flame creating a halo-like effect behind his head seeming almost to identify him as an agent of divine vengeance. And giving Hart credit for the magnificent staging of this sequence in no way detracts from the credit due to cameraman Joseph August, who achieved some superb effects of maddened cowboys racing through the flames, almost like vague demons tortured in some primitive hell.

It should not be forgotten that *Hell's Hinges* was a 1916 production. Griffith was the giant among directors then, with no immediate rivals; DeMille, in any case only a commercial and not an aesthetic rival, was just beginning; Herbert Brenon, Chester and Sidney Franklin, Maurice Tourneur, and a handful of others were of more importance but certainly Hart's ability, if more restricted, was quite comparable to theirs. Undoubtedly, Hart's enormous popularity as an actor (his films had to stand up to competition from Doug Fairbanks, Mary Pickford, and Charlie Chaplin) tended to make people overlook his directorial ability.

Hart's peak and decline

Another classic followed soon after, a film that Hart himself regarded as the best he had ever made—*The Aryan.* One of its major assets was the lovely and sensitive performance of Bessie Love, who had been recommended to Hart by Griffith. She was particularly suited to Hart's requirements in heroines, and it is surprising that he did not use her to a much greater extent. Triangle's original synopsis for *The Aryan*—described as "The Story of a White Human Heart Turned Black"—bears repeating in its original vernacular:

The hard cruel face of a man who has learned to hate, looks into the trusting countenance of a girl whose whole life has known nothing but love and trust. The man has sworn vengeance on the whole white race, and especially its women, because of a vile deed that one woman had done—a deed that has left its black impress on his very soul. The trust of the child, her confidence that he will help her and the other white people who have besought him for food and shelter, at first makes no appeal to the man who hates. She shall be one more victim of his vengeance, her companions shall suffer with her. He glowers at her, and sneers at her pleas.

Still the great dark eyes follow him about, with no indication of fear or doubt. He has told her that he will show no mercy to her or to the white women of her party. Very well—she will not believe him. He is a white man, she can see that, although he lives among half-breeds and Indians, and she knows he will run true to the creed of his race—to protect its women.

He does. He bursts the shackles of hatred and revenge which have held his spirit in bondage, and justifies the girl's absolute confidence in him.

The Aryan took exactly one month to shoot, during which time 15,485 feet of negative were used, of which less than 5,000 feet of film were used for release. Hart was improving as a director with each film, and putting more time, effort, and money into them. *The Aryan* cost $13,531.67, with Hart earning $1,125.00 for the month's work. But in proportion to the money his films were earning for Ince, Hart's own salary increases were ridiculously small; tension and ill will were gradually increasing between the two men, and Hart's suspicions that Ince was unfairly exploiting him was one of the contributing factors.

In late 1917, Hart left Triangle, after having made several films: *Truthful Tulliver, The Gun Fighter, The Square Deal Man, The Desert Man* (his first association with Lambert Hillyer, who wrote the screenplay, and who later directed 25 of the 27 Hart pictures for Paramount), *Wolf Lowry,* and *The Cold Deck.*

Triangle was in sore financial difficulties, due to the flop of a number of expensive features with big *theatrical* names. Triangle's publicity was poor, and there was little real showmanship behind the company. Fairbanks and Hart were terrific box-office draws, but comparatively little effort was made to exploit them, with all the publicity directed at stage imports like Billie Burke and DeWolf Hopper. The company planned a complicated financial merger with Famous Players, later Paramount, controlled by Adolph Zukor. Ultimately, the merger fell through, but in the process Zukor took over Griffith, Sennett, Ince, Fairbanks, Hart, writers Emerson and Loos, and a number of other top personalities. Triangle vainly tried, for four years, to overcome this staggering loss and get back on its feet.

Even without the Zukor intervention, Hart would most probably have left Triangle in time, since his relations with Ince had become extremely strained, on the personal as well as the financial side. It is characteristic of Hart that he could endure unfair pay, knowing that Ince was making a fortune from him, but he could not tolerate Ince's curious dislike of Hart's pony, Fritz. Hart refused to let Ince use Fritz in any more films, and he promptly put the pony out to pasture. Fritz "himself" announced his resignation from the screen with ads in the trade papers, giving obviously phoney reasons for "his" decision. Exhibitors saw through the ad—as Hart had doubtless intended that they should.

Nevertheless, despite his increasing dislike of Ince, Hart was a man of principle. He had a contract with Ince, and although it could doubtless have been broken in some way, he decided to honor it. Thus, Ince was able to make his deal with Zukor in the newly formed Artcraft Productions.

It was after Hart had severed his connections with Triangle, that all of his old films began to appear with different titles, often in totally different versions. A dummy company named W. H. Productions was formed to release them (and old Sennett comedies, too). The practice didn't hurt Hart's new films nearly as much as Triangle had hoped it would, but Hart, furious, obtained from the Federal Trade Commission a ruling that when a film was released under a new title, its original title would have to be displayed along with it. That ruling still exists today, although it is often violated.

Hart's first film, *The Narrow Trail,* for Artcraft was a promising start. Hart had his familiar crew with him, Joe August photographing, and now Lambert Hillyer directing. It was not only one of Hart's best films, but also a sort of synthesis of all that he had expressed before: sentiment, reformation, action, a love for his horse. The climactic race contained some of the best riding shots of Hart ever taken, and included several running inserts of Hart—a technique he seemed not to favor, for they were rarely used in his pictures, and then usually only for shots of stagecoaches (as in *Wild Bill Hickok*) and not individual riders.

Although *The Narrow Trail* was the first film Hart made for Artcraft, it was actually the second to be released, coming out in January of 1918;

William S. Hart in Wild Bill Hickok (*1923*).

prior to it, *The Silent Man* had been released in late 1917. Original excerpts of *The Silent Man* appeared in Warner's 1943 film, *One Foot in Heaven*. Fredric March, playing a Methodist minister, goes to a movie theatre for the first time, determined to know the "evil" at first-hand so that he can denounce it. Instead, he is quite converted to films by the moral and Christian lesson in *The Silent Man*. It was a charming sequence in a touching, usually under-rated film.

Despite his higher budgets and the prestige of an Artcraft release, Hart showed no signs of slowing down, or concentrating on fewer, but bigger, pictures. *Wolves of the Rail* was released in January, 1918, and *Blue Blazes Rawden* (with Jack Hoxie, later a top Western star, in a supporting role) followed one month later.

With *The Tiger Man* and *Selfish Yates,* there came the first signs, not of a decline, but of a mild stagnation. The pace was beginning to slow, and the repetition of incidents and characters was becoming more obvious. Some of Hart's best films were still ahead of him, but the uninterrupted flow of one top Western after another was over.

Although *Selfish Yates* featured some interesting episodes, it was probably his slowest, and most routine, subject to date. *Shark Monroe* was a good deal better, and somewhat off-beat. A melodrama in the style of *The Spoilers,* it was largely set in Alaska, and contained a sequence of which Hart was presumably rather fond, since he duplicated it more than once. Bursting in on the heroine's wedding to another man, he forces the minister to marry the girl to *him* instead, and then forcibly abducts her. Such ungentlemanly conduct was rare in a Hart film, and when it occurred, there was a great deal of account-settling to be done before the hero finally considered himself worthy of the girl whose love he had taken rather than won!

Katherine MacDonald, apparently the one woman that Hart really loved, was his leading lady in *Riddle Gawne,* a good action film that offered a solid role to Lon Chaney. Hart's emotional makeup generally convinced him that he was in love with most of his leading ladies. He proposed to Katherine MacDonald a dozen times—without success. There was a brief engagement to Anna Q. Nilsson, and one to Eva Novak. Jane, Eva's sister, refused him. He married only once, his bride being Winifred Westover, his leading lady in *John Petticoats.* Winifred was twenty years younger than Hart, and although it was she who pursued him in the days of their courtship, it was also she who ended the marriage. She was granted a divorce on February 11, 1927, less than six years after their marriage. In the interim, a son, William S. Hart, Jr., had been born, in 1922.

Then, in as a complete an about-face from anything he had done before, or anything he was to do afterwards, Hart made *Branding Broadway,* with Seena Owen as his leading lady. It was a delightful film, one of Hart's most enjoyable, but completely in the light-hearted vein of Douglas Fairbanks, in particular, and, to a lesser degree, Tom Mix. Playing a Westerner brought to New York by a millionaire to watch over his wayward playboy son, he disported himself with distinction in a dress suit, and made the most of his ample comic opportunities. For once, action was introduced for its own sake, the pace was sprightly, and there was little or no sentimentality. The fights were staged with tremendous gusto, and in a hilarious climax Hart on horseback pursued the villain through the streets of New York and finally captured him with a lasso in the wilds of Central Park. *Branding Broadway* stands up remarkably well today, quite as well, certainly, as Douglas Fairbanks' very similar *Manhattan Madness.* Hart seems to have enjoyed himself immensely in the lead, but he probably regarded the film as casually as would a great painter his doodles. At any rate, he never again made such a carefree film. Not the least of *Branding Broadway's* many merits was the shooting of the film in Manhattan; the chase through the streets in the climax was, of course, doubly effective due to the use of authentic locales.

Hart was a stickler for using authentic backgrounds when plots called for them. One of the best remembered of all images of William S. Hart occurs in *The Narrow Trail;* in full Western regalia, with Stetson and deadly looking guns, he strides confidently and casually down one of San Francisco's most exclusive residential boulevards.

Hart returned to serious business with *Breed of Men* (filmed on location in Chicago, with many scenes shot in the stockyards), and *Square Deal Sanderson.* The latter was a good, straightforward action picture of the old school, with Hart playing a cowboy who saves a girl's ranch by posing as her brother. *Square Deal Sanderson* had a strong climax in which the heroine, about to be assaulted by the villain, is saved by Hart who throws a lasso over the transom window, and literally hangs the villain he cannot see.

Jane Novak and villain Robert McKim were back with Hart in his next film, *Wagon Tracks,* a spectacular, though still only five-reel, Western of a covered wagon trek. It was the success of this film that decided Paramount to make *The Covered Wagon,* although it was to be another four years before the plan was realized. Then came two disappointing films, *John Petticoats* and *Sand.* The first was made on location in New Orleans, with Hart cast in a typical role as "Hardwood" John Haynes, a rough and ready frontiersman suddenly thrust into society life. The plot was heavy, complicated by a suicide, psychological motivations, and other factors at which Hart was never at his best. *Sand* got back to the essentials of plot, but not to the vigor of pacing and direction. It marked the return to the screen of Fritz, the pony, and was President Woodrow Wilson's favorite Hart film. But the film was not nearly up to the standards set in *The Aryan* or *Hell's Hinges,* mainly because the story was needlessly protracted.

Disappointing as *Sand* was, Hart's next film proved that it was still

William S. Hart and Anna Q. Nilsson with Richard Headrick in The Toll Gate (*1920*).

far too early to say that a definite decline was in progress. *The Toll Gate* ranks as one of his four or five best pictures, and was also his biggest money maker. In this film there can be no doubt that Hart gave the best that he had, for he was now free of Ince entirely, having formed his own company.

The Toll Gate, then, was the first film made under the new arrangement. It reverted to the basic essentials of the Hart formula, and yet there was a surprising restraint in the sentimental passages which added poignancy, absent from many of his other films. Hart was again the outlaw, "Black" Deering, and again he was reformed by a good woman, Mary Brown (Anna Q. Nilsson), and her son, "The Little Fellow" (Richard Headrick). The film had more suspense and dramatic values than usual, and the outcome was genuinely in doubt until the last moment. Sincerely in love with the heroine, and she with him, Hart was pitted against her worthless husband, who had deserted her. The two men finally confront each other, and following a vicious fight on the edge of a cliff, Hart literally throws the man to his death. Having earned the respect and admiration of the sheriff's men by deliberately casting away his freedom at one point (in defense of the heroine), he is offered an amnesty. The heroine pleads with him to marry her, for her sake, and that of her son. But Hart, feeling unworthy of her, and knowing that, even though justified, he killed her husband, rejects his one chance for happiness, and returns to the lonely life of the outlaw, even though he knows that he cannot expect to survive for more than a year or two. It was a moving and exciting film, and an auspicious start for the William S. Hart Company.

One of Hart's occasional non-Westerns followed: *The Cradle of Courage.* But even away from the range, the Hart code held: he played an ex-crook who returns from the war and, finding that he now cannot return to a life of banditry, becomes a policeman. Episode followed episode in which his strength and honor were tested.

The Testing Block, a six-reeler released in December, 1920, based on one of Hart's ideas, was one of the most interesting of his later pictures. Hart played the leader of a motley crew of outlaws ". . . collected by the broom that swept hell . . ."

Hart's films now were becoming larger in scale, and there were fewer of them. He followed 1920's *The Testing Block* with *O'Malley of the Mounted* in 1921. It was a run-of-the-mill Hart film, rather carelessly made in general, with some poorly edited action sequences. The climax departed interestingly from Hart's formula in that Hart, becoming convinced of the innocence of the man he has been set out to trap—and respecting the outlaws he has now come to regard as friends—refuses to complete his mission, resigning to return as an ordinary ranger to claim the hand of Eva Novak. In 1921 he made another non-Western, *The Whistle.*

Then *White Oak* followed in which Hart once again used the sister-motif. Hart played a river gambler, out to revenge himself on the man who had seduced his sister, indirectly causing her death. (Attempting to commit suicide by drowning herself, she was rescued, only to die of pneumonia.) It was powerful and beautifully photographed, but again— and this was particularly harmful at seven reels—slow-moving and overly sentimental. Better, but still short of its full potential, was *Three Word Band,* an unusual film, in which Hart played three different roles, the hero's role, that of his father, and that of his brother. The hero's role was a title role deriving from the character's clipped speech in three-word sentences ("Get out, quick!" or "Go to hell!"). The part was colorful and Hart had many opportunities to differentiate the three characters, one of which was the stoic Governor of the State. He played each part to the hilt, and he was aided by some first-class camera work. The film as a whole was a trifle confusing; it inclined to an excess of dialogue subtitles, but otherwise it finds a place among Hart's more interesting works.

Travelin' On (1922) was perhaps the last of what one may term "vintage" Hart films: already there were unmistakable signs that Hart's reign was almost over, and that public opinion had shifted in favor of the more colorful and more "streamlined" Tom Mix.

Unfortunately, Hart had only himself to blame. One had to respect Hart's love for the *real* West; at the same time, one had to admit that his work had become unashamedly sentimental, in its own way as cliché-ridden as the slick little "B" pictures he detested so much. He was growing older, too, finding it difficult to maintain the pace set in his earlier films. Hart still rode hard, and fought hard, but such sequences were kept to a minimum, while the pictures themselves seemed to grow longer. This slowdown in the pace was thrown into even greater relief by the accelerated pace of Westerns generally. *Wild Bill Hickok,* which opened with a delightful subtitle, Hart apologizing to his audience for not looking the least bit like Hickok, and asking his "friends" to accept him as he is, was an intensely personal work, superb in its action scenes, but surprisingly inaccurate historically as a result of Hart's romantic overindulgence with the facts, and excessively maudlin in its sentimental overtones.

Although *Wild Bill Hickok* made money, Adolph Zukor and Jesse Lasky, who released Hart's films through Artcraft, a division of Famous Players, told Hart that exhibitors were tiring of his pictures. Hart, disbelieving them (and not without some cause, for although Zukor and Lasky promised to do so, they failed to produce any documentary evidence in the form of exhibitors' letters of complaints), went calmly about his business, making what was to be his last film under Zukor and Lasky, *Singer Jim McKee.*

Unhappily, it was quite the worst film he had ever made, and seemed to lend no little credence to the complaints reported by his studio heads. Hart was touchy about his age, and insisted on playing a youthful hero in all his films, or in any event, the hero on whom age rests lightly, the man still capable of winning the love of a girl. This had earlier produced some illogical plots, but Hart went quite overboard in *Singer Jim McKee.* It was an absurd production, with a rambling story-line that included every favorite Hart incident. The film as a whole resembled a heavy melodrama, and it was far from the tight and realistic treatments the public had come to expect of Hart at his best.

It was also a sad decline from *Hell's Hinges* and *The Toll Gate,* all the more depressing because it was a decline brought about not through studio supervision or any other external factors, but by Hart himself.

Singer Jim McKee was the last straw for Zukor, who told Hart bluntly that from now on he would have to submit to supervision. He would continue to star, but in studio-picked stories and with studio-picked directors.

If this ultimatum seems rather harsh on the basis of only one really bad picture, it should be remembered that there had been increasing signs of this decline in Hart's recent pictures, and obviously the studio had to check him before he ruined himself as a property.

Hart, needless to say, refused the ultimatum. He probably honestly felt that *Singer Jim McKee* was a fine film, and since his principles were far more important to him than a regular salary check, he left the Lasky studio, and to all intents retired from films.

It seemed for a while that his old tradition might be revived when he returned to the screen in 1925 with *Tumbleweeds* for United Artists. Not only was it his comeback picture, but it was his first real epic, and, with a budget of $312,000, by far his biggest venture to date. Those who expected Hart to have given in, to have made the sort of Western that audiences apparently wanted (and that Zukor had earlier demanded that Hart make) were sadly mistaken. In *Tumbleweeds*, Hart reverted to type without compromise. It was austere, factual. Although showing his age more than ever, he still played an ostensibly young man, he still won the heroine at the end, and he even engaged in some skittish comedy scenes. The sentimental scenes had their usual high intensity,

William S. Hart fights his own gang, one at a time, to prevent their kidnapping the beautiful girl member of a traveling show troupe. From The Testing Block *(1919).*

The simple, glass-roofed stage at Inceville. William S. Hart in The Devil's Double (*1916*).

and the climactic reunion scene was typical Hart emotion at its peak.

In many ways, *Tumbleweeds* was one of the best of the Western epics: it was staged on a truly lavish scale, but again, Hart's refusal to introduce action for its own sake, and his refusal to "streamline" development made it seem more than a little slow and dated. The giant land rush sequence notwithstanding, its epic qualities were appreciated and noted far less than were those of *The Covered Wagon,* a film in many ways inferior to *Tumbleweeds.*

Nevertheless, *Tumbleweeds* was a much greater success than *Singer Jim McKee* had been. Only in his use of Lucien Littlefield as a comic partner—an odd touch for Hart—was there a sign that, probably unconsciously, Hart had noted the existence of this cliché in the newer Westerns. A stickler for authenticity, Hart hated fakery of any kind, and thus there is fairly little stuntwork in the land rush sequence, possibly to its minor detriment. The crashing of a wagon is rather crudely arranged at one point, and this is typical of Hart, and a flaw that is noticeable in *O'Malley of the Mounted* and other films. If Hart had to resort to tricky stunt work to get an action effect, he usually chose to avoid it, or to get around it as well as possible by editing.

The land rush itself, as the Cherokee strip is opened to settlers, was a mighty sequence, generally superior to the similar, and imitative, rush in Wesley Ruggles' *Cimarron*. It contained at least one shot of sheer poetry—Hart, galloping at top speed on his horse, rides over the crest of a hill, with the camera angled in such a way as to give the impression of man and rider literally flying through space. (The ground level was just below the frameline of the image.) Unusually fine editing distinguished the land rush sequence, and particularly the build-up to it. Between the subtitle, "Ready for the signal for the maddest stampede in American history" and the actual start of the rush, there are 684 frames, split up into twenty-five separate shots, the shortest of which runs for only five frames (about a fifth of a second). This sequence is almost mathematically constructed, the shots of the tense, anxious homesteaders running twice as long as those of the disinterested cavalry observers. There is also a simple, and telling, shot immediately preceding the rush itself. As noon, the hour for the rush, is reached, the cavalrymen fire a cannon. There is a quick shot of Hart's horse, alone, tethered to a tree; it is startled by the noise, and breaks free. Then a cut to the mass activity of hundreds of wagons and riders beginning the rush, the stampede for land.

Early in the film, there is one poignant moment when Hart and his riders, on the crest of a hill, watch the great trail herds being driven from the land that is soon to be made available to all settlers. As the herds drift by, Hart removes his hat sadly, and remarks: "Boys, it's the last of the West." And the others remove their hats reverently, and watch as an era passes into history.

Hart's comment was in some ways a prophetic one. With the exception of Edward L. Cahn's *Law and Order* (1932) and possibly John Ford's later *The Wagonmaster*, *Tumbleweeds* was the last of the old breed of Westerns. It was also Hart's last Western. Despite good reviews in New York and excellent business in its New York première, United Artists disliked the film and sought to cut it to five reels. Hart prevented this; United Artists hit back by deliberately mishandling the film, booking it into minor theaters where its commercial potential could not be realized. Hart then took the case to court, charging United Artists with breaching a stipulation in their contract, one calling for them to exert their best efforts on the film's behalf. (United Artists later went through a series of similar cases with other dissatisfied independent producers.) Hart won his case; in fact he never lost one of his many legal battles, despite wrangles with other important individuals and corporations. However, his victory was only a technical one, for the damage had been done. While he recouped his production costs, he estimated that he had lost half of a million dollars in unrealized profits. Discouraged, he retired from films, while still remaining on the fringe of the industry. He made a guest appearance in King Vidor's Marion Davies film, *Show People*, and was the subject of one or two *Screen Snapshots* shorts at Columbia. He coached both Johnny Mack Brown and Robert Taylor in their respective versions of *Billy the Kid*, and sold his old story, *O'Malley of the Mounted*, to Fox for a remake with George O'Brien. While it was a competent enough Western, it bore little resemblance to the original except in the bare outlines, and Hart was so disgusted that he refused to sell any more of his properties for remakes. Instead, he settled on his Newhall ranch and wrote. Hart's books are heavy going, deliberately couched in rough Western vernacular, full of a rugged but far from rhythmic poetry. Nevertheless, they are well worth the effort it takes to read them, and his autobiography, *My Life East and West,* is particularly readable, even though Hart's tendency to romanticize produced some inaccuracies. *Tumbleweeds,* then, marked William S. Hart's farewell to the screen.

In 1939, the film was reissued in the United States by Astor Pictures, with music and effects added, and an eight-minute prologue. This prologue was photographed at Hart's Horseshoe Ranch in Newhall, and it is unquestionably one of the most moving reels of film ever made. It is virtually the film of a man delivering his own obituary.

Hart, dressed in his beloved Western costume, walks slowly over the hill and up to the camera to address the audience. He is old, but still a fine figure of a man. He stands there before us more as a representative of the old West itself than as a silent picture star. In a firm, beautifully modulated voice, Hart tells the audience of the picture's background; he explains what the opening of the Cherokee Strip meant to

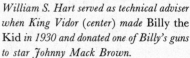

William S. Hart served as technical adviser when King Vidor (center) made Billy the Kid *in 1930 and donated one of Billy's guns to star Johnny Mack Brown.*

both the white man and the Indian. Then he goes on to discuss Western pictures, and as he tells how sorry he is that he is too old to make more of them, and how he misses little Fritz, his pinto pony, there are tears in his eyes. It is a magnificent, superbly touching speech, spoken with all the force and authority that Hart must have given to his Shakespearean roles; it was made in only two or three takes. Apart from being one of the longest speeches recorded on film, it is also, obviously, one of the most deeply felt. Some of the words, from a person other than Hart, might even seem unnecessarily sentimental. But from Hart, every word is so thoroughly sincere, that one can only be moved beyond measure by the whole experience. Its emotional impact apart, it is also a reminder of what a truly fine actor Hart was; had he only been a little younger, he might well have taken the place in sound Westerns ultimately secured by Gary Cooper (and Henry Fonda in his Ford films).

Hart off-screen

Off-screen, Hart was much like his celluloid hero. His love of animals, especially of horses and dogs, was passionate and sincere. Any wrangler working for him who failed to loosen his horse's cinch during the lunch break, or who was otherwise cruel or thoughtless, was dismissed on the spot. He lived quietly on his Newhall ranch, avoided any kind of scandal, drank like a gentleman, and loved a hard game of stud poker more than any other kind of relaxation. His reaction to misfortune was always unpredictable. He merely shrugged off the news that he had lost a large investment in a Dakota bank. While shooting *John Petticoats* on location in New Orleans, he was told that Ince had stolen the Hart company books. "I'll be damned!" he exclaimed—and went right on shooting. However, Lambert Hillyer recalls that when a woman bumped into Hart's brand-new car and dented his fender, he wasn't fit to work with for days. But characteristically, Hillyer reports, Hart did not vent his spleen on the driver, for to Hart every woman was a lady. He was a loyal friend, too, but a man with an obstinate streak, and once an enemy, he was an enemy for life.

Hart's close friends included Western lawmen Wyatt Earp, "Uncle Billy" Tilghman, and "Bat" Masterson, as well as Will Rogers, artists Charles Russell and James Montgomery Flagg, and even Pat O'Malley, a reformed outlaw who had ridden with the Al Jennings gang. He drew no lines, racial, religious, or social. As the late G. W. Dunston, one of Hart's oldest friends, and a motion picture projectionist until his death in 1957, once remarked: "Hart was a Christian—and it showed in every one of his films."

He planned to return to the screen on at least one occasion in the early Thirties. Hal Roach was planning a large-scale Western along the lines of *Wagon Tracks*, and just at that time Hart was preparing to do a Peter B. Kyne story at RKO. Hillyer was to have been associated with both ventures. Both failed to materialize—mainly because the passing of years had not lessened Hart's determination to make Westerns his way or not at all. Among his requirements remained the stipulation that he *still* play the ostensibly young hero who wins the girl in the fadeout.

Hart's regard for the truth of the old West on the screen could, in fact, be affected by only one thing—a sincere wish not to hurt anyone's feelings. A case in point was his film, *Wild Bill Hickok*. Although he had not known Hickok personally, he knew a great deal about him from his father, and from others who had been contemporaries of the famed frontiersman. Thus Hart was able to construct a reasonably accurate, although artistically sentimentalized version of Hickok's life, this accuracy even extending to the little known fact that in his later life, Hickok began to go blind. (Hart achieved some interesting effects at this point in the film by having his camera go out of focus.) One of the legendary stories concerning Hickok is his gun battle with the McCanless boys, who jumped him at a relay station. What really started the fracas was

Robert Taylor, a later "Billy the Kid," visits Hart in his retirement on his Newhall Ranch. Behind them is the grave of Hart's pinto pony, Fritz.

The half-life-size bronze statue of William S. Hart, awarded to the best bronc-buster at the 1926 Wyoming Frontier Days celebration in Cheyenne.

never recorded, but it is an established fact that Hickok killed at least four men in the battle. When it was known that Hart was going to incorporate this incident into his picture, relatives of the McCanless clan wrote him, asking that their family name not be dishonored. Hart, realizing that there were undoubtedly two sides to the story of that battle, and not wanting to cause distress to any McCanless descendants, willingly changed the names in his film.

In 1943, Hart's sister Mary, whom he loved dearly, and who had written several books with him, died. She had been ill for years, as a result of injuries received in an automobile wreck. Hart lost much of his zest for living, and his eyesight began to fail. He wrote G. W. Dunston: "At times I can hardly see at all," and added: "There is nothing I can attribute my illness to, except that I believe it is caused by the deep grief I feel over the loss and absence of my darling sister. At times it seems to be too great a burden to carry. She was in all reality the better part of my existence."

He died in Los Angeles on June 23, 1946, and was buried in Greenwood Cemetery, Brooklyn, alongside his mother, father, two sisters, and the baby brother who had first been buried in Dakota.

He left an estate of well over a million dollars. Relatively little was bequeathed to his son: Hart was rather disappointed in the way the boy turned out. To him, he just didn't measure up, but knowing Hart, and the rigorous yardsticks he applied, this may not have been due to any real shortcomings on the part of his son. There had been no actual ill will between them, and Hart did leave his son some money, although not enough to permit the younger Hart to fall back on it without earning his own way. This, too, was typical of the man. The bulk of the estate, after bequests to several charities, including fifty thousand dollars to the Society for the Prevention of Cruelty to Animals, was left to Los Angeles County. In his lifetime, Hart had also given fifty thousand dollars to the City Park Commission, to effect improvements on his old West Hollywood estate, which he had also given to the Commission as a park. He added: "I'm trying to do an act of justice. I'm trying to give back to the American people what the American people so generously gave me."

The bequest of his estate to Los Angeles County carried with it the stipulation that his Horseshoe Ranch be turned into a public park, and his home a museum for the Western material he had assembled. For years, the ranch, with the WS brand on the front gate, was sealed, with barbed-wire fences to keep out trespassers. Valuable deposits of oil on the land were said to be the reason for the indecision concerning the future of the property. But finally Hart's wishes were respected, and the ranch was opened to the public as a museum. Beautifully maintained with care and respect by a custodian and staff, it is not exactly a huge tourist attraction, but stands as a fascinating and invaluable landmark to students of both Western history and Western film history. Livestock is maintained there, and the corrals and other aspects of work-a-day ranch life remain as they were, unglamorized for exhibition purposes. The graveyard for Fritz and Hart's many other pets is neatly kept. And Hart's workrooms remain, too, with many of his scripts, props, costumes, guns, and saddles intact, representing a marvelous collection of Western lore.

The ranch, situated atop a hill (and overlooking Harry Carey's former ranch) is truly a majestic sight. One can well imagine how happy Hart must have been to retire here—and in his final years, perhaps, how lonely. At sundown, with its solitude, and the great expanses of rolling hills on every side, it must have harmonized especially well with the sentimental "close to God" philosophy that had always been so pronounced in his activity, but which became even more emphasized in his last years. No more appropriate setting could be found for this final adieu of a grand old man who loved truth of the West and the Western with a passion and a devotion rarely shared later by other human beings.

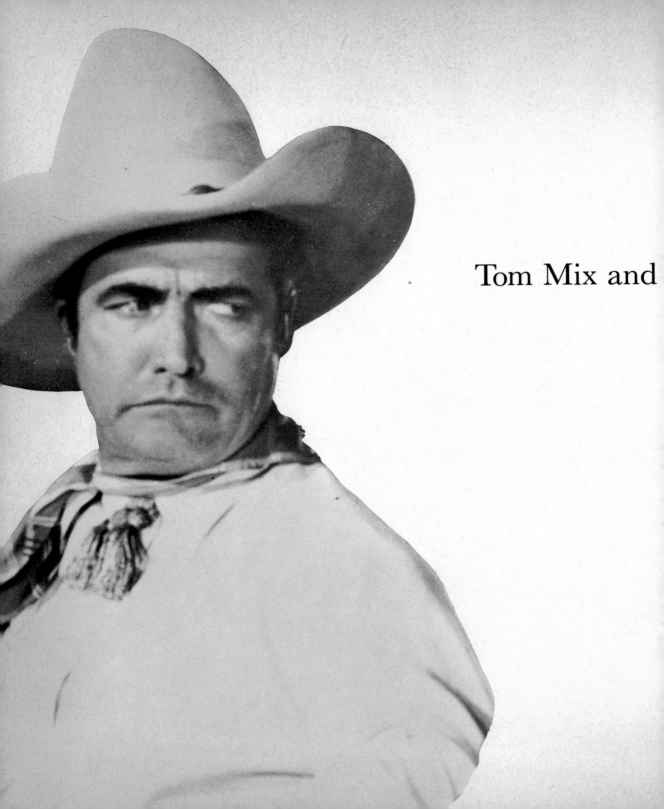

Tom Mix and

showmanship

6

If William S. Hart brought stature, poetry, and realism to the Western, Tom Mix unquestionably introduced showmanship, as well as the slick, polished format that was to serve Ken Maynard and Hoot Gibson in the Twenties and Gene Autry and Roy Rogers in the Thirties. His influence as such outlived that of Hart in the long run. Mix, born in 1880, in Clearfield County, Pennsylvania (and certainly not "in a log cabin north of El Paso," as so many romanticized biographies put it), was blessed with a colorful and adventurous early career. While the Western background attributed to him is authentic, it was a background that he drifted into in his twenties and not one that he was born into.

Having unsuccessfully tried to enlist in the Navy while still in his teens, Mix settled for the U. S. Army instead, and saw action in the Spanish-American war; field artillery then was horsedrawn, and a soldier automatically went through much the same training as a cavalryman. He then saw service in the Philippine insurrection, and later he fought at Peking in the Boxer Rebellion, as a member of the American Expeditionary Force.

Mustered out of the Army upon his return to America, he was soon back in action again—this time breaking horses that were being sent to the British Army for use in the war against the Boers. He accompanied a shipment of horses to the British troops in Africa, and remained there for a period as a wrangler.

The African sojourn over, the wanderer migrated West and assumed a rather nomadic existence in Texas, Oklahoma, and Kansas, working at first as an ordinary cowpuncher, and later joining the Miller Brothers' 101 Ranch, one of the finest, and certainly the most famous, of all the Wild West shows. Officially acting as livestock foreman, Mix talked himself into a position as a rodeo performer, and became a champion prize winner in the 1909 rodeos at Prescott, Arizona, and Canon City, Colorado. During those barnstorming days he formed a close friendship with Will Rogers, and saw action as a law enforcement officer—with the Texas Rangers, as a sheriff in Kansas and Oklahoma, and as a deputy U. S. marshal for the eastern division of Oklahoma. Studio publicity has undoubtedly colored some of this phase of Mix's career, but documentary evidence does exist confirming that Mix's law enforcing activities were quite as rugged as his later movie adventures. The story of Mix's capture of the notorious New Mexico cattle rustlers, the Shonts Brothers, could have been taken from any one of his later Western thrillers for Fox.

But he was beginning to show tentative signs of settling down. Having bought a ranch in the Cherokee territory of Oklahoma, he married Olive Stokes, the third of his five wives. But far from retiring to a sedate ranching life, Mix's career was just beginning, and it was the acqustion of the ranch that directly led to his entry into motion pictures. The Selig Company in Chicago was looking for a good ranch location, and for someone who knew the surrounding country. Informed of this,

Tom Mix in a typical action scene from one of his last Fox vehicles, Hello, Cheyenne (*1928*).

Mix immediately offered both his services and his ranch to Selig, who accepted, dispatching a unit to shoot a documentary film entitled, *Ranch Life in the Great South West,* a simple and straightforward little work depicting the processes involved in rounding up cattle and shipping them to the eastern markets. The director was Francis Boggs, whose career came to a tragic end shortly afterwards. While directing on Selig's open-air stage in Los Angeles, he was shot down and killed by a crazed man.

On this, his first association with Selig, Mix acted in the capacity of general adviser, taking charge of the cowboys, always available, just out of camera range, to shoot or rope any animal that got out of control. When the film was finished, Mix assumed that his work for Selig was at an end. Thus, struck by *wanderlust* again, he drifted into Mexico joining Madero's forces, and at one point was even set up before a firing squad.

Upon his return home, Mix learned that the Selig Company had been trying to find him, and promptly left for Chicago to investigate. Possibly, the mere thought of doing something new prompted his decision to join Selig again, for his earlier association with the Colonel had not been markedly promising or rewarding. As a now permanent member of the Selig Company, he repeated his role as a "safety man" keeping troublesome animals in control, doubling in tricky scenes in Selig's popular jungle and wild animal adventures. He later recalled having been asked to battle a pair of wolves, barehanded. Ultimately he started to act, both in Chicago and California, one of his first appearances for Selig being in *Back to the Primitive,* which starred Kathlyn Williams.

Soon he was permanently attached to the company's California studio, and between 1911 and 1917, he made between seventy and one hundred one- and two-reelers for Selig, with predominantly Western backgrounds. In many Mix functioned as star, author, and director, and it is probably because of this that so many of the films looked like artless affairs shot with little or no preparation. This is no discredit to Mix, since his background, anything but an artistic one, hardly qualified him to step right into a writer-director's role. The wonder is that with his limitations, he turned out so many films so quickly.

The pictures fluctuated between simple, folksy comedies in the Will Rogers vein (*Mrs. Murphy's Cooks, Why the Sheriff Is a Bachelor*) to more conventional Westerns (*In the Days of the Thundering Herd, Pony Express Rider*) which often were mere showcases for Mix's spectacular riding stunts. Many of these little films, e.g. *Sagebrush Tom* and *Mr. Haywood, Producer,* are of particular interest and value to film historians today, because they were comedies built around the business of making Westerns. They featured backstage shots of the Selig studios, glimpses of sets and old cameras, close-ups of Selig's notes with instructions to the crew, etc. *Sagebrush Tom* had a comedy sequence in which Mix, shown an ad for the Italian *Quo Vadis,* attempts to restage the fight with the bull in his Western corral. The quality of these shorts varied considerably; some had surprisingly vigorous action material, but others were dreary. As a group, they were generally below the standards of other Western shorts being made at the time. They were not even representative of the best Selig Westerns, for certainly films like *The Range Law* (1913) with William Duncan were superior.

During these seven years, Broncho Billy Anderson was at the peak of his fame, soon to retire, and Hart had been introduced, graduating in this same period from two-reelers to five-reel features. If any one of Mix's films in this period really stood out, it was probably *Chip of the Flying U* (1914) in which he co-starred with Kathlyn Williams. It was a good action story by Peter B. Kyne, and was directed by Colin Campbell, who also directed one of Selig's most successful action features, *The Spoilers.*

Although this latter film seems fairly ordinary today, and its famous fight between William Farnum and Tom Santschi eclipsed by later screen battles, it was a tremendously popular action film, perhaps because of the unusual realism of the sets and exteriors. Its popularity exceeded even the De Mille-Lasky production of *The Squaw Man,* directed by De Mille in Hollywood in late December, 1913, principally because the Mix film production enjoyed better weather conditions and could also take advantage of Hollywood's laboratory facilities.

The Squaw Man's chief claim to fame is its quite erroneous allegation that it was the first feature film made in Hollywood. However, it and Selig's *The Spoilers* were both among the early really successful Westerns. *The Squaw Man* was remade twice by De Mille, both at times in his career when he was retrenching, with future policy still undetermined. *The Spoilers* was remade four times.

Although the Mix period with Selig was generally uneventful, this was due more to company policy than to any shortcomings on the part of Mix. Selig was mostly interested in, and geared for, the production of shorts, limiting Mix to one-, two- and three-reelers. Committed to quantity, he had no time to develop his own screen personality, or to enlarge the scope of the films themselves. Nevertheless, the films proved to be a useful training ground for Mix, and they *did* improve as they went along. When he joined Fox in 1917, there was no uncertainty or faltering; he became an immediate star attraction.

Only then did Selig realize the commercial potential of the old Mix films and he immediately began by re-editing the old shorts. Some of these "new" Selig-Tom Mix Westerns, films like *Twisted Trails* and *The Heart of Texas Ryan,* are still in circulation and show, if not cohesion, at least considerable ingenuity. One complete reel of *Twisted Trails* is taken from a film in which Mix did not even appear, and serves merely to establish the predicament of the heroine (Bessie Eyton) in running away from an unwanted marriage. An earlier reel had established Mix as a wandering cowboy; then, at the beginning of reel three, an inserted subtitle reads: "Thus were the twisted trails of the boy and girl joined together" —whereupon Mix meets the heroine, an accident she has had having thrown them together. The remainder of the film consists of one of their co-starring two-reelers. Neither Mix nor Fox was too concerned over these manipulations, but Fox stressed that Mix had been seen previously *only* in comedies (a statement that was far from correct) and that his new films were his first as a Western star.

When Fox signed Mix in 1917, his real career began. Although Mix began with a two-reeler, *Six Cylinder Love,* written, produced, and directed by Mix himself, he switched immediately to features like *Durand*

of the Badlands, directed by a former Ince man, Richard Stanton. These were good films, endowed with strong production values, skilled direction, and excellent locations. A decision was soon made to create a unique film personality for Mix; Fox did not want Mix to become a carbon copy of Hart. The new star's films were to contain strong comic elements, making a special play for the juvenile trade. Early films in this category were *Cupid's Roundup* and *Six Shooter Andy,* directed by Chester and Sidney Franklin. They used popular juvenile stars from the recent successes, *Jack and the Beanstalk* and *Aladdin and His Lamp.*

One year later, when Mix's film career at Fox was just getting under way, that of William S. Hart was at its zenith. But by 1920, in terms of audience popularity, Hart's career began a gradual decline with Mix taking over unquestioned supremacy in the Western field. His films for Fox over a ten-year period literally made the company, just as the Autry Westerns in the mid-Thirties put Republic on the map. The lush Theda Bara-Annette Kellerman period behind him, William Fox was only moderately successful when Mix joined his company. Just as, at

Warners, Rin Tin Tin helped pay for the costly but unprofitable prestige features with John Barrymore, so did Tom Mix's films enable Fox to encourage the production of such classic, but financially unsuccessful films as Murnau's *Sunrise.* Fox.openly admitted Mix's value, giving him the full "star treatment." The cowboy had his own production unit, an elaborate private bungalow—everything that went with the status of a Hollywood star in the movies' most colorful era.

By 1925, Mix was being paid seventeen thousand dollars per week and he was earning every cent of it for the studio. Mix wrote and directed only one of his features under the Fox contract, *The Daredevils,* made in 1919. Direction *per se* interested him hardly at all, but he was concerned with the overall conception of his Westerns, so much so that, in their own way, they were as much personal productions as were the films of William S. Hart. Aimed at a wide audience, they were breezy and cheerful, "streamlined" *entertainment* that rarely attempted a realistic

A production shot from Tom Mix's Just Tony (1922); *the muscular assistant in the striped shirt is George O'Brien, soon to be a Western star himself.*

re-creation of the West as it was, offering instead action and excitement spiced with a boyish sense of fun.

Mix went out of his way to devise little stunts and "bits of business" which were utilized for their own sake, regardless of story continuity or their own probability. Mix's screen character never drank, swore, or even used violence without due cause. His scripts usually saw to it that he was never required to kill a villain, or even wound him if it could be avoided. Instead, he would capture and subdue them by some elaborate lasso-work, or by some fancy stunts. His idealized Western hero, possessed of all the virtues and none of the vices, helped usher in the code of clean-living, non-drinking, and somewhat colorless sagebrush heroes, a code that remained in force until the early Fifties, when Bill Elliott, playing the tough Westerner characterized by Hart, began to restore the balance to a more realistic level.

Almost all of the Mix films were made on location, far away from the studio. He made a point of using National Park sites for many films, often writing and constructing the films deliberately so that these locations could be exploited as an integral part of the plot. He once stated: "I want as many people as possible to know what wonderful possessions they own, and to stir up in them a desire to see these places." There was hardly a location of importance and beauty that the Mix troupe failed to cover, although it appeared that he had a special fondness for Colorado.

Like William S. Hart and John Ford, Mix had his own crew on whom he could rely. Lynn Reynolds directed more than a dozen of Mix's Fox Westerns. Cliff Smith and Lambert Hillyer, old Hart alumni, were two more directors in whom Mix frequently put his trust. John Ford directed two Mix films, *Three Jumps Ahead* and *North of Hudson Bay,* and William Beaudine, George Marshall, Edward Sedgewick, Jack Conway, Lewis Seiler, Jack Blystone, Gene Forde, and Edward Le Saint were others who at one time or another directed Mix.

In his choice of cameramen, Mix favored Daniel B. Clark, a former soldier and division boxing champion who had been with Fox since 1919, after Mix had joined the studio, and who had started to work for Mix as a still cameraman. Clark was soon assigned as an assistant cameraman under Ben Kline and Frank B. Good, and later promoted to the head position for *Just Tony*. Clark and Mix, both alike in so many ways, and both rugged adventurers with army backgrounds, hit it off together right away. Clark shot all of the remainder of Mix's Fox Westerns—more than forty films which were characterized by superior photography of these exceptionally beautiful locations.

Mix's films were of sufficient importance to warrant name leading ladies, and among those who appeared opposite Mix at Fox were Colleen Moore, Patsy Ruth Miller, and Lois Wilson.

During his stay at Fox, he was instrumental in getting a number of other cowboy actors launched in their careers. Buck Jones began as a trick rider with the Mix unit, and was soon afterwards placed by Fox into a starring series of his own, patterned after the Mix films. John Wayne also got his first break with Mix, who got him a job as a prop boy. And George O'Brien worked for some months as an assistant cameraman with the Mix unit. Upon leaving Fox to join another unit, O'Brien drifted into acting; he was making so little progress that he had signed on as a galley slave in Frank Lloyd's *The Sea Hawk* when John Ford finally contacted him and gave O'Brien the role in *The Iron Horse* that was to bring him fame.

All told, Mix made more than sixty features for Fox, among them such off-beat subjects as *Tom Mix in Arabia* and *Dick Turpin*. The latter was an elaborate and carefully made "special," but although it earned money, and although Mix went through his traditional riding stunts, the sight of Tom Mix in period costume, dueling with a sword instead of a six-shooter, did not sit too well with his fans, and in his next film he reverted permanently to the costume and character that were expected of him.

Mix was consistent in his screen roles: he avoided the reformed-outlaw type, and that of the dude who went West to make a man of himself. Nor did he attempt the role of the cowpuncher who tames and marries the willful heiress, something that most Western stars have done at least once in their careers. Mix had very definite ideas about the sort of Westerner he should play, and his own words are to the point: "I ride into a place owning my own horse, saddle, and bridle. It isn't my quarrel, but I get into trouble doing the right thing for somebody else. When it's all ironed out, I never get any money reward. I may be made foreman of the ranch and I get the girl, but there is never a fervid love scene."

Mix's simplified and apparently cliché description of his own format hardly does justice to the films. His Westerns might not have been either "poetic" or "adult," but they were well written, with three-dimensional characters, sensible motivation, and often highly imaginative plots. Among his more notable Westerns at Fox were *Rough Riding Romance* (very much off the beaten track in that it had a Ruritanian background), and *Tumbling River* (in which Tony, Tom's horse, was given a frisky colt as a partner).

Just Tony was Tom's own tribute to his horse, much as Hart had made

Pinto Ben and *The Narrow Trail* a tribute to Fritz. The film had some exceptionally fine animal footage and, as always, was loaded with action; Dan Clark recalls it as being one of the best of the Mix films. Lambert Hillyer's choice as the best is *The Lone Star Ranger,* adapted from two Zane Grey stories. *The Rainbow Trail,* made when Mix was at the absolute height of his career, was another outstanding Western, and contained some of the finest stunt work ever filmed.

Mix was wise enough not to let the success of his pictures influence him into making them "bigger" and more pretentious. Even at his peak, he never abandoned the five- or six-reel feature. *The Great K & A Robbery,* shot on location in Colorado, using the Denver and the Rio Grande Western Railroad, was another top Western notable for its stunting. In one scene Tom escaped from the villains by hanging from an aerial cable, sliding down it to land on Tony, while on another occasion he and a gang of villains engaged in a no-holds-barred fight atop a fast-moving freight train. Since Westerns with railroading backgrounds (out of fashion nowadays, alas) were popular with audiences in the days of silents, Mix, with his boyish love of adventure, wrote train sequences into his films whenever he could. Having written the trains in, the next move was to write in as many fights, chases, and stunts revolving around the trains as possible. Dan Clark recalls that he set up his cameras on every conceivable part of a locomotive during his days with Mix—and for that matter, on almost every other type of vehicle, including the cage of an aerial cable. *No Man's Gold* (1926), for instance, contained a typically whirlwind finish; Tom capturing the villains by sweeping down on their shack at high speed in a steel ore bucket suspended by a cable.

Unfortunately, most of the great Mix Westerns are no longer in existence, the chemical effects of time on old film in this case having been assisted by a disastrous fire at Fox, in which many valuable prints and negatives were burned. But at least single prints of two Mix films from the Twenties have been saved, *Sky High* and *Riders of the Purple Sage.* It is perhaps sad that the latter, an atypical Mix film and one of the weakest at that, should remain while others, far better, have apparently vanished for all time.

Sky High, however, is about as typical a Tom Mix film as one could hope to find, as exhilarating and thrilling now as it was in 1922. Incidentally, it would seem to substantiate the claim that Mix rarely if ever used a double. Certainly *all* Western stars, at one time or another, have used doubles for action scenes, but Mix used them far less than most. Mix, himself, was quite touchy on this point; his unit included a few stuntmen who could take over for him in certain scenes if necessary, but they and the rest of the crew were sworn to absolute secrecy. *Sky High* seems not to have taken advantage of these daredevils at all, for Tom tackles villains, falls from a horse, and hops over rocks along the rim of the Grand Canyon, all with the camera grinding away at close range.

Riders of the Purple Sage gave Tom few opportunities for such stunting, and was perhaps the only Western he made in the more restrained William S. Hart vein. Somber and austere, even a little bloodthirsty, it was based on a typically complicated Zane Grey plot. It seemed too heavy a vehicle for high-spirited Tom Mix, and he seemed ill at ease having to take his material so seriously. But, substandard or not, *Riders of the Purple Sage* confirmed again what real production values Mix put into his movies, and what superb camerawork Dan Clark could create.

Enjoying fame and success, Mix lived now like an Oriental potentate. He built an enormous mansion in Beverly Hills, complete with swimming pool and an English butler. His cars were custom built, with hand-tooled leather upholstery and fittings of silver. He dressed lavishly, and began the fashion, later exploited by Autry and Rogers, of wearing outfits that more resembled uniforms than range clothing. One of his more garish items of apparel was a horsehair belt, fastened with a diamond-

Riders of Death Valley (*1932*), *one of Mix's last Westerns.*

My Pal the King (*1932*), *a typical Mix feature combining Ruritanian adventure with Western heroics. The boy-king is Mickey Rooney.*

studded buckle, and emblazoned with the slogan: "Tom Mix, America's Champion Cowboy."

When Mix's Fox contract came to a close, he moved to FBO, an energetic independent company that specialized in first-class Western and other action films. It was then under the direction of Joseph P. Kennedy, John F. Kennedy's father. Mix's Westerns at this new studio retained both the format and the previous high standards, although the budgets were slightly smaller. Because of an incomplete contract at Fox, Dan Clark was unable to join Mix at FBO, but they worked together again in Mix's sound Westerns for Universal and Mascot.

The FBO series was short-lived. The sound era was ushered in and the company was reorganized as RKO. Their initial specialty was very "talkie" adaptations of stage plays, to the exclusion of Westerns. In the early Thirties, however, Mix, again with his own unit, made an excellent series of sound Westerns for Universal. The formula never varied: escapes, tricks, showmanship, stunts. In one film, *My Pal the King* (a Ruritanian adventure with Mickey Rooney as a boy-king), Mix stepped "outside" the movie for a moment, directly addressed the audience, and asked that it try to put itself in the shoes of the child in the movie who was about to see his first rodeo. It was a touching moment, and offered an interesting glimpse of another Tom Mix.

Sound did not improve the Mix Westerns, for when he recited dialogue he was often unconvincing. He put little meaning or expression into his lines, and his speech was often slurred until it was partially incoherent. But the films were still enjoyable. Casting was still good, as was the direction. The first *Destry Rides Again* was one of the films made at this time, and like most of them it was quite elaborately mounted when one considers how quickly and cheaply it was made. These films would have made a reasonable, if not notable, farewell to the screen. But unfortunately Mix chose to make his farewell in a 1935 serial for Mascot, *The Miracle Rider*. Overlong, slimly plotted, and cheaply made, it was a sorry affair. Mix's speech had deteriorated further and, while he still rode well, most of his action was handled by doubles. (This was at least partially a matter of economy, allowing two units to operate simultaneously.) However, the film was a solid financial success, both in its serial and feature versions. It was earning money as late as the Fifties on television in the United States and in cinemas abroad.

Mix's last years were spent in characteristically energetic fashion. In 1932 he married again, this time Mabel Hubbel Ward, a trapeze artist, and before Universal brought him back to the screen, he announced his "retirement," joining the Sells Floto Circus. He was still a magnificent sight, husky, over six feet tall, handsome in a rugged way, with a sun-tanned, deeply lined face. He dressed always in his solid white outfit, with big peaked sombrero, and black boots; Tony was with him, of course. He was paid ten thousand dollars a week by the circus, and motored across the country with it in a lavish Rolls Royce. Obviously prosperous, he didn't need to return to films, and apparently at that time had no intention of doing so. In an interview early in 1931 he stated that he—and Tony—liked the circus, that he felt fitter than he had in years, and that, although in his late fifties, he felt like a man of thirty. Despite his athletic appearance, his many injuries, both from combat in earlier years and from movie mishaps later on, must have had their effect on him. His body was literally a mass of scars, while shattered bones were held together with surgical wire.

Even after *The Miracle Rider,* he remained active in show business. In 1935, he hit the road again with the Tom Mix Wild Animal Circus. In all probability he had little control over it, and was merely being paid for the use of his name. But it was a popular show, and seemed to please his admirers. However, as far as the entertainment business was concerned, it was his last venture.

Five years later he was killed in an automobile accident near Florence, Arizona. On October 12, 1940, his car failed to make a curve at a detour sign and turned over; the great cowboy's neck was broken. So, at sixty, Mix died in keeping with the way he had lived. A statue of a riderless pony has been erected to mark the spot of his death. At Fox, they have remembered Tom Mix, too; one of the big sound stages there bears a bronze plaque dedicating the stage to the memory of "Tom Mix and Tony."

Douglas Fairbanks and

John Ford:
1913–1920

7

*"The 'dreamed reality' on the screen
can move forward and backward
because it is really an external
and ubiquitous virtual present.
The action of drama goes
inexorably forward because
it creates a future, a Destiny;
the dream mode is an endless Now."*

SUSANNE LANGER

During Tom Mix's Selig period, a gradual standardization of the Western began, leading ultimately to the beginnings of the "series" Western with set stars (Harry Carey, William Russell, Roy Stewart) and formats. Triangle, which released the Hart pictures, had other interesting Western subjects, the best of them made, as we have seen, by or under the supervision of D. W. Griffith. Ince's Westerns, as *The Deserter* and *The Bugle Call,* for example, continued to be well-made "spectaculars," but they were little more than expanded versions of his earlier two-reelers. Griffith, at the head of Fine Arts, his subsidiary at Triangle, was not only producing such interesting Westerns as *The Wild Girl of the Sierras,* with Mae Marsh, Robert Harron and Wilfrid Lucas, but also spectacular films of the caliber of *The Martyrs of the Alamo,* dealing with the 1836 war between Mexico and Texas. Highlights of this picture were the battles at the Alamo and San Jacinto. This period in western history was later covered again in sound Westerns, among which we may mention Republic's *Man of Conquest,* and *The Last Command,* Universal's *The Man from the Alamo,* Allied Artists' *The First Texan,* and more recently John Wayne's *The Alamo.*

By far some of the most delightful and off-beat of the Triangle Westerns were those starring Douglas Fairbanks. Their quality was astonishingly uneven; some, like *The Americano* and *Flirting with Fate,* were both clumsy and slow; others, like *His Picture in the Papers* and *American Aristocracy,* were brilliant films, not only exciting in their action, but subtle and inventive in their comedy. *His Picture in the Papers,* in particular, with its satire on the American craze for publicity, was a little gem of the film art.

Several of Fairbanks' thirteen films for Triangle were Westerns, among them *The Good Bad Man, The Half-Breed* and, best of all, *Manhattan Madness.* The latter was to prove a blueprint for the best of Fairbanks' later pictures for Artcraft, casting him as the irrepressible modern youth, happily unconcerned with making a living, existing only for adventure. Fairbanks played the role of a Westerner who came to his staid New York club and regaled its members with tales of his exciting adventures in the West. Determined to show him that the metropolis on the Hudson can be as vigorous a place as Texas, the clubmen fake a kidnapping, and give the modern d'Artagnan full rein to go through his paces. In the process, he triumphs over all obstacles—including hordes of villains—that are placed in his way.

The best of Fairbanks' films (before *The Mark of Zorro* set him making costume dramas) were all madcap adventures, with as much comedy as action, with both elements beautifully interwoven, films not intended to be taken seriously for a moment. It is unfortunate that Fairbanks'

The classic "High Noon" shoot-out was satirized by Douglas Fairbanks as early as 1916 in **Manhattan Madness.**

Douglas Fairbanks, the eternal optimist in the face of all odds. From The Knickerbocker Buckaroo *(1919), one of the best of many Westerns he made prior to 1920.*

greatness is frequently measured by such films as *Robin Hood* and *The Thief of Bagdad;* these films were pretentious affairs, and one can only assume that many critics and historians of the cinema have either forgotten, or are totally unaware of his earlier and livelier work.

The best of Fairbanks' Westerns for Artcraft, made just before he switched to United Artists, are of the highest quality. They include *The Man from Painted Post, The Knickerbocker Buckaroo* and *Headin' South*. Occasionally he made a weak film like *Arizona*. *Arizona* was based on a serious play ill-suited to Fairbanks' style and personality. He injected some fine action and comedy moments into the opening and closing reels, but otherwise it was a generally stodgy, if handsomely mounted film.

Fairbanks' Artcraft Westerns were some of the best action pictures ever made; they also were some of the most diverting, with their rollicking sense of fun, and the implicit demand made on the audience to take them any way but seriously. Among the most frequently used directors on these films were Victor Fleming, Allan Dwan, and Arthur Rosson, while William Wellman figured prominently in one of the best, *The Knickerbocker Buckaroo*.

In 1918, while Mix was beginning to get star-billing at Fox, and

Keith of the Border (*1918*), *starring Roy Stewart.*

while Hart and Douglas Fairbanks were making some of their best films for Artcraft, the outlook for Westerns in general was far from bright. Few were being made and most of them were individual films, not part of any established series. Despite the success of the Hart and Mix films, the field apparently needed the stimulation of *The Covered Wagon,* five years later, to return Westerns generally to public favor.

At Triangle, Roy Stewart had taken over as the studio's number one Western star. He was an acceptable replacement, but a poor substitute in acting ability and star quality for William S. Hart. Worth noting of Stewart's films are *The Law's Outlaw* and *Faith Endurin',* directed by Cliff Smith.

As always in a period of decline, a number of "gimmicks" were introduced to add novelty. One of these was the wide-screen development of

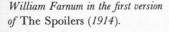

William Farnum in the first version of The Spoilers (*1914*).

the Paralta Company. *A Man's Man,* an action picture starring J. Warren Kerrigan and directed by Oscar Apfel, used this innovation and advertised it in the following way: ". . . compared with our wide screen, the old screen is like looking at part of the stage of a theatre through a square hole." An early sound system which had had some success in 1913 in a number of shorts made by Edison was now used again. In *The Claim,* directed by Frank Reicher for Metro Pictures Corp., Edith Storey sang "Annie Laurie." Apparently, synchronization for that particular sequence was so complicated that most exhibitors preferred to run the film as a silent.

A number of basically non-Western stars now ventured into the field for the first time. Harold Lockwood's first Western was *The Avenging Trail,* directed by Francis Ford; William Desmond at Triangle began to add Western roles to his usual characterization of the "romantic adventurer." William Farnum, still remembered from *The Spoilers,* appeared in a number of outdoor pictures, among which were *Rough and Ready, The Conqueror,* and *The Heart of a Lion.* Franklyn Farnum also attracted a following in Westerns like *The Fighting Grin,* a comedy shot in Arizona that leaned heavily on the Fairbanks format.

A good percentage of the action series films made by the American Film Company and starring stolid William Russell contained Western themes. One of the Westerns directed by Henry King for that outfit, *Six Feet Four* was a curious forerunner of King's *The Gunfighter* in that it was

William Desmond in Deuce Duncan (*1918*).

Cecil B. DeMille directing Mary Pick-ford and Elliott Dexter in A Romance of the Redwoods, *a solid and appealing little Western, made before his "spectacle" career began in the early Twenties.*

a Western almost without action or exteriors. The bulk of the film was shot indoors with the narration dependent on dialogue subtitles. It was very much of a misfire, but very interesting in the light of King's later work.

Paramount, on the other hand, put romantic idol Wallace Reid into a number of Western subjects, among them *Nan of Music Mountain.* Essanay offered a version of *Ruggles of Red Gap,* Harry L. Wilson's story of the English butler suddenly introduced to the rigors of the West. First National kept the Indian hero prominent in films like *The Sign Invisible.*

With Westerns in limited production by independents, the bulk of the really top Westerns made in the years immediately preceding 1920 came from three notable sources. The first was, of course, Fox with the Tom Mix films, sold to the public on the basis of their adventurous stories and the daring stunts Mix provided. The second was Artcraft with the Douglas Fairbanks pictures, which were sold on similar lines, and the Hart films which were advertised quite differently. Trade papers carried announcements declaring: "William S. Hart pictures are always inspiring —they make folks breathe deeper," or, in publicizing *The Narrow Trail:* "Better a painted pony than a painted woman." The third source was Universal which made some first-class Western serials with Eddie Polo, Neal Hart, and other stars, good quality program Westerns such as *The Wolf and His Mate,* and most notable of all, those films combining the talents of star Harry Carey and director John Ford.

John Ford had started in Universal's studios in 1917, using the name Jack Ford, and directing Carey in two-reelers. In *The Scrapper,* Ford not only wrote the colorful story, but also starred. The story as outlined in

Moving Picture World of June 4, 1917, is as follows: "Buck the Scrapper loses his girl, who goes to the city when she is bored with the ranch. There, unemployed, she is innocently thrust into a house of questionable repute. When Buck and his friends bring a cargo of cattle to the city to sell, he is lured by a lady of the streets to the house and finds his girl there as she is being attacked. Buck fights her assailant, and takes the girl back to the West."

Already, it seems, Ford thought nothing of presenting his Western hero as a man human enough to be lured into a bordello. With his first feature, Ford scored an instant success. The film was *Straight Shootin'*, with Hoot Gibson supporting Harry Carey. This time *Moving Picture World* commented: ". . . a cleancut, straightforward tale. Both the author and the director are to be congratulated upon having selected compelling scenes and situations for the production. The Western panorama is set forth in clear, attractive photography and the riding and fighting episodes are enacted with dash and enthusiasm. So successful is the offering that it deserves to rank with *The Virginian* and *Whispering Smith*."

The Secret Man, Bucking Broadway, Phantom Riders, and *Hill Billy* further enhanced Ford's reputation. *Wild Women* (1918) was something of an excursion into the Fairbanks mold. As the synopsis put it: "No rarebit fiend dream was ever half so vivid as the visions that follow the imbibing of too many Honolulu cocktails. Cheyenne Harry and his ranchers drink freely after winning the rodeo, and wild dreams of shanghaiing and the South Seas follow."

Ford was happy making Westerns, and for the time being continued to make nothing else. *A Fight for Love* was a large-scale Western dealing with the efforts of the Canadian Mounties to stamp out whiskey running to the Indians; *Bare Fists* was a sentimental drama, somewhat in the W. S. Hart vein. Then, in 1919, came *The Outcasts of Poker Flat* based on Bret Harte's story. *Photoplay* commented: "Two remarkable things are Harry Carey's rise to real acting power, and director Ford's marvellous river locations and absolutely incomparable photography. This photoplay is an optic symphony." Ford, as can be seen, was already going out of his way to secure fine locations. *Ace of the Saddle,* his next, was photographed in the picturesque Rio Grande Valley.

In only two years, John Ford made some twenty horse operas and established himself as the foremost director of Western dramas, with the possible exception of the quite different William S. Hart. *The Iron Horse,* a very substantial achievement, was now only four years away; with it would come new discussion concerning the truth of the old West, and it would further implement the saga of the frontier as explored on the screen.

"They went with axe and rifle,
When the trail was still to blaze,
They went with wife and children,
In the prairie-schooner days,
With banjo and with frying pan—
Suzanna, don't you cry!
For I'm off to California,
To get rich out there or die!"

STEPHEN VINCENT BENÉT, *Western Wagons*

James Cruze's *The*

and

Covered Wagon
John Ford's
The Iron Horse

8

In 1923 Westerns were generally out of favor, at their lowest point since the pre-Hart days of 1913. Hart was faltering and the films of Tom Mix were the only ones that carried any weight at the box office. Lesser Western stars such as Roy Stewart had failed to attract the attention of any of the more important directors and, save for a few good isolated program features, e.g., Griffith's *Scarlet Days,* King Vidor's *Sky Pilot,* the non-series Westerns were generally commonplace.

But 1923 was also the year of *The Covered Wagon,* whose importance as a major event in Western movie history cannot be stressed too strongly. The first genuinely epic Western and, incidentally, the first American epic not directed by David W. Griffith, it gave a tremendous boost to the Western genre now in its twentieth year. Only fifty Westerns were made in 1923, but the success of James Cruze's film was such that the following year saw the number had almost tripled. Until the elimination of "B" Westerns in the mid-Fifties, the annual Western output never fell below that figure again, and usually exceeded it.

Although numerous imitations over the years have made *The Covered Wagon* appear to be quite commonplace—so much that to a contemporary audience the film seems slow and pedestrian, often crudely faked—its effect then proved startling. Its plot—a wagon trek to California, with villainy and romance added to round out the story—was extremely simple. What amazed the public was the film's sheer size and splendor, and the revelation that a Western could achieve the epic stature.

Most impressive was the magnificent photography, the work of Karl Brown, formerly an assistant cameraman with Griffith, and later the director of such notable films as *Stark Love*. Vast panoramas of the long wagon trains winding across the plains, the impressive scope of such episodes as the Indian attack, the fording of the river, and the buffalo hunt—all these convinced movie audiences that the first twenty years of Westerns had but scratched the surface of the magnificent potential of the outdoor film. The sudden success of the film seemed, rather unfairly, to eclipse the notable earlier work of Hart, Griffith, and Ince, for the implication was that now, at last, *The Covered Wagon* had brought real maturity to the Western.

Certainly, *The Covered Wagon* is a film of major importance. It was the first epic Western and it acted as a powerful stimulant to the faltering Western field. But because it was such an influential film, the legend seems to have sprung up that it was also a great film.

In actual fact, *The Covered Wagon* was, its photography apart, of negligible creative value. Like so many Paramount films of that period, it lacked real plot. Paramount's policy at that time seemed to concentrate on quantity to the exclusion of other considerations. One Wallace Reid or Mary Miles Minter program feature followed the other with frightening rapidity. The production values were slight, the script values often mediocre. It should be remembered that Rudolph Valentino's dispute with Paramount was over being pushed into products of this type.

It is no coincidence, therefore, that Paramount had fewer important pictures, in the aesthetic sense, in this period than any other studio, or that Paramount's best films were those which *had* a "plus" factor in the scripts, films like the two Brenon-Bronson films, *Peter Pan* and *A Kiss for Cinderella,* based on James Barrie's plays.

In *The Covered Wagon,* admittedly, theme is more important than plot. Also, James Cruze was on his own once the film got under way; but the assembly-line writing and the overall Paramount attitude were part of the script well before the cameras rolled, and could not be altogether removed by Cruze. Cruze, in any case, was not a really creative director, but rather a highly competent man who was less likely to compromise than most.

The basic weakness of *The Covered Wagon* lies in its script, which is more apt for a "B" picture than for an epic. The theme of the wagon trek to California admittedly remained foremost in the film, of more importance than the personal difficulties of hero and heroine, but it was not handled in the heroic sense of Ford's building of the railroad a year later. We are never told just *why* the trek is taking place, or exactly what is to come from it. The impression is created that this is an enterprising group of farmers, seeking to better themselves, and willing to risk danger and hardship to find a haven in Oregon and California. But lacking is the vital, dramatic sense of the opening up of new frontiers, the carving of an empire from the wilderness, the bitter struggle against nature's elements. There is little sense even of the period, except for the dates provided by the film's subtitles, and casual references to Brigham Young, the Mormon leader, and Abraham Lincoln, references that in themselves are unnecessary and seem inserted to "authenticate" the background. Nor is the cinematic reconstruction of the period helped by the relative significance of the film's incidents: a conventional fight between hero and villain is given far more prominence than an event like the discovery of gold in California, which is treated in a completely offhand manner.

The panoramic scenes of the wagon train, the near-documentary scenes of a river-crossing, of campfire singing, of a burial followed by a birth (today this seems too facile, but regarded in context and period it was an effective and original touch), of the hazards of snow and mud . . . all this is set off by an orthodox account of a somewhat ludicrously idealized hero (J. Warren Kerrigan), and a heroine (Lois Wilson) who loves him, loses him through misunderstandings fomented by the villain, and ultimately wins him in a traditional studio formula ending!

The arrival at the promised land: The Covered Wagon (*1923*).

Another detracting factor was the role of the villain played by Alan Hale. The role was well acted, but written unsubtly, in a completely black vein. Here was a villain without a single redeeming feature. In general, then, two elements, near-documentary originality and strictly formula writing, are constantly at odds with each other in *The Covered*

A potentially exciting sequence staged in an unexciting manner; Cruze shoots the runaway horse episode from The Covered Wagon *in a single uninterrupted long shot.*

Wagon, preventing unity. The production, too, is stolidly paced (perhaps deliberately, to stress the monotony of the trek) and surprisingly unexciting.

The big action sequences suffer occasionally from unimaginative inclusions which strike a false note. For example, the buffalo hunt is marred by patently false studio-shot riding close-ups in which the actor clearly is doing nothing more than bouncing up and down in front of a cyclorama; if no running inserts shot on location were available, certainly none at all would have been preferable to a piece of obvious fakery. And the Indian fight itself (discussed more fully later) loses much of its punch when one considers the basic improbability of its circumstances: as William S. Hart pointed out, somewhat scornfully, *no* wagon boss would be stupid enough to court disaster by camping his train overnight in a blind canyon.

One would like to be generous to *The Covered Wagon* because it could so easily have been a great film, as well as an important one. But if only for its superb Western vistas, impressive to this day, and for its fine supporting performances from Tully Marshall and Ernest Torrence (ideally cast as a couple of hard-drinking frontier scouts), *The Covered Wagon* is well worth seeing—and, of course, its influence on other film-makers was great.

Surprisingly, it was almost accidental that the film emerged in the form we know. Initially Emerson Hough's novel had been purchased to be filmed as a vehicle for Mary Miles Minter. She ultimately balked at the prospect of a lengthy and uncomfortable trip on location, and contrived to have herself cast in another film scheduled to go before the cameras at the same time. Thus, the property, handed over to James Cruze, was cast with then-minor stars (J. Warren Kerrigan, Lois Wilson, Ernest Torrence, Alan Hale) and a film quite different from the one initially planned was then mapped out. Cruze from the first was for shooting the film away from the studio, and some of the locations he used are still among the most impressive to be seen in any Western film, particularly those of Snake Valley in Nevada and Antelope Island in Great Salt Lake, the last the location for the buffalo hunt.

To facilitate managing the hundreds of Indian extras employed in the production, Cruze had the services of Col. Tim McCoy, then an Indian agent for the government, a man who knew the Indian sign language fluently, and who subsequently escorted a party of Indians to England to appear at the film's première at the London Pavilion. One year later McCoy himself turned to acting and became one of the better Western stars.

In the wake of *The Covered Wagon*'s enthusiastic reception, Cruze's reputation as a director grew, and four years later he became, at seven thousand dollars per week, the highest paid director in the world, while the box-office value of the actors who had appeared in the film rose considerably, as well. The film inspired a number of other films, quite logically, and omitting mention of the many "B" imitations, three major epics were made as a result of Cruze's film, two of them made by Paramount again. *North of 36* (1924), a sequel to *The Covered Wagon,* directed by Irvin Willat, an old Ince man, offered Lois Wilson and Ernest Torrence in their original roles, with Jack Holt replacing Kerrigan to great advantage. The film had its success.

Cruze's own follow-up, in 1925, was *The Pony Express,* a lavish affair with Ricardo Cortez, Wallace Beery, and Betty Compson (Mrs. Cruze) that was more or less ignored by the public; it had many of the faults of

The Covered Wagon and few of its virtues. Apart from a well-staged Indian attack for its climax, there was little action and the film too often bogged down in romantic, political, and historical intrigue. Cruze's own respect for historical accuracy provided the film with a further weakness in that the villain, Jack Slade, played by George Bancroft, got away scot free despite a career of robbery and murder. Nevertheless, the film was vastly superior to the slow-moving 1953 version with Charlton Heston.

Both *North of 36* and *The Pony Express* occasioned little comment, and they are generally ignored by historians. Quite a different matter, however, was the third epic film inspired by Cruze's work: *The Iron Horse,* directed for Fox in 1924 by John Ford, when he was twenty-nine and had already made nearly fifty films, thirty-nine of them Westerns which gave him a reputation as a shrewd director. He had always gone out of his way to secure first-class locations, his scripts were strong (sometimes incorporating unusual elements of fantasy), and were written either by himself or by writers like Jules Furthman, later one of the most prolific of all screen writers, his credits to include the Jane Russell vehicle, *The Outlaw.*

Prior to *The Iron Horse,* Ford's longest film had been the seven-reel *Cameo Kirby* with John Gilbert; and at two hours and forty minutes, *The Iron Horse* is still Ford's longest film and his only *real* epic. For the statistically minded, *The Iron Horse* contained 1280 separate scenes and 275 subtitles! Ford was well schooled in the Western field and, loving Westerns, he obviously saw in *The Iron Horse* an opportunity to make a Western on a grand scale, and that is precisely what he did.

Of course it was an enormous spectacle depicting an inspiring event in a nation's progress, but it was, in fact, an expansion of his earlier, less important Westerns—*Hitchin' Posts,* for example, which also contained elements of the epic with its spectacular sequences in the last reel of the Cherokee Strip land rush. In short, *The Iron Horse* was faster, much more exciting than *The Covered Wagon,* yet less of an event in film history.

Perhaps because he was able to lavish so much care, time, and money on the type of film most dear to him, *The Iron Horse* has remained Ford's favorite—or at least it was in 1953 when he so stated in an interview. Although the veteran director has also gone on record as disliking certain of his films that critics consider among his best, most specifically, *They Were Expendable,* it is significant that Ford should prefer *The Iron Horse* to the generally higher esteemed *Stagecoach* (1939).

The cast of *The Iron Horse* was particularly interesting. For his star he selected George O'Brien, formerly an assistant cameraman with Tom

Cameras prepare to shoot the fording of the river sequence for The Covered Wagon.

Mix, a stunt man who was actually better known as the son of San Francisco's chief of police. He soon became one of the top Western stars in both the silent and sound eras, directing ten films, in addition, and starring in eight of them.

In one of his subsequent films Ford introduced the team of George O'Brien, Janet Gaynor, and Margaret Livingston, who were used immediately afterwards by Murnau in his non-Western poetic masterpiece, *Sunrise*. Fred Kohler, who had been used by Ford earlier in *North of Hudson Bay*, and who was really missing three fingers as called for in the script, was also cast, and subsequently became one of the best-known Western villains of all time. George O'Brien's brother Jack had a prominent part, and Madge Bellamy made a good heroine. Such Ford reliables as J. Farrell MacDonald and Chief Big Tree were also featured, and George Wagner, who later became a leading writer-director, played Buffalo Bill. Charles Bull, cast as Lincoln, was actually no actor at all, but a Reno judge discovered by Ford. Francis Powers, one of the comic leads, was a playwright rather than an actor. The film's subtitles were written by Charles Danton, then dramatic editor of the *New York World*.

Ford emulated Cruze by shooting his film almost entirely on location, in the Nevada desert. There was little or no studio work in the film; all of the cabin's interiors, for example, are authentic, with constant activity taking place outside the windows. Apart from an obviously painted backdrop of a canyon, there were no artificial sets at all. It was a monumental undertaking, since there were more than five thousand extras and it required almost one hundred cooks to feed them all.

The unit built two complete towns, used a train of fifty-six coaches for transportation, issued a daily newspaper, and in general lived under the same conditions as had the original workers on the railroad. The huge cast lists a complete regiment of U. S. Cavalry, three thousand railroad workers, one thousand Chinese laborers, eight hundred Pawnee, Sioux, and Cheyenne Indians, two thousand horses, thirteen hundred buffaloes, and ten thousand head of cattle, thus providing enough "accessories" for an authentic segment of life in the old West.

Apart from the extensive use of outdoor locations, Ford followed few of the precedents set by Cruze and Griffith in their earlier epics. Cruze, for example, played down action sequences unless they were an essential part of the plot. In *The Covered Wagon* he used that old Western stand-by, the heroine's runaway horse, only as a means to an end, in this case, to increase the hatred between the hero and the villain. The actual business of the runaway was handled in a single long shot, and was over in a matter of seconds. Ford, on the other hand, passionately played every action sequence for all it was worth.

The grandiose sequences of Indian fighting in both films illuminate the two directors' widely differing approaches to identical problems. Cruze's Indian battle was staged on a massive canvas, yet it was sharp, concise, and almost underplayed in a documentary manner. Once the camera shot a scene with a hundred charging Indians, Cruze was finished with them, and would move to something else. Ford, instead,

Tim McCoy, not yet a player, was employed by director James Cruze to handle the tribes of Indians used in The Covered Wagon. *Here McCoy looks on as Cruze presents a gift to one of the actors.*

deliberately constructed his action scenes so that they built steadily. His cameramen, George Schneidermann and Burnett Guffey, photographed the same charge from half-a-dozen different angles, with variety in the action. He intercut with other footage, and slipped away from the vast battle panorama on which hundreds of Indians were in the process of encircling the trapped locomotive (which is one of the finest and most exciting Indian fighting sequences ever filmed) to scenes of the rescue party in another locomotive, or to a detachment of Cavalry scouts galloping into the fray.

Another notable aspect of Ford's battle scenes was his dynamic use of the moving camera. During the early Twenties the camera for the most part remained largely stationary; a too mobile camera was regarded with suspicion as an "arty" European trick. Throughout most of *The Iron Horse*, too, the camera is stationary, but during the action sequences Ford loaded it on trucks, to the front of the locomotive, shooting from the top of the train. This technique permitted the groups of galloping riders to come into the camera's range simultaneously, effectively capturing in this way the rhythm of the action. The fluidity of this kind of camera work, plus the breathtaking effects of brilliant editing raised these great battle scenes to a pitch of magnificent excitement quite denied those in *The Covered Wagon*. These scenes in themselves fully justified the use of the term "epic" in connection with *The Iron Horse*, a memorable film indeed.

In other ways, however, it deviated rather surprisingly from epic tradition. The central theme of a man hunting his father's murderer was a common theme of the "B" Western (although it was also used in *The Big Trail*) and it frequently became more important than the construction of the railroad itself. In addition, despite the historical framework, Ford seemed to play down the factual aspects of the story. Abraham Lincoln was unnecessarily written into the narrative, primarily for the satisfaction of producer William Fox, who for years had been deeply interested in Lincoln and whose plan to present a biography of the sixteenth President on the screen had been shattered by a similar film from a competitor.

Unlike Griffith, who accompanied all his historical tableaux with subtitles giving exact dates, places, and other information, Ford paid scant attention to the few historical events that he did recreate accurately. The famous track-laying race, which culminated in ten miles being laid in a single day, is presented without any reference to the fact that in 1924 it *still* constituted a record, and that, in the 1860's, Vice President Durant of the Union Pacific Railroad had bet ten thousand dollars that it could

John Ford directs Indians, including Iron Eyes Cody, in The Iron Horse (*1924*).

not be done. Yet Ford went out of his way to obtain authentic props, or at least so Fox's publicity agents claimed. The original trains "Jupiter" and "116" are shown in the final sequence, for example; Wild Bill Hickok's vest pocket Derringer gun was used, and so was—although this sounds rather too much like a publicity story—the original stage-coach used by Horace Greeley. Even George O'Brien's horse, Bullet, was selected because, having won the annual St. Louis-to-San Francisco Race, it held the title of "Champion Pony Express Horse."

The Iron Horse still contains some of Ford's best and most typical work, despite the number and quality of some of his later works. Its weakest sections are its broad slapstick interludes, which represent the least successful ingredients in Ford's Westerns. There is little difference, for example, between the knockabout dentist sequence in *The Iron Horse* and the rough-house humor of *The Searchers* which he made in 1956. But photographically *The Iron Horse* is superb, with many shots now almost his trademark, the grouping of the Indians on the crest of a hill, for example, or the small band of riders fading into the dusty sunset.

Though *The Iron Horse* did not duplicate the critical acclaim of *The Covered Wagon*, it enjoyed huge popular success in the United States, and it did earn the praise of governmental and educational bodies. One critic termed it "An American Odyssey," a description that someone has applied to almost every Ford film since then, and in Ford's oeuvre, it certainly represents an extremely important film to which he gave both his enthusiasm and dedication.

The Iron Horse had run for a year at the Lyric in New York, Fox was still taking no chances, and it was sold using three different advertising campaigns. One followed the epic pattern, exploiting Erno Rapee's original music, "The March of the Iron Horse," then very popular. The second campaign—for the women presumably—spoke of a non-existent triangle and promised "Woman Against Woman In A Romance of East And West, Blazing The Trail Of Love And Civilization." The third approach was to concentrate on O'Brien, then being built into a top box-office name. "The George O'Brien Smile Is Spreading The Spirit Of Happiness Over The Seven Seas," claimed one advertisement, while another offered: "He's Not A Sheik Or A Caveman Or A Lounge Lizard—He Is A Man's Man And An Idol Of Women."

In any event, with O'Brien, the music, and the full-length novel based on the film (not vice versa) to exploit, the film went on to top business in the United States, but inexplicably failed in Great Britain. Paul Rotha, the British critic, once attempted to explain this by claiming that the British had no sympathy for railroads being con-

The track-laying race in The Iron Horse.

structed across trackless wastes. To generalize, then, while in many ways a more interesting and certainly a more exciting film, *The Iron Horse* was less objective than *The Covered Wagon* and initially was less influential.

Cruze's film was imitated over and over again until the silent era ended, particularly in Paramount's Zane Grey Westerns; even then its influence continued, right through such sound films as *The Big Trail, Kit Carson, California* (a particularly loose remake of *The Covered Wagon*), and John Ford's *The Wagonmaster*. There were, of course, inherent technical problems to duplicating *The Iron Horse*. And yet, odd scenes in Russia's documentary *Turksib* and Great Britain's *The Great Barrier* (dealing with the construction of the Canadian Pacific Railroad) suggested that many of Ford's ideas had been noticed and appreciated.

Turksib, written and directed by Victor Turin, often had a special similarity *visually,* in panoramic scenes stressing the immensity of the open wilderness, and comparing it with the seemingly small locomotive challenging its right to remain a wilderness. And, as in *The Iron Horse, Turksib's* climax was a race against time to finish the road. The cutting, however, was far more studied and complex than it had been in Ford's film. Ford's final race to complete the track in time was dramatic and convincing, but it was so much a foregone conclusion that the deadline would be met, that it did not generate the desired excitement. Victor Turin, in *Turksib,* made his climactic race the highlight of the film, a rapidly cut montage in which dramatically brief subtitles were as important as the images into which they were so skillfully cut.

This form of editing, often done to excess in Russian films merely because it was expected from a school that had been evolved by Eisenstein and Pudovkin, enabled the climax of *Turksib* to transcend completely the more immediate problem of the railroad's construction. The dramatic shots of the train almost jubilantly racing through the wilds towards its nearing destination, accompanied by such titles as "The line MUST be completed!" were stirring, and the audience must have felt itself called to serve the cause of national progress of every kind. So effective was this final sequence from several viewpoints that the film's final title, "And in 1930 the line *was* completed" (actually added after the completion of the railroad) seemed weak and anti-climatic.

American epics, and particularly those built around railroads such as *The Iron Horse* and *Union Pacific,* have come to far less dramatically satisfying conclusions because they failed—even in the war years—to recognize a certain inherent dramatic potential; they did not draw on the nation's pride—and epics are peculiarly able to do this. Both *The Iron Horse* and *Union Pacific* made the same mistake of treating the material purely historically, as a *fait accompli*. They approached the theme of national development as though the ultimate in progress had already been achieved. They looked back, respectfully, at the pioneers who had helped to bring that "ultimate" into being, but they did not see the continuing need for the pioneering spirit. There *were* traces of such a recognition—that this spirit could still usefully exist in contemporary America—in an occasional film like King Vidor's *Our Daily Bread,* but unfortunately never in the Western, the genre most suited for an exposition along these lines.

Strangely, as the influence of *The Covered Wagon* began to wane in the late Thirties, that of *The Iron Horse* grew. De Mille's *Union Pacific* (1939), dealing with the construction of the same railroad, not only used a vaguely similar plot, but repeated many sequences intact. One episode, an Indian attack on a supply train, even duplicated the composition and camera work of Ford's film.

In more recent times, the wagon train theme has not proven popular, while that of the railroad has gained in importance. *Kansas Pacific, Santa Fe, Canadian Pacific, The Denver and Rio Grande* are among the films which utilized scenes or sequences originating in *The Iron Horse.* There have been many better Westerns than *The Covered Wagon* and *The Iron Horse,* but none that were more influential on the whole structure of thought concerning the creative cinematic presentation of these and related aspects of the saga of the West.

The Twenties

Despite the tremendous success and influence of *The Covered Wagon* and *The Iron Horse*, the immediate result was not a cycle of epics. Ford waited two years before he made his next large-scale Western, *Three Bad Men*. Based on Herman Whittaker's novel *Over the Border* (it is often erroneously confused with Peter B. Kyne's *Three Godfathers*, a story that has been filmed several times), it was a sentimental Western distinguished by a magnificently staged land rush sequence.

Harrison's Reports, a trade publication, noted at the time ". . . from a production point of view, 'Three Bad Men' comes up to the standard of 'The Covered Wagon'; in some respects it even surpasses it. In the history of the picture business, in fact, there has never been a picture in which such an array of prairie schooners has been used." *Harrison's Reports* was a publication for exhibitors with only two functions: it editorialized against unfair producer-distributor tactics, and it provided the exhibitor with detailed descriptions of film plots and, to a lesser degree, merits. It is invaluable as a reference in terms of *plot* material; less reliable for its critical opinions, since, in order to be impartial, it had several reviewers turn in opinions which were then welded into one review by a writer who had not seen the film.

However, *Three Bad Men* had many of the flaws of dramatic construction that marred *The Iron Horse*, and it did not repeat its success. Apart from *The Pony Express*, James Cruze made no further Western epics. The

9

other prestige directors of the time—D. W. Griffith, King Vidor, Cecil B. De Mille—showed no apparent interest in tackling Western themes. As we shall see, the newly popularized epic Western made little headway in terms of quantity production, but did serve to stimulate a tremendous upsurge in both the quality and quantity of "B" Westerns.

The assembly line begins

Prior to *The Covered Wagon,* the average "B" Western had been influenced more by W. S. Hart than by Tom Mix. This was partially due to the fact that it was easier to copy a *style,* such as Hart's austerity, than a man of the personality and prowess of Mix. Thus, even little Westerns like Aywon's *Another Man's Boots* (1922) were patent copies of Hart; *Another Man's Boots,* in particular, seemed a blatant plagiarism of Hart's *Square Deal Sanderson* of a year or two earlier. The plot was lifted intact from the Hart film, and star Francis Ford closely followed Hart's acting style, with its reliance on facial close-ups in scenes involving the hero's romantic suffering at the hands of the heroine. A minor comic vein, pitched to reflect contemporary American viewpoints (there was a barroom gag kidding prohibition; another on the trend of thought that a man's wearing of a wristwatch was a sign of effeminacy) alleviated the austerity of *Another Man's Boots,* and differentiated it from Hart's film. *Another Man's Boots* was a well-made little Western, but typical of so many "B" Westerns prior to *The Covered Wagon*—cheaply made, and resigned to the proposition that the "B" Western was and always would be mired in a fairly unimportant rut.

With the Western so much back in favor after the success of *The Covered Wagon,* and apart from the general "streamlining" of smaller Westerns and the granting of slightly higher budgets to them, the next event in the history of Western movies was the development of a whole new crop of Western stars, some of whom, like Hoot Gibson, were promoted from two-reelers. Gibson's short Westerns for Universal had

Ken Maynard menaced by that familiar heavy, Charles King, in Between Fighting Men.

been of a "folksy" variety not unlike the old Mix shorts for Selig. However, they were much more carefully made and, though limited in action, were lightheartedly humorous. Gibson was quite able to take care of any action that came his way, and the format he created in his shorts was so successful that, for the most part, he retained it in his features. Other stars, like Ken Maynard and Bob Steele, were launched with less background training into starring vehicles. Maynard had made an impression as Paul Revere in the Marion Davies production *Janice Meredith,* and he was immediately thereafter signed for a series of independent Westerns. Steele, the son of director Robert N. Bradbury, appeared in his father's picture, *With Sitting Bull at the Spirit Lake Massacre,* under the name of Bob Bradbury, Jr., and soon thereafter was given his own series at FBO. A dozen other Western stars emerged in this period, from Tom Tyler to Jack Perrin; the latter, a former Triangle and Sennett extra, had appeared in straight dramatic roles in Erich von Stroheim's *Blind Husbands* and other pictures, making little impression until he began making Westerns. He and other stars of the period will be considered later in the chapter at greater length.

It should be remembered that in the Twenties the double-bill was virtually unknown, and therefore even the "B" Western, supported only by a comedy short and the newsreel, had to draw an audience. Initially, at least, this sudden increase in the production of small Westerns established and maintained a surprisingly high standard, but as their mass production continued, and increased, the inevitable decline set in. This decline was brought about not by a decline in the quality of films made by the major companies—for MGM and First National in particular brought real production value and creativity to their Westerns—but by the entry into the field of hordes of opportunistic independent producers working with meager budgets and generally second-rate talent.

The Weiss Brothers fell into this category. Through their Artclass productions, they offered Buddy Roosevelt, Wally Wales, and Buffalo Bill, Jr., in eight Westerns apiece. The Weiss Brothers had already then developed to a fine art the business of making films with the least possible outlay; as recently as 1945 they issued a "new" film called *The White Gorilla,* which was literally eighty percent stock shots from a *silent* serial, *Perils of the Jungle.*

Another independent, Anchor Distributors, offered Al Hoxie in eight of the cheapest and worst Westerns ever made, *The Ace of Clubs* setting some kind of record for pointless boredom, and eight more with Bob Reeves. Hoxie and Reeves achieved little stature even in this short period, and were quickly forgotten.

Supplementing their eight Ken Maynard films, the Davis Corporation made eight with Ben Wilson and Neva Gerber, a once-popular serial team that had fallen from favor, and no less than fifteen Westerns per year with Al Ferguson, an unattractive-looking fellow who normally specialized in villains' roles. Sierra Pictures presented a series of six Westerns with Al Richmond, six with Bob Burns, and six two-reelers with Fred Hawk, while a group of two-reel Westerns—these with a comic edge —starred Bill Patton and were directed by Al Herman for the Tennek Film Corporation. But that was not all: Ruth Mix, Tom's daughter, billed as "A Chip Off The Old Block," much to Tom's annoyance, made a group of cowgirl Westerns that tried to recapture atmosphere of the early Mix films by stressing elaborate stunt work and trick riding. From her first film, *That Girl Oklahoma*, Ruth Mix went on to a lively, if not spectacular career that lasted some ten years. Two lesser figures, Art Mix (a very distant relation of Tom's) and Bill Mix (no relation at all), dressed like the original and were billed as his brothers until the courts forced them to desist; neither of them made much of an impression on Western audiences, and Art Mix, a very short man, with a most un-heroic appearance, soon drifted into villains' roles. Bill Cody Westerns were released through Pathé; FBO launched Buzz Barton, a child star, as a novelty Western star along with their other featured players who, at one time or another in the Twenties, included Bob Steele, Tom Tyler (teamed with Frankie Darro), Tom Mix, Fred Thomson, and Bob Custer. Rayart, forerunner of Monogram, had producer Harry Webb turning out Jack Perrin Westerns like clockwork, and supplemented these by a lesser series starring Pawnee Bill, Jr., and the Rayart Rough Riders.

Slightly better were a group of allegedly historical Westerns produced by Anthony J. Xydias for Sunset Productions: *With Buffalo Bill on the U. P. Trail, With Custer at the Little Big Horn, With Sitting Bull at the Spirit Lake Massacre.* They were competent in their way, but fell far short of their potential. Strong casts (Roy Stewart, Edmund Cobb, Bryant Washburn, William Desmond), good camera work, and interesting plots had the audience anxiously awaiting large-scale climaxes, the kind not available in a stock-shot library, but small budgets ruled out any effective alterna-tive, and so the grand climaxes never materialized. The long-awaited massacre in *With Sitting Bull at the Spirit Lake Massacre* consists of a handful of Indians *running* into the attack; Bob Steele rides to a cavalry outpost to bring back the troops for a pitched battle only to be told by a lone sentry that *all* the troops left that morning! The film grinds to a frustrating close, with the hero realizing that nothing can be done to prevent the

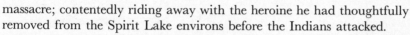

Harry Carey, who starred in Westerns from 1910 to the late Thirties and then switched to character roles.

massacre; contentedly riding away with the heroine he had thoughtfully removed from the Spirit Lake environs before the Indians attacked.

Pete Morrison, William Fairbanks, Neal Hart, Guinn "Big Boy" Williams, Yakima Canutt, and Earle Douglas were others who appeared in these cheaply made Westerns for Sunset, Anchor, and similar companies. Few of these small outfits had sufficient means to own their own branch offices, or exchanges, and there were no *national* distribution outlets for the bulk of these products made on the assembly line.

In the midst of such frenetic activity, with Hollywood firmly established as a production center and with the advent of the star system, some of the old "heroes" of the West remained in their saddles, but many new ones had already arrived and more were to come.

Harry Carey and Buck Jones

With the failure of Hart's *Singer Jim McKee,* upcoming Western stars were naturally no longer anxious to imitate either Hart's style or the content of his stories. Breezy, energetic Tom Mix, the very antithesis of Hart, exerted the greatest influence, but by now even he was a veteran; rather than go in for outright imitation, most stars tended therefore to *elaborate* on the Mix concept of the Western hero.

Thus, the slick, "streamlined" Westerner, immaculately groomed and flashily dressed, began to take over, and the "new look" was best represented by Hoot Gibson and Ken Maynard, both first-rate "performers" (although Maynard was an indifferent *actor*). Both could fight and ride which was essential in their roles, but they were predominantly showmen. Neither had any great love for the Western as such, nor any desire to be particularly creative. The breathtaking but flamboyant and often unnecessary trick riding stunts in Maynard's films, and the prominent comedy content of Gibson's, were two steps which advanced the divorce of the Western from actuality. Only two Western stars remained in any way in the Hart tradition: Harry Carey and Buck Jones. In actual fact, Carey's taciturn characterization predates Hart's in that he was active in early Biograph Westerns for Griffith. Perhaps partly because his leathery and non-youthful appearance so dictated, Carey avoided the "streamlined" Westerns that Maynard, Gibson, and Fred Thomson made so popular. His were always Westerns of the old school, sometimes a little slow on action, but always strong on plot, with a definite sign of Hart's influence. Carey's *Satan Town,* for example, was a very creditable lesser *Hell's Hinges.* Respect for womanhood was a staple ingredient with Carey, and in *The Prairie Pirate,* a good Carey film for Hunt Stromberg in 1925, this extended to another typical Hart plot motivation—the death of the hero's sister (she commits suicide when threatened with rape by the villain) and the tracking down of the man responsible. Both Hart and Carey had almost Victorian streaks concerning their heroines, who were always shown as symbols of helplessness and purity, to be protected and loved only remotely, until events had proven the heroes thoroughly worthy of them. Carey's pictures were certainly stronger in story content than those of his contemporaries, but significantly he was never as popular as either Ken Maynard or Hoot Gibson.

Buck Jones somewhat resembled Hart in both facial characteristics and in his realistic dress, but there the similarity ended. Fox used him in a series designed as a second-string group to reflect the formats laid down by the fabulously successful Mix Westerns. "Second-string" in this instance does not mean second-rate, for the Jones Westerns were good ones, backed by solid production values, although more concerned with showmanship and lively action than with creating a realistic picture of the West. Only in his personal performance, underplayed and rugged, and in his clothing, far less gaudy and flamboyant than the outfits worn by Mix, did Jones follow the Hart line. As in the Mix films, the Jones Westerns were split evenly between straightforward action pictures and light Westerns with a marked comic content. He seems to have been impressed with comedy's value, for, Hoot Gibson apart, he was the only Western star to really stress comedy featuring *himself* rather than the "official" comedian who afflicted so many "B" Westerns. The comic content in Jones' Fox Westerns of the Twenties was generally on a fairly high level, but in the Thirties Jones injected a surprising amount of "hick" comedy into his pictures. However, even this was used with some discretion, and it never interfered with plot or action.

Typical of the Jones films with a pronounced comic content were *The Gentle Cyclone,* directed in 1926 by W. S. Van Dyke, with Buck acting as mediator between the heroine's two perennially scrapping uncles, and *The Cowboy and the Countess,* made in the same year. This last film opened on a luxury liner with Jones and his Western cohorts en route to Europe. Of course, there was a good deal of comedy built around the situation of the Western cowboy in high society; one of the best gags had the Westerners puzzled by the liner's menu. Unable to understand the foreign language, they were forced to draw pictures to describe what they wanted to eat. Much of the action took place in Europe, with the heroine's father attempting to marry her off to a rascally nobleman to whom he has financial obligations.

Along far more traditional lines and full of first-rate riding and other stunts by Jones were *Good as Gold,* directed in 1925 by Scott R. Dunlap, and *Timber Wolf,* set in a lumber camp. Jones is a fighting lumber boss who forcibly abducts the heroine to prevent her from marrying the villain, who is both the proprietor of the local dance hall and a bootlegger. His intention, of course, is first to "tame" her and then to marry her.

Despite the tradition of the Western hero as a man who naturally respects womanhood, the theme of the heroine's forcible abduction by the hero, and his "taming" of her, was quite popular in the Twenties. Its watered-down remnants persisted until the Thirties, but its implications varied. The moral difficulties were overcome by having the hero appointed either the heroine's guardian or the custodian of her estate. Conflict then had a legal basis, as he sought to prevent her from selling the ranch, or refused her permission to marry the villain. In these cases, sympathy was very much on the side of the hero, since the heroine was invariably presented as a headstrong heiress who very much needed taming.

Fred Thomson

After Mix, Fred Thomson was possibly the most popular Western star of the Twenties. He was well liked not only because his films maintained high standards, but also because his blameless off-screen life and his reputation as a former minister earned him the respect and support of even those moviegoers apathetic to Westerns at a time when Hollywood's morals were constantly under fire. He was a first-rate acrobat, and his slick films for FBO were little more than Western equivalents of the stunting adventures made by Richard Talmadge for the same company. These Westerns were lively, full of fun and action quite obviously designed to please the youngsters; many, such as *A Regular Scout* in which Thomson boosted the cause of the Boy Scouts, had a definitely salutary effect on American youth. *The Tough Guy*, in addition to its strong action, contained some good comedy in a children's orphanage. *The Bandit's Baby*, made in 1925, again had some unusual comic elements, including a proposal scene quite distinct from the usual shamefaced marriage proposals made by most Western heroes. Referring to the heroine's infant brother, Thomson remarks: "Gosh, Esther, I don't want to get hitched up, but I'll do anything to get that baby"; to which the heroine replies, "All right, Tom, I'll do anything to get that horse."

In another Thomson Western of the same period, *Silver Comes Through*,

Buck Jones and Silver.

Fred Thomson, Helen Foster, and baby Mary Louise Miller in The Bandit's Baby (*1925*).

there is another effective blending of sentiment, comedy, and thrills. The opening reel finds Thomson fighting and subduing a mountain lion to rescue a little white foal which, of course, grows up to be Silver King, Thomson's white horse. The climactic thrill is provided by a cross-country race; the villains kidnap Thomson and his horse, but they both escape by making a spectacular leap from a moving freight train, and return to win the race on schedule. Tremendously exciting and well made though they were, logic and conviction were frequently abandoned in these films. *Thundering Hoofs,* for instance, contained one of the most "epochal" moments in any Western. The sagacious Silver King has just found the body of the hero's father; a title informs us that "Silver King had one last duty to perform," and then fades into a beautifully back-lit scene of the stallion reverently tapping the top of an immaculately constructed grave. Not only does it have a neat cross at its head, but a jar of flowers as well . . . and the implication certainly is that Silver King did it all himself! *Thundering Hoofs* also had a humorous sequence in the style of Douglas Fairbanks: Thomson, calling on the heroine, is pursued over the hacienda by an irate father and jealous suitor, and escapes by swinging from chandeliers, hanging on vines, climbing up walls, and the

Fred Thomson and Ann May in Thundering Hoofs (*1924*).

A chase across rooftops was a Ken Maynard film specialty. From The Wagon Show (*1928*).

like. The rest of the film was up to the high standards of action in Thomson's Westerns, with a beautifully cut and photographed runaway stagecoach episode, and a fine climax in which Fred, jailed by the villain, makes a spectacular escape, finds his way to the bullring, and arrives just in time to battle a bull with his bare hands to save Silver King from being gored to death.

Thomson's FBO Westerns were all beautifully mounted films, expertly staged, and excellently photographed. Many of the scripts were by Marion Jackson, often confused with another writer, Frances Marion who was married to Thomson. Following his FBO period, Thomson moved to Paramount to make some large Westerns presumably intended to replace those of Bill Hart. *Jesse James*, directed by Lloyd Ingraham, whitewashed the old outlaw even more than did the Tyrone Power version of 1939; no bank robberies of any kind are shown, and in fact the only crime that Jesse commits in the entire film is a mild stagecoach holdup! Undoubtedly, the film was intended more as a Thomson vehicle than as an authentic historical Western, and yet, it had its fine moments, particularly several spectacular Civil War battle scenes early on in the film. It was the first Thomson Western in which he died at the end, and ironically, it was to be his last film. He died shortly afterwards, at the end of the silent era.

Ken Maynard

Ken Maynard's rise to popularity roughly paralleled Thomson's. After his debut in *Janice Meredith,* Maynard made a series of cheap Westerns for the Davis Corporation, films like *The Grey Vulture*. These were inexpensive but entertaining, with plenty of stunting action for Maynard, and a tendency to rather bizarre comedy. One film opened with a long sequence in which Maynard dreamed that he was one of King Arthur's knights; another had a long "bathing beauty" interlude. These films were later reassembled into a none-too-cohesive serial entitled *The Range Fighter*. Maynard really came into his own, however, upon joining First National in 1926. He was put into a quality series beginning with *Senor Daredevil*. By no means "B" pictures, these were seven-reelers, and often spectacular in their action content. As *Harrison's Reports* commented, in reviewing *Senor Daredevil:* "If the subsequent Westerns which First National has announced with this star will contain only one-half the entertainment that 'Senor Daredevil' possesses, those who buy them will have nothing to worry about . . . it is an exceptionally good Western . . . has a story that is entirely different from those seen in the past . . . thrills aplenty . . . Mr. Maynard is a wonderful rider who displays his horsemanship frequently."

Senor Daredevil had for its climax a spectacular sequence of Maynard racing a food convoy of wagons to a town starved and besieged by villains. One or two critics compared this sequence with the chariot race in *Ben Hur* for the excitement it generated, and this is not hard to believe; although this particular Western is not now available for reappraisal, other First National Maynard films are, and *Red Raiders,* in particular, confirms that the praise for *Senor Daredevil* was probably more than justified.

Directed by Al Rogell and produced under the supervision of Harry Joe Brown (who later teamed with Randolph Scott on a number of Westerns in the Forties and Fifties), *Red Raiders* is a particularly illuminating example of the really slick and well-made Westerns of the Twenties. Aside from consideration of the stars involved, *Red Raiders* is quite as *big* a picture as *Stagecoach* and other epics. The action is staged on a massive scale, and the entire picture seems dedicated to the proposition that action matters far more than plot. (This was not typical of Maynard's First National group, which was usually strong in the scenario department, too.) Indeed, there really is no plot to *Red Raiders,* merely a situation (Indians being led on the warpath by a hotheaded chief dedicated to wiping out the cavalry), and no real villainy. The film has no white "heavies" and the Indians are presented merely collectively as the motivated villains of the piece, although they *are* presented sympathetically and as human beings, a comparatively rare note in the Twenties, midway between Ince's *The Heart of an Indian* and Daves' *Broken Arrow.* The subtitles, incidentally, present several little footnotes to Indian lore, and introduce one of the Indian players as White Man Runs Him, last surviving participant in the Little Big Horn battle.

Red Raiders is both a showcase for Ken Maynard's amazing riding skill, and for the use of the running insert. Few Westerns have used the riding close-up as consistently—and as dramatically—as did this picture, and its effectiveness is doubly apparent when *Red Raiders* is contrasted with such other silent Westerns as *Another Man's Boots,* or such "talkies" as *Man from the Black Hills,* in which not a single running insert is used. The camera work on *Red Raiders* was that of Sol Polito (later one of Warners' top cameramen on Errol Flynn and Bette Davis sound films); the running inserts were shot from a camera car sometimes carrying as many as four Bell and Howell or Mitchell cameras. As well as being used for *really* close work (Maynard's riding, and one tricky stunt in particular where a wounded man is being dragged in the dust by his galloping horse, and Maynard, hanging precariously backwards out of his own saddle, swooping the man up—this being shot in such extreme close-up that the shadow of the cameraman was visible briefly) the running inserts were used to tremendously dramatic and spectacular effect in long, panoramic shots of the large-scaled action. The Indians charging, and a mad stampede of covered wagons, were rendered all the more exciting by the camera's extreme mobility. One of the most effective shots was an extreme long shot of the troop of cavalry appearing on the crest of a hill; the men and horses race down the slope onto a flat plain, and string themselves out into a long line for the charge. As this gets under way, and the riders near the camera, the camera itself begins to move, tracking rapidly backwards, but moving slightly slower than the cavalry troop, which eventually thunders right "into" the camera. Creative photography of this type was at its peak in the Westerns of the Twenties, and never more so than in the Ken Maynard series for First National.

Other new stars

Hoot Gibson, who combined comedy and modern story lines in his very popular Universal Westerns of the Twenties.

The Hoot Gibson features for Universal were quite different, but they were also "streamlined." They were light on action and heavy on bantering comedy, and yet fairly realistic in style. *The Texas Streak,* written and directed by Lynn Reynolds, was an enjoyable comedy-action Western with Gibson playing a Hollywood extra stranded in the West. He overcomes some rather mild villainy, and is rewarded with a real Hollywood contract. *Painted Ponies* had rather more action and stunts than was usual in Gibson films, which was due in all likelihood to the direction of Reeves Eason. Others, *The Man in the Saddle,* for example, went sadly overboard on comic content. Occasionally Universal put Gibson into a "special" and afforded him much better material. One such film was *The Flaming Frontier,* a spectacular account of Custer's "Last Stand" at Little Big Horn. The political and historical backgrounds were sketched in with general accuracy, and the battle scenes staged on a lavish scale. Dustin Farnum, as Custer, appeared in support of Gibson, and Edward Sedgwick directed.

Another Universal Western star was Jack Hoxie, who had started out in straight roles under the name of Hartford Hoxie in such films as *The Dumb Girl of Portici.* However, he remained in vogue only briefly. He was a beefy, amiable cowboy, athletic enough, but rather a poor actor. His films made a point of stressing the collaboration he got from two four-footed associates: his horse and his dog. This element, no doubt, contributed to his popularity among youngsters. Before his Universal Westerns, Hoxie made a cheap but interesting series of pictures for independent producer Anthony J. Xydias. Rather light in action, they were enjoyable little films. *Galloping Thru,* based on a story, *The Fog Man,* concerned a fairy tale the heroine tells her young brother. A mysterious rider on a white horse appears out of the fog at night to defeat goblins, and this fantasy was interestingly presented in the early portion of the film. When Hoxie appears on the scene, the youngster naturally identifies him with the hero of the fairy tale, and good camera work of Hoxie riding out of the mountain mists substantiates his belief. The rest of the film had Hoxie assuming the role of the family's protector when a thief frames the boy's father on a robbery charge. Hoxie's later Westerns were all fairly routine in conception, never more than five reels in length. *The White Outlaw, Red Hot Leather,* and *The Wild Horse Stampede* were among the better ones. *Harrison's Reports* summed up the Hoxie series fairly accurately in its review of *A Six-Shootin' Romance* (1926): "A fair Western. There isn't much new in it, everything being stereotype. There is some action, a little human interest and a little suspense, but not enough of any one of these elements to give one heart failure. The direction is not bad."

Leo Maloney was another star in the rather plump Hoxie tradition and made his Westerns for Pathe. On the whole, his was a good series, with generally well-constructed scripts. Maloney frequently directed his own Westerns, and occasionally wrote them, too. *The High Hand, The Outlaw Express,* and *Two-Gun of the Tumbleweed* were among those in which he both starred and directed.

FBO, as we noted earlier, had a most impressive stable of Western stars. A series with Tom Tyler was novel in that Frankie Darro, then a very minute youngster, teamed up with Tyler in many of the adventures; Darro had some good comic material in these pictures. In *The Cowboy Cop,* for instance, he was amusing dressed in top hat and tails and dancing the Charleston. Lesser series with Bob Custer and Yakima Canutt were much better than average, and among the most exciting of all the FBO Westerns were those with Bob Steele. Although they were overly melodramatic and almost serial-like in their plot structure, the action was continuously hair-raising. Steele was not a big man, but he had a cheerful boyish expression, he was a good rider and an even better fighter. *The Mojave Kid* was one of his best for FBO, and its plot is typical of the much larger-than-life but really rugged material that distinguished his Westerns at that time. He played the son of a man who had mysteriously disappeared in the desert; a man himself now, he overhears outlaws discussing his father in connection with treasure hidden in an old Aztec ruin. He trails them to their hideout, to discover that the outlaw leader has a granddaughter (Lillian Gilmore), with whom he falls in love. He discovers that his father has been held prisoner for twelve years by the outlaw for having refused to reveal the hiding place of the treasure. Thinking that this time he will talk, the villains flog his son before him. But Steele breaks loose and holds the outlaws at bay. The outlaw leader agrees to free Steele and allow his father and the girl to go with him if Steele can beat one of the bandits in a fist fight. Steele agrees to fight, wins, and leaves. But the outlaws renege and go in pursuit. In order to keep *his* word, their leader explodes a dynamite charge on the trail, killing himself and all but three of the gang. These keep up the pursuit of our hero, but are ultimately killed. Finally, hero marries heroine, and the long-lost father and his wife are reunited. Robert N. Bradbury was responsible for the excellent direction; based on a story by Oliver Drake, *The Mojave Kid* was excellent material of its type.

FBO had one other highly popular series, starring Buzz Barton. In reviewing the first of the group, *The Boy Rider* directed by Louis King, *Harrison's Reports* had this to say: "Thirteen year old wizard Buzz Barton . . . is a miniature Tom Mix, Ken Maynard and Fred Thomson all in one. He can ride almost as well as any of these players, can throw a lariat as well, and has a winning smile . . . And he can act. He will capture the child custom first, and the child custom will attract the adult afterwards."

Barton's series started late in 1927, just before "B" Westerns went into a temporary eclipse due to the coming of sound movies. His second Western, *The Singleshot Kid* (like the first, directed by Louis King and written by Oliver Drake), was as good as the first; the third, *Wizard of the Saddle,* only slightly inferior. Barton arrived on the scene a little too late to make a really big impression, but he remained active in Westerns through the Thirties, principally playing in support of Rex Bell and Francis X. Bushman, Jr.

The fine Tim McCoy Westerns for MGM were not the star vehicles other cowboy players made in this period. For the most part they were fictionalized re-creations of various phases of American frontier history; lavishly produced, they were almost all directed by either W. S. Van Dyke or Reginald Barker. But surprisingly, the Russian director Tourjansky made one of them. *Winners of the Wilderness* was perhaps the most elaborate of the group. It dealt with pre-Revolutionary days when the Canadian French plotted to conquer the Ohio; McCoy was cast as an Irish officer in the British army. One of the highlights of the film was a spectacular attack on a French fort by British troops headed by General Braddock, and their defeat at the hands of the French and their Indian allies. In *California,* the conflict between the United States and Mexico in 1845 was taken up, after which California was added to the Union. Again, there were some truly spectacular battle scenes, most notably in the ambush of General Kearney's command by the Mexican army. *War Paint* and *The Law of the Range* (with Joan Crawford) had more conventional plot-lines, but *The Frontiersman* reverted to the historical format in a story dealing with Andrew Jackson's attempt to suppress the Creek Indian uprisings. These MGM Westerns with McCoy were on an even larger scale than were the Maynard films for First National, although they were more pretentious and generally slower paced, with occasional long stretches between their action highlights.

Universal's Pete Morrison Westerns of the Twenties have been strangely forgotten, and yet, although short (usually under five thousand feet) and made cheaply, they were often quite fresh and unusual, particularly in the plots. *Blue Blazes,* for example, had a typical "city mystery" plot: an Eastern financier is murdered, and his money disappears. Twenty years later his granddaughter goes West on a slender clue, hoping to avenge the murder and recover the money. The mystery comes to a thrilling climax with a cloudburst swelling the river and deluging a mountain cabin. Another first-class Pete Morrison Western, *Triple Action,* featured some good stunting acrobatics.

Among the most enjoyable Westerns of the Twenties were those with canine stars. Rin Tin Tin was the undisputed monarch of this realm, of course, but most studios had their own dog stars, ranging from Peter the Great, Napoleon Bonaparte, and Strongheart, down to Universal's rather moth-eaten imitation of Rinty, Dynamite. (Dynamite appeared with Edmund Cobb in some uneven Universal Westerns, of which *Wolf's Trail* was probably the best, and *Fangs of Destiny* the weakest.) Rinty was more than just a well-trained dog and a beautiful animal; he was an actor. Overblown as that statement may seem, it is nevertheless true, as almost any scene in *The Night Cry* will prove. Rinty's acting ability grew with each picture, many of which were Westerns. In his early films (*Where the North Begins,* for example) there were several scenes in which he stared at the camera, waited for his instructions, and *then* went through his paces. Not so in his later pictures; Rinty now knew exactly what to do, and did it faultlessly. He had a way of running into a situation, "sizing it up," and then, having decided on the wisest course of action, following it. All of the later Rin Tin Tin films had at least one situation in which he had to *emote,* to rely *entirely* on facial expressions, rather than on cute action. In *The Night Cry* there was a sequence in which Rinty, suspected of killing sheep, returns forlornly to his master's cabin. He puts his head on the table between his master (John Harron) and mistress (June Marlowe), and in a single take, expresses hope, grief, tolerance, and finally joy, when at least one friend is found in the person of the couple's baby. Rin Tin Tin's writers were forever dreaming up dramatic dilemmas such as this one for the canine star—and he always played them to the hilt.

His films represented great income for Warners, helping more than once to pay off the losses on the costly prestige films with John Barrymore, much as Tom Mix helped pay off the mortgage at Fox. They were also something of a phenomenon: they were cheaply made, and often so naïve that they seemed at least twenty years behind the times, and yet so well directed (by Chester Franklin, Howard Bretherton, Mal St. Clair, Herman Raymaker, and others) and so well photographed (Edwin Du Par did some fine work in *The Night Cry*) that their primitive plots were accepted almost casually. Delightful in the Rin Tin Tin films were the very human problems requiring instantaneous decisions facing the dog. In *Tracked by the Police* he has to choose between saving his canine friend Nanette (trussed up in chains and tossed into the torrent by the villains) or rescuing the heroine, who, temporarily blinded, is hanging precariously from a crane that dangles over a sabotaged dam. He decides in favor of his human friend, but by sagaciously working complicated levers and mechanisms, he brings the flood waters under control and *both* females are saved!

Rinty always played his big dramatic scenes as if his life depended on it. In *Where the North Begins,* a particularly successful film from every standpoint, he fights off the villain while a baby is taken to safety by her nurse. When the baby's mother returns, she finds only Rinty, and a part of the baby's clothing that has somehow become soaked with the villain's blood. Naturally Rinty is suspected of the worst, and clears himself only after several reels of self-torment and sagacious detective work. Another good one, *A Hero of the Big Snows* (like *The Night Cry,* directed by Herman Raymaker), presented Rinty with an almost identical situation, and in addition had him rehabilitate the disillusioned hero who, as a reviewer of 1926 put it, ". . . neglected not only his appearance but also his home, until Rin Tin Tin, who was unwilling to live in a dirty hole, made him feel ashamed of himself, forcing him to give the house a thorough cleaning and make himself look presentable." Rin Tin Tin's importance should not be underestimated. Many film historians never even mention Rinty, only because they have never seen him, and consider his films outside the scope of film history. Nothing could be further from the truth. Rin Tin Tin was as good a Western star, in his own way, as any of them, and a good deal more intelligent than some.

Rin Tin Tin, having disposed of the badmen, turns the switch that will stop the sabotage they have wrought on a massive dam project. From Tracked by the Police *(1927).*

Directors William Wyler and William K. Howard

The early Twenties, more notable for their creation of Western stars than directors, did witness, however, some very notable directors emerging from the ranks of the horse operas. William Wyler served his apprenticeship with Universal's Westerns, starting in 1925. He had come to America in 1921, joined Universal's New York office, and shortly thereafter moved to the coast to specialize in foreign publicity work. In 1923 he had been one of several assistant directors on *The Hunchback of Notre Dame.* Although by 1925, Universal had a regular schedule of Western *features,* starring Harry Carey, Hoot Gibson, Art Acord, and others, they still maintained their output of two-reel Westerns, not least as a training ground for stars and directors who seemed possibilities for upgrading to feature work. Wyler's first was *Crook Buster,* released late in 1925. From that year on, Universal's Western shorts were known as Mustangs, and between 1925 and 1927, when they finished, some 135 of them were made. Fast-paced and well mounted, they were made in three days, and cost only a little over two thousand dollars each. Wyler directed twenty of this series, others being handled by Ray Taylor and Vin Moore, among others. One of them, *Ridin' for Love,* was also written by Wyler, the only time he has ever taken a script

The Bank Hold-up.

credit. Among Wyler's interesting two-reel films were *The Fire Barrier,* marked by a spectacular forest fire climax which was, in all probability, stock footage from some more ambitious film; *The Ore Raiders,* rated by reviewers as one of Wyler's best and most action-packed films; and *Daze of the West,* Wyler's last Mustang short. Written by Billy Engle, it was a satirical Western, and presumably Wyler's first encounter with comedy.

Paralleling the Mustangs, were the Blue Streak Westerns. Wyler directed five of fifty-three, the others being handled by Cliff Smith, Albert Rogell, and Dell Henderson. These were generally short and snappy, five reels being their official length, usually something less than five thousand feet. *Lazy Lightning,* starring Art Acord, and released in December, 1926, was Wyler's first feature. *The Border Cavalier* starred Fred Humes, and was Wyler's last Blue Streak Western, but by no means his last Western for Universal. Thereafter they referred to their Westerns as an "Adventure Series," heralded by the symbol of a stampeding elephant. Wyler's work in this new group included Ted Wells' first picture, *Straight Shootin',* a film with some effective comic moments, and *Desert Dust,* another Wells vehicle which placed more emphasis than usual on the romantic element. Reviewers generally agreed that *Thunder Riders,* Wyler's last "B" Western, was rather inferior, but none of the Universal Westerns (apart from the specials with Hoot Gibson and occasionally Jack Hoxie) drew especially enthusiastic comment, for, in comparison with the slicker Mix pictures and the fine FBO releases, they seemed rather too standardized.

Wyler was to make only three more Westerns in his career (up to 1961): *Hell's Heroes* (1929), *The Westerner* (1940), and *The Big Country* (1958). Next to Wyler and Ford the most interesting directorial talent to emerge from Westerns in the period was that of William K. Howard, who did not specialize exclusively in Westerns in his early years.

For some reason, all trade biographies give Howard's first film as *East of Broadway* (1924). Actually, by then he had already made nine pictures, with a marked stress on action and melodrama. Some lively Richard Talmadge stunt thrillers were among them. Of these nine pictures, one was a particularly pleasing Western: *Captain Fly by Night* (1922). Based on a story by Johnston McCulley, it was a rather obvious attempt to cash in on the success of Fairbanks' *The Mark of Zorro* (also, of course, written by McCulley) and quite imitative in places. The picture moved fast, and was extremely well photographed and edited; Howard was a dynamic visual director and even when his plot material was negligible, he held interest with the excellence of his camera work: shots were well composed, the angles were well conceived, and intelligent use was made of the moving camera. Famous Players-Lasky signed Howard late in 1924 for a number of pictures, the most ambitious of which was *Volcano*. Too lurid to be suited to Howard's taut, realistic style, and marred by some unconvincing special effects, it was not a particularly good film. Far more successful were four large-scale Westerns in the studio's Zane Grey series: *The Border Legion, The Thundering Herd, The Code of the West,* and *Light of the Western Stars.* The best of these was *The Thundering Herd,* starring Jack Holt, Tim McCoy, and Noah Beery, and featuring as its climax a spectacularly staged stampede of covered wagons across a frozen lake. *Light of the Western Stars,* again with Holt, was also good with a suspenseful second half more than compensating for a slow beginning. The climactic situation in which the hero is permitted to walk the streets unarmed, prevented from escaping by the presence of the villain's men, and knowing that he will be killed at sundown unless ransom money arrives by then, was a natural for Howard's melodramatic flair.

When Cecil B. De Mille formed his own production company, shortly thereafter, Howard joined him. Having made three Rod La Rocque vehicles, Howard wrote and directed the picture that has since been regarded as one of the greatest films for the silent period, and a most notable Western: *White Gold* (1927). It is unfortunate that the film is not available for revaluation. No prints have survived in the United States, while only one is known to be held in France, and the negative is no longer in existence. *White Gold* (the title refers to wool) had a Western setting, but its story—that of a Mexican dancer who marries and goes to live

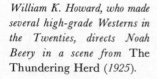

William K. Howard, who made several high-grade Westerns in the Twenties, directs Noah Beery in a scene from The Thundering Herd (*1925*).

on a lonely sheep ranch, with its strange, stylized treatment of sex and jealousy—far removed it from the category of the average horse opera. Although based on a play by J. Palmer Parsons, it was almost an original creation, written and conceived in visual and nonstatic style by Howard. There were only five people in the cast, with Jetta Goudal, Kenneth Thomson, and George Bancroft forming the triangle. The reviews were unanimous raves, and even *Harrison's Reports,* inclined to be overly critical of films that were judged by exhibitors as being too artistic to be commercial (*Greed, Potemkin,* and *Metropolis* were all found wanting on one score or another by the publication), was unstinting in its praise: "From the standpoint of production, scenario construction, directing and acting, 'White Gold' compares most favorably with the best German films that have been brought to America. The production style is of the same order as 'The Last Laugh.' Deeper psychology is revealed in this film than in any other ever produced in America."

The Producers Distributing Corporation made every effort to sell the film, to both exhibitors and the public, but unfortunately *White Gold* turned out to be a resounding box-office flop. Despite this, the film was not without influence. Victor Sjostrom's powerful *The Wind,* starring Lillian Gish and Lars Hanson, made in 1928, was remarkably similar in many respects, although far less studio-bound. It contained one of Lillian Gish's finest performances as the city wife who almost goes mad from the loneliness of life on a small Western ranch. The melodrama of *White Gold* was repeated in the situation of a lecherous neighbor (Montague Love) who attempts to seduce the wife. Terrified, she kills him in self-defense, and tries to bury him during a fierce sandstorm. There is a strikingly macabre moment when the fury of the wind whips the sand from the shallow grave, revealing the rigid corpse lying below. As in so many films of the period there was no code-enforced "moral compensation" for the justified homicide, and the conclusion had the wife finally adjusted to a life in the wilderness, reconciled with her husband.

Far more surprising evidence of the influence of *White Gold* can be found in one of Universal's "Adventure Series," *Wild Blood,* produced early in 1929. Director Henry MacRae and cameraman George Robinson took a story that already had elements of *White Gold* in it (the bored Western girl, tired of drudgery, is prepared to sell herself to the villain merely to get to the excitement of the city) and gave it a strangely stylized visual treatment. There were a preponderance of moving camera work, an interesting dream effect utilizing a *rocking camera* and split-screen, and other visual devices whose direct inspiration was both *White Gold* and the German cinema.

Other aspects of the Twenties

Two films that should not be forgotten were *The Round Up,* an interesting Western satire with Roscoe "Fatty" Arbuckle, and *The Last of the Mohicans.* This last film was perhaps not thoroughly "Western," but so essentially American-Frontier in its spirit that it deserves a mention. It was made by the brilliant French director Maurice Tourneur who was responsible for some of the most visually exquisite films turned out in the United States between 1915 and the end of the silent era. Even in the early days, Tourneur's breath-taking compositions never dominated plot or action: his pictures *moved,* and their action was staged on a spectacular scale. Tourneur's version of *The Last of the Mohicans* was by far the best of the many versions of this James Fenimore Cooper tale.

By 1921, Universal was probably the most active Western production company. One of the biggest hits of the year was Douglas Fairbanks' *The Mark of Zorro,* his first real costume picture, but one in which he retained the economy, sense of fun, and lively tempo that had marked his earlier pictures. The year 1925 was probably the industry's most prolific year "outdoors," with Westerns of every size and type, ranging from MGM's *The Great Divide* with Conway Tearle, Alice Terry, and Wallace Beery, to Associated-Exhibitors' *Twisted Triggers* with Wally Wales. Petite, charming Betty Bronson—sadly wasted by Paramount since her captivating performance in *Peter Pan*—lent distinction to a rather loosely constructed but otherwise interesting Western, *The Golden Princess,* directed by Clarence Badger.

Hal Roach's series with Rex, King of the Wild Horses, included *Black Cyclone,* with Guinn "Big Boy" Williams as the hero; some neat special effects—stop-motion work using models, manipulated much as were the monsters in *King Kong*—produced an unusual sequence in which a wild horse fought a mountain lion. Buster Keaton made a sadly disappointing Western satire in *Go West,* although the opening reel was hilarious. Thereafter, it declined into uninspired imitation-Sennett slapstick and, although amusing, was far below Keaton's standards.

First National filmed their version of Custer's "Last Stand," in a nine-reel picture entitled *The Scarlet West.* Clara Bow and Johnnie Walker were co-starred with Robert Frazer, cast as an Indian who has been educated in a white school, and is an officer in the American Army. The reawakening of interest in the Indian as a Western hero was carried a step further in Paramount's *The Vanishing American.* Since this film is not at present available for re-examination, reprinted here is an original review of the film by *Harrison's Reports:*

While Hart and Fairbanks occasionally kidded each other, Fatty Arbuckle kidded the whole Western genre, as in this scene with Wallace Beery from The Round Up (*1920*).

William Farnum, a stage actor who became one of the most popular stars of the pre-1920 period, as the hero of the Zane Grey story, Last of the Duanes (*1918*).

Whether Famous Players-Lasky knew what they had in their hands when they decided to film this Zane Grey story, or simply discovered it after it was made, just as the old prospector of the West happened to discover the most paying gold mine when the burro on which he rode happened to kick off an edge from a gold-bearing quartz vein, disclosing the glittering gold, it is hard to tell. But one thing one can tell—that "The Vanishing American" is a picture that will live in one's memory after hundreds of others have faded away. Two things are disclosed by "The Vanishing American": that the plains of the West are inexhaustible material for motion pictures; and that Richard Dix is an ACTOR. It took Zane Grey to prove the one theory, and director George B. Seitz the other.

The story deals with the vanishing Indian, starting with the cliff dwellers of more than two thousand years ago, who, because of the sense of security that had come to them from living in caves on the inaccessible sides of cliffs, became lazy. Finally a more sturdy and warlike race descended upon and exterminated them. Years later, the whites subdued the Indians and the American government placed them on reservations, promising them peace and security if they would live there. But they were systematically robbed, murdered, and decimated by the greed of government Indian Agents and unscrupulous settlers. Among these remnants of a once-proud race is Naphaie, son of a chief. He places much of his faith in the white schoolteacher (Lois Wilson) of the Indian children, who is both kind and sympathetic. When war is declared, Naphaie and other Indians join the colors, proud to serve as Americans. In France they acquit themselves honorably, but only a handful return from the savage fighting with the Germans. When Naphaie and his followers reach their home again, they find Brooks (Noah Beery), a thief and a murderer, installed as the Indian Agent, their homes confiscated by him, and their women and children forced to live as best as they can in the desert. The Indians revolt, but just as they are about to attack the whites, Naphaie tells them that the schoolteacher has just returned from Washington with the news that Brooks has been discharged. The Indians surround the blockhouse in which Brooks is holding them at bay with a machine gun. He is killed by a well-aimed Indian arrow. But in the fighting, Naphaie, who has been trying to stop the carnage, is shot down by a stray bullet. Bidding his people to obey the government, he dies, the brave son of a disappearing race.

The Zane Grey tradition

While there undoubtedly was a Grey tradition in literature, there was no clear-cut transference of that tradition to Westerns in general or

Buster Keaton, defeated by the mechanics of city life, is equally defeated by the vastness of the West. From Go West *(1925).*

even to those adapted from his works; certainly not in the sense that there is a William S. Hart tradition or a John Ford tradition. When one looks for a reasonably realistic, as well as entertaining literary picture of American crime and underworld life, one may turn to an author like Dashiel Hammett. Yet Edgar Wallace and S. S. Van Dine are more readily associated with the accepted—and more colorful—notions of crime. So it was with Zane Grey. Grey didn't create a tradition; he exploited one already existing, cunningly manipulating plots and characters so that he never seemed to descend to cliché. He deliberately gave his characters odd, hard-to-pronounce names like Dismukes in *Riders of the Purple Sage* and Guerd Larey in *Wanderer of the Wasteland;* he rounded out his plots with so many characters and so many ramifications that traditional action, though well represented, seemed almost incidental. Any evaluation of Grey's worth as a writer lies outside the scope of this history, but it is reasonable to state that his prolific output represents good solid commercial writing, on a slightly higher level than Clarence E. Mulford and W. C. Tuttle admittedly, but commercial nonetheless. *The Vanishing American* apart, none of Grey's novels were ever made into really important movies, while the less publicized work of A. B. Guthrie and James Warner Bellah has formed the basis for many outstanding Westerns.

The Grey "tradition" is rather a *veneer* than anything radically new in style or content, and thus there is no common denominator for the filmed works of Grey—unless it is a more pronounced emphasis on plot and character. Because of the popularity of Grey's novels, an attempt was made to retain the values of his stories rather more than in the case of other writers. The four versions of *Riders of the Purple Sage* (1918, 1925, 1931, 1941) deviated but little from one another. Surprisingly, the fourth version made in the Forties was the best, perhaps because in the earlier adaptations, the ebullient personalities of Tom Mix and George O'Brien seemed somewhat at odds with Grey's rather grim, revenge-seeking hero. The final version was used to introduce a new Western star (George Montgomery) who had no previously established screen personality to overcome.

Grey "tradition" varied from company to company, too; at RKO the trend was to slick, polished little Westerns, and thus the Grey works were either selected for their conventional action content, as in *Nevada*, or rewritten to conform to a less austere pattern as in *West of the Pecos* and *Sunset Pass*. Fox always had to bear the Mix and George O'Brien personalities in mind. The best, as a group, were undoubtedly those that Paramount made in the Twenties, when story and production values were given primary place, and star value considered only after them (although with players like Jack Holt, Noah Beery, and Tim McCoy, Grey's characters were singularly well served). Apart from a feeble remake of *The Vanishing American* in the Fifties, it has been some time since the screen has given us any Grey material—due in part to the competition on television of a "Zane Grey Theatre" which maximized the value of his name, while distorting the old values of his works. Few of the films included in the series were actually based on his originals, and many were decidedly modern in the heavy psychological mold—the very antithesis of his stories.

Boom years

The Indian motif was continued in 1926 with *Braveheart,* in which Rod La Rocque was starred as a college-educated, football-playing Indian, who returns to lead his people in the ways of the white man. Paramount's Zane Grey films continued with some fine entries, including *Born to the West, Forlorn River* with Jack Holt, and *Desert Gold* with Neil Hamilton. One of Rin Tin Tin's competitors, Peter the Great, made an enjoyable action film entitled *Wild Justice.* MGM's *The Barrier* was a well-made Rex Beach melodrama, with Henry B. Walthall stealing acting honors. *The Devil Horse,* well directed by Fred Jackman, offered action, good stunts from hero Yakima Canutt, fine photography by George Stevens, and well-staged Indian attacks.

One of the most spectacular Westerns of the year, sadly forgotten today, was *The Last Frontier,* directed by George B. Seitz, an eight-reel epic which had been started under Ince, and temporarily shelved following his death. The Indian fighting scenes were spectacular: wave upon wave of mounted Indians, hundreds strong, galloped into battle, dramatically photographed from high vantage points. Even a fine buffalo stampede sequence had to give way before these magnificently staged Indian fights.

Westerns in 1926 were enjoying their biggest boom of the silent period; even a sedate and cultural center like Baltimore, at its Garden Theatre, turned out in greatest numbers to see a Western—Tom Mix's *The Best Bad Man.*

The boom continued into 1927. Old series were sustained, new ones were started. But it was the last really big year for the silent Western. Paramount, still not sure how to use the unique talent of Betty Bronson following her excellent, if unsuccessful *A Kiss for Cinderella,* had her mark time in her second Western, *Open Range.* A competent film, it had plenty of action, with Lane Chandler as the hero, and Yakima Canutt doubling for him in stunt scenes.

Gary Cooper made *Nevada,* another Zane Grey Western, for Paramount; and the old situation of California under the Mexican flag, almost becoming Russian territory, was given another treatment in First National's *Rose of the Golden West,* made by that underrated director, George Fitzmaurice, with Gilbert Roland and Mary Astor as loyal Californians, and Gustav Von Seyffertitz engaging in his customary efficient villainy. Director Richard Thorpe and star Wally Wales worked together on a number of diverting films made cheaply, among them *The Cyclone Cowboy* and *Tearin' into Trouble,* the last with Walter Brennan quite prominently cast. FBO continued strong with their several series. First National made the best logging melodrama in years with *Valley of the Giants* starring Milton Sills and Doris Kenyon. Charles Brabin directed this particular version of the rugged Peter B. Kyne story, which had been made earlier with Wallace Reid, and was to be made twice again in color in the sound era.

One of the most interesting off-beat "B" Westerns was a six-reeler from First Division, directed by Paul Powell, entitled *Death Valley.* For a Western, it seemed unusually depressing and sordid, featuring some stark scenes of the hero and villain, alone in the desert, nearly mad from thirst. The underlying theme was the greed for gold, and the villain's murder of his female partner, followed by a flight across the desert, suggests more than the casual influence of Stroheim's *Greed.* The villain meets his end in a bizarre fashion, too: quite mad, and already near death from thirst and exposure to the sun, he is struck down by a rattlesnake.

The *Death Valley* was made again with *no* plot changes, exactly nine-

Betty Bronson, a top star who was being mishandled, and Lane Chandler, then on equal footing with Gary Cooper as an upcoming new Western favorite, were teamed in Open Range *(1927).*

teen years later, this time with Robert Lowery and Helen Gilbert in the leads, and Nat Pendleton as the maddened thief who dies of snake bite. The only change was a negative one: it was photographed in the blurred green of Cinecolor.

The sound era

It was inevitable that sound should eventually come to the screen. There had been experiments, by Edison and others, in the earliest days, and periodically throughout the Twenties, in films like Griffith's *Dream Street,* unsuccessful attempts had been made to hasten its arrival. But the revolution in 1928 was total; sound, initially on disc, soon on track, had come to stay, and before its use in movies became absolute, the Western suffered a resounding set-back. The genre seemed somehow "symbolic" of the silent era, and therefore something to be shunned; Westerns seemed to offer little opportunity for the full exploitation of the new medium. All that mattered in those early days of the new era was that a film *talked* incessantly, and often to the exclusion of all else. Camera movement stopped, plot stopped, action stopped, while the characters stood around and talked at length. This is not to imply that only bad films were made: veterans like King Vidor refused to abandon their technique and mastery of style—his *Hallelujah* remains one of his best films from any period; newcomer Rouben Mamoulian, making his first film, *Applause,* refused to let his technicians tell him about the "limitations" of sound, and made a picture that was *visually* a film first, and a "talkie" second. But these were exceptions; movies which "talked" on endlessly, like *The Locked Door* and *The Racketeer* set the rule. The Western, recognizing that its appeal lay still primarily in its clean-cut action, made small attempt to let dialogue dominate; curiously, however, it allowed itself to be slowed down so that its pacing matched the now-fashionable slowness of sound films. Victor Fleming's *The Virginian,* for example, an interesting film, and perhaps still the best version of this classic Western tale, suffered especially in this respect. A leisurely story in any case, it seemed almost artificially slow in its measured pacing. With a minimum of action and a normal amount of dialogue, it seemed to be full of unimportant incident, with the expectation that something significant would emerge at some point from that incident. However, it was beautifully photographed and well acted, especially by Richard Arlen as the tragic rustler, while Gary Cooper and Walter Huston were a fine pair of protagonists.

But sound was not the only element that affected the Western; something else had happened at almost the same time: Lindbergh flew the Atlantic, capturing the imagination of millions of Americans. It was remarked at the time that the Western was ready for a quick burial. Among the most significant examples of this mentality was an editorial by James R. Quirk which appeared in the April, 1929, issue of *Photoplay:*

"History will be several generations along before we can get a real focus on the results of Lindbergh's epochal flight and character. Great as was his initial accomplishment, it will fade into the background when compared to his effect on national thought and manners. Lindbergh has put the cowboy into the discard as a type of national hero. The Western novel and motion picture heroes have slunk away into the brush, never to return.

Within the past two years, Western pictures, always surefire profit earners, have lost their popularity. Western novels and Western fiction have fared a similar fate. The Western picture has gone the way of the serial thriller. The cow ponies are retired to the pasture with the old fire horses. Zane Grey and Harold Bell Wright are following Horatio Alger and Oliver Optic.

Tom Mix, Hoot Gibson and Ken Maynard must swap horses for aeroplanes or go to the old actors' home.

The great open spaces are now landing fields, and the bears in the mountains cannot hurt Little Nell because Little Nell is thumbing her nose at them as her lover pilots her over the hill tops.

They used to lure the dimes out of little boys' pockets with lithographs of Tony and Silver King jumping Stetson hats over ravines, and two-gun men shooting daylight through dastardly Mexicans who had insulted the ranch-owner's daughter.

But little boys have changed their ideas since Lindy flew the Atlantic, and save their dimes until they can see Sam Browne belted lads plugging aeroplanes marked with German crosses, or air mail heroes winging through the fog and the night to save the honor of Clara or Corinne, Greta or Colleen. That's just one little thing that Lindy's done."

Photoplay, which has little in common with the magazine of the same name today, was the most influential and intelligent of the fan magazines of the Twenties. It was respected by Hollywood, and not merely used by it; its articles and editorials were excellent, its reviews discerning, and its "fan padding" at a minimum. Through the years, it took cognizance of the popularity of the Western and reviewed the bulk of them while lesser magazines merely shrugged them off. In retrospect, some of editor Quirk's editorials can be seen to be blatantly wrong; but the majority were far-sighted and intelligent.

During the first two years of the sound film, no really important large-scale Westerns were made and, influenced by this apparent slackening of interest in large Westerns, fewer "B" Westerns were produced. MGM ceased production entirely on the Tim McCoy series and never resumed any kind of "B" Western schedule. FBO, which had the Tom Mix series, likewise stopped production when internal changes transformed the company into RKO RADIO, which then launched a group of very talkative literary and stage adaptations. It was not until two years later that one of these adaptations, *Cimarron,* unexpectedly returned the Western to favor with the RKO front office, and prompted a reinstatement of series Westerns on their production schedule.

Fox's *In Old Arizona,* made in 1929, inadvertently convinced the skeptics that the Western could utilize sound beneficially; director Raoul Walsh, who had planned to star in the film until an eye accident made it impossible, made no real attempt to exploit his sound track as such. It was a big film, still the best of the many Cisco Kid adventures, and doubtless its sheer size and gusto would have made it just as successful even had it been shot as a silent. But simple scenes combining sound and picture, such as bacon frying over an open campfire, somehow excited the critics who now foresaw a great future for the sound Western. Visual action remained more important than dialogue. However, if *speech* was to add little to the Western, *sound* was instead to add a great deal. Sounds of action—stampeding cattle, gunshots, etc.—and the use of traditional Western folk music, particularly in the films directed by John Ford, definitively added another dimension to the genre.

Uncertain about the future of the sound film, and in any event having to cater to both silent and sound exhibitors, many companies issued their Westerns in the 1927–1930 period in both sound and silent versions. Dialogue was usually concentrated into one or two sequences, the rest of the film being mainly a matter of music and sound effects. Dialogue was there solely to exploit the novelty of sound, and added little, if anything to the plot. Because of the then cumbersome sound equipment, the films were shot on long box-like sets, with almost no camera movement. Such sequences, of course, seemed pointlessly static in the purely silent versions. For example, Ken Maynard's *Lucky Larkin* has some barroom comic interludes which brought the whole plot to a grinding halt for half a reel at a time. And films like Hoot Gibson's *The Mounted Stranger,* which had always placed more stress than most on comedy, seemed particularly slow.

As late as 1930, some Westerns were being put out in both silent and sound versions. Universal's serial, *The Indians Are Coming,* was so released, becoming the studio's *last* silent serial and *first* talkie serial simultaneously. It proved to be a strange mixture of techniques: the sections where direct sound, that is to say, principally dialogue, was not used but where sound effects and music alone were utilized, remained typical of the silents of the late Twenties. There was an almost overabundant use of the moving camera for lengthy tracking shots, one of which traveled from outside the Western town, right up the main street, and into a close-up of the saloon, an exceptionally smooth and long shot that was re-used many times during the course of the serial. Of course, the tendency was reversed whenever the direct dialogue sequences took over. To make the most of the dialogue, the romantic interest between Tim McCoy and Allene Ray became more pronounced than was common in serials, and some chapters came to their conclusion on a dramatic rather than melodramatic note, the crises being prompted by words rather than by physical action.

The Western as a whole fared much better than most films in this transitional change of a period. The average non-Western, content to rely on the pure novelty of sound, usually offered seven reels of nothing but talk, with a total repudiation of camera movement and a near-abandonment of all other types of film grammar. The Western instead, by its very nature, remained fresh and fast despite the commercial necessity of occasional slow stretches. Strangely enough, comparatively little was done to introduce music. Ken Maynard occasionally featured singing groups in his films, and in fact frequently sang himself, but perhaps due to Maynard's own limitations as a singer, and the fact that he still adhered to the traditional Western, the idea for musical Westerns did not catch on at that time.

The success of *In Old Arizona* naturally spurred interest in the large-scale sound Western epic. The immediate outcome was the remaking of several established Western favorites. *The Virginian* was sold not on its own considerable merits, nor on star value, but on the angle: "Now you can see and hear this classic story."

Approximately a year later De Mille used the same approach on his third version of *The Squaw Man*. But, of course, the novelty of sound in a film genre which really used it so little, was bound to wear off. Luckily, a new novelty attracted a great deal of attention. Almost forgotten now is the fact that between 1926 and 1932 Hollywood, which had already tried and discarded three-dimensional films, was experimenting with various types of wide-screen presentations. For a while it seemed that seventy-millimeter film (the same film now used in the Todd-AO process) might well become standard, but at the time the revolution was premature and the movement died out. At least two important Westerns were shot, however, for wide screens on seventy-millimeter film, with, of course,

Sound was big news when The Virginian *was released (1929).*

standard thirty-five-millimeter versions being shot at the same time. They were *Billy the Kid,* directed by King Vidor for MGM, with Johnny Mack Brown and Wallace Beery, and *The Big Trail,* another Raoul Walsh "special" for Fox. Scenes of the vast wagon train winding across the desert, fording a flooded river, and literally being hauled over mountains, were especially effective because they were suited to the widescreen treatment, and no film since, even in the period of Cinemascope, has even approached the effectiveness of this footage. By now, too, Walsh had developed more constructive ideas concerning the use of music. The grand scale of the Indian battle in the film was made doubly effective by the sudden introduction of a furious agitato with Indian themes; otherwise, music in the film was still used sparingly.

The Big Trail also proved the fallacy of the executives' theory that sound Westerns would lose the traditional foreign market for Westerns. These people thought that it would not be worth the trouble to dub or subtitle a film in which dialogue was not of prime importance. *The Big Trail,* however, proved a great success overseas.

In this period, great importance was attached to foreign versions of films. These were versions shot at the same time, but with different players, a different director, and sometimes even a completely different approach, despite the same basic script and sets. All of the big action scenes could be used intact, with occasional cut-in close-ups of the foreign players; the German version of *The Big Trail,* for example, was especially well put together. Dialogue taking a second place to action, the sequences that had to be re-shot, on the original sets, of course, were relatively few and comparatively simple. Although German audiences were deprived of John Wayne except in the long shots, Germany's exhibitors had a much more profitable product.

Hollywood's practice of making alternate versions of its films did not last long; as soon as the cheaper processes of dubbing and subtitling were found to be acceptable overseas, the more elaborate method of making foreign versions was abandoned, except for occasional shooting of additional scenes to increase the marketability of a film in a given territory.

Billy the Kid, The Big Trail, and *Cimarron* in themselves constitute the cycle of epic Western of 1930 to 1932. It was a short-lived cycle and not a prolific one, but it did restore the Western to the front rank in box-office popularity and paved the way for the boom period in "B" Westerns from 1932 to 1942. These factors combined demonstrated conclusively that the genre was not ready for burial as *Photoplay* more than intimated; instead it was very much alive and kicking, to the delight of its supporters.

The Western

"*True, most of the characters
in the movies are better dressed and
live more luxuriously than do their
counterparts in real life.*"

HORTENSE POWDERMAKER

costume

10

Western costuming by Hollywood seems to have been governed more than anything else by changing concepts of the Western itself, and by tailoring to the requirements of individual Western players. Special films like *The Iron Horse* and *Shane* apart, relatively little concern seems to have been displayed over absolute authenticity of wardrobe. It became customary for the hero to dress in simple but clean-cut fashion, and the hero with a waistcoat or a jacket was rare indeed. It was equally customary for the gambler to advertise his trade by wearing a long black frock coat.

Undoubtedly the most completely realistic Westerns, insofar as costume is concerned, were those made by Ince between 1910 and 1913. With the star system not yet a potent factor, authenticity of reconstruction was one of Ince's main concerns, and his films were in part sold on the basis of their authenticity. It was fairly easy to be authentic under the circumstances; he was shooting his films in the West and about a West that was almost contemporary.

Compare, for instance, the utter realism, almost to the point of drabness, of the costuming in his films, with the costuming in the earlier *The Great Train Robbery*. The explanation for the difference is that Porter's film, shot in New Jersey, tried to duplicate the West, while Ince was able to reflect it.

The costuming in *The Great Train Robbery* is mainly a matter of suggestion; by their large, wide-brimmed hats and their boots, we

Ill-fitting and over-large necker-chieves, Eastern hats and shirts, and the "expected" sheepskin chaps—the initial inaccurate costuming of Westerns not made in the West. From a Broncho Billy Western, The Girl in the Triple X (*1911*).

know that these men are supposed to be Westerners. But the suspicion remains that the hats and boots were rented, and the rest of the wardrobe furnished from the players' closets of old clothes. Too many of the "actors" looked like Easterners masquerading as cowboys in clothing that was obviously unfamiliar to them.

Somewhat amateurish though it appeared, the costuming in *The Great Train Robbery* and other early Edison Westerns was still—understandably —superior to the costuming in French "Westerns" of the same period. *The Hanging at Jefferson City,* one of a series made by the French director Durant, seemed to rely solely on its barroom set, and on its exteriors—none too convincing in themselves—to convey Western atmosphere. Costuming was sketchy in the extreme, the average outfits looking like everyday French farmers' clothes, with only the broad-brimmed hats to act as a common denominator between the variety of costumes. The Law was presented in the form of two individuals in nondescript uniform, resembling, if anything, U. S. cavalrymen. These lawmen both bore enormous silver stars on their chests to designate their official capacity, but so outsized were these badges that they almost reduced the lawmen to the comic proportions of traditional American comic-policemen in strip cartoons or, a little later with the Keystone Kops, in movies.

The Broncho Billy films made in the interim period were, however, much more realistic in this respect, without going to the extremes that Ince did. Managing to avoid a "phoney" or theatrical look, they struck a satisfactory balance between the two. As the first Western star in his own right, the rather beefy Anderson cut quite a striking figure without being either drab or garish. He wore a simple and modestly colored shirt, often a waistcoat (apart from Hart and, occasionally, Mix, few other Western stars did this) and leather cuffs, adorned with a single star, around his lower arms. These cuffs were, of course, an essential part of the working cowboy's equipment. As he roped cattle, he would dig the cut-off heel of his boot into the ground to provide a firm anchor, and loop his rope around a cuff, which provided the protection from friction and rope burns. Authentic or not, they apparently were too cumbersome for the movie cowboy, and apart from Anderson and Hart, they never quite caught on with Western leads. Rather they seemed limited to actors playing villains or old-timers; for example, a lesser villain, Earl Dwire, wore them frequently, and Raymond Hatton, playing a grizzled old-timer in several series of Westerns, used them as an integral part of his costume. Hatton's, at least, seemed to be the real article, for they were well scarred with rope burns.

One part of the Anderson costume that never caught on were the sheepskin chaps. Chaps were never really an accepted part of the movie cowboy's costume, although Ken Maynard, Buck Jones, and Tom Mix frequently wore leather chaps. But the sheepskin chaps remained a part of Broncho Billy's era. After that, they were worn for the most part by players enacting the roles of dudes (Jack Benny in *Buck Benny Rides Again,* Stanley Fields in *The Mine with the Iron Door,* or William Boyd, masquerading as a dude in *Sunset Trail*). The appearance of an actor in these chaps always brought forth gales of laughter from the supporting cast of "hardened Westerners." Apparently New Yorkers and Englishmen were the principal dudes exported to the West; both fell back on sheepskin chaps, and on "city" riding habits to emphasize their milquetoast characters.

William S. Hart's insistence on authenticity in all matters pertaining to the West extended especially to his costume. Because of this, Hart frequently looked far from neat, but he never once took on the slick "circus" appearance of so many other "cowboys." Hart wore drab frock coats, often shiny with use and dusty from much traveling, and the cheap, sturdy, gaudily colorful shirts that the old frontiersmen loved so much. They had to be of strong material, to meet rugged frontier activity and weather, and they had to be cheap, to meet the cowboy's pocketbook. Hart wore these trappings casually, neither exploiting their authenticity nor avoiding them because of their vulgarity. His outfit varied according to the role he played, but he always wore a Mexican sash beneath his gun belt. This item, never actually used by Hart in his films, and never copied by any other Western star, was a vital part of the cowboy's working equipment, for with it he tied the hooves of a steer after he had roped it. The authenticity of Hart's costumes was never approached by any other Western star, nor did most stars even want to take on such an unglamorous appearance.

Tom Mix, the next great Western star to appear after Hart, went to quite the opposite extreme. Mix openly admitted that his screen character was not intended to parallel that of the authentic Westerner. Mix was essentially a showman, and his costume perfectly reflected this "circus" approach. It was Mix who evolved the costume that practically looked like a uniform.

This sort of costume was not entirely foreign to the real West, but it was the kind of costume that a cowboy would buy to indulge his vanity at a rodeo, or at a similar special event. It was impractical, and certainly uneconomical, as an everyday working outfit. Along with the meticulously designed colored shirts and intricately carved boots, Mix also introduced gloves to the Westerner's outfit—a piece of clothing seldom worn by the real cowboy. In Mix's case, they were a necessity, for his hands were soft and prone to injury; but most of the subsequent Western stars, without his reasons, imitated him and likewise wore

Tom Mix: the "circus" approach.

gloves. Mix's fantastically embroidered shirts and trousers decorated with gold braid (actually his most extreme outfits were reserved for off-screen appearances) particularly influenced Gene Autry in the Thirties, and Autry in turn was imitated by another, if lesser, singing cowboy, Jimmy Wakely.

Autry's most distinctive items were shirts, usually jet black affairs, ornamented with gold braids. When Roy Rogers took over as Republic's leading cowboy, going in as much if not more for music as for action, his outfits went even further than Autry's, and his pictures often looked more like a Romberg operetta than a story allegedly set in the West! This "streamlining" of costume, started by Mix, was developed through the Twenties, mainly by lesser Western stars like Yakima Canutt and Edmund Cobb, who specialized in elaborate all-white outfits. Many costumes were deliberately imitative of Mix. Ken Maynard, Hoot Gibson, and Buck Jones all dressed neatly, attractively and colorfully. Although their costumes were far less realistic than Hart's had been, they successfully avoided being labeled as "dudes." In their final years as stars, in the Forties, Maynard and Gibson did give in to the flashier outfits, but Jones never did, his only concessions to the trend of individual clothing styles being his pointed white Stetson and a very distinctively designed

Gene Autry and Champion.

gun belt. The gun belt itself underwent fewer changes than any other part of the Western costume. In the Thirties, Monogram and Republic seemed to favor functional belts always jammed full of deadly looking cartridges. Bill Elliott wore his belt in such a way that the guns rested in their holsters butt forward, calling for the spectacular cross draw. And in the Twenties, Fred Thomson had sometimes worn a strange-looking all white gun belt. It was a clumsy affair, looking for all the world like a child's toy. It took much away from his otherwise tough, capable appearance. For obvious reasons, very few Western stars used the holster string—a cord which tied the holsters tightly to the legs, facilitating a fast draw. This was principally a device of the professional gunfighter, and for a Western hero to use it might suggest either an unhealthy knowledge of the art of gunfighting or an unfair advantage taken over an opponent. Hart, of course, had used this device frequently, and William Boyd, Bill Elliott, and others did on *occasion*, but it was never stressed in any way.

Strangely, the "B" Westerns of the Thirties adopted on a large scale a costume pattern which had been only mildly prevalent in the silent era: symbolic clothing. This was even more surprising since, with the advent of sound films, the need for obvious visual symbolism had been obviated. The pattern was largely based on black and white clothing, the colors representing evil and good respectively. The hero would wear a spotless white Stetson, as much white as possible in his costume, and would ride a snow-white horse. The villain, needless to say, wore a black hat, usually more shapeless and less heroic in size than that of the hero, a completely black outfit, and rode a black horse. Sometimes a black mustache was added, and the mustache itself became almost a symbol of evil, heroes with mustaches in the Thirties becoming quite rare; Jack Holt was one of the very few who survived the taboo. The trend to white hats was led by such stars as Charles Starrett, John Wayne, Bob Livingston, Ken Maynard, Buck Jones, Tex Ritter and Bob Allen. Starrett at Columbia wore the largest and most spotless white Stetson that ever gleamed from a screen at a near-blinded audience!

One of the very few exceptions to the rule was William Boyd, who as Hopalong Cassidy, affected a rather strange outfit. For one thing it was simple and workmanlike, lacking any hint of the garish; yet in its way it was quite as unrealistic as the near-surrealistic outfits of Mix. Completely consistent from picture to picture—until the much later films in the Forties—it was a uniform no less than were the outfits of Mix and Rogers. It defied convention by being totally black, but, of course, Boyd still rode a flawlessly white horse.

Another to reverse the black-white symbolic pattern was Tim McCoy, who at Columbia in the early Thirties adopted a black outfit, topped by a gleaming white sombrero. Later he dropped the white hat, replacing it with a black one, too. McCoy was always immaculate. His clothes were not fancy, but they were obviously of the finest fabrics, spotlessly clean, and neatly pressed. He hardly looked like a working cowboy, but since he invariably played a lawman posing as a gambler or an outlaw, this discrepancy mattered little. McCoy's somber appearance in black made him seem like Nemesis in person, for outlaws in any case. He would walk slowly into a saloon, letting the swing doors flap behind him, and would stand there silently surveying the scene, glowering grimly at any obvious renegade, and flashing his eyes from side to side in a manner that became almost his trademark. Whether the outlaws accepted him as friend or foe, from that moment on, they knew that they had met their master! Such a scene was included almost automatically in the majority of McCoy's later Westerns, and they depended in large part on his striking costume for their ultimate effect. McCoy was a bit of a ham at heart, and played such scenes to the hilt. He also had a fondness for masquerading as a Mexican bandit, and appropriate scenes were written into many of his pictures, giving him the opportunity to wear a colorful costume, and to engage in flamboyant theatrics with a Mexican accent.

Bill Elliott: costume picturesque but generally realistic, gun holsters reversed for faster cross-draw.

Charles Starrett: a tasteful compromise between neatness and practicality.

William S. Hart, in workmanlike garb, is galvanized into action by the pleas of a plain cotton-frocked heroine, circa 1919. To the left, Roy Rogers, all rodeo frills, prepares to launch into a song with similarly uniformed Jane Frazee, circa 1950. Hart was spared the sight of this final debasement of the genre he loved so much.

Before turning to black outfits, McCoy favored colorful buckskin costumes. These were never gaudy either, but were always a little too neat and fresh for complete conviction. He looked more like the star of a Wild West show than an actual frontiersman, which was a pity, for McCoy was not "phoney," only a little too theatrical, and his pictures were of the better sort. More realistic buckskin outfits were worn by Johnny Mack Brown in some of his Universal serials like *Wild West Days* and *The Oregon Trail,* and by Buck Jones in films like *White Eagle* and *Dawn on the Great Divide.*

One of the very few Westerns to really defy the conventions of the Western dress, Hollywood style, was Ford's *Stagecoach*. John Wayne wore, instead of a belt, suspenders, and juvenile audiences in particular found this most distressing: they thought he looked half-dressed and not very glamorous. The costume has not been worn since.

In the Forties, for reasons which no one has yet explained, the large Stetson, considered almost a trademark of the Western since the earliest days, began to disappear slowly—to be replaced by a much less spectacular Stetson, equally widebrimmed, but with a much flatter crown. Tim Holt, Johnny Mack Brown, George O'Brien, Charles Starrett, and Roy Rogers all adopted this as their regular headgear, and in due time all the Western stars, even those of negligible stature like Lash LaRue, made the changeover.

John Ford's flair for accurate costuming was apparent from the start. George O'Brien in The Iron Horse.

Johnny Mack Brown: costume fashionable, tasteful, hardly realistic.

Costume changes in other stock characters in the Western—the heroine and the Indian for example—have been less distinctive. Female garb seems to have been changed primarily to reflect contemporary fashion rather than to re-create authentic Western fashions. In early Westerns, the trend was to high, demure bodices and to long skirts. In the Twenties, the heroine dressed in practical blouses, and skirts were shorter. There was no longer quite the same hesitation about showing something of a well-shaped female leg, in Westerns or other films, but fashions were still modest. In the late Thirties and early Forties, legs *were* exploited in Westerns. Short skirts and ankle boots came into vogue, and musical numbers, which frequently provided excuses for chorines in tights to go through their paces, were contributing factors. Once the Western really exploited sex, following *The Outlaw,* the Western heroine took to provocatively tight and unbuttoned shirts and blouses, equally undersized men's trousers, silk stockings, flimsy negligees, and similar accessories.

Costuming of the Indian has not radically changed in itself; rather have the movies increasingly explored the backgrounds of radically different tribes in order to show that the feathered headdress was no more typical of all Indians than is the bowler hat of all Englishmen. Many Indians, particularly the more peaceful ones, and those that lived near whites, adopted many of the white man's clothes, especially colored shirts and trousers. But, perhaps to stress that Indians were not quite as civilized as whites, the movie Indian always seemed to wear his shirt outside of his trousers! A few films like *Apache,* however, did treat the Indian in the white man's clothing in proper perspective.

In recent years, we have seen something of a return to the style of dress of the old Ince films, due mainly to certain inherent tendencies in "adult" Westerns and the influence of television series. From this return to more realistic and at times drab costuming, a new sort of uniform has become identified with the hero. As exemplified by Gary Cooper in *High Noon* and more typically by Hugh O'Brian in his Wyatt Earp series for television, this uniform consists of various items of everyday apparel subtly combined to produce a dramatic effect which emphasizes black. The hero appears as a starkly dramatic figure, a black upholder of the Law silhouetted against gray surroundings, visually a man of obvious destiny, force, and leadership.

The Thirties

11

"Collectivism is indispensable in the film, but the collaborators must be blended with one another to an exceptionally close degree."

VSEVOLOD I. PUDOVKIN

The cycle of epic sound Westerns started in 1929 and 1930 was short-lived, but the renewed faith in the genre as such brought a boom in the production of the modest "B" Westerns, a phenomenon which lasted at full strength for a decade and a half. The veritable Golden Age of the "B" Western materialized in the early and mid-Thirties, with cheap production costs, ready markets, and high profits. And when the boom seemed in danger of burning itself out, the musical Westerns of Gene Autry came along to enjoy even greater popularity. Although the sound era introduced new important Western stars, the leading ones, initially at least, were those who had reigned supreme in the silent era, too: Buck Jones, Ken Maynard, Tom Mix, Tim McCoy, and, to a lesser degree, Hoot Gibson. Only one of the silent Western stars, Art Acord, failed to make the transition in sound Westerns. He found his voice unsuitable for the sensitive recording apparatus, a big problem, but one that careful vocal training could have overcome. Most of the top stars of silent films—Garbo, Barrymore, Swanson, Chaney—easily made the transition, but Acord did not persevere; perhaps realizing that his vogue was over, he drifted into crime, served a prison term for rum-running, and finally committed suicide. Bob Steele and Tom Tyler never quite made it to the top rank in the sound era, although the quantity of their output for independent studios equaled if it did not exceed that of their more popular contemporaries. Of minor stature were the Westerns made by a dozen or so lesser heroes of the sagebrush. Bob Custer, one of the poorest actors of them all, appeared in some lively serials and "quickie" Westerns with Rin Tin Tin, Jr., of which the feature, *Vengeance of Rannah* is one of the more interesting. Conway Tearle, a minor movie idol only a decade earlier, was sadly reduced to such pedestrian Westerns as *Judgement Book.* Wally Wales (better known in later years as a villain under the name of Hal Taliaferro) was another holdover from the silent days, appearing in many cheap independent Westerns. Trick roper and rodeo performer Monty Montana failed to catch on as a Western hero, probably because the few starring vehicles he made, of which *Circle of Death* is typical, were too ineptly produced. Lane Chandler, who had appeared in a number of silent Westerns for Paramount, had a brief starring period, but soon drifted into traditional "hero's pal" roles. Fred Kohler, Jr., son of the famous actor but a rather colorless personality, after a few starring "B" Westerns remained at best on the periphery of the field for years. Some of his little Westerns were surprisingly good, especially *Toll of the Desert,* which had plenty of action, a solid script, and moving finish very much in the Zane Grey tradition. Kohler, as an honest sheriff, hangs the outlaw leader whose courage and code of honor he has always admired, unaware that the outlaw is actually his own father.

Probably the best of the lesser Western stars of the Thirties was Rex Bell, a good-looking and considerably better-than-average actor whose period of popularity was surprisingly brief. His Westerns were often good-natured and humorous, with a fairly realistic approach to traditional plots. At another time Bell might have been far more popular, but when he arrived on the scene, the Western market was already glutted with names. Cheap companies like Resolute gave him plenty of action and even good plots in *Gun Fire* and *Saddle Acres,* for example, but an absolute minimum of production value. He did, however, make a good series of Westerns for Monogram, married Clara Bow, and gradually retired from the movies, returning only occasionally to appear in such films as *Tombstone, Dawn on the Great Divide* and *Lone Star.* In the years before his death in 1962 Bell devoted himself almost exclusively to politics, and in 1955 he was elected Lieutenant-Governor of Nevada.

Among the real old-timers only Harry Carey remained consistently active as a Western star in sound films, appearing in both serials (*Vanishing Legion, The Devil Horse*) and in "B" pictures constructed along the lines of his silent Westerns. However, most of his sound Westerns—*Wagon Train,* or *Last of the Clintons,* for example—lacked the *really* strong plot elements that had distinguished his better silents, films like *Satan*

Town and *The Prairie Pirate,* and seemed rather slow-moving. Jack Mul-hall alternated between heroics and villainy, as did Walter Miller and William Desmond. Only two *new* Westerns stars of real caliber emerged during the early years of sound. George O'Brien had, of course, starred in *The Iron Horse* for Ford in 1924, and in other silent Westerns, but had always been considered a straight leading man rather than a Western star. Fox put him into a fine series of Zane Grey Westerns. The other newcomer was another Ford discovery, John Wayne, who had played a minor role in that director's *Men Without Women* and achieved stardom in Raoul Walsh's *The Big Trail.* Wayne, under contract to Warners, appeared in a remarkably good series of Westerns produced for that company by cartoon-maker Leon Schlessinger.

One of the most surprising trends of this period was the temporary abandonment of "streamlining" in the "B" Western. "Streamlining" and lush glamour were considered essential in the Hollywood product: the early, halting days when the "movies" became "talkies" were over. In films like *Grand Hotel* or even fairly routine programmers like *Jewel Robbery,* the movie audiences were getting the ultimate in films that literally dripped veneer from every frame. It was a wonderful era of super-sophistication, an era in which the delightful fantasy of *Trouble in Paradise* could rub shoulders with the stark realism of *Public Enemy.*

Producer-stars

Westerns, however, did not generally follow the trend to more glamorous products, and for a while many of them were austere in the Hart tradi-tion. One of the reasons for this was that Tom Mix, Ken Maynard, and later, in 1935, Buck Jones had their own production units and handled their films in a personal and individual way. But just as Hart had some-times lost perspective through too little supervision, so it was to a degree with Jones and Maynard. With Jones especially, there was a tendency to be "arty" and to play down action in favor of unusual dramatic elements. *Stone of Silver Creek,* for example, almost repeated the austerity and evangelistic fervor of Hart's *Hell's Hinges,* since it was mostly de-voted to the methodical conversion and reformation of a saloon-keeper (Jones) by a minister's daughter. There was no physical action until a lively final reel packed in sufficient riding, fisticuffs, and shooting to satisfy the customers. At times, too, Jones became a great believer in comedy, casting himself as a "dumb" cowhand mixed up in affairs somewhat beyond his comprehension. These films were usually weak in all departments. He more than made up for them with good Westerns

Buck Jones, Tim McCoy, and Raymond Hatton in Monogram's "Rough Riders" series.

like *The Crimson Trail, Outlawed Guns, Border Brigands, Rocky Rhodes,* and *When a Man Sees Red,* all fine products of his Universal period.

Certainly, Jones' Westerns for Universal were superior to those of Maynard, who filled his films with action, and especially animal action involving wild horses, but who, unfortunately, as a writer-director-producer was completely without discipline. He did not always fill all three capacities but the official directors of the films—Alan James was frequently used—were usually no more than right-hand men for Maynard, who made the films the way *he* wanted. But for this lack of discipline, Maynard, who was good-looking and a really fine rider, might well have built himself into the leading Western star of the sound era.

Maynard's off-beat approach to Westerns frequently led him into plots, written by himself, which were so outlandish as to be completely unbelievable. In *Smoking Guns* made in 1933, the main titles, backed by strange pseudo-classical and distinctly non-Western music, give way to a scene which immediately places the audience into the middle of the story. Maynard accuses the villain of unspecified crooked activities, and the villain responds by threatening Maynard with the same fate that overtook his father. There is no elaboration on any of this. In a scuffle the villain is killed by a henchman; Maynard is blamed, but manages to make his escape. He is next seen, bearded and white-haired, in a crocodile-infested jungle swamp, presumably in South America. Hot on his trail is Texas Ranger Walter Miller, who captures him. They become firm friends during their trek back to civilization. As they paddle through swamps, Miller suddenly becomes wildly delirious and shoots at a swarm of crocodiles; the canoe overturns, and Miller is badly mauled by a crocodile. Then, in an incredibly written sequence, Maynard casually announces that, having lived with the jungle Indians, learned many of their medical secrets, it will be a simple matter for him to amputate Miller's leg with a red-hot iron before gangrene sets in. Miller, understandably skeptical, shoots himself. At this point Maynard discovers that he is an exact double for Miller, a development that is quite unacceptable in spite of the men's heavy beards. Maynard decides to return in Miller's place, and manages to fool even those people who knew both men intimately.

Nor was there any attempt at serious acting in Maynard's Westerns, and this together with the absence of any logic in the tales told, made it difficult for adults to accept his films as seriously as they accepted those of Buck Jones. But the best Maynard Westerns, like the silent *Red Raiders,* and his early sound films, *Dynamite Ranch* and *Fargo Express,* are among the best Westerns made by any star. And to Maynard—rather than to Gene Autry—belongs the real credit for the introduction of the musical Western. Songs in Maynard's films were never introduced for their own sake, and they were integral parts of his films for some five years prior to the advent of Autry and Rogers. *Strawberry Roan* had its plot built around the theme of that popular Western song. Maynard had a pleasant voice and frequently accompanied himself on the fiddle. Songs in his Westerns were usually sung around the campfire episodes, introduced logically to provide moments of relaxation between melodramatic action. They remained essentially masculine affairs, quite without dance-hall singers or even a vocally inclined heroine.

The "old look" in Westerns was further sustained by Paramount in the excellent series of high-class "B" Westerns based on the novels of Zane Grey, a series started in the Twenties which was to continue until the early Forties. Although "B" in running time and budget (with occasional rare exceptions such as Gary Cooper's *Fighting Caravans,* a rather disappointing imitation of *The Covered Wagon* in sound), these films had exceptionally good production values, strong scripts, excellent cameramen, directors, and casts.

Director Henry Hathaway made some of the best early sound films in this group. After *The Lives of a Bengal Lancer* (1934–5) he was promoted from "B" films, left Westerns to return almost twenty years later with *Rawhide,* which he directed for Fox. But Hathaway's flair for fast, smoothly staged action has never again been used nearly as effectively as it had been in those early Paramount Zane Grey subjects. Many of the films in this group (*Desert Gold, The Thundering Herd, Man of the Forest, To the Last Man, Light of the Western Stars*) had been made earlier as silents. Paramount re-used whole sequences intact from the silent originals, often matching up the footage quite cleverly by re-employing many of the players from the old versions, casting them in the same roles in the remakes, and garbing them in identical costumes. Thus, some of the credit we have just given to Henry Hathaway for *The Thundering Herd* rightfully belongs to William K. Howard, who directed the original version: Howard's brilliantly staged stampede of wagons across a frozen lake was used again in the sound version and it still proved impressive and thrilling. However, Hathaway can take full credit for *To the Last Man* (1933), which had a minimum of stock footage. Its stark plot spanned many years and concerned a longstanding feud between families. The film and feud ended with only one representative of each family (Randolph Scott and Esther Ralston) remaining alive, determined to end the futility of clan warfare there and then.

Other excellent Paramount Westerns adapted from Grey's novels were *Nevada* with Buster Crabbe and *Thunder Trail,* based on Grey's *Arizona Ames* and starring Gilbert Roland. However, with the exception of the last two or three films in the series, all maintained a remarkably high standard.

The "B" Western

The qualitative difference between the independently made Westerns and the "B" pictures of the major studios was quite staggering, especially after the early days of sound. The independents (Resolute, Puritan, Spectrum, Ambassador, and others) often turned out such a primitive product that at first glance it seemed to have been made at least ten years earlier than those of contemporary major-studio Westerns. One major contributing factor was the poor quality of the camera work. Also, the original silent speed of sixteen frames per second (as opposed to twenty-four for sound speed) was used on Westerns, due both to the work of inefficient second-unit camera crews, and to a then-prevalent belief that speeded-up action lent excitement to fast action scenes. This near-hysterical pacing of the action, plus the lack of realistic sound effects (fight scenes were often played completely silent or with general "scuffing" effects ineptly dubbed in later), combined with the lack of incidental music (and especially the lack of agitatos in chase scenes) gave one the impression of viewing a speeded-up silent film without the benefit even of a theater pianist! The lack of musical scores was, in fact, the greatest drawback to these early independent Westerns, for they were often very lively little adventures which would have enjoyed more popularity with occasional background music. The most useful function performed by these very cheap Westerns was that they provided a good training ground for several stars and directors: John Garfield and Rita Hayworth made their entry into movies by this route in the Thirties; among the directors apprenticed in this way were Joseph H. Lewis, an editor on Mascot serials who developed into one of the best directors of "B" Westerns, ultimately graduating into high-bracket melodramas (*Undercover Man, Gun Crazy*) in the Forties and Fifties, and Edward Dmytryk, who made an interesting little Western, *Trail of the Hawk.*

Most of the independent Westerns of the Thirties were simple affairs, built solely around action. Films like *Gun Fire,* a Resolute Western of 1935 starring Rex Bell, and *Tangled Fortunes* with Francis X. Bushman, Jr., were almost non-stop parades of fistic encounters, chases, and riding stunts. They were made cheaply and prolifically, in groups of eight, but as always there were refreshing exceptions to this pure rule of action. A series starring Tom Tyler for newly formed Monogram Pictures in 1931 featured occasionally original stories, and superior scripting, at least in concept, even if it lacked some polished dialogue. One film in this series, *Partners of the Trail,* even went so far as to eliminate villains entirely in telling a remarkably adult story of a playboy who has come West to escape the consequences of having killed his wife's lover. He finds himself

Tom Santschi, Boris Karloff, and the grand old man of many Westerns, Lafe McKee, in The Utah Kid *(1930).*

battling with his conscience when chance throws him into friendly contact with the man who has been blamed for the crime. Even apart from the unusual plot-line, there were other distinctly original touches, including a drunken scene in which the hero scrawls his name on the adobe walls of his cottage. The explanation for the use of such themes in early sound Westerns must lie in the fact that writers and directors were able to make films for a generally freer screen in those pre-Code days. Certainly after 1934 *all* films adopted a far more conventional and less biting format, and the Western cooperated with the "reform" even more than did the gangster film and the risqué comedy.

Forgotten Westerns

The Western common today is the film that is neither an epic nor an insignificant quickly made picture, but such Westerns were comparative rarities in the Thirties. Yet a number were made, and some were unusually good, two of them quite classic of their kind. One was William Wyler's *Hell's Heroes,* the best of several versions, including one by Ford, of a sentimental Peter B. Kyne story; the other, Edward L. Cahn's *Law and Order,* made in 1932 for Universal. Cahn's film was and is sadly underrated. It is an almost forgotten film, the only sound Western perhaps, apart from King Vidor's *Billy the Kid,* to recapture successfully the primitive quality and stark realism of the early Hart films, not only in plot, but also in characterization, photography, and direction.

For *Law and Order* to refute the trend toward "streamlining," and to return wholeheartedly to the original concept was a courageous move

Andy Devine (center) and Walter Huston (right) in Law and Order *(1932).*

Yakima Canutt (closest to camera) takes a horse fall in the Battle of San Jacinto sequence from Man of Conquest (*1939*).

Warner Baxter, Bruce Cabot, and Margo in Robin Hood of Eldorado (*1936*). *This still, one of several selected for newspaper serialization, carried this caption: "In the dim light they saw Rosita, naked save for a few torn strips of clothing, lying across the bed with her head and arms hanging down on one side."*

indeed. A straight tale of four lawmen cleaning up a wide-open town, it was slowly paced and never exploited action for its own sake, but it was climaxed by one of the most savage gunfights ever put on film. Its flawless construction, photography (the camera seemed to dart in and out of the action like a participant rather than a spectator), and editing quite outclass the similar, more highly touted, but vastly inferior climactic battle in *High Noon*. Although based on a novel, *Saint Johnson*, itself based on the life of a famous lawman, most of the characters and incidents seemed to derive more from the career of Wyatt Earp. Devoid of feminine interest, save for a realistic dance-hall trollop without a heart of gold, *Law and Order* starred Walter Huston, Harry Carey, Raymond Hatton, and Russell Hopton as the law enforcers, and Ralph Ince as the leader of the "heavies."

Despite the quality of the film, its director, Edward L. Cahn, was, and is, comparatively unknown. A former editor who had worked under Paul Fejos, Cahn's directorial work on *Law and Order* was his first—and unquestionably his best. Even more than the late E. A. Dupont (who made only one *great* picture, *Variety,* but had at least several interesting near-misses), Edward Cahn was a one-film director. He soon became a specialist in economical rather than creative shooting, and spent his time shooting vapid "B" pictures.

Some of the credit for the film's unusual quality must be shared: the script was written by John Huston. It is interesting, and a little sad, to compare Huston's script with that used for Universal's remake in 1953 under the same title. Although the plot's essentials remained the same, all the strength and subtlety of the original were removed, replaced by scenes of violence or unnecessarily suggestive eroticism. (While the original film had *no* leading lady, this one had *two!*) The very touching scene in the original in which the honest lawmen were forced to hang an accidental killer (Andy Devine) became a tried-and-true lynching by the villains in the new version.

Apart from *Law and Order* and *Hell's Heroes,* the Westerns which were neither epics nor "quickies" were mainly limited to an interesting group of films put out by RKO, of which *The Last Outlaw, Powdersmoke Range,* and *The Arizonian* were the prime examples. *The Last Outlaw* concerned a

Nelson Eddy and Jeanette MacDonald in The Girl of the Golden West *(1938).*

reformed Western badman trying to go straight in the modern West and coming up against city racketeers. It was a well-made film and featured Harry Carey, Hoot Gibson, Tom Tyler, Henry B. Walthall, and Fred Scott—the latter seen as a singing cowboy when the hero takes his girl to the movies, thereby ridiculing Hollywood's idea of the West. *Powdersmoke Range,* based on one of the William Colt MacDonald books in his *Three Mesquiteers* series, was billed as "The Barnum and Bailey of Westerns" and rounded up not only most of the reigning Western stars (Hoot Gibson, Bob Steele, Harry Carey, and others) but also many of the old-timers, William Desmond among them. Such a cast rather got in the way of the action and plot, but it was an enjoyable novelty. In *The Arizonian* RKO returned to the old school with a straightforward tale of honest lawman Richard Dix cleaning up a corrupt town run by Louis Calhern.

Partial renaissance of the epic

Between *Cimarron* in 1931 and *Stagecoach* in 1939, relatively few large-scale Westerns were made, and even fewer that could justly be termed epics. MGM produced an interesting if romanticized version of the Joaquin Murietta story in *Robin Hood of Eldorado.* Warner Baxter played the famous outlaw, and William Wellman directed. Otherwise, MGM seemed to prefer their Westerns to have the flavor of operettas, as in the Nelson Eddy—Jeanette MacDonald films, *Rose Marie* and *The Girl of the Golden West,* and even in *Let Freedom Ring,* a strange historical Western played straight, but marred by the inept dramatics of Nelson Eddy in an allegedly he-man role. Warners, until the firm made *Dodge City* much later, limited their outdoor "specials" to logging melodramas of the Peter B. Kyne type. *Valley of the Giants* was a first-rate specimen of its type, lavishly staged, and full of exciting action, but *God's Country and the Woman* was not up to it. Both were in Technicolor, as was *Heart of the North,* a first-rate vehicle for Dick Foran, promoted from the ranks of "B" Western heroes. But none of these could properly be called epics; they had neither the scale nor point of view.

Perhaps the most interesting epic of the mid-Thirties and, despite its faults, the best, was Universal's *Sutter's Gold.* Initially the Soviet director S. M. Eisenstein was to direct, and British actor Francis L. Sullivan to star. The role finally went to Edward Arnold, who was perfectly cast and delivered a dynamic performance as the Swiss immigrant and dreamer who discovered gold in California and finally died poverty-stricken and crushed. There was discussion over the script in Eisenstein's proposed treatment and, after an interim period in which Howard Hawks took over and even directed a few scenes, James Cruze was finally selected as the director. Cruze had been slipping since the last days of the silents, and made only independent features, many of which were not without interest, although none were able to restore his faded reputation. Then, an excellent little picture for Columbia, *Washington Merry-go-round* proved to be a "sleeper," and Cruze was back in favor again. He directed *Sutter's Gold* with enthusiasm, and in many ways it can be considered the final piece of a trilogy begun with *The Covered Wagon* and *The Pony Express*. It certainly had the epic sense of those two pictures—and a good deal of their silent technique, too. Cruze found it hard to devise effective transitions in his episodic story (which traveled half-way around the world and included political intrigue in its melodramatic action) and often reverted to subtitles reminiscent of the silent era to cover gaps in continuity. ("Wagons rolling Westward . . . endlessly Westward" was one subtitle that would have made perfect sense in *The Covered Wagon*.)

Cruze spent a fortune making *Sutter's Gold*. There were costly jaunts to location, mob scenes, a spectacular gold rush, large-scaled battle sequences. Unfortunately, for a film without a "name" star, it cost far too much, literally wrecked the old regime at Universal, and was one of the biggest losses in the company's history. Fortunately for Universal, James Whale shot *Show Boat* at the same time, also an expensive picture, but one so tremendously profitable that it enabled the company to survive and go on to other, newer things.

Sutter's Gold was in many ways a very good film, and its major sin was in losing money. It finished Cruze as a director of top products, but he did continue to turn out some quite enjoyable little "B" thrillers.

The responsibility for the survival of the epic seemed to fall squarely on the shoulders of Paramount in the Thirties. The company's Western output had fallen mainly into the "B" category since *Fighting Caravans* and *The Virginian* made in the early days of sound. After that Paramount specialized more and more in rousing outdoor adventure. In the mid-Thirties, Paramount switched the emphasis to the epic Western in four films, none of which had the virility and pace of the more expertly made Zane Grey Westerns. The quartet made up an interesting collection of different aspects of Western history. Cecil B. De Mille's *The Plainsman* was a very much romanticized account of the lives of Wild Bill Hickok (Gary Cooper), Calamity Jane (Jean Arthur), and Buffalo Bill Cody (James Ellison). Jean Arthur represented a monumental error in casting, and only the supporting actors (Fred Kohler, Dorothy Burgess, Porter Hall, George Hayes) were consistently convincing. The climactic

Sutter's Californians repulse the Mexican attackers in a scene from Sutter's Gold (*1936*).

Indian battle, too long delayed, was exciting but marred by the excessive use of back projection.

Frank Lloyd's *Wells Fargo* was a grandiose production, but the epic theme of national progress was too often lost sight of by excessive attention to historical details and the business aspects of the Wells Fargo organization. An artificial love triangle further slowed the proceedings, which came to life only twice: in a brief attack by Indians on a stagecoach, and, more notably, in a spectacular action sequence showing a troop of Confederate rebels attacking a wagon convoy.

King Vidor's *The Texas Rangers* was livelier, making better use of the camera's potential. It, too, was disappointing since it represented little more than a series of incidents, most of them drawn from Texas Rangers records. It was at least superficially authentic. The action highlights, particularly an Indian attack, were directed by Vidor with all the sweep and flair for spectacle so much in evidence in his earlier films, *The Big Parade* and *Billy the Kid*. But it was a spotty film, marred by conventional characterization and incredibly banal dialogue. Its action highlights, a stirring musical score, and especially fine camera work all made it a Western that was worth studying if not a great one. With all its defects, however, it was a far better film than Paramount's anemic Technicolor remake, *The Streets of Laredo*, which omitted the spectacular Indian fighting scenes, replacing them with a sadistically brutal horsewhipping scene. *The Texans,* made in 1938, was the least impressive of Paramount's large Westerns of the Thirties, but one of the most enjoyable. With no particular historical background it was content to travel the well-worn trails of *The Covered Wagon.* Conventional enough, it had some exciting action sequences and likable performances from Randolph Scott and Joan Bennett. Above all, its production was thoroughly competent.

Hopalong Cassidy

The Plainsman, Wells Fargo, The Texas Rangers, and *The Texans* were all made by Paramount between 1935 and 1938. Although the company did not realize it then, they were making a far greater contribution to the Western film with a much less ambitious project—the *Hopalong Cassidy* series, representing the work of veteran producer Harry Sherman. They went on to become the most successful "B" Westerns ever made, excluding possibly the Autry musical Westerns. Initially Paramount had no thought of making a series of Cassidy films, nor were these adaptations of Clarence E. Mulford's old-school stories even thought of as traditional Westerns. Although William Boyd, a former De Mille star of the silent era, was finally cast, he was no youngster, nor did the first film in the series, *Hopalong Cassidy,* suggest that he was. The dialogue explained that he was getting along in years and no longer a very active man; and the bulk of the physical action was handled by his younger "sidekick," Johnny Nelson, very ably played by James Ellison. This shunting of action away from Boyd served two purposes: first it remained faithful to the character of Cassidy as created by Mulford; and secondly it allowed Boyd to remain principally an actor.

Although he had made one or two Westerns before, such as the interesting minor "A" production of *The Painted Desert,* the film which had brought forth Clark Gable as a new villain of note, Boyd was still ill at ease on a horse. All his hard-riding scenes were done in extreme long shot and doubled by Cliff Lyons. However, within a year he had learned to ride well, and *The Bar 20 Rides Again* was the first film in the series to feature close-ups of Boyd riding. Fisticuffs were usually played down until quite late in the scenes and many of the films, particularly *Cassidy of Bar 20,* seemed remarkably light on *all* kinds of action except gun-slinging.

The initial Cassidy Westerns (*Hopalong Cassidy, The Eagle's Brood, Heart of the West, Three on a Trail, Call of the Prairie,* and *The Bar 20 Rides Again*) were all based to a large degree on Mulford's original books and, therefore, in terms of plot content they were quite superior to most of the contemporary "B" Westerns.

They were constructed in an identical manner, often re-using the same footage: a deliberately slow "build-up" to a climax of astonishing speed and vigor. After five or six reels of minor skirmishing, the last reel had a "hell-bent-for-leather" posse either speeding to rescue Boyd or being led by him after the outlaws. These climaxes were constructed with sweeping trucking shots, slick intercutting of running inserts with long panoramic scenes, and really creative, tension-building editing. The excitement in these sequences was increased by the sudden and appropriate introduction of background music for the first and only time in the film. The startling addition of a rousing agitato (the one most used was "Dance of the Furies" from Gluck's "Don Juan") literally had the younger element jumping up and down in their seats, while adults responded to this dramatic device, too! The construction and this use of background music was original in the Hopalong Cassidy Westerns, and it was imitated to excellent effect by two producers in particular—Scott R. Dunlap in such first-rate Jack Randall Westerns as *Riders of the Dawn* (a perfect example of the influence of one "B" Western on another) and by Sol Lesser in his Principal Westerns for Fox release, films like the very good Smith Ballew subject, *Western Gold*.

Nearly seventy Hopalong Cassidy Westerns were made in all, some of them even attaining a limited top-feature status with running times sometimes as high as eighty-eight minutes. Despite occasional unusual plot ingredients (mainly when the scripts were based on Mulford originals) the plots were, for the most part, strictly formula affairs. There was never any "adult" material that might prove distasteful to youngsters, nor was there much of an attempt at an accurate representation of the old West.

William Boyd as Hopalong Cassidy in Range War (*1939*).

William Boyd and villain Clark Gable (opposite) in the climactic showdown of The Painted Desert *(1930).*

If Boyd followed convention, he did not follow cliché. Boyd's Cassidy was soft-spoken and gentlemanly, not given to brash treatment of the ladies or to exhibitionistic displays of riding and stunting. A mild romance between Cassidy and an old sweetheart was revived on infrequent occasion, and it never was allowed to come to fruition. Romance in the Cassidy Westerns was largely limited to gentle comedy at the expense of Cassidy's perennially love-sick young companion, James Ellison in the earlier films, Russell Hayden later on. There was hardly ever any sentimental "small-boy appeal," and little comedy except that which arose naturally from the story. Towards the end of the series, in the Forties, producer Harry Sherman switched his distribution from Paramount to United Artists, and the first group of Westerns under the new regime were of a generally much higher standard: one thinks of *Hoppy Serves a Writ* in particular as being among the best Westerns Boyd had made. However, shortly thereafter Sherman terminated his interest in the series, and Boyd took over as producer-star. Unfortunately, he failed to sustain Sherman's high standards. His new films were almost totally devoid of action, lacked good scripts, and were produced on very limited budgets. Boyd himself was nearly bankrupt when he finally ceased production on these inferior Westerns. His return to prominence on television is discussed elsewhere.

The heroine

One of the few real changes in the format of the Western in the Thirties was in the character of the heroine. Formerly it had been the tradition for the heroine to be beautiful but helpless, a tradition thoroughly established by William S. Hart, whose heroines were usually as passive, though not as comically absurd, as those of Buster Keaton. Previously her main function had been to provide motivation: it was her cattle, or her ranch, that was being stolen by the villain. If she had a father or a brother to protect her, they were usually eliminated early in the proceedings. One of the strangest clichés of all was the fact that the heroine never had a mother! Occasionally some casual reference would be made, the father perhaps saying, "If your mother were alive . . . ." but even that was rare, and the heroine usually appeared to be the offspring of but a single parent! The hero's romantic interest in the girl was rarely emphasized, despite the inevitable last reel "clinch." Sex was present in the Western only when the villain forced his attentions on the heroine, provoking the timely appearance of the hero and the inevitable fight. And even then, the heavy was usually trying to win the girl only for her property. Naturally there are exceptions to these generalizations, but for the most part the heroine *did* fill this passive and stodgy role.

In the Thirties, however, there was a change. The heroine became more self-reliant, more athletic, and even sexier. While it took the Fifties to introduce the nude bathing scene as a cliché, it was not unknown in the Thirties. Esther Ralston's diverting, if unnecessary, swim in the nude in *To the Last Man* was followed by a surprising climax in which she engaged the villain in an all-out fight to save the hero!

The situation of the heroine about to be reluctantly married off to a lecherous villain was, of course, not unknown, in silent Westerns either, but sound provided new opportunities for exploiting this line, especially in Paramount's Zane Grey films in which the badman in question was invariably Noah Beery. His fruity delivery of his lines, expressing uncontrolled lust, added a vigor to such films as *The Thundering Herd* and *Man of the Forest*.

Some Westerns even went so far as to have a cowgirl heroine (the first since Ruth Mix) and to give her billing and prominence in the plot over the male lead. Such was the case in *The Singing Cowgirl* which starred Dorothy Page. While romance remained a minor element in the "B" Western, its importance was rising. The standard "city" triangles—two men in love with one girl or two girls after one man—began to invade even the "B" Westerns, ranging from those like *Gun Fire,* made on the cheap at Resolute, to the far more intelligent Sol Lesser production of *When a Man's a Man*.

Musical Westerns further increased the heroine's participation and made her more of an active partner than a passive leading lady. While this trend became far more emphasized in the Forties and Fifties, its beginnings can be noted in many of the early Gene Autry and Roy Rogers Westerns; in fact, Roy Rogers and Mary Hart (later known as Lynne Roberts) were billed as "The Sweethearts of the West." The Western heroine took her cue from the times, too, in the matter of dress. Figure-fitting, semi-transparent blouses and very tight trousers began to replace crinolines increasingly.

It was no mere coincidence that Westerns like *When a Man Rides Alone* seemed to go out of their way to show their heroines in light, tight clothing, mounting their horses with the camera close by.

Gene Autry and Roy Rogers

The musical Western cycle got under way in 1935 at Republic. Formerly known as Mascot, the company had previously concentrated on cheap action pictures and serials. In the last months before Mascot reorganized, Nat Levine, the firm's head, discovered Gene Autry, a former telegraph

Roy Rogers and Trigger.

operator and a singer on radio. Autry and his friend Smiley Burnette, a rotund low comic and hillbilly singer, were cast initially in two Ken Maynard vehicles. They had bit parts in the serial *Mystery Mountain*, but in what amounted to guest star roles they sang three numbers in succession in a Maynard feature, *In Old Santa Fe*. This film, considered a "special" for Mascot and directed by David Howard, was an unusually good Western, in many ways a sort of blueprint for the pattern that Autry himself was later to follow. Set on a dude ranch, its villainy combined modern racketeering with such traditional Western elements as stagecoach robbing. There was a pronounced musical element, and even Ken Maynard sang several numbers; Autry and Burnette attracted at-

A poster of the late Thirties. The emphasis on action lessens, and appeal is based mainly on the star's name. Added credits promise the customers musical and comedy content as well.

The musical Western at its most lunatic—show-girls, politics, and the West incongruously interwoven in Colorado Sunset *(1939).*

tention and were promptly starred in a serial, *Phantom Empire,* a ludicrous affair for the most part, mixing traditional Western material with a science-fiction story about an underground kingdom! Autry was presented as a radio star, and part of the "suspense" evolved from his escaping from various predicaments in time to meet his radio deadlines. *Phantom Empire* had the usual Mascot fast pacing and frenzied action and the film was popular. Autry played "himself" and thereafter, with the exception of *Shooting High* at Fox, was always cast as "Gene Autry." This was something that none of the other Western stars had ever done, but after Autry's innovation the practice spread and at various times in their career Roy Rogers, Bill Elliott, Johnny Mack Brown, Whip Wilson, Allen Lane, Sunset Carson, Ray Corrigan, Jimmy Wakely all used their own names in their movie adventures.

Phantom Empire established Autry as a completely new brand of Western hero, and, billed as "The Singing Cowboy" he was thrust into a series of musical Westerns, while Smiley Burnette went along to provide comic relief. Autry's films achieved tremendous popularity and put Republic on the map. The earlier ones, reportedly made for as little as fifteen thousand dollars, soon turned him into more than just another Western star. He was often listed as one of the ten top money-making stars alongside such names as Clark Gable and Bette Davis, and

at one time he even appeared in fourth place! Of course, Autry made perhaps eight films a year while Gable and Davis rarely made more than two or three. Although Autry's place in Western history is an important one, it is difficult to regard him as a serious Western star: he was a popular singer who had something new to offer to Westerns at a time when they were slipping back into the doldrums. A weak and colorless actor, and only a passable action performer, he could ride well, however, and with the help of Republic's overworked stuntmen doubling for him, he won an enormous following almost overnight.

Republic always made the best fast-moving Westerns. Their photography was always first-rate, the stunting the best in the field, and the musical scores, in terms of *incidental* music, not songs, exceptionally good. The scores of William Lava were particularly vigorous, as were those of Cy Feuer, later a prominent Broadway impresario, who composed in the Lava manner. This production knowledge brought unusual quality to the early Autry films. Pictures like *Tumbling Tumbleweeds* and *Red River Valley* combined excellently staged action with really strong and above-average plots, and a sensible proportion of comic foolery and songs. *The Yodellin' Kid from Pine Ridge* was another enjoyable film in this group, although it was an off-beat Western that actually had a Southern locale set in the turpentine forests of Florida.

In films like *Boots and Saddles* (1937), the musical and comic content was increased, however, to a degree where it almost completely dominated the proceedings. The film had a lively chase and several stunts midway through the picture, and a large-scale overland race for its climax, but otherwise it moved slowly, and the villainy was merely sandwiched in between songs and overlong comic routines. As Autry's popularity grew, his budgets were raised, and the musical and other non-Western ingredients became increasingly elaborate. The presentation of traditional Western action in modern, overly "streamlined" Western surroundings, together with an up-to-date chorus line, made the films ludicrous, little more than parodies of the orthodox Western.

Republic then developed a second singing cowboy in Roy Rogers. Publicity proudly sold him as a sensational discovery who had made his first film appearance for Republic with the starring role in *Under Western Stars*. Actually, Rogers (whose real name was Leonard Slye and who hailed from Duck Run, Ohio) had followed Autry's route to stardom by appearing in bit roles. Under the name of Dick Weston he had been one of the singing troupe, "The Sons of the Pioneers," and he had also been seen in Charles Starrett Westerns at Columbia and—embarrassingly—with Autry himself in several films. Ironically, in *The Old Corral* he had even had a fist fight with Autry who then forced him to sing a song at the point of a gun! For a while Autry resented Republic's "build-up" of Rogers, even though Autry remained their number one star of Westerns. He quarreled with the studio and left the screen for a time, finally returning with the promise of better vehicles. Although the first film under the new deal, *Gold Mine in the Sky,* was a routine Western, better ones followed.

While Autry was "in the saddle" Republic generally gave Rogers and his films less play. His pictures, while maintaining a high standard in the musical Western field, were more cheaply produced and never given the commercial exploitation Autry's films received. When a hit Western song was purchased by Republic, it was always Autry who was starred in the Western "special" built around it, the classic example of this being the enormously successful *South of the Border.* Another factor working against Rogers was his youthful appearance and slim build; he appeared no match for the burly villains that he was pitted against. Apparently his writers thought so, too, and often seemed to shun action in his pictures. Fisticuffs were rare in Rogers' Westerns until the Forties. Then, when the musical Western had lost its novelty and the tough thriller was in vogue, Rogers' Westerns almost went overboard in the brutality of their fights, fights in which much Trucolor blood was shed. Nevertheless, Rogers' films were not, until the early Forties at least, the virtual parodies of authentic Westerns that Autry's had become. Autry's little troupe of hillbilly performers (The Cass County Boys and others of

Indian athlete Jim Thorpe in one of his many minor movie roles. With Tex Ritter (left) and Slim Andrews in Arizona Frontier *(1938).*

their ilk) continued to grow in size and activity, and live action continued to be of only secondary importance.

Autry actually was just a shrewd businessman who had no great interest in or respect for the Western as such. He realized that his value as a show business personality (taking in also radio, rodeos, and ultimately television and his own production companies) depended on his almost comic-opera approach to the Western. He also had the happy knack of being able to hide his shrewdness behind the amiable façade of the hill-billy singer; he was both a popular idol of the people, in the manner, if nothing else, of Will Rogers, and at the same time a highly successful businessman. Roy Rogers, on the other hand, had none of Autry's business acumen and was to suffer for it in future years when the two Western stars, in business on their own, were to be in direct competition with each other.

Autry's imitators

Naturally, the immediate success of Republic's musical Westerns prompted copies from other studios. Usually imitations cannot help but be inferior to the original, but in this case there was an exception to the rule. Warner's singing cowboy hero, Dick Foran, was not only vastly superior to Autry as a singer, but he was a much better actor at dramatics and action as well, and his Westerns had exceptionally high production values. They were slick, glossy productions in which the action content remained dominant, while songs remained songs and never became production numbers. Films like *Cherokee Strip, Land Beyond the Law, Moonlight on the Prairie,* and *Devil's Saddle Legion* (some of them remakes of silent Maynard Westerns or early John Wayne "talkies") were exceptionally fine low-budget Westerns, well written and refreshingly free from low comedy. One of the perennial villains and supporting players in the series was Gordon Elliott, a Warner contract player since 1926, who was apparently getting nowhere. For an actor who had specialized in drawing-room material, he made a surprisingly convincing Westerner. Shortly after these Foran films at Warners he branched out as a Western star in his own right at Columbia, developing a unique and effectively austere style.

Autry, Rogers, and Foran apart, the new musical Western cycle produced some interesting new heroes in Tex Ritter, Jack Randall, and Bob Baker; lesser ones in Fred Scott, John King, and Smith Ballew; and—much later, well into the Forties—a vastly inferior crop in the ineffectual Jimmy Wakely (an obvious Autry imitator), Monte Hale, and perhaps the most inept Western hero of them all, Eddie Dean. All of these actors imitated Autry's formula in the musical content of their films, but not in the musical treatment. These movies were still essentially Westerns in which songs were only incidental.

Tex Ritter was discovered and exploited by an imaginative independent producer-director, Edward Finney. An authentic Westerner with a broad Texas drawl, Ritter specialized in traditional folk songs rather than in the modern "Western" ditties of Autry, and was himself a writer of Western songs. His films were vigorous, often staged on a surprisingly large scale, but their quality varied. Some were built almost entirely around stock footage, the interpolation of complete Indian attack sequences from Thomas Ince's *The Deserter* (1915) into *Roll Wagons Roll* (1937), for example, only too apparent, even to the untrained eye. Nevertheless, the Ritter-Finney Westerns maintained a generally high standard.

Westbound Stage, *Down the Wyoming Trail* (with a fine reindeer stampede sequence), and *Rolling Westward* were among the best of a Monogram series. Their only persistently negative factors were appallingly crude and repetitious musical scores by Frank Sanucci. Jack Randall, a former bit player, unfortunately arrived on the scene a little too late. He had a fine voice, superior to those of most of his rivals, but the market was flooded with musical Westerns, and when Monogram presented Randall as one more singing cowboy, there were audible protests from exhibitor groups as a result, songs were deleted from completed Randall Westerns, and the bulk of the series made as normal action Westerns. This was a pity, for Randall could out-sing most of the others, and had he been introduced a year earlier he might well have become one of the top singing cowboys. Randall was also a first-rate action star, performing many of his own stunts without a double; in *Overland Mail*, for example, he leaped from a galloping horse to a speeding stagecoach with the camera recording the whole action in close-up. The initial films in the Randall series were produced by veteran Scott R. Dunlap, who had been associated with Griffith in his early days, and had directed many of the best silent Buck Jones Westerns for Fox. Dunlap put real production value into his Westerns in terms of good scripts, good directors, top cameramen, and magnificent locations. Best of them all was *Riders of the Dawn*, a strong story which featured one of the most flawlessly constructed, staged, and photographed concluding reels ever put on film: a chase across saltflats that compares more than favorably with Ford's chase in *Stagecoach*. The unusual and dramatic placement of the camera and the perfect employment of running inserts helped to make this a memorable episode, and one of the best of its kind. Randall's career was sadly cut short: while working on a serial at Universal, he was thrown from his horse and killed.

Another singing cowboy who missed was Bob Baker. A pleasant personality, he was put into a series of musical Westerns by Universal but unfortunately, they were pedestrian, extremely low on action content. Although they had average production values and good directors (Joseph H. Lewis made some of the better ones), their lack of action prevented their popularity with juvenile audiences. Baker made a good number of solo starring Westerns before he was switched to a co-starring series with Johnny Mack Brown. These, for a change, had plenty of action, but Baker, although officially co-starred, actually did little more than sing a song or two and back up Brown in the action. He made only six Westerns with Brown before dropping out of the series, and his activity thereafter was very limited—he never returned to starring roles in musical Westerns.

Fred Scott was another singing cowboy who lasted for only a few years. His Westerns were made for an independent company, Spectrum, and although cheaply made, they were often enjoyable. Scott was billed as "The Silvery Voiced Baritone," and while his pictures and his voice were good, his personality and acting had little to speak for them. *Ranger's Roundup* was probably his best film.

Jack Randall (center) and villain Ed Coxen (right) in one of the best of the "B" Westerns of the Thirties, Riders of the Dawn *(1938).*

The singing cowboy myth: well-groomed, colorfully garbed cowboys sing on the range, in the sheriff's office, on the ranch, at every opportunity. From Courage of the West *(1937); in the center are Bob Baker, Glen Strange, and Lois January.*

Other stars

In the very early Thirties Warners made a fine series of John Wayne Westerns, many of them recalling the adventurous spirit of the silent Fred Thomson films. *Haunted Gold*, for example, had an exceptionally good sequence, the hero escaping by climbing up a crumbling mine shaft, a sequence that featured elaborate set construction and many bizarre and effective camera angles. Another sequence in the film had Wayne and the villain battling it out in a large ore bucket, suspended over a yawning chasm. The bottom falls out and the villain tumbles to his death; Wayne is left dangling on a rope to be saved only by the intervention of his horse.

Never a maker of great Westerns, Columbia was one of the most consistently reliable producers of competent and fast-moving assembly-line Westerns. Their really early sound Westerns with Buck Jones and Tim McCoy deserve to be rated above the "assembly line" category. More-

Randy Rides Alone (1934), with John Wayne and Alberta Vaughan.

over, in the mid-Thirties Columbia introduced some new Western stars, of whom Charles Starrett was the best and also the longest to survive. The early Starrett films, particularly *Two Gun Law*, were interesting and enjoyable. But later plots tended to be too standardized, and this was also true of the casts. A Columbia "stock company" of Western players (Dick Curtis, Ernie Adams, Edward Le Saint, Jack Rockwell) supported

Starrett and made the films look too much alike. Two of the early Starrett films that stand out were *The Cowboy Star,* in which he played a dude Western star who cleaned up a racketeering gang, and *On Secret Patrol,* one of several Westerns filmed in Canada.

Columbia also starred Jack Luden, a generally uninteresting Western star, and Bob Allen in short-lived groups of pictures. Allen was essentially a straight actor (he had appeared in *Crime and Punishment* and other films at Columbia) and was rather colorless, but his films, especially *Ranger Courage* and *When Rangers Step In,* were on the whole very good. In the mid-Thirties, too, Columbia put Ken Maynard into a group of good Westerns, such as *Lawless Riders, Avenging Waters,* and *Heroes of the Range.*

The series that followed marked a return of Buck Jones to Columbia in Westerns that varied in quality to an amazing degree: *Overland Express* was a quality film of Pony Express days, but *Law of the Texan* and *California Frontier* were cheaply made, ineptly directed, and certainly among his weakest films. An attempt was made to bring Jones "up-to-date" (the formula had worked quite well in his previous Columbia series) by putting him into contemporary settings. In *Heading East* he played a Western rancher who came to the big city to smash a gang of racketeers that was victimizing lettuce-growers (!), and in *Hollywood Roundup* he played a double for a singularly unpleasant Western star played by Grant Withers.

Columbia's last Western star discovery of the Thirties was Gordon Elliott, a former bit player who zoomed to unexpected stardom as the hero of a serial, *The Great Adventures of Wild Bill Hickok.* He went on to make two more serials and a long-running series of "B" Westerns. The first two of these, *Frontiers of '49* and *In Early Arizona* (suggested very loosely by the Wyatt Earp story) were unusually elaborate, carefully plotted, full of prime action. But after this promising start, it was not long before the Elliott films declined badly and became cheap, unexciting assembly-line products. Columbia also made a few interesting films out of series. Into this category fell *Heroes of the Alamo,* a competent historical Western with Lane Chandler, and the sadly neglected *The End of the Trail.* This fast-paced and dramatic Western, an adaptation of a Zane Grey novel, starred Jack Holt and provided an unexpectedly moving climax. The hero (Holt) has killed the villain (C. Henry Gordon), who had cold-bloodedly killed a child. Sentenced to death, Holt walks alone to the gallows leaving his heart-broken best friend, the sheriff (Guinn Williams), and his fiancée sitting alone in his former cell playing a little tune on a record player.

George O'Brien.

George O'Brien was Fox's top Western star in the Thirties, and his films were excellent examples of expertly made, yet economical, grade "B" pictures. Exceptionally good was *Fair Warning* (1931), directed by Alfred Werker, with George Brent among the supporting players. Full of action and stunts and well played by O'Brien with his usual sense of lively fun, it was a fine film of its class. Later Fox stopped making their own Western series, instead releasing those made independently by Sol Lesser. These were split into two groups, one with Smith Ballew and the other with George O'Brien. The Smith Ballew films were musical Westerns. Ballew was a likable but rather thin and decidedly non-muscular Western star; he had a pleasant voice and could handle action well enough, but he failed to establish himself with the public. *Rawhide* (which for novelty had Lou Gehrig, the baseball player, appearing as himself in a prominent supporting role) was his best film. The George O'Brien group, while far below the standard of O'Brien's previous Fox series, contained nevertheless some interesting films. Best of all was *When a Man's a Man,* based on a tale by Harold Bell Wright; an unusually intelligent Western, its strong story values more than compensated for its relatively light action content. Character development was especially strong, for it was one of the few minor Westerns to present a rejected suitor (Paul Kelly) in a sympathetic light. Generally speaking, the Lesser O'Brien series put too much stress on comic and romantic digressions, and not enough on action; some of the films, *Dude Ranger,* in particular, seemed to go out of their way to *avoid* action. O'Brien, however, was fine in comic situations, and his cheeky sense of fun injected life into what would otherwise have been very routine Westerns.

Monogram remained consistently active in the Western field during the Thirties, first with cheap but creditable little "B" Westerns with Tom Tyler, Bob Steele, Bill Cody, Rex Bell, and John Wayne; and later with Tom Keene, Jack Randall, Tex Ritter, and Tim McCoy. After a temporary hiatus following the changeover from FBO and the brief abandonment of "B" Westerns, RKO re-entered the field in the early Thirties with some high-caliber Tom Keene vehicles (*Freighters of Destiny* was one of the best) and a few interesting Westerns with Creighton Chaney (Lon Chaney, Jr.). George O'Brien made a series of independent Westerns, similar to those for Fox, for RKO release. These also tended to overemphasize comedy, films like *Hollywood Cowboy,* although one "special" in the group, *Daniel Boone,* was well made on a surprisingly large scale, adopting a sensible proportion of comedy to action. The O'Brien Westerns took a distinct upswing when RKO began producing them within their own organization. They were well above average with their strong plots and some splendid action sequences. O'Brien rarely used a double of any kind; if films like *Trouble in Sundown* and *Border G-Man* were a trifle slow in terms of action, then *Racketeers of the Range, Prairie Law,* and *Lawless Valley* more than made up for the deficiencies. The latter is probably the best Western O'Brien made, if one excludes his prime Fox period, with an intelligent script, first-rate action, and a fine cast headed by Walter Miller and the two Kohlers, Fred, Sr., and Fred, Jr. O'Brien's Westerns were more popular with adults than most "B"'s, not only because he could act, or because he was remembered with affection from the Twenties, but also because his light touch with humor never failed to please.

The leading maker of Westerns in the sound era was Republic, whose schedules in the Thirties were a trifle complicated. Take, for example, the independent Westerns of A. W. Haeckle starring Bob Steele and Johnny Mack Brown, some of which were made directly for Republic and some for his own company, Supreme, which for a time released through Republic. The Haeckle Westerns were routine and undistinguished as to plot and direction, but also fast paced and full of action. The Steele films were given the greater production values, and *Cavalry* stands out as being the best. The Brown films were strictly assembly-line products, but Brown himself was one of the best of the Western stars, a fine athlete and a pleasing performer (he had of course been a "top-liner" at MGM in the late Twenties and early Thirties, playing opposite Garbo, Crawford, Mary Pickford, and other great female stars).

Republic for a time was merged with Monogram, but the association was brief. When he left Monogram, John Wayne switched to Republic for a good series of historical Westerns (*Winds in the Wastelands* and *The Lawless Nineties* among them), many of which featured Ann Rutherford as the heroine, and which had Yakima Canutt involved predominantly in the action. The Wayne films were made on a fairly large scale, and they provided much stock footage for later Westerns. Republic never made a *really bad* Western in this period, and even the weakest had elements to recommend it.

Apart from this series and the Autry and Rogers musical Westerns, Republic also produced one of the best Western series any studio has ever made—the "Three Mesquiteers" group. Dedicated to action first, last, and always, but with pleasant comic moments provided by Max Terhune, a ventriloquist, they carefully avoided the "streamlined" plots and muscial elements of the Autry and Rogers films. Based very loosely on the stories of William Colt MacDonald (and after a while, only on his *characters*) the films strangely contradicted each other with regard to

A poster of the early Thirties in which the emphasis is on theme. The approach is simple and direct. There are no catchlines, and the appeal rests only on the type of film and the star's name.

the periods in which they were set. The first in the series, *The Three Mesquiteers,* was set in the period right after World War I. *Pals of the Saddle* (1938) dealt with contemporary America, and the violation of the Neutrality Act by foreign spies. *Covered Wagon Days* dealt, of course, with a much earlier period, while others in the series were again up-to-date, concerning themselves with racketeering and counterfeiting (*Come on Cowboys*); the crooked exploitation of a state orphanage (*Heroes of the Saddle*); gambling syndicates that fix horse races (*Riders of the Black Hills*); and escaped Nazi spies (*Valley of Hunted Men*).

The films were consistent, however, in delivering first-class Western action. The photography was sharp and clean, the musical scores effectively animated, and the action fast and furious. *Heart of the Rockies, Outlaws of Sonora,* and *Range Defenders* can be considered the best of this very fine series. Ray Corrigan, Bob Livingston, and Syd Saylor played the leads in the first film, but Saylor dropped out immediately and Max Terhune took over. John Wayne assumed Livingston's role a few years later. Other stars who were involved as the Mesquiteers at one time or another were Bob Steele, Tom Tyler, Rufe Davis, Jimmy Dodd, Raymond Hatton, and Duncan Renaldo. Leading ladies involved in their escapades included Louise Brooks (the lovely star of *Pandora's Box* and *Diary of a Lost Girl* in what was to be her last American film, *Overland Stage Raiders*), Carole Landis, Rita (Hayworth) Cansino, and Jennifer Jones—the latter appearing under her real name, Phyllis Isley, several years before *The Song of Bernadette*.

Each independent company had its own series of cheap Westerns, and some companies, like Resolute, made *only* Westerns. Particularly good were the Westerns of Ambassador Pictures, normally directed by Sam Newfield, cheaply produced, with a maximum of outdoor work and a minimum of interiors, but for the most part very competent and full of fast action. They starred Kermit Maynard, the slightly older brother of Ken, and a brilliant trick rider. He had started out in silent Westerns as Tex Maynard, but never quite achieved real stardom. He was a much better actor than Ken, however, and when "talkies" came in he became more active, first as a stuntman and bit player (as in Mascot's serial, *Phantom of the West*), and later as an established star. Kermit's popularity never approached that of Ken, probably because he never graduated from the "independent" market, but he was a likable player and did extremely well in his limited sphere. The riding sequences and chases in his films were always extremely well photographed, and often gave his little action Westerns, such as *The Red Blood of Courage, Whistling Bullets,* and *Galloping Dynamite,* significant production value.

Among the many other independent companies operating were Spectrum, Tiffany (in the very early Thirties they made some unusually good Ken Maynard films: *Texas Gunfighter, Whistling Dan, Branded Men*), Puritan (producers of one good Tim McCoy, *Bulldog Courage,* and many amazingly slow and generally inferior ones), and First Division (for whom Hoot Gibson appeared in some interesting, if rather crude, Westerns).

The number of Western stars who appeared in both major studio (including for our purposes, Republic and Monogram) products and in those of the independents was relatively few. Ken Maynard and Tim McCoy were the biggest stars to follow this course, each appearing in any number of series for producers of marked difference in stature, ranging from Universal and Columbia to Sam Katzman's Victory Pictures. The bulk of the lesser Western stars stayed firmly within the boundaries of the independent market, the greatest number of them, like Bob Custer, Edmund Cobb, Wally Wales, Reb Russell, Bill Cody, and Rex Lease, never achieving any major status. Basically, most of these players were just good-looking athletes who were not good enough *actors* to get by in the sound era. It was not merely a question of voice; sometimes it was even a matter of literacy! Jack Hoxie, a very popular Universal silent Western star, is said to have been unable to read his scripts; he projected as rather an oafish cowboy in sound films, and thus he, too, was limited to the lowest grade Western outfits. As the *Motion Picture Herald* remarked in reviewing a typical independent Western of 1931, *Westward Bound:* ". . . the actors appearing in this film may have been sufficiently competent in the days now gone, of the silent, gun brandishing cowboy pictures, but they are hardly capable in the era of talking films. The lines are spoken for the most part with an utter lack of all the rules of elocution."

With the renewed popularity of the "B" Western following in the wake of the musical Westerns, the late Thirties saw the horse opera at its all-time peak in terms of quantity production. The epic Western had made a tentative return in 1936, and had vanished almost immediately, but in 1939 (and in the first two years of the Forties) more Western stars than at any other period in movie history were all working simultaneously. No less than thirty Western stars, including old-timers like Buck Jones, Ken Maynard, and Tim McCoy, were grinding out groups of eight Westerns a year each, making an approximate total of 240 "B" Westerns in a given year. This situation was to continue for a few years before a decline began. The re-emergence of the epic in 1939 with *Stagecoach* and *Union Pacific,* and the steadily increasing production costs in the Forties were to contribute greatly to this decline, but it was after all a quantitative decline from a rather staggering high.

The Western serial:

its birth and
demise

Serials were, comparatively speaking, late in reaching the screen, coinciding with the arrival of the feature film of five reels or more, and came into being primarily as novelty attractions. In 1913, the Edison company's "What Happened to Mary?" series was put into production to tie in with a newspaper serial of the same name. Its principal importance was in getting the serial film started, although it was not essentially a serial in construction, but rather a series, a group of shorts featuring the same character and with a slight connecting theme. The adventures were usually melodramatic, often involved physical action, and always resolved themselves within the episode.

The Hazards of Helen, made in 1914, although a railroad series, had, however, definite elements of the Western serial in its construction and action ingredients. *The Perils of Pauline,* also begun in 1914, has come to be regarded as the prototype of silent serials but it was actually still a series film in that episodes did not end on notes of suspense, and in that there was really no cohesive story line. Parts of it took place in the West, making it the first serial to contain western material. Perhaps because of its title and star (it marked the serial debut of Pearl White) *The Perils of Pauline* has acquired an undeserved reputation as the greatest of silent serials. Although important as a milestone, and vastly entertaining today, it is a surprisingly crude serial, with abysmally poor writing, barely adequate photography,

and, occasionally effective moments of cross-cutting excepted, very primitive editing.

All told, in both silent and sound eras, slightly more than four hundred serials were made. Most popular in the silent era were what we can somewhat ambiguously term "adventure" serials. These action thrillers do not fit into any other set classification and include such items as *Scotty of the Scouts, The Fortieth Door,* and any number of fire-fighting and circus stories—two themes that disappeared from serials completely after

Carol Wayne and Monte Blue in the Columbia serial, The Great Adventures of Wild Bill Hickok (*1938*).

the first few years of sound. In second place, with sixty titles, came the Western. (In the sound era, the category increased to eighty titles over a somewhat longer period of time.) The Western can therefore be considered the genre that was given priority in serials, since the "adventure" groups is really a collection of groups. And the total of sixty titles would actually be increased considerably if one also included the borderline cases such as *The Tiger's Trail* and *The Perils of Pauline* which had pronounced, if not exclusive, Western ingredients.

Despite the enormous success of *The Perils of Pauline,* it wasn't until nearly two years later, in 1916, that the first completely Western serial was made. This was *Liberty,* a twenty-episode film made by Universal. Directed by Jacques Jaccard and Henry MacRae, it starred Jack Holt, Eddie Polo, Marie Walcamp, and Roy Stewart. MacRae was a better production supervisor than he was a director, although prolific in both capacities. His personally directed serials usually had less inventiveness and polish than those of George B. Seitz, W. S. Van Dyke, and Spencer Gordon Bennet, the three best serial directors of the silent period.

By 1920, the Western serial was firmly established in both major and independent studios, and steadily growing in popularity. Among the most notable of that year were *North of the Rockies,* the first serial directed by George Marshall, and Universal's eighteen-episode *The Moon Riders,* marking Art Acord's serial debut. The leader in 1921 was *Winners of the West,* the first of the "historical" Western serials, and made by Universal who maintained their supremacy in that particular type of Western serial right through the sound period. By 1924, the annual total of Western serials was up to nine, and from then on to the end of the silent period, there was little fluctuation in the number made, or in the stars and directors involved. (William Desmond, Walter Miller, William Duncan, and Art Acord were the principal stars; Ray Taylor, W. S. Van Dyke, Spencer Bennet, George Marshall, and Reeves Eason the leading directors.)

Universal and Pathe, the foremost producers of serials, were joined in 1927 by Mascot, the forerunner of Republic, with three ten-episode serials, two of which were Westerns. Mascot's *The Vanishing West* (1928) was one of the last and most interesting silent serials. Directed by Richard Thorpe (later better known for his expensive MGM swash-bucklers) it was ballyhooed extensively for its "all-star" cast headed by Jack Perrin, Leo Maloney, Yakima Canutt, William Fairbanks, and Eileen Sedgwick.

Action first and foremost was only a partial requirement of the silent serials; indeed, many of the pre-1920 serials were singularly lacking in physical action. Exciting stunting only came into its own in the mid-Twenties, particularly in the Pathe serials, which were always strong on inventive action and provided real thrills. Many of the daredevil escapes and stunts were truly imaginative and provided real thrills.

They still do, perhaps especially today, in a Cinemascopic age which has so often substituted pseudo-sophistication and so-called "adult" material for the obvious and unassuming thrills and charming adventures which so characterized the films of the Twenties.

Silent serials were also unusually strong on plot values: involved mysteries, a romantic element, and one or more "mystery" characters whose identities were not revealed until the closing reel of the last chapter, were all essential ingredients. The serials proved a valuable training ground for many top talents, too, such players as Constance Bennett, Charlie Chase, Warner Oland, Laura LaPlante, Warren William, Lionel Barrymore, and, in the sound era, Jennifer Jones, George Montgomery, and others, including, of course, writers, directors, and cameramen.

The primacy of the Western among the many types of serials is both surprising and a reconfirmation of the enormous popularity of the genre. For the serial could really bring nothing new to the Western: its patterns of action had been firmly established, unlike the mystery film, which could still expand and exploit its potential in a serial format. The Western serial had to be accepted as a Western rather than as another serial; it was in competition with large numbers of feature-length and two-reel Westerns, which was not true to the same extent with other types of serials. And yet, despite this handicap, the Western retained its supremacy throughout the serial's forty-year history.

Inevitably, when a standard Western was expanded to ten, thirteen, or fifteen episodes, it became even more standardized than usual. Railroad building or covered wagon treks were themes, of course, particularly suited to serial treatment because of the tortuous and necessarily episodic nature of the subjects.

Elements of mystery were injected into the Western serial to further exploit the protracted development. Often, when the villain was not a "mystery man" whose identity was a matter of conjecture, then the hero was. The classic example of this was Republic's *The Lone Ranger* (1938). Since there is a limited variety of physical action in the Western, the end-of-episode climaxes—and the subsequent escapes—did tend to become rather stereotyped. Falls from cliffs were popular, as was the hero caught beneath a herd of stampeding cattle or horses, or trapped in a burning building, or lying unconscious in a runaway wagon, or blown up in mine disaster, or about to be lynched by a maddened mob.

Republic undoubtedly made the best Western serials for the same reasons that they made the best non-serial Westerns. Republic's best included *The Painted Stallion, The Vigilantes Are Coming,* and especially *The Lone Ranger.* At a time when the serial in general seemed to be losing its appeal and box-office value, this stylishly made, actionful production restored, for a while at least, audience and exhibitor enthusiasm for the serial.

The Lone Ranger, *one of the most successful serials of the Thirties.*

Universal maintained high standards, too, with their Buck Jones and Johnny Mack Brown serials, which had plenty of fast-paced action and excellent photography. But independent serials of the Thirties tended to be rather inept, their crudity emphasized by the fact that they often chose very ambitious themes which simply could not be treated adequately on a shoestring budget. For example, *Custer's Last Stand,* a sixteen-episode serial, fell back heavily on obviously ancient stock footage, and the final "Last Stand" was little more than a mild skirmish between several dozen horsemen. To counterbalance its inadequate action, it had a top-heavy plot which seemed to incorporate most of the standard Western themes within its framework: the Indian princess hopelessly in love with the hero, the hero seeking the man who killed his brother, the cowardly Army officer who must redeem himself . . . and similar old chestnuts, here dealt with only superficially anyway. Its principal virtue was its strong cast—old-timers such as William Farnum, William Desmond, Jack Mulhall, Frank McGlynn, Josef Swickard, and others—supporting Rex Lease, Dorothy Gulliver, Reed Howes, George Cheseboro, Chief Thundercloud, Bobby Nelson, and other reliables of the independent producers of the Thirties. In the repertory company tradition of the old Biograph days, many of the players doubled up. For example, Ted Adams, heavily bearded, played Buffalo Bill in one episode, and a scoundrel in another. Generally speaking, *Custer's Last Stand* is typical of the lower grade of independent serial: slowly paced, stodgy, and of little interest apart from its cast.

Independent serials made less headway in the sound era than they had in the silent, and by 1938, serial output had dwindled to twelve per year, four each from Columbia, Republic, and Universal. In later years, the number was cut to three, and then two, from each studio, with reissues making up the difference so that each studio could offer exhibitors the required contractual package of four, sufficient to supply a theater's annual need.

The decline of Western serials paralleled the decline of "B" Westerns generally; just as *Gordon of Ghost City,* made in the early Thirties, had been strong, virile stuff of the same caliber as Universal's regular Westerns, so did later serials like *The Oregon Trail* reflect the "streamlined" but standardized action of "B" Westerns of the late Thirties. Apart from the presence of Johnny Mack Brown as the star, and the still effectively edited climaxes, *The Oregon Trail* was a pedestrian affair, loosely constructed, and excessively reliant on stock footage. So carelessly was it put together at times that the beginning of one episode did not even match the end of the preceding one. In one episode Brown was left beneath the hooves of a stampeding herd; the following episode made no reference at all to the stampede. Nevertheless, with all their shortcomings, Universal's Western serials did have fast action, good casts, and excellent scores. And, to their credit, Universal did occasionally try really hard with specific serials. In 1941 they claimed that their *Riders of Death Valley* was the most expensive serial of all time. Certainly it was made on a very large scale, with good location work, fine photography, and care taken in the musical and other departments. (Mendelssohn's "Fingal's Cave Overture" was surprisingly, but most agreeably, used as background music.) However, most of the increased budget seemed to have been used on a particularly strong cast (Dick Foran, Buck Jones,

Charles Bickford, Lon Chaney, Monte Blue, Leo Carrillo, Noah Beery, Jr., William Hall), for "corner-cutting" showed, certainly in the repetition of previously seen footage. This work showed signs of carelessness too—sometimes it was a little too obvious that Rod Cameron was doubling for Buck Jones, even in straightforward non-action scenes.

Columbia's Western serials were often produced on a surprisingly large scale, particularly *Overland with Kit Carson,* and were certainly full of action, but their scripts were always extremely weak. Plot were almost nonexistent, and the serials—which ran to fifteen episodes—were little more than series of fights, escapes, intrigues and counter-intrigues. Republic certainly maintained the highest overall standards in Western serials, doubtless because for that studio the serial had always been more of a "bread-and-butter" item than it had been for either Universal or Columbia. During the war years, Republic made a short-lived, but interesting, move to restore the serial to favor. The vigor of the renaissance made the serial's sudden decline after the war an unexpected shock. The independently produced serial had, of course, completely disappeared by now. Universal attempted to inject new life into their serials by such innovations as eliminating synopses to identify previous action, and substituting naïve dialogue explanations. When so-called added story values were introduced, they usually diminished the essential action.

The Royal Mounted Rode Again, had a particularly inept and unattractive hero in Bill Kennedy (he later switched to villain roles) and the dialogue strangely went out of its way to emphasize his lack of athletic ability. When one of the villains escapes, Kennedy is urged to pursuit, but demurs "because he has too much of a head start." His crony, an old-timer, then offers him a horse, and when Kennedy still appears reluctant, adds "It's a very gentle horse." Since this was not done for comedy, one can only assume that everyone concerned was getting a little tired of this pedestrian serial, and that uncalled-for lines and situations were slipping into it. This suspicion is further heightened by a fantastic climax in which the saloon, headquarters of the villains, is suddenly revealed to be a made-over river boat. The "saloon" then hoists anchor and steams away down a river, the existence of which had never been hinted at before.

By 1948 Universal had made its last serial, leaving the field to Columbia and Republic; but by that time rustlers and master criminals had become things of the past; the atomic age now exerted its influence on serials. Mad scientists gleefully plotted the destruction of the world, and the inhabitants of other planets, unmindful of the lessons of *Flash Gordon* ten years earlier, set their sights on conquering the Universe, and especially the Earth. The anti-Communist feeling also found its way into serials, and not a few were used for crude propaganda. Nationalities were never mentioned, of course, but since the villains were invariably named Ivan or Boris, and spoke non-stop about the "unimportance of the individual," the "liberation of the people," and "the liquidation of the leader's enemies," it became fairly obvious that world peace was not being threatened by Samoans.

Western serials had little to offer in the way of competition to Hollywood versions of the present and the future. Columbia and Republic cut down the number of Western serials to only one each per year. At Republic, the slickness and speed of the serials, to a degree, compensated for their tired subject matter, but Columbia's products had still less to recommend them. Republic's last few serials, including *The Man with the Steel Whip,* another Western deriving from the Zorro theme, were pitiful shadows of the company's former fine episodic adventures. Republic eased out of the field a few months ahead of Columbia, leaving to Columbia's *Blazing the Overland Trail,* produced in 1955 and released in 1956, the distinction of being the last serial made in the United States—unless of course some completely unforeseen circumstances should bring about a revival.

Rising production costs and television are the reasons given for the decline of both the "B" Western and the serial. Not only was television using many of the film serials' heroes (Kit Carson, Wild Bill Hickok, The Lone Ranger) for its own *series,* but it was also reviving many of the best serials from their peak period—the mid-Thirties. These elaborately mounted affairs and television's own expensive filmed series put the contemporary, very cheaply made, movie serials on the hopeless defensive.

Today it seems that the serial in general is a matter only for history. While television can utilize old movie serials, its programming is such that it would find expensive new serials, filmed to its own format, rather cumbersome under television conditions. The present television series films have no continuity, other than of character, and so can be used in any order for reruns, or, of course, run singly.

So far, the only real serials to attract the attention of television producers have been soap operas. With the plethora of theatrical Westerns already on television, and the medium's endless supply of its own Westerns, it does not seem possible that television will restore the serial. Certainly, it is even more unlikely that the movie industry will do so. With all the great Western stars either dead or in retirement, and, since it is sure that any serials that resulted from renewed interest would inevitably be cheap and inferior to their predecessors of the Twenties and Thirties, perhaps the death of the serial is just as well.

The good badman, Wallace Beery.

The Forties

Renaissance of the epic

While it is true that the Depression in the United States persisted into the late Thirties, conditions had improved to the extent that a new national optimism took root. Hollywood reflected this new spirit in a return to inspiring themes of national progress, and naturally the Western featured prominently in this trend. However, this important theme in the genre merely served to re-establish the epic Western as a box-office commodity, and it did not noticeably sustain itself beyond the first two films of the new cycle.

Although Cecil B. De Mille's *Union Pacific* was inferior to John Ford's silent *The Iron Horse,* while covering virtually the same ground, it was a better film than De Mille's previous Western, *The Plainsman.* Its story of empire-building took in all the spectacular elements one would expect from a De Mille version of the construction of a mighty railroad: Indian attacks, a train crashing into a chasm as it tries to forge its way through a snowbound canyon, a pay roll robbery, wild fist fights, strikes organized by selfish political interests anxious to delay the building of the railroad and the inevitable brawl in which the railroad workers wreck a crooked gambling saloon. *Union Pacific,* which starred Paramount's popular team, Joel McCrea and Barbara Stanwyck, was an exciting large-scale Western but not an inspiring one. The sense of national pride was not as strongly present as it had been in *The Iron Horse* and indeed it was largely ignored by the producers until the rather mawkish climax was

13

reached. Here, the weak but basically decent Robert Preston redeems himself in the traditional style by killing the villain, saving the hero's life, dying in the process. Explaining the turn of events to the heroine, hero McCrea merely remarks: "He'll be waiting for us, Molly—at the end of the tracks," whereupon a brief epilogue showed the rapid progress of the Union Pacific railroad through the succeeding decades, a huge streamlined monster screaming towards the camera for the "End" title.

John Ford's *Stagecoach* of the same year appealed less to a nation's pride in design, but far more so in its ultimate execution. A sort of *Grand Hotel* on wheels, and based on the above-average Western novel *Stage to Lordsburg* by Ernest Haycox, it followed a familiar pattern: a group of widely assorted characters (perhaps too much of a cross section to be completely logical) are placed in a dangerous situation—Geronimo is about to attack. This situation forces their true characters to rise to the surface. In keeping with tradition, too, those who display the most nobility are the social outcasts (a gambler, an outlaw, and a prostitute), while the most "respectable" member of the party (a banker, played by Berton Churchill) turns out to be least worthy, a man with neither courage nor principles.

Author Ernest Haycox is said to have been influenced by de Maupassant's *Boule de Suif* in his creation of the dance-hall prostitute who

James Ellison (Buffalo Bill Cody), Helen Burgess (Mrs. Cody), and Gary Cooper (Wild Bill Hickok) in De Mille's The Plainsman (1936).

"He'll be waiting for us, Molly—at the end of the tracks." The last line from Union Pacific (1939) *with Barbara Stanwyck and Joel McCrea.*

John Ford directing Stagecoach *(1939), with Bert Glennon at the camera.*

is the heroine. Certainly, there are superficial similarities in both the action of the two tales and in the conception of the heroine's character. The basic differences, of course, are stressed by the fact that Haycox's heroine redeems herself in the eyes of all by her courageous actions during the Indian attack, while de Maupassant, less sentimentally, more cynically, and perhaps more honestly, shows the passengers turning on her, despising her again, once crisis and her own usefulness are past.

Although designed more as a Western melodrama than as an historical Western, nevertheless, its carefully etched backgrounds—the establishment of telegraphic communication, the patrolling of the frontier by the cavalry, the role played by the stagecoach in the opening up of the West—made it a far more important contribution to Hollywood Western lore than *Union Pacific*.

Film historians—in particular, some European critics—have tended to overrate *Stagecoach* as a film and to regard it as the yardstick by which

The climax of De Mille's Union Pacific, *the linking of the rails.*

The stagecoach and its cavalry escort cross Monument Valley in a scene from Stagecoach.

all Westerns should be measured. The reasons for this exaggerated evaluation are at least partially sentimental, for the theme itself was an obvious one. It was John Ford's first sound Western, and the first for which he was to use Utah's Monument Valley for his principal location. It was also a film that rescued John Wayne from the rut of "B" pictures in which he had marked time since *The Big Trail,* a decade earlier. *Stagecoach* should be seen in its true perspective as a film more important in the development of Ford than in the development of the Western itself. Certainly it was one of the most flawlessly constructed and beautifully photographed of all Ford Westerns. Even the ending—the time-honored duel in the streets—though perhaps anti-climactic after the magnificently staged chase across the salt flats, was so well photographed and directed that it still sustained interest. The whole film, however, was far more a matter of Ford's lovely, sentimental images and sweeping action, and Yakima Canutt's brilliant second unit direction of stunt sequences, than a completely *true* picture of the times. William S. Hart pointed out somewhat scornfully that such a prolonged chase could never have taken place, the Indians being smart enough to shoot the horses first!

Cult of the outlaw

In 1940 the tendency to glamorize outlaws began in earnest, most notably in Henry King's somewhat pedestrian but enormously successful

Jesse James. Of course, outlaws had been presented on the screen before in at least a partially sympathetic light, but now the tendency was almost apologetic, and sought to prove that virtually all of the West's more notorious badmen had been forced into a life of crime by a combination of unfortunate circumstances, not the least of which were the activities of crooked law enforcement officers.

Jesse James was followed by, among others, *When the Daltons Rode, Billy the Kid, Badmen of Missouri* (the Younger brothers), and *The Return of Frank James,* the first of Fritz Lang's three Westerns. This last film, in typical Lang style, glamorized the colorful villainy of John Carradine as opposed to the dull heroics of Henry Fonda. Lang went one better in his next, *Western Union,* which told of the construction of the telegraph lines, by so stressing the character of the outlaw (Randolph Scott) that he became, in effect, the film's hero, quite overshadowing the "official" heroes (Robert Young and Dean Jagger). Incidentally, through a deal made with the Zane Grey estate, Fox advertised the film as "Zane Grey's *Western Union,*" although it was merely a screenplay written by a Fox contract writer; no such book had ever existed. Following the release of the film, interest in the nonexistent book by Zane Grey's fans was so strong that a book based on the film was actually written, published,

Daniel Boone (George O'Brien) and the white renegade Simon Girty (John Carradine) in Daniel Boone (*1936*).

The good badman and the bad badman meet for the showdown. Humphrey Bogart, traditionally dressed in villain's black, and James Cagney square off in The Oklahoma Kid (*1939*).

and credited to Zane Grey, who had died in 1939, two years earlier!

The cause of the whitewashed bandit was furthered by a series of Wallace Beery Westerns at MGM in which he played the role the public so closely associated with him, that of the lovable rogue. His pre-1940 Westerns at Metro (*The Badman of Brimstone,* for example) had their sentimental elements, of course, but they stopped short of presenting Beery as a completely sympathetic scoundrel. In the post-*Jesse James* period all this was changed, and in films like *The Badman of Wyoming* and *Bad Bascomb* his nobility acquired mawkish proportions. *Bad Bascomb,* made in 1940, was a particularly distressing example of this sentimentalizing process, for the entire film was devoted to the reformation of an apparently ruthless outlaw by a small child, played by Margaret O'Brien. The film had two rousing climactic reels and one of the best Indian attacks on a covered wagon train that the Forties had to offer, but the lugubrious fadeout in which Beery, having saved the wagon train at the cost of his freedom, bids farewell to a tearful Margaret as he is taken away by the law to face the hangman, was one of the grimmest moments movie audiences had to face that year.

A particularly good film in the "lovable rogue" category was Warners *The Oklahoma Kid* starring James Cagney and Humphrey Bogart. Few large-scale Westerns have been as faithful to the traditions of horse opera as was this picture, which completely avoided the stodgy pretentiousness that afflicted *Billy the Kid* and so many other big-budget Westerns. It was fast, vigorous action all the way, complete even to the last-reel fist fight in the saloon. At the same time it had a number of pleasing variations on standard Western clichés; at one point, the hero rides into town just too late, for once, to save his father from being lynched by the villains. Another great asset was the creative camera work of James Wong Howe. Perhaps unwittingly aiding in sustaining the old-time Western flavor was the film's unnecessary but pleasing use of subtitles to cover gaps in time and place. One subtitle bridging a gap tells us: "A hundred miles away the Kid continued to play his cards the way he saw them," a subtitle that could have been lifted from any Ince Western.

Undoubtedly *some* of the Western badmen had been, at least partially, victims of circumstance (the woman guerilla and later bandit, Belle Starr, is a case in point), and others, such as the Civil War renegade, Quantrill, may well have been inspired by unselfish motives, but this cycle of the Forties followed a set pattern: to completely idealize "popular" outlaws like Jesse James and to create *complete* villains from more complex and less "exciting" figures like Quantrill and even John Brown. This standardization was furthered by the "B" Westerns: in these films

Billy the Kid, Jesse James, and others were transformed into conventional Western heroes so that stars like Buster Crabbe, Bob Steele, and Roy Rogers could, without offense, play them. As always, this conformity soon became tiring. When producers of horror films in this period, for example, found customers less interested, their first move was to offer two monsters for the price of one (*Frankenstein Meets the Wolf Man*) and later three or four (*House of Frankenstein* offered the monster, the Wolf Man, Dracula, a mad doctor, and a psychopathic hunchback). So it was with the Westerns. First, comparatively obscure Western badmen were unearthed and given the whitewash treatment (Sam Bass, Jack McCall). Then, Hollywood's writers contrived to have Jesse James, Belle Starr, the Daltons, Sam Bass, Quantrill, and sundry others join forces for organized crime waves which belonged more to the gangster era than to the old West. In most of *these* whitewashing was not even attempted in order to provide the requisite amount of brutality and viciousness expected of such a line-up of outlaws; needless to say, any pretense at historical accuracy was likewise abandoned. Some of the more interesting of these films were made by RKO Radio (*Badmen's Territory, Return of the Bad Men, Best of the Badmen*), usually as vehicles for Randolph Scott; seldom did any U. S. marshal ever have to face such an array of concentrated villainy, in reality or on film.

Historical Westerns

Apart from the group of "badman" Westerns, the early Forties saw a tremendous upsurge in historical Westerns, particularly at Warners. In *Dodge City,* swashbuckling Errol Flynn switched to cowboy heroics. Although his mild manner, careful diction, and well-groomed appearance seemed to mark him as an unlikely Western hero, the film itself was well made; while not markedly original, it was certainly one of the most elaborate and exciting films of the "towntaming" school.

Three other elaborate Flynn vehicles followed. *Virginia City* was a well-plotted adventure of gold robbery during the Civil War with Flynn representing the North, aided by his perennial movie cronies, Alan Hale and Guinn Williams, and Randolph Scott representing the South. Humphrey Bogart was cast none too convincingly as a Mexican bandit. It was fast moving, flawlessly photographed, and well scored. *Santa Fe Trail* which followed, and which preceded *High Noon* by several years in having a theme song, "Along the Santa Fe Trail," to publicize the film well ahead of its release, was a fairly accurate reconstruction of the campaign against John Brown's abolitionist movement. It was climaxed by a well-staged reconstruction of Brown's abortive attempt at Harpers Ferry to start a slave uprising. The third film, *They Died With Their Boots On,* was a rather ponderous and far from accurate account of General Custer's career. However, it rates mention as one of the few films to deal with the Civil War, the subsequent opening up of the West, and the Indian Wars. Many films (*Run of the Arrow* in more recent years) have taken this period as a general background for an *individual* story, but *They Died With Their Boots On,* viewing the period from a predominantly military point of view, did succeed in presenting an interesting picture of several phases of the West's history linked into a cohesive whole.

Thereafter Flynn's vehicles became increasingly routine. *San Antonio* still retained strong production values, plenty of vigorous action (including a gun duel that had obviously been patterned on the one in *Stagecoach*), and featured a wonderful "slam-bang shootup" at the end, in which a whole saloon and most of San Antonio was cheerfully wrecked.

For some strange reason Paramount, which made absolutely first class "B" Westerns (the Zane Grey series, the Hopalong Cassidy Westerns, the Harry Sherman productions) seemed incapable of turning out satisfactory Westerns on a larger scale, exceptions perhaps being *Union Pacific* and *The Texas Rangers.* Paramount's record in the Forties was particularly disappointing. De Mille's entry in this period, *Northwest Mounted Police,* an elaborate Technicolor epic with a huge cast headed by Gary Cooper, Madeleine Carroll, Robert Preston, Paulette Goddard, and Preston Foster, was an incredibly dull production with literally no action until its twelfth and final reel. The only Paramount Western of this period that did achieve a measure of excitement was *Geronimo,* a fine example of a film put together with little more than Scotch tape. The cast was economically drawn from Paramount's contract roster. The heroine, Ellen Drew, had a particularly easy time of it: after smiling at the hero in reel one, she was involved in a stagecoach accident and remained in a coma until the fadeout; she actually had not a single line of dialogue in the entire film. The script was a meticulous reworking of Henry Hathaway's earlier film, *The Lives of a Bengal Lancer.* Each detail was carefully copied and transferred from India to the West, the only difference being that the earlier film had had no heroine, which doubtless accounted for Ellen Drew's sketchy role. The spectacular action sequences were all borrowed, with complete disregard for qualitative differences, from Paramount's stock library. Thus *Geronimo* was enhanced by the action highlights from *The Plainsman, Wells Fargo,* and even silent material from *The Thundering Herd.* Nevertheless, despite costing per-

Errol Flynn as General George Custer in They Died with Their Boots On *(1941).*

haps a tenth of what De Mille had spent on his *Northwest Mounted Police, Geronimo* was vastly more entertaining.

MGM in the early Forties was still considered the studio of the top stars, the center of Hollywood's traditional glamour and luxury. Perhaps because of this, it seemed to hold Westerns in comparatively low regard, making fewer of them than any other studio. In 1939, both Nelson Eddy (in a very strange, multi-starred historical Western called *Let Freedom Ring*) and Robert Taylor (cast opposite Wallace Beery in *Stand Up and Fight,* a story of stagecoach-locomotive competition) had failed to make the grade as Western heroes. In the Forties, Taylor tried again in *Billy the Kid* (1941). This film had one fine chase sequence, but otherwise was boring, cliché-ridden, and not at all a suitable vehicle for the actor at that time. In the postwar period a more mature Taylor proved surprisingly suited to Westerns and appeared in half-a-dozen good ones for MGM. Gable, also "too valuable to be wasted" in Westerns in the Thirties and early Forties, made several for MGM, Fox, and United Artists in the postwar years. Spencer Tracy, a more rugged type, and Robert Young, regarded by MGM as a second-string Taylor, teamed in *Northwest Passage.* Directed by King Vidor in 1940, it was hardly a Western in the accepted sense, but worthy of note here inasmuch as MGM at that period was making so few films even casually related to the Western. A spectacular adaptation of the first of Kenneth Roberts' two novels on Rogers' Rangers, it was to be followed by an adaptation of the second, and more interesting, book dealing with the actual search for the Northwest Passage, but this second film was never made. *Northwest Passage* has a place in the general history of the Western for being one of the most viciously anti-Indian films ever made. Hatred for the Indian is apparently justified only by a sequence in which Indian tortures of a particularly revolting nature are described by a member of Rogers' Rangers, a man whose brother was put to death by the Indians. The motivating factor for the Rangers' raid is revenge, and the raid is actually a carefully planned massacre, in which Indian men, women, and children are wiped out ruthlessly. The Indian's side of the question is never presented, and the only sympathy shown for the Indian is achieved in barbaric, if not perverse fashion. One of the Rangers, having gone mad with hatred of the Indians, sustains himself through a period of near-starvation by secretly eating from the severed head of an Indian he had hacked to pieces during the massacre. Despite this barbarism, the audience's sympathies are directed to the plight of the poor, mad white man (who subsequently kills himself) rather than to the Indian victim of such atrocities.

Such "specials" as *Northwest Passage* and *Billy the Kid* apart, MGM almost totally ignored the Western in the early Forties. There was a half-hearted attempt to make a group of minor "A" historical Westerns with James Craig (*The Omaha Trail, Gentle Annie*), but these were unusually incompetent films, sadly lacking in action, and they were soon discontinued. Probably MGM used this handful of lesser Westerns as a training ground for new talent; then, too, every studio needed a few co-features for their more important pictures.

William Wyler's The Westerner *(1940) with Gary Cooper and Walter Brennan.*

At other studios some interesting Westerns were being made. *Kit Carson* was one of these, directed by that old serial maestro, George B. Seitz, for United Artists. Its spectacular Indian attack sequence, almost a full reel of large-scale, well-organized mass action, was one of the best things of its kind since *The Big Trail*. And at a time when Indians were being depicted in the conventional fashion as unmotivated savages, this film made quite a point of stressing the inhumanity of the treatment meted out to them by the Army. Unfortunately, *Kit Carson* seems to have had financial difficulties; apparently the money ran out and the last reel was finished off very cheaply, robbing the film of a dramatic last punch.

One of the most outstanding Westerns of this period was William Wyler's *The Westerner,* a strange, moody, unevenly paced vehicle for Gary Cooper. Its austerity and unglamorous picture of the West made it unpopular. Judge Roy Bean, one of the old West's most colorful characters, as played by Walter Brennan, emerged as a much more interesting protagonist than hero Cooper; indeed, Bean later became the central character of a popular television series. Intelligently cast, the action content unusually well handled (the fights were often clumsy, as they should be when farmer fights cowhand, and as they seldom are when Western star fights stunt man), *The Westerner* was a serious work, indeed.

Columbia's Western record in the period is a peculiar one. Like Paramount the company was expert at turning out slick, action-packed "B" Westerns; like Paramount, too, Columbia seemed unable to translate that expertise into the making of their large-scale Westerns. *Arizona,* made for Columbia by Wesley Ruggles as his first epic since *Cimarron,* was a large, ambitious undertaking in the old style of Vidor and Griffith. It told an important story—the development of Arizona—on a vast, sprawling canvas. It had the integrity neither to glamorize nor to introduce action for its own sake. Its careful reconstruction of the old mud-adobe town of Tucson has been preserved by the State of Arizona as a historical monument. Some sequences were beautifully staged and photographed: using miles of telephone wire to boom his instructions over a vast area, Ruggles created a memorable panorama of the people of Tucson watching the Union troops withdraw, their ranks spread over miles of country, burning the wheat fields as they leave. Yet despite such great moments, *Arizona* was an even duller film than *Wells Fargo.* It seldom moved or inspired, and thus it lost the epic quality that had distinquished Ruggles' *Cimarron.*

Possibly the fault lay with the original story by Clarence Buddington Kelland, better known as the creator of Scattergood Baines, a homespun small-town philosopher, than as a writer of national epics. It outlined the early history of Arizona by telling the parallel story of one of that State's pioneer women, a rugged opportunist named Phoebus Titus, rugged, yes, if the script can be relied upon, but not of sufficient stature to warrant being used as the symbol of a State's growth.

Columbia took no chances with subsequent epics: *Texas* was all action, as were *Desperadoes* and *Renegades*. Somehow ever since, Columbia's large-scale Westerns have looked like expanded "B" Westerns, despite Technicolor and important star names.

John Ford's further contributions

Twentieth Century-Fox's output of Westerns in the Forties was not exceptional. The "B" films were limited to a series of Cisco Kid adventures with Cesar Romero, none particularly remarkable, and four Zane

Barbara Stanwyck and Joel McCrea in The Great Man's Lady (*1942*).

Wyatt Earp (Henry Fonda) greets his fiancée from the East (Cathy Downs) in John Ford's My Darling Clementine (*1946*).

Grey films—*Riders of the Purple Sage* and *The Last of the Duanes* (both good, with George Montgomery), and *Sundown Jim* and *The Lone Star Ranger* (both weak, due largely to inept performances by ex-football star John Kimbrough). Fox's really big Westerns, *Jesse James,* and its sequel, and *Western Union,* have been mentioned earlier. There were many others, but few made a lasting impression. One of the most enjoyable was *A*

Ticket to Tomahawk, a light-hearted film with some musical elements which still managed to treat its Western material seriously. It was in many ways a better film than the more highly touted *Annie Get Your Gun*, although the music, of course, was less ambitious. Harry Sherman's *Buffalo Bill*, directed by William Wellman, was far too sentimental, as was another Wellman Western of the same period, *The Great Man's Lady*, made for Paramount, but it was an interesting and colorful film. Its great battle—Indians and the cavalry fighting to the death in the middle of a shallow river—was certainly exciting and the spectacular staging was in large part responsible. Although readily recognizable because of its distinctive locale, this complete battle sequence was re-used twice by Fox in the Fifties, once in *Pony Soldier,* and again a year or so later in *Siege at*

A scene from John Ford's Wagon-master *(1950), one of the most poignant Westerns of recent times.*

Red River, one of Leonard Goldstein's "Panoramic Productions" for wide-screen. Critics with short memories were easily fooled. To a man they praised the battle scene that was over a decade old, and pointed out how much better wide-screen films could present this sort of mass action than the "old-fashioned" small screens!

From the studio's rather routine assortment one outstanding film emerged in the period. It was John Ford's retelling of the Wyatt Earp legend in *My Darling Clementine,* adapted from the book *Wyatt Earp, Frontier Marshall* by Sam Hellman and Stuart Lake. The story had seen service before, of course, including a Fox version in 1939 (*Frontier Mar-*

shall with Randolph Scott as Earp and Cesar Romero as Holliday) which contained several incidents repeated by Ford in his film. Among these was the capture in the saloon of a drunken Indian, played by Charles Stevens in *both* versions. Ford's account of Earp's story was leisurely and effectively non-spectacular. The exciting action sequences, particularly a chase after a stagecoach and the climactic duel at the O. K. Corral, were filmed with authority, but action as such was not allowed to dominate the development, playing thus a relatively small part in the proceedings. Shot largely in Ford's beloved Monument Valley, the film was quiet, sensitive, and a visual delight, next to *Wagonmaster* perhaps the most satisfying of all Ford's Westerns. It was not an enormous commercial success, but it did prove popular enough, and the critics were almost unanimous in their praise. *The New York Times* remarked: ". . . Ford is a man who has a way with a Western like nobody in the picture trade . . . a tone of pictorial authority is struck—and held. Every scene, every shot is the product of a keen and sensitive eye—an eye which has deep comprehension of the beauty of rugged people and a rugged world. Fonda . . . shows us an elemental character who is as real as the dirt he walks on." And *Time* commented: ". . . horse opera for the carriage trade . . . [Ford's] camera sometimes pauses, with a fresh childlike curiosity, to examine the shape and texture of a face, a pair of square-dancing feet, a scrap of desert landscape, or sunlit dusty road. The leisurely lens—a trick Europeans frequently overdo and Hollywood seldom attempts—makes some of Ford's black-and-white sequences as richly lifelike as anything ever trapped in Technicolor." Victor Mature appeared as Holliday, with Walter Brennan and Tim Holt as the leaders of the Clanton clan.

Ford's three subsequent large-scale Westerns (for Argosy, releasing through RKO) were *Fort Apache* (1948), *She Wore a Yellow Ribbon* (1949), and *Wagonmaster* (made in 1949, but not released until 1950). *She Wore A Yellow Ribbon,* unashamedly sentimental, strikingly photographed in vivid Technicolor, is regarded by many as the most typical Ford Western of all, although the far less elaborate black-and-white *Wagonmaster,* a Western almost completely neglected, was a much superior production. The values of *Wagonmaster* have been rather distorted by Europe's John Ford "cult" (with its headquarters seemingly in and around London's *Sight and Sound* publication) which has blown it up into an Odyssey and read into it values—and meanings—that Ford doubtless never intended. *Wagonmaster* is a beautiful *little* film, Ford expressing his love of both the West and the Western film, using incredibly lovely images and a moving score of Western hymns and folksongs to pay tribute to the old Westerner as an *individual,* not as just one of a special breed of men, or as a crusader for national progress. *Wagonmaster* is as close to a genuine Western film-poem as we have ever come, but attempts by Ford's admirers to enlarge it beyond that do both it and Ford a disservice. *Wagonmaster* is a film that should be seen, felt, and, above all, *fairly* evaluated.

A social Western: The Ox-Bow Incident

Fox's other outstanding Western of the Forties was William Wellman's *The Ox-Bow Incident,* adapted by Lamar Trotti from the novel by Walter Van Tilburg Clark. The sheer power and dynamism of the film derive directly from the original novel, which is followed faithfully but for minor details. This is no discredit to the picture, but critical appraisal has tended to shift emphasis and credit to the contributions of Trotti and Wellman. Wellman's direction was certainly very competent; he had a subject to which, for the first time since his powerful late Twenties and early Thirties' films (*Beggars of Life, Public Enemy*) he could really devote all of his considerable talents. He created powerful images, stark characters, disturbing thoughts—or rather he *reflected* them, for they all were inherent in the original work. He added little creativity of his own, but certainly the film would have been a lesser film with another director at the helm, for another director might have overlooked the power, starkness, and significance of the original source.

   The story is a grim and depressing one. A posse takes out after a gang of cattle thieves. Some members of the posse are ranchers who have a right to be concerned; others are drifters, suddenly sucked into the frenzy and blood-lust; others still are men for whom the proposed lynching provides an outlet for their own sadism, with the resulting guilt, if any, to apply to the group rather than to them as individuals. They corner three men (Dana Andrews, Anthony Quinn, and Francis Ford) who could be guilty. But the evidence is only circumstantial, and the men violently protest their innocence, an innocence which they claim can be easily proved in a day's time. Their pleas sway some of the posse but the personal magnetism of the posse's leader, an ex-Confederate army officer, welds the bulk of the party into an organized force demanding the execution of the three men. At dawn the next day, still protesting their innocence, the victims are hung. After the lynchings, positive proof comes that the men were innocent. Although the sheriff who has brought this news declares that the executioners will be tried and punished, clearly, any such punishment can only be nominal. The instigating ex-officer, still without remorse for his sadistic act, commits suicide: it is the *mistake* he cannot abide.

The Ox-Bow Incident was a surprising film to have been made in 1943, when the wartime trend, particularly at Fox, was to all-out escapism. The film was also made without any concessions to box-office standards. The hero and his friend (Henry Fonda and Henry Morgan) were hardly heroes in the accepted sense, being little more than ineffectual observers. The martyred men, too, were without heroic qualities. "Lovable" character actress Jane Darwell played a cold-blooded woman rancher, fair-minded, but harsh and not easily given to sympathy or mercy. The comedy relief (Paul Hurst) was deliberately offensive. The only concessions, if any, were to sentimentality in the climax, a sentimentality which tended to vitiate some of the tragedy's harshness. Great stress is laid, in the film as in the book, on a farewell letter that the leader of the doomed men writes to his wife. One of the posse, in sympathy with him, tries to use the letter to convince others that such a man could not be guilty, but he fails because the doomed man himself angrily protests its use for that purpose when its contents are so sacred to him and his wife. At no point in the book is the letter actually read or any of its contents divulged. In the closing scene of the film, however, as the disconsolate townspeople gather in the saloon, Fonda decides to read the letter to them. The result, inevitably, is a sad letdown, and a weak anti-climax. In moments like these the screen treatment fell far below the literary and dramatic standards set by the novel.

One other film, Lewis Milestone's *Of Mice and Men* (1939), provides a perfect example of the successful adaptation of such material to the screen. Milestone's film was a minutely faithful adaptation of Steinbeck's novel, but it was also a completely separate entity as a film. It can be judged as a piece of film art quite divorced from its origins, while *The Ox-Bow Incident,* an important and courageous film certainly, has an artistry which merely duplicates, never transcending that of the original work. This achievement in itself is so rarely accomplished that such a statement is automatically praise rather than criticism, but *The Ox-Bow Incident* has been so highly praised on its own ground that it is perhaps time to restore the balance.

Trotti and Wellman, incidentally, tried to recapture much of the spirit of *The Ox-Bow Incident* in their later, more conventional Western, *Yellow Sky,* with Gregory Peck, Anne Baxter, and Richard Widmark. Some situations, much of the stark atmosphere, and the opening sequence (cowboys lazily surveying a painting of a plump nude in the town's saloon) were repeated *in toto*.

Parodies and satires

In the Forties, with the phrase "adult Western" still almost twenty years away, Westerns were sophisticated enough to stop taking themselves so seriously and to start poking fun at themselves. This was not an entirely new development, of course. Well before 1920, Mack Sennett had kidded Westerns mercilessly in satires like *His Bitter Pill,* and Fairbanks had genially poked fun at the cult of the Western hero. But although there had been a great many films of this sort, they could not be said to represent a trend any more than it could be said of *Ruggles of Red Gap* or Laurel and Hardy's *Way Out West* in the Thirties. But in 1939, such a trend did begin with Universal's *Destry Rides Again,* directed by George Marshall. Its success can doubtless be explained by its very definite novelty and for the opportunity it gave Marlene Dietrich to display the talents she had made famous. It was a "different" Western, certainly, but the differences made dyed-in-the-wool Western devotees shudder, especially those who recalled with pleasure the old Tom Mix version. To them the new *Destry Rides Again* seemed a betrayal of the Western, and their opinion has not changed with time; here is one case where nostalgia for the past has not worked its magic on the celluloid image. Quite to the contrary, the 1939 film seems slower and more

Anthony Quinn, Dana Andrews, and Francis Ford as the innocent victims of the lynch mob in The Ox-Bow Incident (*1943*).

James Stewart and Marlene Dietrich have it out in Destry Rides Again (*1939*).

Abbott and Costello with Douglas Dumbrille (center) and Iron Eyes Cody (right) in a burlesqued Western, Ride 'Em Cowboy (*1942*).

pointless today, especially with a likable and intelligent third version around, starring Audie Murphy and released by Universal in 1955.

Perhaps the one solid contribution of *Destry Rides Again* to Western films was a particularly fine score by Frank Skinner, one of the best ever composed for a Western, and put to good use by Universal in areas other than film ever since. The film also stimulated a certain levity towards the Western, and a number of satires resulted. *Trail of the Vigilantes* happily disposed of its somewhat witless lampooning in the first four reels, and thereafter got down to the serious business at hand. Much of the action was admittedly tongue-in-cheek, but it was so well staged with all the customary Universal zip, that no one really minded.

One of the most enjoyable of all Western satires was the Marx Brothers' *Go West,* which, combining Groucho's rapid-fire patter with Keatonesque sight gags, reduced to shambles Western plotlines, villainy, and action. Its climactic locomotive chase suggested a close study of Keaton's *The General,* and when it didn't score on its own fast slapstick or its wisecracks, is was making short work of Western plot and dialogue clichés. Even the inevitable romantic interest was played for its cliché value. No *cycle* of Western satires ever really evolved, however, although it soon became familiar routine for comedians to go through their established patterns against Western backgrounds (Jack Benny in *Buck Benny Rides Again,* Bob Hope in his two *Paleface* films and *Fancy Pants,* Martin and Lewis in *Pardners,* and Abbott and Costello, whose *Ride 'Em Cowboy* was one of the best of this species).

Destry Rides Again (1939) did not influence these films directly, but its success must have induced producers to further explore the field of "novelty" Westerns and to settle, somewhat unimaginatively, for the broad comic approach. When *deliberate* satire was attempted, as in the King Brothers' *The Dude Goes West,* it was usually far too heavy-handed and less amusing than the purely slapstick approach. However, the tongue-in-cheek Western *has* enjoyed more of a vogue since 1939, and even stars like Gary Cooper (*Along Came Jones*), John Wayne (*A Lady Takes a Chance, North to Alaska*), and Rod Cameron (*Frontier Gal*) have taken a broad comic approach in certain Westerns, although it is perhaps no coincidence that these ventures were not among their most popular efforts.

The "B" Western

The Forties were characterized by the proliferation of "B" Westerns. At RKO, when the George O'Brien series came to a close early in the period, Tim Holt became the studio's leading cowboy. An excellent series of Zane Grey Westerns, initially with Bob Mitchum and later with James Warren, completed the field for that studio. At Universal, the Johnny Mack Brown series provided some of the best and fastest Westerns, full of action and made with excellent production values; particularly notable were the musical scores and first-class camera work (the running inserts and fast tracking shots in Universal's Westerns in general put to shame those of any other studio). Among the outstanding films were *Desperate Trails, West of Carson City,* and *Riders of Pasco Basin.* Stories were unified, but rarely remarkable; action was the key element and such directors as Ford Beebe, Ray Taylor, Lewis D. Collins, and particularly Joseph H. Lewis never failed to produce works of at least some interest. The camera placement and imaginative cutting in *Arizona Cyclone* (1941), for instance, made it not only one of the very best of its series, but also a model which demonstrated that real cinema sense and style could be injected into basically hackneyed material. Lewis used running inserts to excellent advantage, and his sweeping shots of chases in *The Boss of Hangtown Mesa* (1942) were exceptionally good. When the Brown series came to an end, Universal starred Tex Ritter and Russell Hayden in several films, picking up Rod Cameron and later Kirby Grant.

As in the Thirties, the best Paramount Westerns were the "B" Westerns of Harry Sherman, who brought the Zane Grey series to a close in 1940 with *Knights of the Range,* with Russell Hayden and Jean Parker, and *Light of the Western Stars.* Thereafter, with the exception of a Tito

Guizar Western, *The Llano Kid,* Sherman was to concentrate on the Hopalong Cassidy films and some Paramount "specials" with Richard Dix (*The Round Up, Cherokee Strip,* and *Tombstone, The Town Too Tough To Die*). Quality rose with the budgets when Sherman switched his distribution to United Artists. *Buckskin Frontier* was easily the best of all Sherman's Dix films, a fine "pocket *Iron Horse,*" and an excellent example of how to make a relatively inexpensive Western look like an epic. It ran only seventy-five minutes, and its climax was a particularly exciting affair, with fine mass riding scenes, and a monumental knock-down, drag-out fight. The next film, *The Kansan,* made on an even larger scale, was a more routine tale of a lawman cleaning up a wide-open town. After these two tales of action, Sherman's *The Woman of the Town* seemed both pretentious and ponderous, although *Motion Picture Herald* enthusiastically reviewed it as a throwback to the great days of *The Covered Wagon* and the Bill Hart Westerns. Starring Albert Dekker, Barry Sullivan, and Claire Trevor, it told the story of newspaperman-lawman "Bat" Masterson in rather sentimentalized fashion. Later Sherman concentrated on a number of exraordinary Westerns, films like *Ramrod* (with Joel McCrea, Veronica Lake, Don DeFore, and Donald Crisp), directed by André de Toth, and *Four Faces West* (with Joel McCrea, Frances Dee, Joseph Calleia), directed by Alfred E. Green. The first was an austere, violent, suspenseful story of a range war, the second a gentle and sensitive story of an outlaw on the run. Both were Westerns that William S. Hart would have endorsed, but both proved to be unsuccessful with audiences that wanted *The Outlaw* and *Duel in the Sun.*

Sherman's plans for a series of big Westerns for Eagle-Lion never materialized; the company collapsed, and Sherman himself died soon after. He may have been a less dedicated creator than Hart, but he loved the West and the Western film just as sincerely. He frequently turned up in bits in his own Westerns, driving a mule team or a chuck wagon with obvious pleasure, having the time of his life behind a grimy shirt and a set of grizzled whiskers.

In the late Forties, United Artists replaced the Hopalong Cassidy Westerns with a series of Cisco Kid Westerns, starring Duncan Renaldo, made by Krasne and Burkett. They had their lively moments, were fast, but they were cheaply made and generally inferior to another series which Monogram had just made. United Artists also had their share of the nondescript Westerns that were being made in such increasingly large quantities. Typical of these was Jules Levey's production of *Abilene Town* with Randolph Scott. It had some good action sequences, but a disappointing climax in which an expected battle failed to materialize. The critics noted that Randolph Scott looked tired and showed his age. They expected him to withdraw from the field momentarily. Instead, he had more Westerns ahead of him for Fox, Paramount, Warners, and Columbia than he had made to date!

At Republic, in the meantime, the musical Westerns of Gene Autry and Roy Rogers rose to alleged half-million-dollar budgets; they placed undue stress on musical production numbers, and were eventually whittled down to normal size. Autry left Republic eventually, and Rogers, with his "King of the Cowboys" billing, became the studio's top Western star.

Among other Republic Western series of the Forties (not, of course, all in production simultaneously) was *The Three Mesquiteers*. While the post-1940 entries in this group were not as good as the earlier ones, it nevertheless remained near the top of its category. Other series starred Bill Elliott, Sunset Carson, Monte Hale, Allen Lane, Donald Barry, and Eddie Dew. Bill Elliott became the chief rival to Autry, Rogers, and Boyd, the reigning Western kings for some time. Monte Hale was brought in as another singing cowboy to replace Rogers, in the event Rogers was drafted into the armed forces. Eddie Dew's tenure was brief: introduced initially as "John Paul Revere, the Gentleman Cowboy," he actually took second billing to comic Smiley Burnette in his Westerns. The films themselves were good, but Dew didn't catch on with the public and he was replaced by Bob Livingston. Sunset Carson was a big athlete, with a broad Southern drawl. His films were jammed with action, and were very fast-moving, but Carson himself was a poor actor, and his period of popularity was brief. (He wound up in a cheap series for Astor Pictures, shot on sixteen millimeter and blown up to thirty-five for theatrical release.) Action was the one common denominator of the Republic "B" Westerns, but so expertly were they all made that despite the lack of script values, they avoided having the mass-production stamp all over them, just as the Johnny Mack Brown Westerns at Universal had done.

The Westerns of PRC (Producers Releasing Corporation) were shoddy, cheap, carelessly made, badly photographed, and ineptly directed. Plot values were nonexistent for the most part, and since the casts were identical in almost every film (Edward Cassidy as the heroine's father, Charles King, John Cason, Lane Bradford, Jack Ingram, Jack O'Shea, and Terry Frost as the villains, Bud Osborne as the sheriff, Stanford Jolley as the banker or saloon owner) it was virtually impossible to tell one film from the other! Only in their Eddie Dean Cinecolor Westerns did PRC devote real care. But Dean himself, although a good singer, was a poor actor with an unattractive face and singularly inept at action.

PRC's pictures were rushed through so quickly that there was just no time for acting, for preparation, or even for retakes when mild mishaps occurred. On more than one occasion the hero missed his step leaping into the saddle, and the camera just kept on grinding while he then proceeded to mount in a more orderly fashion. One classic incident marked *Gentlemen With Guns,* a low-grade Buster Crabbe Western. The hero pursues the villain, and as he draws abreast of him, one or the other audibly cues, "One . . . two . . . three . . . HUP!," at which signal the hero's double leaps on the villain, and both fall, not to the ground, but to a soft mattress well within camera range! Not even the cheapest independently made Western of the early Thirties would have let such carelessness get by. The scripting was of an equally carefree order, it being sufficient for the villain to brush up against the hero, snarl, "I don't like your face!" and launch into an otherwise unmotivated fist or gun fight.

During PRC's less than ten-year career, their Westerns starred Buster Crabbe, George Houston, Bob Livingston, Tim McCoy, Bob Steele, James Newill, Bill Boyd (another Boyd, not Hopalong Cassidy), Tex Ritter, Dave O'Brien, Eddie Dean, and Al "Lash" LaRue. A former adolescent player in the "Dead End Kids" vein, LaRue was a most unattractive personality. His unusual walk and his hard-bitten, Bogart-like face made him more suitable for villain's than hero's roles. His "gimmick" was an ability to crack a bullwhip realistically, performing simple tricks with it. It was a "gimmick" he needed, since he was a poor rider and required a double for most of his action scenes. PRC gave him Al St. John as a comic partner. Despite LaRue's shortcomings, his Westerns were otherwise competent, a notch above normal PRC standards.

Unconvincing, standardized action in a cheap Western of the Forties, Fighting Vigilantes *(1947), starring Lash LaRue (right) and former Sennett comedian Al St. John (left).*

Scriptless, witless, ad-lib knockabout cheapened many "B" Westerns of the Forties. Emmett Lynn, Charles King, and Al St. John in Colorado Serenade (1946).

Undoubtedly the best series made by Monogram during these years was that known under the collective heading of "The Rough Riders." Buck Jones, Tim McCoy, and Raymond Hatton were starred as three veteran U. S. marshals. Possibly each film was a little too much like the other. Plots, which always gave the key role to Jones, were similar both in their construction (the three marshals work undercover, one of them poses as a member of the gang, all three finally join forces in the showdown) and in their by-play (a running gag in the series dealt with Hatton's attempts to get married and settle down). Although made quickly (in the space of a week or so) these films were well edited and offered fine photography, good acting, interesting action, and stunts.

The first three films in the series, *Arizona Bound, The Gunman from Bodie,* and *Forbidden Trails* (with some exceptionally fine running inserts) were the best. The others still remained uniformly good. One of the series' assets was the stirring music, including a fine agitato, composed by Edward J. Kay, and the "Rough Riders' Song," played over the main titles, main titles which were superimposed over a freeze-frame from Ford's *Stagecoach.* The series was cut short by Buck Jones' death in the catastrophic Cocoanut Grove fire. Jones, safely outside, returned to help others and was finally overcome by the flames.

Monogram then signed Johnny Mack Brown for another series, very much modeled on the Jones pictures. Brown, one of the very best of the post-1930 Western stars, a fine action performer, with an extremely likable personality, was a better actor than most Western stars; he had played many straight dramatic roles opposite Greta Garbo, Joan Crawford, Mary Pickford, and other top stars of the late Twenties before switching to Westerns. He helped to make this series enjoyable at the very least, and Raymond Hatton, one of the few Western comedians who was primarily a character actor, and whose mild comedy fitted into the action without disrupting it, made a perfect foil. Together they made forty-five Westerns before Max Terhune, a much less interesting screen personality than Hatton, took over. The series reached its peak between 1944 and 1945, when Monogram's expansion was just beginning, and when even the "B" pictures reflected the upgrading of production values. The Brown films in this period held to the standards of the best of the "Rough Riders" films, with really polished production mountings, good scripts, and an abundance of action. This was also the peak period of the tough Dashiel Hammett-Raymond Chandler school of detective-mystery films, and perhaps unwittingly, some of the Brown Westerns seemed to reflect much of their spirit, particularly in terse, wisecracking, tough dialogue, and an abundance of really rough fisticuffs. It was during these years that "dirty" fighting, an inheritance from gangster films, crept into Westerns and stayed there. Possibly the best of the Brown Westerns for Monogram was the 1946 entry, *The Gentleman from Texas,* directed by Lambert Hillyer.

Some commercial success was achieved with Jimmy Wakely, a hillbilly singer who had been in many Universal and Columbia Westerns as a specialty musical performer. Wakely himself was a shameless imitator of Gene Autry (he had been a member of Autry's radio troupe at one time), copying his costumes and his mannerisms. The Wakely Westerns were "streamlined" and smoothly made, but had little stature. However, they proved to be extremely popular in rural areas, where Wakely's hillbilly style, and the low-grade humor of Dub Taylor (the "unfunniest" of all Western comedians) and Lee "Lasses" White found a ready reception. One of the last of his series, *Silver Trails,* introduced a new Western star in Whip Wilson, who immediately went on to stardom in his own series. Wilson, a rugged ex-rodeo star who could handle the action well enough, was more adept with the bullwhip than was Al LaRue, but he revealed himself as an indifferent actor. Some care was taken with his first pictures, but they soon degenerated; Wilson's stardom was brief, for he came in at the beginning of the end, as far as the "B" Western was concerned.

In this period Monogram completed the Tom Keene and *Renfrew of the Royal Mounted* series started in the Thirties. Monogram also produced a number of Cisco Kid adventures of which *The Gay Cavalier,* starring Gilbert Roland, was the best, a film true to the spirit and story of O. Henry's original conception. *Beauty and the Bandit* was another excellent picture. Roland's performance was unique in these films; he injected a note of sensitive sadness into what had hitherto been (and was again subsequently) a characterization of sheer bravado. Again, as seemed automatically the case in eight out of ten Western series, quality declined towards the end. *Robin Hood of Monterey* had standards far below those set by the earlier one; however, all of the Monogram Cisco Kid films with Roland were quite a few notches above the average.

During the Forties, Monogram also made two quite successful efforts to repeat the success of the "Three Mesquiteers" Westerns. The initial try was an obvious take-off with a team known as "The Range Busters," with Ray Corrigan and Max Terhune, two of the original Mesquiteer team, and John King. The pattern, too, was very much along Mesquiteer lines as far as plots were concerned, but the films were much cruder than Republic's had been. They had plenty of action, but very little polish. There was also no real cohesion to the series, which switched from the old West to the new, and had the boys battling both Nazis, in *Cowboy Commandos,* and Japanese, in *Texas to Bataan.* It was, however, an enjoyable minor series. The other series, "The Trail Blazers," was devoted to fast action and a maximum of stunt work, with old reliables such as Ken Maynard, Hoot Gibson, and Bob Steele in leading roles. The best film of this series was *The Law Rides Again,* carefully made, with plenty of fast and furious action.

The *Durango Kid* Westerns, starring Charles Starrett in the role of a masked Robin Hood, was a series of fast action pictures, but one was too much like the other. They proved very popular, however, lasting until well into the Fifties.

The Japanese and Nazis got quick and efficient handling in Westerns during the war. A scene from Texas to Bataan *(1942).*

BLAST A JAP
WITH SCRAP

At Columbia, where the Bill Elliott and Charles Starrett Westerns had declined in quality and popularity, a new deal was ushered in with the signing of Tex Ritter and Russell Hayden, restoring pep and vitality to the studio's horse operas. The regular "B" features were supplemented by a string of dreadful so-called "musical Westerns" which were popular in rural areas, a market for which they were primarily intended, to be sure. Their "life" depended on hillbilly music and simple knockabout comedy provided by Slim Summerville, Andy Clyde, and other veteran comedians. These cacophonous works were happily abandoned when Gene Autry joined Columbia. His Westerns became more realistic in style and omitted the big musical production numbers previously so much a part of his films.

Autry's first, *The Last Round Up,* was also his biggest—and very probably his best. It was an intelligent, well-directed Western, one of the most ambitious ever made as part of a so-called "B" Western series. It, and one or two subsequent Autry Westerns, had faint notes of social criticism in their plea for better conditions for the contemporary Indians, but these notes were never overplayed. The next two Autry films were not quite as good, but nevertheless still of a very high order (*Loaded Pistols, Riders of the Whistling Pines*). Later there were signs that it was uneconomical to continue the series on such ambitious lines. A decision to produce them in Cinecolor was abandoned after only two pictures (*The Strawberry Roan, The Big Sombrero*), and thereafter Autry put out his films in Monocolor (black-and-white prints run through a sepia bath). Running times were shortened. Nevertheless, until the end of the Forties, with such films as *The Cowboy and the Indians, Mule Train, Riders in the Sky,* and *Sons of New Mexico*, Autry did manage to maintain a reasonably high standard.

By the end of the Forties, however, "B" Westerns started to relinquish their hold on the field, as the time approached when they would become little more than memories, and part of a history.

Trends in

Jennifer Jones

the postwar Western

Siegfried Kracauer's book, *From Caligari to Hitler,* interestingly outlined how the post-World War I films of Germany reflected the crushed and disillusioned spirit of the German people. The basic value of the work, in view of the trends in German cinema of post-World War II, confirmed that many of his conclusions were not only correct, but also being repeated a quarter of a century later in an astonishingly like fashion.

Surprisingly, these same trends began to appear in English and American films. Kracauer's theories were confined to the film expression of a defeated people. Great Britain and America were instead among the victors in the struggle; in 1918 their films had reflected only optimism, but in 1945 they contained many of the same German introverted psychological examinations. And, as in Germany, those tendencies were channeled in America towards murky psychological dramas and mysteries that were combinations of violence and pseudo-psychiatrics (*Somewhere in the Night, Murder My Sweet, Spellbound*) and out-and-out sex dramas (*Scarlet Street*), while British films like *Odd Man Out* and *Good Time Girl* were even closer parallels to the defeatist films of Germany.

The Western was by no means immune to these influences, and three new elements made their bow in the genre as a result of the postwar gloom and "psychology" that settled on American films. They were, in order of their appearance, sex, neuroses,

14

and a racial conscience. All had been *used* as plot elements in Westerns before, but they had never succeeded in establishing themselves as *integral* parts of the simple and uncomplicated Western tradition. At first the three new elements went their separate ways, but it was not long before they came together to produce an entirely new kind of Western. For example, *Reprisal!*, a Columbia Western made in 1956, with Guy Madison as an Indian who passes for white, with little commotion incorporated all three.

Sex

Sex was the first element to establish itself, obviously because there had been precedents, and it seemed safe to tamper with the iron-clad Western tradition when the new product would sell so well. *Destry Rides Again* had abounded in raucous, obvious, and unerotic sex—and reaped a huge success. Howard Hughes' *The Outlaw* had used blatant suggestiveness, and the physical equipment of Jane Russell, as its sole advertising angle. Its long trail of censorship hassles and the fact that it *did* deliver the goods it advertised tended to obscure the fact that it was really a good Western in its own right. One of the better film biographies of Billy the Kid (no more accurate than the others, but less sentimentalized), it would in fact have been a *very* good Western but for the obtrusive eroticism. The frequent tussles between Billy and Rio were not only blatantly suggestive, but also frequently sadistic. Some of the dialogue accompanying these sequences had an unexpectedly raw flavor, and the already abundant Russell bosom, further enhanced by an ingenious "heaving" brassière designed by Howard Hughes, injected one more obvious erotic note. What angered so many opponents of the film was not the erotic emphasis alone, but the minimal *importance of the woman*,

Rio (Jane Russell) ponders the only way "to keep Billy warm" in The Outlaw *(1943). Jack Beutel as Billy the Kid and Walter Huston as Doc Holliday.*

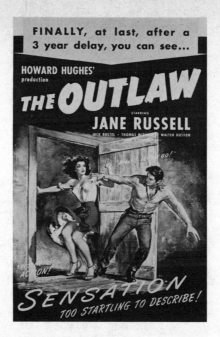

A typical early Thomas Ince poster selling the old excitement and glamor of the West in an unrealistic, dime-novel fashion. Contrast this with the poster for The Outlaw *in which action is referred to only in one minor catchline; the appeal is solely erotic.*

even on a sexual level. There is no sincerely motivated love story in *The Outlaw,* and Rio's role was more that of a machine gratifying lust than of a genuine object and subject of passion. Many looked upon the film as a deliberate insult to womanhood, specifically pointing out the scene in which Billy and Doc Holliday gamble and cannot decide whether the winner should take Rio or a horse. The higher value is ultimately placed on the horse, and the logical conclusion is drawn that in the West a woman was an enjoyable luxury, but a horse was an absolute necessity!

The "Western" aspects of the film were, however, good in many respects. The lightning-fast draws of Billy the Kid in the film's fast and violent gun duels were well photographed; the backgrounds and simple sets had a convincing air to them. Veteran actors Walter Huston and

Thomas Mitchell were fortunately on hand most of the time to compensate for the histrionic limitations of Beutel. One well-directed sequence had Doc Holliday (played by Huston) literally shooting pieces out of Billy's cheek and ears, and yet, despite its patent brutality, it was handled in a casual manner that made it seem far less sadistic than some of Billy's calculated mistreatment of Rio.

The film's climax offered a surprising juxtaposition of defiance of, and compromise with, the prevailing Production Code. After an obviously lengthy and initially forced sexual liaison between the two protagonists, there is a ludicrously casual reference to a marriage performed by "that stranger on the white horse." This line was, of course, dubbed in later as a minor sop to protesting pressure groups, and in view of the preceding action, it is a ridiculous piece of dialogue. Yet even while authorizing such concessions, Hughes refused to change the film's ending, in which both transgressors (Billy the legal as well as *moral* offender, Rio at fault morally only) ride off into the sunset. A neat plot twist of writer Jules Furthman had Sheriff Pat Garrett (played by Thomas Mitchell), officially credited by all historians as the man who finally killed Billy the Kid, actually aiding in a deceptive plot by burying another body in Billy's name, fully aware of the fact that Billy had escaped. This fairy-tale ending has, of course, no basis in fact. In Hughes' film, outlaw and mistress (or wife, if one accepts the additional line) ride off in heroic, poetic silhouettes, the sort of fadeout normally reserved for builders of empires and men of otherwise manifest destiny. The film made producers feel that with certain concessions to censorship and enough production gloss to disguise a lack of taste, Westerns with large doses of sex *could* get by the censors. This was proven by the first big follow-up to *The Outlaw,* King Vidor's *Duel in the Sun* (1945).

Duel in the Sun featured sex in such large doses that it was promptly nicknamed "Lust in the Dust" and encountered considerable censorship opposition; but, due no doubt to its "prestige" background (a top director and producer, all-star cast, first-grade writing, musical scoring, etc.) and a glossy presentation of erotic elements that in *The Outlaw* had seemed much cruder, it overcame this opposition without much difficulty, going on to become one of the top grossing films of all time. One of the few genuinely "big" Westerns in recent years, it had an epic sweep and scope almost in the Griffith tradition, a sweep that unfortunately was limited by a trite story of passion which took precedence over the more important theme of empire building in the early West. It replaced the happy ending of the novel with a starkly tragic ending, but this may well have been a move to forestall censorship. There were traces of the racial theme, too, for the point was often made that the heroine was a half-breed, but the fact was used more for the exotic quality it lent to the love scenes than for any genuinely dramatic purposes.

As a Western, *Duel in the Sun* contained many fine moments, some excellent performances, and exceptionally good photography. One better remembers the beautifully staged mass-riding sequences of the ranchers assembling to wreck the railroad than the sexual elements, which were manifest in the inevitable nude-bathing episode and several hard-breathing seduction scenes. Griffith was a frequent visitor to the set, and he and Vidor must have had some wry comments to make on the subordination of spectacle—of which they were past masters—to the titillations of sin and sex!

If not a great film, *Duel in the Sun* was probably the very best film possible from such an approach and such a script; it certainly contained far more artistry and genuine merit than any of its successors. It is interesting to compare it to Vidor's subsequent Western, *Man Without a Star* (1955).

Gregory Peck, the lecherous "hero," and Jennifer Jones, the good but weak and sensual heroine, in Duel in the Sun *(1945).*

The approach was basically the same: an emphasis on sex, attempting to give it "stature" by placing the erotic aspects against an impressive background, in this case, the struggles of the cattle barons in Texas' early days. But in the ten years between the two Vidor pictures a sort of decay had set in. The sex had become more blatant, less seriously motivated; while one could believe in and understand the desperate affair between Gregory Peck and Jennifer Jones in *Duel in the Sun*, the mutual seduction of Jeanne Crain and Kirk Douglas in *Man Without a Star* was both unconvincing and almost unmotivated, in fact a merely clumsy contrivance, created not out of plot necessity, but out of the arbitrary decision to stress sex for its own sake, with the entire affair treated as a huge joke.

This levity extended even to deliberately poking fun at the bath as a sex-symbol. The bathtub in American films has assumed the same sort of sexual association as the bed in French films. The bathtub is, of course, a somewhat anemic symbol, since its immediate association is with nudity rather than with sex, but perhaps this is appropriate because eroticism in American movies after the moral "purge" in 1933 had been anemic anyway. As a result of Cecil B. De Mille's exploitation of rather pointless bathtub scenes, and the use of the bubbles, showers, and sundry other species of the bath as a never-fail prop for cheesecake publicity stills, the bathtub became Hollywood's principal inanimate symbol—the human body being quite animate—for the suggestion of sex, supplemented, of course, by a monotonous reliance on unmotivated beach scenes.

Man Without a Star, which kidded sex, did so, at least partially, by kidding its symbol, but the bathtub gags became rather strained after a few reels. The use of a bathtub for mildly "sexy" scenes in Westerns was, of course, not uncommon before *Man Without a Star*. *Kit Carson* (1940) included a robust scene in which Jon Hall (Carson) and his cronies unknowingly share a communal bathhouse with heroine Lynn Bari, the two sexes being separated by a small wooden partition. When the soap slips under the partition, Jon Hall dives for it and the discovery is made. De Mille, of course, brought his familiar bathtub sequence into *Unconquered*, with Paulette Goddard up to her neck in suds, and there were other similar scenes. But the idea was usually handled casually and in good taste. Vidor's attempts to simultaneously exploit and satirize the traditional formula misfired, and far more genuine humor was to be found in John Ford's *The Searchers* (1956), in which a refreshing switch was made: unseductive male (Jeffrey Hunter) in the bath and disinterested female (Vera Miles) as observer.

Added to the superfluous sex was the heavy emphasis on sadistic brutality, manifested principally in fight scenes and beatings, in which the protagonists were ripped with barbed wire. The introduction of physical barbarism was one more element incorporated into the Western's stock-in-trade since *Duel in the Sun*. The progression—or regression—from the one Vidor film to the other is not one that went in a straight line, influenced as it was by the "neurotic" and "racial" influences, but it is consistent in that the erotic element has steadily increased. The nude bathing scene of *Duel in the Sun* was a center of controversy at the time, being considered the very antithesis of the "healthy" Western. Today this same scene has become so contrived that it is taken for granted and generates less excitement than the more standard action that it often precipitates. For example, Yvonne de Carlo bathing nude in *Shotgun* (1953) provokes a violent brawl between Sterling Hayden and Zachary Scott.

Shotgun was actually a remarkably good minor "A" Western, which to a degree anticipated *Run of the Arrow* in its presentation of the Apache Indians as both reasoning human beings *and* as cruel warriors. Expertly directed by Lesley Selander, it featured two grand fights and an unusual duel on horseback, Apache style, in its climax. Other assets included some exceptional color photography by Ellsworth Fredericks (who later achieved his peak in William Wyler's *Friendly Persuasion*) and an interestingly off-beat hero. Sterling Hayden was by now fairly familiar as the rugged, hard-bitten Westerner, but there were added nuances in his role this time. For a "hero," he was frequently callous, when callousness served a justifiable end, and his drab sweat-soaked costume was utterly appropriate for his role as a lawman on a long and lonely mission. There was, of course, the customary quota of the "new" clichés, centered principally on sadistic violence (the killing of a sheriff with a shotgun fired full in the face, an outlaw trussed up in an elaborate rattlesnake trap, the slow death of semi-villain Zachary Scott, pinned to a tree by an Indian spear through his stomach—hero Sterling Hayden provides him with a gun with which Scott subsequently kills himself—and the aforementioned duel) and sexual emphasis (frequent references to the girl's somewhat doubtful past—she is characterized as a dance-hall girl who has "been around," which in Westerns is synonymous with prostitution—heated love scenes between hero and heroine, and especially a nude bathing scene).

Nudity, of course, still sells, and many of the advertising campaigns of Westerns containing nude bathing episodes have been built around that ingredient. Independent Westerns like *The Oklahoma Woman*, *The Yellow Tomahawk*, and *Flesh and the Spur* seemed to have been made for no other purpose. This form of cinematic expression reached its logical

The Stagecoach Hold-up.

ultimate in *The King and Four Queens* in which, reversing the usual procedure, hero Clark Gable is discovered bathing "in the altogether" by one of the film's four heroines. *The King and Four Queens,* incidentally, is dedicated entirely to the proposition that sex is *the* ingredient that matters most in the modern Western. The film has literally no action, concerning itself exclusively with the romantic dalliances (always frustrated) of Gable with four lonely widows. In this way it defeated itself; in the golden pre-Code era, considerable fun would have been extracted from such a situation. Today, the watchful Production Code prevents the ultimate in humor from emerging. Since the film has nothing else to offer, it falls flat, innocuously and pointlessly. However, this inflated stress on sex brought with it a more realistic presentation of men and women, people presented again in the realistic fashion of William S. Hart. Hart's realism was, of course, achieved differently, but in the post-war Western, the depiction of men and women with normal (and even often abnormal) drives, went far toward knocking them from their pedestals of purity.

A minor "A" Western from Columbia, *Three Hours to Kill,* presented the unusual—for a Western—situation of the hero (Dana Andrews) returning home after many years to find that a casual affair he had had before he left has made him the father of the heroine's child. Nor did "tidy" scripting bring this to the expected happy ending. In recent years, too, more than one Western hero (Glenn Ford in *Jubal*) has himself been an illegitimate child. Columbia's *Jubal* (1956) typifies the increasingly dominant place that sex is taking in the Western. The film, which incidentally aimed a few arrows (none-too-barbed) at religious intolerance, is primarily a story of lust rather than of crime, pursuit, empire-building, or any of the other staple ingredients of Western film. The middle-aged rancher (Ernest Borgnine) finds his appetite for his young wife (Valerie French) never satisfied; she, in turn, is both a tramp and a nymphomaniac, who finds his attentions boring. The woman, who is also the mistress of ranch foreman Rod Steiger, suddenly switches her attentions to a wandering cowhand (Ford). The latter, in turn, rejects her seductive advances and expresses an ardent love for the virginal daughter (Felicia Farr) of the leader of a religious sect! From this welter of repression and frustrations comes a very heavy-breathing tale of lust, murder, and general neurosis.

With the exception of minor and fairly infrequent realistic touches, the invasion of the Western by sex has been a commercial, rather than an aesthetic, advantage. There is no great merit in having Marla English bathe nude in *Flesh and the Spur*, less still in an even more sug-

gestive sequence where she is staked out on an anthill, but unfortunately the lesser Western has arrived at a point where only that type of content will give it the pitch it needs to sell, in the mind of some producers, at least.

Is it merely a coincidence that some of the best Westerns of recent memory—particularly John Ford's superlative *Wagonmaster* (one of the few sound Westerns to really deserve the description, "poetic") and George Stevens' *Shane*—have still been Westerns basically in the old mood, stressing the austerity of the frontier, and telling their stories in a superbly pictorial manner? The other Ford Westerns of the same period (*Fort Apache, Rio Grande, She Wore a Yellow Ribbon, The Searchers*) and, to a lesser degree, Zinnemann's *High Noon,* Jacques Tourneur's simple and very pleasing *Wichita,* and John Farrow's *Hondo,* were also devoid of sensational eroticism and, significantly, can be counted among the best Westerns of the period. Perhaps the most graphic demonstration can be made by comparing two somewhat lesser films made by the same director for the same studio, lesser films, that is, in terms of budget and industrial importance, but not necessarily in merit.

The first, *Panhandle*, was made for Allied Artists in 1947 by director Lesley Selander, at that time one of the expanding company's biggest pictures. A completely "pure" Western in terms of plot and tradition, as well as in a moral sense, it was a tale simply told. The boundaries between good and evil were as obvious as they had been in *The Covered Wagon* and *The Iron Horse,* and the action was not markedly original, although exceptionally well executed. Harry Newman's photography was in the same extremely able, but not showy, vein. In many ways it was a very fine film, and quite superior to the many larger-scale Westerns that star Rod Cameron made for Universal and Republic. Selander followed up with another for Allied, *Stampede;* not quite as good, and with rather too many "trimmings" in terms of plot ramifications and superfluous characters, but again an intelligent and traditional horse opera. These two films were both made prior to 1950, when the sex "gimmick" had already begun to catch on. When Selander made *Cow Country* for Allied in the early Fifties, a regression was all too obvious: to the still basically straightforward plotline sex, brutality, and a hint of an evaluation of racial relationships had been added. The erotic material revolved primarily around pretty Peggie Castle, an old hand at this sort of thing, who was systematically seduced by one of the villains; when he ultimately refused to marry her, she took a bullwhip to him in a sequence which looked most striking on the promotional material, but was no help in repeating the success of the earlier and far superior *Panhandle.*

Neuroses

"Neurotic" Westerns such as *Pursued* and *The Furies* as a species in themselves had a short life, but when the erotic was added as it was in Joan Crawford's ludicrous *Johnny Guitar,* or when racial themes were injected (primarily dealing with the Indian, of course), such films continued to be made. Some Westerns in the immediate postwar era were straight psychological dramas, not always too convincingly transposed to the West, which reflected much of the fashionable pessimism then so prevalent in European cinema. One of the most typical was Warner's *Colorado Territory,* which, with a little dramatic license, one might compare to Marcel Carné's story in his *Les Portes de la Nuit.* Hero and heroine seemed pursued throughout by an inevitable and malevolent destiny: circumstances were *always* against them; and despite their innate goodness and a determination to "go straight," it was just not to be. And the gloomy ending exactly paralleled the final scenes of Carol Reed's *Odd Man Out;*

cornered by the sheriff's posse, the heroine shoots at the pursuers, deliberately draws the posse's fire, and she and hero Joel McCrea die in a bullet-ridden embrace.

Another Warner film of the same era, *Pursued,* came to a happier ending, after having taken an equally depressing route. This film took advantage of dream images and dialogue borrowed from current psychiatry. More interesting—and one of the best of its kind—was a strange Western entitled *The Capture.* Starring Lew Ayres and Teresa Wright under the direction of John Sturges, it was a well written modern Western set in a little mining community. It dealt with a basically decent man's struggle with his conscience upon realizing that he has killed a man unintentionally. While admitting to the illegality of his act, he questions whether he was morally wrong, taking refuge in flight. It was one of the few Westerns to take as its main concern the question of a killing under extenuating circumstances and the responsibility of the individual to decide for himself the *extent* of his guilt in a land where lawlessness is fairly common. As in so many films of this type, the conclusion was far too facile, but the journey to that disappointing end of the road was a most rewarding one.

Henry King's much-imitated *The Gunfighter* (1950) introduced something of Greek tragedy into its story of an outlaw's last hours. It also brought what soon became a new cliché to Westerns: the motif of the inheritance of a killer's mantle, the compulsion of young "punks" out to make a name for themselves to shoot and kill (preferably, for greater glory, in a fair fight) a feared gunman, and to then find themselves facing the knowledge that the same fate awaits them. This thematic cliché has turned up with startling rapidity since King's film, which, incidentally, was a far more stylish and intelligent film than one had come to expect from this veteran actor-director from the early days of silents, a man who had once established himself as a leading creator of Americana in silent films like *Tol'able David,* and sound ones like the Will Rogers version of *State Fair.* But *Romola* and *Stanley and Livingstone,* as well as *Jesse James* among his few Westerns, were typical spectaculars with nothing very cinematically creative about them, and thus it was somewhat of a surprise when King made *The Gunfighter* and *Twelve O'Clock High* (not a Western), both fine, mature films, within a few months of each other.

In films whose theme has been that of the young hoodlum out to make his reputation by killing a wanted man, sympathy has always been with the older outlaw and almost never with the younger would-be fighter, who is invariably presented as sadistic or maladjusted. While

The youngster "out to make a name for himself" is killed by the reluctant gunfighter. Harry Shannon, Gregory Peck, and Richard Jaeckel (on the floor) in The Gunfighter (*1950*).

this in a sense whitewashes the older outlaw, especially since he is also presented as a man weary of killing, aware that he is doomed, at the same time notions of violence for glory's sake and the temptation to take the law into one's own hands are heartily condemned. But in essence, one is asked to sympathize with a killer and to reject a man whose actions, if not motivations, will benefit law and order!

Of all the films based on this idea (and one of the most recent super-Westerns to include it rather gratuitously was *Gunfight at the O. K. Corral,* directed by John Sturges) only one, *The Desperado,* presented the picture of a normal and likable young man becoming a gunman and giving it up when the circumstances which provoked it no longer applied. Despite its originality, *The Desperado* was nevertheless very much part of a cycle that began with *The Gunfighter.* The youngster, convinced that an outlaw's life is a foolish one, returns home; the older outlaw, unrepentant and unpunished, although, of course, his major crimes took place *before* the film opens, continues on his lonely way, expecting death from an assassin's bullet, or arrest by the law, to bring his career to a close.

Henry Hathaway's *Rawhide* was a film with a similar mood, a more conventional plot, and a conglomeration of neurotic and sadistic villains. It was an interesting work, but Hathaway is better served by sweeping action than by "complexes." Making the most consistent contributions to what one might facetiously term "le Western noir" was Anthony

Mann, a director brought up on hard-bitten city thrillers. His heavy, pretentious approach was well suited to a Western like *The Furies,* which he made for Paramount. A strange, gloomy affair, with touches of both Eugene O'Neill and Daphne du Maurier, Mann gave it the ultimate in low-keyed lighting, somewhat turgid pacing, and oppressive angling of the sets. Unfortunately, he persisted in this approach with Westerns which had less neurotic content. Somehow the trick worked on his black-and-white Westerns; *Winchester 73* was an extremely satisfying horse opera, but as soon as Mann moved into Technicolor Westerns (*Bend of the River, The Naked Spur, The Far Country*) the pretentiousness and the artifice showed through the gay surface of the prints.

A film very much in the Anthony Mann mold was *Track of the Cat,* with Robert Mitchum, another strange, moody Eugene O'Neill-flavored Western directed by William Wellman. Its title was largely symbolic, and the mountain lion, or "cat," though an important plot factor, was never actually seen and assumed near-mystical proportions, representing different emotions to each man who tracked it.

Certainly one of the most off-beat Westerns ever made, it utilized Cinemascope with intelligence and made surprising use of color, with blacks and whites still predominating. In its slow, deliberate pacing, most notably in a grim burial sequence, photographed in a foreboding manner *from* the coffin as it is lowered into the ground, it more resembled the style of Carl Dreyer than the taut, deliberately harsh style Wellman had set in *The Ox-Bow Incident* and *Yellow Sky.*

Doc Holliday (Kirk Douglas) and Wyatt Earp (Burt Lancaster) walk toward the gunfight at the O.K. Corral in the 1956 reconstruction of that famous gunfight of 1870 in Tombstone, Arizona.

A psychological approach to a Western seems effective when it is allied with a traditional Western theme, as it was in *The Gunfighter,* but when the background is merely incidental to a story that could equally well take place in a city or on a desert island, that background of healthy, uncomplicated, outdoor life seems to make the complexity of the protagonists' problems appear both contrived and unimportant.

A Warner Technicolor Western, *Barricade,* seemed to possess quite astonishing vigor in its mixture of neuroses, sex, and violence—until one realized why. The film was a careful remake of Jack London's *The Sea Wolf,* meticulously transposed from ocean to plain, from ship to gold mine, but otherwise unchanged, with Raymond Massey performing ably as London's satanic villain.

Sheer neuroses found it harder than sheer eroticism making headway into "B" Westerns. Films like *The Tall Texan* and *Little Big Horn* had their psychological complications, but there was no indication that tortured psychological Westerns could ever hope to be as popular as the erotic Western, or even as popular as the old-fashioned straight-action horse opera. The purely psychological Western—the term is usually camouflage for a Western devoid of physical action, whether or not it is truly psychological—has been largely limited to a handful of medium-budget lesser "A" Westerns.

Alfred Werker's *At Gunpoint,* its lack of action rather pointlessly stressed by color and a wide Cinemascope screen on which nothing happened, drew rather too obviously on *High Noon* for its theme of civic responsibility. Its plot (a storekeeper becomes an overnight hero when he acci-

A scene from Broken Arrow *(1950)*.

dentally kills a bank robber and just as quickly is shunned by the townspeople when it becomes apparent that the outlaws plan to return for vengeance) was quite unusual and its use as a "hero" of a man without heroic or other distinguishing qualities was an interesting detour from well-worn paths. But a Western needs more than an unusual situation and an off-beat hero to sustain it, and *At Gunpoint* had nothing else. Even so, it was a more successful experiment than was Frank Sinatra's laborious and unconvincing *Johnny Concho,* a study of the regeneration of a bully and a coward. Not only was the "regeneration" facile and unbelievable, but the character himself was so unsympathetic that audiences could not reasonably be expected to *care* what became of him. Again, the *High Noon* theme of community responsibility was trotted out to save the "hero" in the film's "shoot-up" climax.

Racial conscience

The discovery that a "conscience" on racial problems can be profitable box office had been proved by Elia Kazan's *Pinky* and by other films dealing with the Negro question. It was not surprising, therefore, that the theme was exploited in the Western, especially since the "Indian question" was far less touchy and controversial. To Fox's credit the film that really started the Indian racial cycle, *Broken Arrow,* was no catchpenny "quickie." It was, in fact, a sincerely motivated, excitingly told story, based on fact, of the early misunderstandings between the whites and the Indians. Written and directed by Delmer Daves, always one of the most talented (and least recognized) Hollywood directors, it was a moving and sensitive film with some breathtakingly beautiful camera work; the sequence of the wedding between white man and Indian princess was exquisitely done.

Broken Arrow not only presented the Indians for the first time in years as sympathetic human beings with a genuine grievance, but it set a vogue for Indian heroes (Jeff Chandler played Cochise) which has been continued ever since. However, the film did not entirely have the courage of its convictions—or perhaps had Production Code jitters. Whatever the reason, the idyllic marriage between frontiersman James Stewart and Indian princess Debra Paget was not allowed to flourish. The wife was conveniently killed off in skirmishing towards the film's close, a few weak lines of dialogue insisting that her death was not in vain because it had brought Indian and white closer than ever before. Just how, was not explained, but for the next few years, Indian brides of white men were doomed to die before the final reel. Now, changing tastes seem to have permitted at least a few Indian brides to survive!

Prior to *Broken Arrow,* there had been no concerted effort to present the Indian sympathetically since the early days of Ince and films like *The Heart of an Indian.* Such films as *Ramona, Massacre,* and *The Vanishing American* were exceptions rather than the rule, and in any case they were more concerned with telling dramatic individual stories than with pleading the Indian's case. True, the Indian was not always presented as a hostile savage, but even when he was shown sympathetically, he was merely portrayed as a childlike native.

One of the standard "B" Western plots, that of *The Law Rides Again,* for example, concerned Indians threatening to take to the warpath again, usually because they were being cheated out of a few cattle by the local Indian agent. Hoot Gibson and Ken Maynard on most occasions managed to persuade them that the Great White Father in Washington was really their friend, proving it by restoring their stolen cattle. Indians as heroes were also hard to come by, although it was by no means uncommon for the hero to believe that he was an Indian (Buck Jones in *White Eagle,* for example), and to find out just before the fadeout that he was really a white man raised by the Indians, this revelation permitting him to marry the heroine after all.

Broken Arrow changed all that, and a new trend resulted, one based on a racial conscience. Westerns such as *Two Flags West, Tomahawk,* and *The Last Frontier* were positively overrun with crooked traders who cheated the Indians and precipitated wholesale wars, and with neurotic Indian-hating officers who went out of their way to provoke bloody battles! Notable films that, in one way or another, belong in this cycle were William Wellman's quite individual and impressive film, *Across the Wide Missouri* (a Clark Gable vehicle that went through the same, but less publicized, difficulties as did *The Red Badge of Courage* and was finally presented in a much mutilated version), *White Feather,* and the quite gentle and pleasing *Walk the Proud Land.* The parade of routine "misunderstood Indian" epics was endless—from *The Battle at Apache Pass* (again with Cochise in the saddle) through *Sitting Bull, Chief Crazy Horse,* and *The Savage.*

Interest in racial matters in the Western extended beyond the purely action subject. *Broken Lance,* in part, dealt with the prejudice against the Indian wife of a white rancher and her halfbreed son. This film was, incidentally, a remake of Joseph L. Mankiewicz's *House of Strangers,* which had dealt with Italian immigrants in America. There was also a marked decrease in the use of Negroes in Westerns; now that Westerns were stressing the equality of the races, they did not want to remind audiences of the still controversial Negro problem, and the faithful old black retainer, once a stand-by in Westerns, especially those with post-Civil War themes (e.g., *Badmen of Missouri*) became a thing of the past. For a while the Negro remained on the Western scene only in those horse operas made with all-black casts, and designed for exhibition in Negro theaters. There was, at one time, a fairly large market in the South, and in New York's and Chicago's Negro areas, for all-black pictures. These were usually limited to Westerns, with an emphasis on slapstick comedy and music (singer Herb Jeffries starred in a number of films), exuberantly religious features, often (to non-black eyes at least) in apparently very bad taste, and to particularly lurid sex-and-crime melodramas, of which a film magnificently entitled *Dirty Gertie From Harlem* is a typical example. Produced cheaply enough, these films nevertheless felt the pressure of rising production costs and declined in number, and, as in the case of the more orthodox "B" pictures, it was the horse opera that was the first to go.

With the withdrawal of the Negro, both as a *type,* and even as an individual, from the Western, other national and racial types began to disappear. That old comic stand-by, the excitable Chinese cook or laundryman, invariably played by rotund Willie Fung, was an immediate casualty. Of course, when national and political temperament is right, racial types *do* still appear in Westerns: during World War II it was positively amazing how many Nazis turned up on the "frontier" with plots to aid the Axis. Now, to a lesser degree, admittedly, it is an obviously Russian villain who occasionally seeks to upset Western justice. There is some mild justification in Western history for the use of a Russian heavy; at various times the Russians had projects of their own in both California and Alaska. Films like Raoul Walsh's *The World in His Arms* made rather obvious political capital of a plot involving a struggle between Russian and Yankee on what was to *become* American soil. Somewhat more incredible have been instances of "Communist infiltration" into the West on some of television's "Texas Rangers" series. The villains here have done the cliché of being Russian one better; they turn out to be representatives of "satellite" nations, equally bent, of course, on overthrowing the government.

The stuntman

and
the second
unit director

15

The Western has relied for many years on two figures who have not received their due: the stuntman and the second unit director. The stuntman is a highly trained athlete, adept at rough and tumble work, everything from fisticuffs and spectacular leaps to falls from horses and high dives. Some stuntmen specialize in one particular branch of activity while others take on any job that might break another man's neck. If that neck belongs to the star, the stuntman doubles in the individual action sequences. The second unit director, often a former stuntman himself, directs the staging of the action sequences, usually working independently of the film's official director.

Both the stuntman and the second unit director were relatively late to arrive on the scene. There is certainly no evidence that either function had been established prior to 1913; to the contrary, there is ample proof that early Westerns suffered due to the lack of these specialists. There *was* vitality and realistic action in many of the early Westerns, but even the best of them, including the films of Griffith and Ince, of course, frequently showed an unevenness which a stuntman or second unit director might well have prevented.

Falls from horses are, of course, essential to Western action scenes, but in the early days there were few actors capable of executing stunts of this sort well. Indeed, there was little incentive to risk one's neck in a fall which wouldn't add a penny to an actor's pay; the "extra" was employed to play dead, not to be particularly acrobatic about being shot off his horse, and in many early Westerns the audience could see the Indians bringing their horses to a halt after having been shot; they could *then* tumble with far more safety from the saddle. Even "playing dead" seemed to tax the abilities of some extras; an early episode of *The Perils of Pauline* is plagued by a couple of "dead" Indians forever popping their heads up out of the grass to see what is going on. In Griffith's admirable film *Fighting Blood,* there are momentary lapses due to the lack of efficient stunt work. A settler, wounded while driving a wagon at full speed, stops the wagon and *then* tumbles to the dust. Earlier, the excitement of *The Great Train Robbery* had been lessened somewhat by the obvious use of dummies during the latter part of the fight on the coal tender, when the victims were thrown from the train: in later years, such a situation would automatically have called for stuntmen.

Ince's stunt work—if one can term it that, for the phrase had not yet been born—was generally superior to that of Griffith for the simple reason that Ince *specialized* in Westerns and maintained a large crew of riders and cowboys, some of them rodeo trick riders who took riding stunts in their stride. *The Woman* (1913) had a particularly dangerous horse fall in a land rush sequence, so completely convincing and so obviously hazardous that it must be assumed that it was performed by a double for the heroine.

Doubtless one reason for the delayed appearance of the stuntman was the equally delayed appearance of the star. The motivation for the use of a stuntman was the risk involved for the star in tricky bits of business, either because the star was not up to the stunt or—and this was the major factor—because the stunt risked injury to the star. An injured stuntman can always be replaced and the picture can proceed without delay; but an injury to the star inevitably halts or slows production, sending costs soaring. Initially, especially at Biograph, the star system was not permitted to develop, and no actor was considered so important that he could not participate in the action when the plot demanded. Because actors were expected to perform their own physical action in the early Westerns, really dangerous stunting was not written into the scripts by the writers or insisted upon by the directors.

Recently, Spencer Gordon Bennet, one of the most prolific Western and serial directors, related how he had become unofficial stuntman in his first film, Edison's *A Moment of Madness,* made in 1914 and not a Western. In one sequence, the heroine fell off a yacht and was in danger of drowning. The hero of the film, Edward Earle, could not

Pioneer Scout (*1928*) *featured this hazardous stunt scene.*

swim, and it had not occurred to anyone to use a double for him. So he rushed over to a nearby sailor, played by Bennet, and asked *him* to save the girl. Bennet performed the rescue and reunited the heroine with her not very athletic suitor. On the basis of this little anecdote (and a study of the film bears out Bennet's story) we can safely assume that in 1912 the practice of doubling was, if not unknown, certainly still uncommon.

The lack of and need for second unit directors was less apparent in Griffith's films than in Ince's, undoubtedly because sweeping action was such a Griffith specialty that it is doubtful if any subordinate director could have improved on his results. Griffith, however, did use assistant directors hidden away as extras in his crowd scenes. Each had his own bit of action to direct, action predetermined by Griffith who remained in overall control of the scene. Thus, mass action was guided from within as well as from without. This procedure can hardly be considered the real forerunner of second unit direction, but it indicates that Griffith already realized the value of delegating responsibility in action scenes. Second unit direction actually came into its own in the Twenties, partly because of the large increase in the number of spectacles, but also because Hollywood had begun to veer away from mystery serials, placing greater stress on pure action content. Serials were usually shot by two or more units. The first unit, headed by the official director, concentrated on the plot, the studio scenes, and footage with the stars. The second unit would, at the same time, be away on location with a group of stuntmen, grinding out the fast action. Careful editing later would weave the output of both units into one cohesive whole.

B. Reaves Eason and Arthur Rosson

Leading second unit directors were B. Reaves Eason and Arthur Rosson. Rosson worked on most of Cecil B. De Mille's pictures, while Eason was responsible for the mighty chariot race and much of the sea battle in *Ben Hur* (1926), "officially" directed by Fred Niblo. It is ironic that *Ben Hur,* in other respects a dull picture, is remembered only for these two sequences, and such De Mille films as *The Plainsman,* otherwise held in low regard, are redeemed in the eyes of the critics by the well handled action sequences. In other words, the only episodes that Niblo and De Mille did *not* direct are the ones that are held up as examples of prime contributions to the cinema!

Rosson was with De Mille for some twenty years (one of his best creations was the Battle of New Orleans for a film made in 1938, *The Buccaneer*), but by no means exclusively. He also staged the big Indian attack on the covered wagon train in *Kit Carson* and the cattle stampede in Howard Hawks' *Red River.* Much earlier in the silent period he had been both an individual stuntman and a full-fledged director for Tom Mix and Hoot Gibson.

Many second unit directors who excel in their specialty, however, seem to have limited talent outside it. Eason's Westerns were lively, and a serial he directed, *The Galloping Ghost,* was a minor masterpiece of sustained stunting, but his dramatic talent was weak, and whenever the action lagged, he was an indifferent director. But his second unit contri-

Gene Autry's double transfers to a stagecoach in Loaded Pistols *(1949).*

butions, particularly in action involving horses, have been remarkable, ranging from the magnificent climax of *The Charge of the Light Brigade* of 1936 to the gathering of the ranchers in *Duel in the Sun,* the latter done in collaboration with another specialist, Otto Brower. Other typical Eason sequences: the splendid race between cavalry horses and a modern tank in Republic's *Army Girl* of 1938, a sequence that has been re-used as stock footage in many subsequent films; the jousting in *The Adventures of Robin Hood,* and the slapstick harness race in *Ma and Pa Kettle at the Fair.* Fast horse action remained Eason's specialty until his death in 1956. Next to the aforementioned sequences in *Ben Hur* and *The Charge of the Light Brigade,* his best work was probably the re-creation of the Battle of San Jacinto in *Man of Conquest* made in 1939. The film itself, Republic's first attempt to break into the "super-Western" category, was an extremely good one, rather unfairly neglected because it was not made by a major studio or with a prestige director (George Nicholls, Jr., directed). One of the best, and historically most accurate, films of its type, it dealt with the political and military career of Sam Houston (Richard Dix) culminating in the Texans' war of independence against the Mexicans, and the battles of the Alamo and San Jacinto. This last battle represented a triumphant union of stunt *organization* by Eason and stunt *execution* by Yakima Canutt's group of stuntmen. Starting with Houston's forces strung out in a long line, the sequence built rapidly into a magnificent charge as the Texans raced down a slope and ultimately into the San Jacinto River, completely routing the Mexican forces. Rapidly cut, beautifully photographed with a maximum use of the mobile camera, the sequence was as exciting as anything a major company could have produced, and a credit, therefore, to a small company like Republic. Canutt himself took several of the more spectacular horse falls, and the unit as a whole worked out some startlingly realistic wagon crashes and wholesale horse falls in the midst of exploding shells.

Cliff Lyons

In more recent years, Cliff Lyons, a former bit player and stuntman who had doubled for William Boyd and Ken Maynard, has donned the mantle put aside by Eason as the maestro of horse-action second unit work. Both John Wayne and John Ford utilized his services regularly.

In earlier years, manipulation of horse falls revolved principally around a device known as "The Running W"—ropes arranged strategically, and hidden from the camera, over which the horse tripped. The stuntman, knowing when to expect his fall, was prepared; the horse was not. The almost incredible number of horse falls in *The Charge of the Light Brigade* (brilliant editing undoubtedly made many of these falls seem far more brutal than they actually were) provoked the American Society for the Prevention of Cruelty to Animals into action, and the method was outlawed. Stuntmen then developed systems to signal the horse, so that it would fall on command with less risk of injury.

Lyons in his day was the foremost of the horse-fall specialists, and if there was any flaw in his work it was perhaps that it was just a little too perfect, suggesting its preparation. *The Comancheros*, a John Wayne Western made in 1961, in particular had too many scenes in which groups of stuntmen, all obviously acting on the same command, had their horses fall at the same split-second. Lyons' speciality has always remained the horse fall en masse, and he has never quite equaled Eason's work in other areas.

Other second unit directors

Other second unit directors of note include Andrew Marton, who staged the battle scenes in *The Red Badge of Courage* and who occasionally takes over as sole director. When John Huston left the Selznick production of *A Farewell to Arms* (1957), it was Marton who directed until a new prestige director could be assigned. Such was also the case with Willard Van Dyke, who took over *White Shadows in the South Seas* (1928) when Robert Flaherty left the film.

John D. Waters, who directed most of the Tim McCoy Westerns at MGM that were not directed by Van Dyke, also turned to second unit direction, among his credits being sequences from *Viva Villa!* and the

Indian attack from *Ambush.* Richard Talmadge, probably the best all-around stuntman of them all, and an amazing athlete (he doubled for Douglas Fairbanks in some of the most tricky acrobatic stunts from *The Mark of Zorro, The Mollycoddle* and *Robin Hood*) had his own starring series of action pictures in both the silent and sound eras; he, too, became a fine second unit director, principally at Paramount in the Thirties. More recently he staged the bruising, semi-comic fist fights in *North to Alaska.*

Chester Franklin, who died in 1956, was a specialist in animal scenes, and worked on a number of Westerns and semi-Westerns. It was Franklin who directed one of the best of the silent Rin Tin Tin films, *Where the North Begins,* the lovely film *Sequoia,* and the more sugar-coated *The Yearling.* (Only on the first of these films did he receive sole director credit.) Sam Nelson was one of the busiest second unit directors at Columbia, but his work lacked distinction in larger films, and he was best suited to the scores of routine "B" Westerns that were assigned to him. Another man who had always been associated with fairly routine "B" Westerns, Edward Killy, showed that when functioning as a second unit director with a large enough budget, he could produce brilliant action material. The battles and particularly the final charge in *Gunga Din* were his work.

Yakima Canutt

Unique among stuntmen and second unit directors is Yakima Canutt, who led both fields for many years, and who staged the big action scenes for *Ben Hur* (1961) and *El Cid* (1961). A former second-string Western star, Yakima switched to playing villains in the sound era, and at

Falls from horses work better atop a slight incline.

Yakima Canutt (a photo taken in the early Thirties).

Monogram and Mascot quickly established himself as the top stuntman. Being an actor of sorts was a distinct advantage in that he could play prominent supporting roles in addition to handling the falls and fights. One of his most astounding stunts took place in the Mascot serial *The Devil Horse* (1932), directed by stunt expert Otto Brower. Doubling for Harry Carey, Canutt literally fought the horse of the title, hanging by his feet from the horse's neck while it reared, plunged, rolled in the dust and wheeled around at top speed in an effort to throw him. Mascot serials were crudely put together, but they *moved* and serials like *The Devil Horse, The Three Musketeers,* and *The Hurricane Express* provided all the opportunities Canutt and his colleagues could want. Canutt was soon the leading stuntman at Mascot (later to become Republic), Monogram, and at independent studios as well. At Monogram, Canutt was not only the perennial villain in series with John Wayne, Rex Bell, and others, but he was also Wayne's permanent double. In this latter capacity he was often very carelessly photographed: e.g., the director would offer a medium close-up of Canutt leaping into the saddle, and only seconds later did the audience realize that it was supposed to have been Wayne. The last reel often found Canutt, doubling for Wayne, chasing himself!

One extremely hazardous stunt was a Canutt specialty. It usually found its way into the last reel as the villain attempted to make his escape on a stagecoach. The hero raced after the coach on horseback, and as he drew abreast, he would raise his arms to grasp the back of the coach preparatory to the transfer. At this point, of course, there was always a neat cut to a reverse or long shot, enabling the stunt man to take over from the star. Canutt, clutching the rocking coach, hauled himself from the saddle, clung from the back of the coach, drew himself over the top, advanced to the driver's seat, and engaged the villain in some furious fighting. In films where Canutt was also the villain, matters became a trifle confused since Canutt was doubling for the hero, obliging someone else to double for *him!* The only person uninvolved was the hero, who was seen only in close-up inserts shot separately. After fighting on top of the careening coach, the two men would break apart and Canutt would fall between the horses. He would hang for a few seconds from the wooden shaft just above the flying hooves, and finally let go. (An alternative action had the struggling men fall on the horses themselves, the fight continuing for a few moments on the shaft between them.) Then, as the coach passed over him, Canutt would grasp the rear axle, permitting himself to be dragged along. Slowly he would turn over on his stomach, climb to the top of the coach once more, this time to subdue the villain for keeps.

Canutt performed this stunt, with variations, for Jack Randall in *Riders of the Dawn*, for Roy Rogers in *Young Bill Hickok* and *Sunset in Eldorado*, and for countless other players. At Republic, in addition to acting and directing several features and serials, he organized a group of stuntmen with well-trained horses and specially rigged equipment, which he directed (or controlled under another's direction) in large-scale Westerns, as well as in such "disguised" horse operas as *Storm Over Bengal* (1938).

Apart from the Battle of San Jacinto, mentioned earlier, he staged the escape from the prairie fire in *Dakota*, and the dash of the oil-laden wagons through a blazing canyon in *In Old Oklahoma* (1943). In another excellent historical epic, *Dark Command* (1940), he drove a team of horses and a buggy off a high cliff. His expert hand (and he himself) were to be seen in the chase over the salt flats in *Stagecoach* (1939). Canutt, no longer young, has given up personal stunting, but he still directs an occasional "B" Western, *The Lawless Rider* (1954), for example. He was responsible for the expert second unit work on such films as *Ivanhoe* (1952), with its first-rate jousting scenes, and *Helen of Troy* (1956), notable for some brilliant and truly lavish battles. His son carries on the family tradition as a stuntman; it was he who doubled for Charlton Heston in the chariot race crackup in *Ben Hur* (1961).

David Sharpe.

David Sharpe

Not far behind Canutt in ability is David Sharpe, a former child star, also a competent actor, who took many featured roles as well as occasional leads in Westerns. Now in his late fifties, he retains a slim figure and youthful appearance. Sharpe is a fine rider and an all-around stuntman, but acrobatics are his specialties: leaps, falls from horses, wild fisticuffs. He worked on some of Fairbanks' last pictures and seems to have had much of the great star's grace. (Douglas, Jr., utilized his services as both a double and stunt organizer, too.) If anything, Sharpe's stunting is too mechanically slick, and occasionally it dispels conviction.

In *The Perils of Nyoka* (1942), one of the fastest-paced serials ever made, Sharpe doubled for literally everyone in the cast, the heroine included! In the Fifties, he switched to Universal, bringing his athletic prowess to bear as a double for Tony Curtis, Alan Ladd, and others. Some of his best stunting for this studio was in the intelligent and above-average Western *The Man from the Alamo* (1953), in which he doubled strenuously for Glenn Ford. He was also the standard double for Guy Madison in his "Wild Bill Hickok" television series, in which he was often photographed in such near close-up that the substitution was painfully obvious. Of late, Sharpe has been following Canutt's path: coaching stars and directing action sequences.

Fred Graham

One of the leading specialists in really rugged brawls is Fred Graham. His very appearance is usually a tip-off that a free-swinging fracas is on the way. His barber-shop encounter with Arthur Kennedy in Fritz Lang's *Rancho Notorious* (1952) was particularly bloody and singularly unmotivated. Graham's appearance in one non-Western is perhaps worth mentioning: John Ford seemed to be kidding Graham's prolific activity as a movie scrapper when in *The Wings of Eagles* (1957), Fred appeared on both sides of one battle—as a Navy man and as an Army opponent. In one of the two roles Graham sported a small mustache, but since Ford delighted in incorporating full close-ups of *both* Grahams glowering at the camera, he was presumably having a little fun on the side.

Stunting and doubling may, as in the case of Jack Mahoney, Ray Corrigan, Kermit Maynard, and George O'Brien, be an introduction to stardom for some actors, but for others it can sometimes mean the end of the trail. Jim Bannon, who was a promising "B" Western leading man at Columbia in the mid-Forties, later starring in one or two minor series, dropped out of sight only to reappear in the early Fifties as a double for Bill Elliott in fight scenes at Allied Artists.

Apart from the "straight" riding and fighting stuntmen, there must also be even more specialized performers. Burly Duke York did some good scenes fighting wolf-dog Chinook in a series of James Oliver Curwood adventures for Monogram. Poundage is a definite asset in such fights, for even the experienced stuntman needs ample padding, and on a slightly built man padding is a little too obvious. (Padding is particularly noticeable in the scenes in which men of slight stature are struck by Indian arrows!)

Bud Osborne

The apparently straightforward job of stagecoach driving is, however, also very much of a specialized area. The old Wells Fargo drivers had to be as physically fit as the Pony Express riders, and many of their exploits have become legend. There was the famous Hank Monk who, according to Wells Fargo records, "had as many press notices as a prima donna." It was Monk who drove Horace Greeley down the Sierra slopes at a furious pace, catapulted his celebrated passenger through the roof, and calmly told him: "Keep your seat, Horace, and we'll get you there on time!" Even more colorful was Charlie Pankhurst, a whip-wielding daredevil who once routed a gang of highwaymen single-handed. "Charlie" lived to be sixty-six, and only on his death did Wells Fargo discover that its foremost stagecoach driver was, in fact, a woman! In Hollywood Westerns, one player has assumed the role of Hank and Charlie almost exclusively—Bud Osborne. Osborne, a former stunt rider with Buffalo Bill's Wild West Show, has been in movies since 1915, primarily as a villain. His principal distinction has been his ability to handle any kind of wagon or coach, equipped with any number of horses, and to drive it at top speed over the roughest kind of terrain.

Stunt movies

Despite the obvious excitement and drama inherent in movie stunting, there have been few movies about it, and almost no good ones. Two RKO films of the early Thirties, *The Lost Squadron* and *Lucky Devils,* came near to success, but neither dealt with Western stunting. The bulk of the others were primarily cheap action pictures which implied that stunting was mainly a matter of brawn and luck. *Sons of Adventure* made by Republic was inauthentic and unconvincing, despite plenty of

"Bulldogging," a technique for capturing cattle adapted to the capturing of badmen.

action and direction by Yakima Canutt himself. *Hollywood Thrillmakers* was merely a cheaply fashioned parade of old Richard Talmadge stunts, allegedly being performed by William Henry. The basic situation of Fox's *Shooting High* (1940) was genuinely, if unintentionally, amusing. Gene Autry played a cowboy who was hired to double for the star (Robert Lowery) of a Western that was being shot in the cowboy's neighborhood. We see the camera stop grinding on Lowery as Autry, in close-up, walks into the scene and replaces Lowery in order to stunt for him. Then, in almost telescopic long shot, a double performs the stunt for Autry. When the excitement is over, the camera returns to a close-up of Autry grinning amiably and dusting himself off! In an earlier Western, *The Big Show*, Autry played a dual role as both a Western star *and* a stuntman double. Needless to say, both Autrys made liberal use of Yakima Canutt in a wild sequence which took place practically beneath the hooves of a galloping wagon team.

Films like this generate the impression, one largely true, that few Western stars are capable of performing stunts themselves. Obviously most are not, and even those that are, usually, for obvious reasons, submit to doubling. But in all fairness it should be recorded that some stars—Tom Mix and George O'Brien, in particular—only infrequently resorted to doubles, while others—Johnny Mack Brown, Gilbert Roland, Jack Randall, Tom Tyler, and Ken Maynard—on various occasions proved their capabilities with stunts filmed in close-up.

While there is naturally a limit to the number of stunts that can be devised around horses, cliffs, or fight scenes, there seems to be no limit to the number of ways a given stunt can be performed. And quite often a stunt that "misfires" will prove more exciting than a perfectly executed one. A case in point occurred in the 1934 John Wayne Monogram Western, *The Trail Beyond*. The stuntman (probably Canutt) doubling for Wayne draws abreast of the open wagon in which the villain is making his escape. He is to leap onto the wagon from his horse, engage the villain in a fight, and topple with him down a steep incline. But the timing was off. He leaps—and misses—just grabbing the bars on the outside of the wagon instead of landing securely. For a moment he clings there, being dragged along almost under the front wheels. Obviously he realizes that there is no way to salvage the stunt, so he lets go, rolls in the dust, gets to his feet, leaps on his horse, resumes the chase, and does the stunt again—correctly. The photographer had the presence of mind to keep the camera going the whole time, and the exciting sequence was used *in toto*. Such "failures" can be seen only in the cheaper

Stuntman Fred Graham (right) in a fight scene with Johnny Mack Brown from Lone Star Trail (*1943*).

Jumping horses from a fast-moving train, a difficult stunt from When the Daltons Rode *(1940).*

Westerns, where tight shooting schedules often prevent such a scene from being shot over again.

Bulldogging scenes, in which the hero leaps from his galloping horse onto the fleeing villain, dragging him down from his horse, frequently go wrong, too. Usually the actual fall takes place atop a slight incline so that the stuntmen's bodies hit not flat ground, but a slope, enabling them to roll to safety. But the slightest change in the speed of one of the horses can throw the timing off. Sometimes (as happened in *Outlaws of Sonora*) the stuntman misses entirely; more often the fall is not "right" and it is quite apparent from the way the men fell that the one underneath has been knocked unconscious. Sloppy editing such as that in *Smoking Guns*, (1934), will sometimes leave the "hero" lying prone from his fall for a few frames, before the next frame is projected of the suitably dusty hero leaping to his feet to continue the fight. Timing is the essence of all such stunt work, particularly those stunts involving wagon crashes in which the stuntman has but seconds to jump clear before the wagon lands on top of him. In many cases, the shooting of such stunts is almost as tricky as their execution. A camera car racing along in front of a runaway wagon, with the hero perched on the shaft, having just released the horses, is obviously in some jeopardy from the driverless vehicle. The intricate riding stunts in Ken Maynard's silent *Red Raiders* included several shots taken at ground level between galloping horses. Camera crews shooting such sequences are often, by union requirement, given stuntmen's pay themselves.

Through the years, stuntmen or the stars themselves have handled every conceivable kind of action. In *Truthful Tulliver* (1916) William Hart rode Fritz through a plate glass window. In 1942 Buck Jones and Silver did the same stunt the easy way; he rode his horse through an empty frame, but a quick cut to a reverse angle, the throwing into the scene of some broken glass, and the liberal use of sound effects created a convincing illusion. Large-scale Westerns like *Dodge City* and *The Spoilers* have provided field days for stuntmen specializing in fisticuffs, with all-out fights in which saloons have been realistically wrecked—some credit due, of course, to the breakaway furniture used and stairways that collapse when half-a-dozen toughs get on them. Staging fights *between* horses is an art in itself, and one never fully mastered, since the ropes holding each horse back have always been at least partially visible. And one of the trickiest of all horse stunts has never been repeated: in *When the Daltons Rode* (1940), stuntmen rode their horses off a moving train and then down a steep incline parallel to the tracks.

Unfortunately, the importance of the stuntman, except as part of mass spectacle action, has declined in recent years. The increased use of back projection has made it all too easy to fake stunts, even though it is impossible to duplicate the excitement of the real thing. Then, too, the elimination of "B" pictures generally, and of Western and other serials in particular, has meant that the field has automatically become smaller. The lively days of the Thirties when Yakima Canutt and hordes of stuntmen recklessly risked life and limb at Mascot are gone forever, replaced by action created in the studio in front of a process screen, and rendered even less realistic in panoramic Cinemascope. *Sic transit gloria mundi*; so fades the tradition of the exploits of a breed of gallant and brave men.

Rory Calhoun

Exeunt the "B"s, enter

television

16

The stars wane

The early Fifties saw the beginning of the end of the "B" Western. In 1940 almost thirty Western stars were active, but 1950 could offer only a handful: Roy Rogers, Allan Lane, Monte Hall, Rex Allen, Johnny Mack Brown, Whip Wilson, Gene Autry, Charles Starrett, and Tim Holt. Before the final death knell sounded, two more series were begun by Monogram-Allied Artists, one with Bill Elliott, the other with Wayne Morris. A dozen Elliott pictures were made, only half that many with Morris, before it was conceded that even such well-written and above-average "B" Westerns were still uneconomical propositions.

Between 1950 and 1954 *all* "B" Western series were eliminated; Monte Hall was the first casualty, Rex Allen and Wayne Morris were the last. With the sole exception of Randolph Scott, who maintained an average of two minor "A" productions a year for Columbia and Warner Brothers, the industry was entirely without Western stars, a condition that had not existed since Broncho Billy Anderson had made the genre so popular at Essanay in 1908!

There were several contributing factors to the sudden demise of the small-scale horse opera. One, of course, was the fact that the top Western stars were no longer young. Even Johnny Mack Brown, a relative newcomer compared to veterans like Ken Maynard and Hoot Gibson, was in his fifties—one of the few new stars that had been developed since 1940 who approached the stature of the old-timers. Some, like Jimmy Wakely, Eddie Dean, and John Kimbrough, just failed to make the grade and faded from view even before the decline set in. Kimbrough, a former football player, lasted for only two films! Dean had been given all the advantages of fairly elaborate productions by PRC and his initial films achieved above average success through their use of the newly developed Cinecolor. However, these did little to sell Dean personally and soon reverted to black and white. As the *New York Daily News* reported in reviewing his *Hawk of Powder River:* "Eddie Dean's latest is in black and white rather than color but the improvement is hardly noticeable; you can still see him."

The rise in production costs

In 1950, television was inundated with "B" Westerns made from 1930 on, initially just the cheaper independent material, but before long all the polished little Westerns from the major companies, too. Here were a great number of films that in terms of production value and excitement were unquestionably superior to the Westerns that Columbia, Republic, and Monogram were still making. As new television markets opened, and as further blocks of old films were leased to them, the theatrical market for new Westerns diminished. There was little incentive now for the studios to improve their small-budget Westerns; they continued to be made for their limited markets, located in the South and in northern cities with big black populations, but they were markets that were steadily shrinking and the films even there did little more than break even. The big profits from "cheap" Westerns were a thing of the past, and in fact "cheap" Westerns themselves were an illusion. A Western that would have cost fifteen or twenty thousand dollars in the mid-Thirties was now costing sixty thousand, and even this budget was held to only by careful cutting of corners. For example, the expensive running inserts, shot from camera cars, were replaced by the simpler, cheaper, and less dramatic pan shots. Mobile camera work was reduced to a minimum, resulting in long static dialogue takes devoid of movement or intercutting. Casts and even livestock were reduced to skeleton forces, and a maximum use was made of stock footage. Increasingly, Republic and especially Columbia began to build their Westerns around available footage, and the latter studio used it so extensively that they were turning out their "new" Westerns on three-day shooting schedules! The plot of *Laramie*, for example, was arranged so that it could use all the big scenes from John Ford's *Stagecoach*, complete to the chase across the salt flats and the cavalry racing to the rescue. Occasional close-up inserts of Charles Starrett, dressed to match the long and medium shots of John Wayne, furthered the deception.

Only RKO's Tim Holt series made any attempt to maintain worth-

Economy measures: the dramatic and exciting running inserts (below) shot from camera trucks, often in picturesque locations, were supplanted in the Fifties by static scenes (right) shot from fixed ground camera positions, in drab locations only a few miles from Hollywood.

while standards of production value. The films remained full of action, well written, well cast, and intelligently directed. But these virtues, including frequent changes in camera set-up to avoid the long takes that were making the other "B" Westerns pedestrian, took their toll. The Tim Holt films cost as much as ninety thousand dollars apiece without making a dollar more than competitive Westerns which cost two-thirds or even less of that amount to produce.

Thus, despite every possible economy, including the bolstering of current series with reissues, and cutting new output from the standard eight pictures per year to six, and even four, the "B" Western was doomed. Every "gimmick" was tried—even the use of half-a-dozen Western stars in one film—in vain. The last regular "B" series Western to be released, in September 1954, was Monogram's *Two Guns and a Badge,* a Wayne Morris vehicle in the old austere vein, with a simple plot and no songs or other modern accouterments, and even a title in the old manner. It was no spectacular swan song for the "B," but it was an appropriate and respectable close. In addition to being the last of its class, it was also, sadly, the last film of its director, Lewis D. Collins, one of the most prolific directors of expert minor Westerns. He died shortly after its completion.

Doubtless *individual* "B" Westerns will always be made by very small operators on a strictly independent and non-series basis, but the number of these is so small, and their quality so poor, that they constitute no likelihood of a revival or even a limited continuation of the "B" Western as a class in itself. One or two producers reasoned that with all the major companies withdrawing from the field, the market was wide open for cheaply made Westerns. The films that emerged from this mentality were so inferior that most of them, even with low budgets, failed to recoup their costs. One producer of a James Ellison-Russell Hayden series hit on a unique method of keeping his budgets down to twenty thousand dollars per picture. Apart from using a maximum of stock footage, often ancient and poorly inserted, he also put identical casts into each film, shot every chase and fight from several angles, worked on a minimum of two pictures at a time, and came up with a group of six Westerns so identical that it was impossible to tell one from the other! To compound the confusion, he later sold the group to television under completely different titles! Another producer, theater-owner Joy Houck, made an appalling series of Westerns starring Al "Lash" LaRue, built around liberal helpings of sequences from his older starring films, and featuring only a minimum of new and cheaply filmed studio scenes.

One of the more enterprising of these independent Western producers was John Carpenter, who operated in the capacity of actor, writer, director, and producer. Neither Hart nor Mix had tried to bite off quite as much as this! A good enough actor, and certainly a highly competent rider and stuntman, Carpenter was not particularly attractive in appearance, rather too old to catch on with youngsters as a Western hero, and too familiar as a bit player to launch himself as a new personality. Instead, he cashed in on a slight resemblance to Montgomery Clift by dress-

A John Carpenter film, Son of the Renegade *(1953). Example of an overdone attempt at the classic Western.*

ing himself as Clift had done in *Red River!* In his plots Carpenter certainly tried for the unusual, and for what he felt was a realistic reconstruction of the early West, but he crammed so much into his plots that they moved too quickly and illogically, and it was just impossible to take them seriously. The fights were fantastically overdone displays of stunting ability, the gun battles, all gloriously and heroically posed, too obviously emulated—in a critic's opinion—the paintings of Remington, Flagg, and others. To all this, he added a fondness for casting himself in a dual role, and for duplicating snatches of action patently lifted from great Westerns. Carpenter (who also used the name of John Forbes at times) certainly had his limitations as a writer-director, but it was his further shortcomings as a business man and promoter that really doomed his films. Nothing if not enterprising, but a babe in the woods in Hollywood financial circles, Carpenter sometimes found that in his efforts to raise backing he had sold away rather more than one hundred percent of the picture! When money ran out, he would try to finish a film cheaply, using non-union camera crews and shooting in sixteen millimeter, having the results blown up to thirty-five millimeter. More than once, because of unpaid lab bills, the negatives to his films were attached, and it was often a year or two before they were freed for ultimate release. In an effort to keep costs low, or in return for financial support, he used friends and associates in his films as both actors and technicians. Leading ladies like "Texas Rose" Bascom and supporting players like "Big Red" Carpenter, John's brother, added nothing but amateur ineptitude to his films. Only one, *The Lawless Rider,* emerged with a professional stamp on it, as a result of Alex Gordon's production and Yakima Canutt's direction. The majority of his films, of which *Badman's Gold* and *Outlaw Treasure* are typical, emerged mainly as hodge-podge affairs. Carpenter's work does not warrant perhaps the space we have given him, but his activities illustrate particularly well the less-publicized, the independent, side of film-making on poverty row.

Borderline Westerns

Replacing the quickly and cheaply made Westerns, was a newcomer: a new type of "B" Western which made its appearance in the early Fifties. It did not, of course, consider itself "B" in any way. Films in this group were eighty-minute Technicolor Westerns with stars of some stature—Randolph Scott, Audie Murphy, Tony Curtis, Rory Calhoun, Sterling Hayden, Stephen McNally, and others. They were produced by Warners, Republic, Columbia, Paramount, Allied Artists, and especially Universal in quantities almost equaling the cheap Westerns produced by them in earlier years. *Shotgun, Drums Across the River, Santa Fe,* and *Wichita* were among the best of this generally high-standard group. Decidedly a product of the Fifties, they were, in scope and budget, several notches below the standards of such previous, less mass-produced "A" Westerns as *Dodge City* and *Stagecoach,* yet they could boast of considerable production values and often better-than-average scripts. Above all, they presented plenty of slick, fast-paced action, the kind one usually associated with the humble "B" Western. Initially they caught on well with the public as top features.

Universal, having abandoned its "B" series, still needed Westerns and so embarked on these more expensive programmers at a time when other companies like Monogram and Republic were still struggling to sustain their five-reel black-and-white oaters. The competition of these Technicolor Westerns was one more factor which hastened the end of the few remaining small Westerns. Obviously, if the average exhibitor could pay a few dollars more to obtain a color film with Randolph Scott, a film long enough to obviate the need for a co-feature, he had little call to buy the five-reeler with Charles Starrett or Rex Allen.

However, within a very few years these "new look" Westerns were quickly relegated to the supporting feature category. Of course, they were still strong attractions in the rural areas, commanded respectable rental rates, and were good overseas sellers (more so than the regular "B"s, which were too short for the predominantly single-bill European market), but since the costs of color and name casts meant not inexpensive budgets, they were basically not much more profitable than the "B"s they were replacing. Most did show a profit of sorts and since exhibitors and public alike found them preferable to the old black-and-white Westerns available on television, they have become, it would seem, permanent fixtures, although after 1960 their number declined somewhat.

The production value of these Westerns must have discouraged small producers and independents who were still trying to make profitable minor Westerns. An attempt was made by these producers to overcome their competition by loading their own pictures with "gimmicks," most specifically, controversial new "versions" of Western history, and the wholesale exploitation of violence and sex, always a safe proposition commercially. A number of crude and tasteless productions, of which *The Daltons' Women* and *Jesse James' Women* were the most vulgar, were rushed to the market; their principal attractions were blatant sexual suggestiveness and all-out saloon brawls between rather bare-bosomed dancing girls. Fortunately, the very cheapness of these films prevented their ever achieving wide popularity, and they remained merely novelty attractions. (The ultimate was reached in 1961 with some films that were out-and-out exploitations of nudity, of which *The Bare West* is a fairly representative sample.) Fight scenes now were devised to be as brutal as possible; in *Rancho Notorious,* for example, a sixteen millimeter camera nosed its way in and out of the fight scenes in order to capture candidly all the bloody highlights.

Not only the morals turned topsy-turvy in these films, but, more distressing, history was often completely distorted, a good example being provided by *Jack McCall, Desperado.* Initially the film depicted Wild Bill Hickok as a completely unscrupulous renegade, guilty of trafficking with the Indians, in addition to being a cold-blooded killer. Certainly, in previous films, Hickok, who had been played by Gary Cooper, William S. Hart, Roy Rogers, Bill Elliott, and Richard Dix among many others, had been whitewashed and idealized; there is no doubt that there were unsavory sides to his character, and a good deal of his reputation is more legend than facts but basically he was on the right side of the law. A further distortion occurred in the casting of honest-appearing, virile George Montgomery as Jack McCall, the man who callously shot Hickok in the back in order to win fame and glory. The film showed McCall beating Hickok to the draw in a fair fight, with audience sympathy all on McCall's side, his parents having been murdered by Hickok. Historical fact was followed to the extent of having McCall arrested, condemned to death, and subsequently pardoned; this and McCall's marriage made a conveniently happy ending. However, equally conveniently, the producer forgot to note that immediately after McCall's pardon he was re-arrested by Federal troops, retried, and promptly hanged!

Television's grind; re-enter Gene Autry

The gradual abandonment of "B" Westerns for theatrical release and their adoption by television duplicated, in a general way, the situation that had existed in Hollywood with the arrival of sound. The field of Westerns to be made *specifically* for television was wide open; new formats and stars could be created, and already established stars whose thrones had been threatened by the diminishing value of the Western were given a new lease on life.

The first important star to enter the new medium in the late Forties was Gene Autry. Although he was still producing his own theatrical Westerns for Columbia, and encountering hostile reactions from exhibitors who complained that patrons would not pay to see Autry in theaters when they could see him for nothing at home, he twisted the argument's tail by declaring that his television films would, in fact, stimulate extra business for his theatrical ones. At this point, television was relatively new, its effects unknown, and the motion picture industry felt that it constituted a grave threat. Participation in it by top stars was rare, and producers, distributors, and exhibitors alike were up in arms in their determination to withhold cooperation from the new medium. This determination relaxed a good deal in subsequent years when it became apparent to these same people that there was money to be made from television!

In all probability, Autry did not really believe his own assertion that his television films would assist his theatrical ones; it has held true in only one case, that of producer Walt Disney. A shrewd businessman, Autry probably realized long before his competitors did that television was to be the new outlet for the cheap Western, and the *only* consistent one. Under the banner of his Flying A Productions he developed several series in addition to the one starring himself: the "Range Rider" group with Jack Mahoney, "The Adventures of Champion," a horse series, "Buffalo Bill, Jr." starring Dick Jones, and "Annie Oakley" with Gail Davis.

Television's needs

Requirements for television Westerns are far more rigid than they ever were for theatrical releases. For one thing, they have to pass the inspection of sponsors and advertising agencies long before they are broadcast. Each story has to be told in a running time of twenty-six minutes, providing a half-hour show with time out for commercials. In addition, it must be constructed so that the dramatic or action highlight immediately preceding the break for the commercial will be strong enough to hold viewers' attention. Television programming is such that groups of thirteen, twenty-six or thirty-nine shows are required for a series, meaning that the television Western is much more of a mass produced commodity than were small Westerns for theatrical release, which never ran to more than eight a year in any one series.

In order to facilitate quick and economical production, it was necessary to build up a sort of stock company of technicians and actors, much as Griffith and Ince had done in their own short pre-1914 Westerns. Autry assembled a particularly efficient unit consisting of directors like William Witney and John English, players like comedian Pat Buttram, leading lady Gail Davis, character actors Denver Pyle, Lyle Talbot, and Don Harvey, and sundry hillbilly musical groups. Their talents were pooled and applied with the same energy that marked all of Autry's activities.

Mass production for predetermined markets inevitably means that quantity is more important than quality. Television Westerns were certainly no better than the down-graded theatrical Westerns they were supplanting, but since their stories were told in only three reels, they were faster and slicker. In story content, however, they were usually much inferior. Designed specifically for juvenile audiences, but needing adult approval (since it would be the adults who would buy the products advertised by the show's sponsor), the films succeeded in providing action and simple comedy, avoiding elements such as sex, strong drama, or brutality, which might alienate viewers supervising their children's entertainment. Playing it completely safe, Autry and others tended to make fast but completely anemic films: what might have been a mere plot element in one of Autry's prior Westerns would now be strung out into the complete plot line.

The small television screen required a maximum of close-up work, and a minimum of fast intercutting. Producing the films on, or under, budget (thirty thousand dollars being an average figure for a good quality half-hour Western) also produced a tendency to long static takes and lengthy dialogue exchanges. These protracted scenes, plus the stress on close-ups, gave these new "pocket" Westerns a rather "stagey" appearance at times. And the necessity for close-up work had its distinct disadvantages: Autry and some of his colleagues were beginning to age rather visibly, and this did not escape the scrupulous eye of the camera; the use of doubles in action scenes also became that much

Dennis Weaver

James Arness

more obvious. More obvious, too, than in theatrical films were the studio sets. A blank white backdrop with a couple of false trees planted in front of it just could not pass muster as an "exterior." Cheaply made series, such as "The Lone Ranger," staged almost all their action, interior *and* exterior, within these cramped and obvious sets. A few chases, for use throughout the entire series, would be shot in genuine exteriors and intercut with all the patently artificial studio footage. The more expensive and carefully planned television Westerns had to contend with the necessity for haste no less than cheaply made films; shows had to be completed on schedule, to meet an air-time deadline. Sets could be serviceable at best, and rarely compared with the at least workmanlike sets of the cheaper theatrical Westerns.

The television Western was in fact a factory-made product, and with so many limitations placed upon them, it is surprising that many films emerged as well as they did. One reason that they did is perhaps that they were not made by television personnel, but by the same veterans who had been making theatrical Westerns for years. For example, director on some of television's "Cisco Kid" adventures was Lambert Hillyer, maker of some of the best Hart and Mix Westerns.

From a standpoint of action content and modest but efficient production values, some of these television horse operas, especially those of Autry, came out quite creditably. Autry incidentally reduced the musical content of his films considerably, and concentrated more on action than at any time previous.

Hopalong Cassidy

In the wake of Autry's success, the trend was to exploit both Western stars and actual historical figures. In the former category, Autry's number one rival—they had, of course, been rivals in the days of theatrical competition, too—was William Boyd. Boyd was on the verge of bankruptcy when television arrived literally in the nick of time to restore his popularity. In setting himself up as a producer, he had secured the apparently worthless rights to his old Hopalong Cassidy films. He not only earned a fortune leasing these features to television at the time when they were the *only* Westerns of major studio origin to be seen on the home screen but, more important, he reawakened national interest in the Hopalong Cassidy character. This accomplished, he was able to start a completely new series of Cassidy Westerns specifically for television's use. Boyd's tenure as a cowboy on television was brief, but for a while he remained its brightest star, reaping the usual subsidiary benefits. These far exceeded the mere grosses from film rental; also very much involved were the considerable profits which accrued from Hopalong Cassidy comic books, toy guns, Western outfits, and sundry other products, plus revenue from guest appearances at rodeos, circuses, in street parades sponsored by large stores, and even in De Mille's film *The Greatest Show on Earth*. Following in the wake of this success, all of Clarence E. Mulford's Hopalong Cassidy novels were reprinted and completely rewritten to tie in with the uncommon conception of Cassidy as an idealistic and gentlemanly Western hero. Mulford's excellent authoritative picture of the West was therefore completely distorted, to be presented anew on the level of a "B" Western.

Other stars

Roy Rogers, who quit theatrical film production a little later than Autry, was also to be seen in a television series; although popular, it failed to repeat the success of the Autry pictures, perhaps because of a rather more brutal approach to action content. Moreover, Rogers and his leading lady and wife, Dale Evans, are both deeply religious, and their occasional philosophizing did not sit too well with youngsters who were far more interested in gun play than gospel-thumping.

Another Autry rival was a star under contract to him, appearing in a series produced by Autry: Jack Mahoney and his "Range Rider" series. Mahoney was a former stuntman, and this lively series was successfully designed to exploit his outstanding athletic and acrobatic ability. Exploiting characters rather than stars were the series dealing with the Lone Ranger (Clayton Moore), Wild Bill Hickok (Guy Madison), and Kit Carson (Bill Williams). Of course, all these films produced revenue above and beyond television rentals by lending their titles and the names of their stars to accessory products. Theatrical release in Europe added to the profits.

Just as the theatrical "B" had fallen from grace, so in a much shorter time did the television Westerns. The principal contributing factor was the sale to television of old Westerns starring Gene Autry and Roy Rogers, and other Westerns not previously seen on television. They all were naturally of a much higher standard than the television Westerns then being made by the same stars.

As always in such situations, the need for a new "gimmick" was evident, and in 1952 it took two forms: the popularizing of national heroes who were not necessarily Western heroes; second, the skillful application to Western themes of what may be termed a composite of *High Noon* and "Dragnet" approaches, "Dragnet" in particular having been a fabulously successful detective television series, relying for its effect on dramatic understatement and pseudo-documentary writing.

A series such as "Gunsmoke" is perhaps most typical of this second form, the films of which have come to be known as "adult" Westerns, a term bestowed gratuitously upon itself by television. It is true that such films have a more sober and realistic approach than those of Autry and Rogers, and undoubtedly adult audiences view them with more favor. However, juvenile audiences have been found to enjoy them as much. Their "adult" label derives more from the fact that the films are being shown at night when youngsters are presumed to be in bed. "Gunsmoke" has certainly retained the highest overall standard of this new brand of Westerns. Relying more on characterization and drama than on straightforward action, it has handled several near-psychological themes. Its underplayed depiction of the U. S. marshal as a colorless official doing an unglamorous job, derives directly from "Dragnet," while the recurring elements of civic responsibility in the maintenance of law derive from *High Noon*. Unfortunately such elements, gripping and original in individual films, inevitably become stereotyped when they are merely part of a formula. The marshal's human weaknesses and moments of self-doubt in "Gunsmoke" ultimately tend to become as much clichés as the invincible heroism and fearlessness of heroes in Westerns that go to the opposite extreme. "Gunsmoke" was popular enough to survive both imitation and outright parody, and in 1961 it switched from a half-hour format to a full hour. Its influence on other series has been considerable, and one of the better ones to emerge in the wake of "Gunsmoke" was "Wyatt Earp," dealing with the career of the U. S. marshal, played by Hugh O'Brian. Because of the tremendous audience exposure such shows get, their ability to build stars is phenomenal; James Arness, the star of "Gunsmoke," and Hugh O'Brian, the star of "Wyatt Earp," although comparatively unknown at first, soon became important box office properties. O'Brian even appeared in a Broadway play. Such a process, in the old Hollywood days, took years. However, the stars produced in the older and slower manner had greater stature and *lasted*. Robert Taylor and Clark Gable, for instance, introduced in "B" picture supporting roles, remained top stars for thirty years. Arness and O'Brian, on the contrary, featured immediately in big Hollywood films, have had only mediocre success, indicating that their greatest popularity lies with the less discriminating younger audience, and not with the adult ticket-purchasing public.

As frequently happens, a good thing is over-exploited and a decline began. The Earp Westerns soon strove too hard and too self-consciously for effect, especially disturbing being the sustained use of guitar-strummed theme in lieu of a standard musical score. Far from constructive in its effect on juvenile viewers was the soon-defunct "Jim Bowie" series, obviously imitative of Walt Disney's successful "Davy Crockett" film. As played by Scott Forbes, frontiersman Bowie was a vulgar barbarian given to the irresponsible wielding and throwing of a knife. Youngsters who had learned that it was good, harmless fun to imitate the exploits of Roy Rogers, Gene Autry, and other cowboys, naturally found it hard to understand why they should not likewise imitate this latest, but potentially more harmful "herd." Presumably there were audience and sponsor protests, for Bowie after a while began to conduct himself in a more respectable manner, his activity with the knife cut down to a minimum.

New off-beat series sprang up with such monotonous regularity that they outnumbered the staid and unpretentious films of Autry. Even the Westerns that made no claim to adult slants had to have these off-beat elements, such as Kirby Grant's "Sky King" series which dealt with an airborne Texas Ranger. Warner's "Cheyenne" series, built around liberal helpings of stock footage from old Warner epics, attracted a considerable following, although the hero, Clint Walker, was a poor, if muscular horseman, doing his riding on a tame studio horse. John Bromfield, a star of "B" movies, proved quite popular in his "Sheriff of Cochise" series, dealing with the life of a sheriff in a modern Western town. Another lesser player, Douglas Kennedy, also built himself a much larger following in television in a series obviously imitative of "Gunsmoke," called "Steve Donovan, Western Marshal." Even the older character actors cashed in on the television's gold, among them Edgar Buchanan with a series based on a somewhat whitewashed version of Judge Roy Bean's career. Only two new series really followed the old format of action first and last, and to hell with soul-searching! Of these, one was "Sergeant Preston of the Yukon," a rather inept series, despite good directors like Lesley Selander, and the other "Rin Tin Tin." Rinty caught on like wildfire, the series having been so shrewdly contrived it could not miss, with a mixture of three always safe ingredients: the U. S. Cavalry verses the Indians, a small boy, and a dog. These films were all shot at Chatsworth, using John Ford's old Fort Apache set as a center of operations. Cheaply but slickly made, they pleased the youngsters with their fast action, and satisfied the adults with naïve but at least constructive moral lessons which could be passed on to their offspring, such as "rewards must be earned," "honesty is the best policy," etc. The series was, of course, particularly gratifying to manufacturers of accessories, who now found a completely new line of merchandise to peddle, from dog food and canine equipment to cavalry uniforms for the kids.

The Indians came in for a fair share of attention on television, as well. Lon Chaney, Jr., and John Hart co-starred in a series based on characters in James Fenimore Cooper's *The Last of the Mohicans*. The adventures themselves were strictly contrived for television, far removed from Cooper's world. Keith Larsen, who had played Indians in a number of theatrical films, starred in "Brave Eagle," a straightforward action series. Most successful of all was Fox's "Broken Arrow" series, deriving from the film of the same name. The same two protagonists are involved (Tom Jeffords, a mail rider, played by John Lupton, and Apache chief Cochise, played by Michael Ansara) and the issue remained the same (the maintenance of peace between the whites and the Apaches). Written by historian-novelist Elliott Arnold, the scripts had some slight distinction, although the translation of Indian lore into television's terms was superficial at best. Unfortunately the whole program smacked too much of the studio. Apart from the use of a Western town—a standing exterior location set—too many of the so-called exterior scenes were obviously shot on cramped interior stages.

Series continuity, the use of basically similar story lines involving the same people each week, is an important contributing factor to the success of series like "Gunsmoke" and "Wyatt Earp." One well-above average series known as "Frontier," produced by enterprising Worthington Miner, did not have this continuity, and story line and cast were changed each week. It became an early casualty and many felt that it flopped because it lacked the continuity of, as New York writer Philip Minoff put it, "a regularly seen hero who can be identified by a viewer as an impersonal guardian angel."

Failures are, of course, not determined by merit, or on the basis of reviews, but by ratings. Ratings are, however, meaningless; they merely represent a manipulation of figures that can "prove" anything. But a show's sponsor is interested *only* in a high rating since presumably it indicates a large audience for his sales pitch. Despite the spectacular flops and the moderate successes, television Westerns, which, like the theatrical Westerns, have been the "bread and butter" of their industry, have not only maintained their leading position, but also have widened the gap consistently over other types of shows. We have necessarily mentioned only a fraction of the shows produced; every week, to be sure, a new project is announced, and in 1961 alone, about thirty-two Western series were regularly presented on television. This figure was far exceeded in the mid- and late Fifties, when the popularity of the electronic Western was at its dizziest height.

Throughout the Fifties, the television Western went through cycles roughly parallel to the cycles of the theatrical Western: from the early starring vehicles stressing action for its own sake, through racial and off-beat themes, to the "adult" group. We have had such diversified series as "Sugarfoot" (a deliberately inept, non-violent cowboy), "Rifleman," "Rawhide," "Have Gun, Will Travel," and "Outlaws."

One interesting offshoot of these rather laboriously off-beat series has been the topsy-turvy casting. Former heavies of Westerns, players like Tristram Coffin and Douglas Kennedy, have found themselves cast as "character" heroes on the theory that they look like unglamorous *real* people. Conversely, former Western heroes like Ray Corrigan and Johnny Mack Brown, unable to find much work in the new "adult" world of Westerns, have donned dirty suits, let the stubble grow on their chins, and have played villains.

Western series were expanded in recent years to include a number of quite ambitious hour-length shows, the most prominent of which are the "Zane Grey Theatre," mentioned earlier, and "Wagon Train," which starred Ward Bond until his death and which presented different dramatic stories each week within the framework of a prolonged wagon trek. It attracted such great directors and stars as John Ford and Bette Davis, and prompted other hour-length Western shows to use name talent, too. A serious loss in the field has been that of "Bonanza," after fourteen years of uninterrupted international success and top Nielsen ratings in the United States. The death in 1972 of Dan Blocker, the colorful Hoss of the Cartwright family of the Ponderosa, dealt a severe blow to the show, which, after having been revamped in a desperation move, sank to the fifty-second spot in the ratings and was taken off the air in January, 1973. A detailed coverage of all of these television Westerns would really require a book in itself, and since so few are of real merit or importance, we have allowed ourselves the luxury of generalization.

In one field, however, television made little attempt to duplicate Hollywood: the field of the documentary. This area, implying high cultural and educational standards, has a frightening sound to the great majority of television producers. But there have been a number of interesting television documentaries relevant to the West. Tim McCoy made an engaging series of fifteen-minute shows in which he talked about Western history and lore—basically a lecture series in which his talks were illustrated by film material culled mainly from old theatrical features. NBC, in the mid-Fifties, devoted a ninety-minute show to the history of the Western, and to the making of a current Western. In 1961, a moving and impressive program called *The Real West* debunked many clichés, relying exclusively on old paintings and photographs of Western life as it was—and is. Gary Cooper, in the last year of his life, was poignantly effective as the narrator. One other program devoted itself to the career and credo of William S. Hart. Such isolated events, however, can do but little to brighten the rather dismal overall picture. The television Western can never hope to compete with the grandeur of such theatrical Westerns as *The Searchers* (1956) and *Shane* (1953). And television has taken over the "B" Western completely, has compressed it into its own peculiar formula, and at the same time rendered it commercially useless in a theatrical sense.

The grand thrillers of the type made by Buck Jones, Tom Mix, Ken Maynard, and Fred Thomson are in this way taken from us for all time, and the loss is one for which the grand-scale epic of Ford or Vidor, no matter how well done, can never really compensate.

The Western's international audience and the

international Western

17

An extremely valuable survey of the communications behavior of the average American was undertaken in the fall of 1947 at the National Opinion Research Center of the University of Chicago by Dr. Paul F. Lazarsfeld and Miss Patricia Kendall. This survey, whose statistical nature precludes our delving deeply into the subject here, produced evidence based on a sampling of over 3,500 Americans, evidence which incontrovertibly gave the lie to the prevailing notion that the mentality of the average movie patron was that of a ten-year-old. The evidence was assembled after exhaustive research into the frequency of attendance at motion picture theaters and the preference for different types of films at various age and educational levels. Nevertheless, those who should have studied this report, the people who make films in America, persist in their misconceptions, persisting therefore in the production of films which *are* keyed to the mentalities of ten-year-olds. However, in some circles at least, mature thinking is on the increase; even Cecil B. De Mille could write in the Fifties: "I do not abide by the belief popular in certain quarters that motion picture stories should be told to fit an audience level of ten or twelve years. This is a most erroneous concept."

That same year the survey was made, 1947, witnessed a serious falling off of attendance in motion picture theaters, due in large part to television's increasing competition. The pure novelty of television was

in itself a tremendous factor in the decline of movie audiences; so was the desire of the average American to devote more time to relaxing outdoor activities, after the tense war years. Yet the Western has retained its great influence. In the United States the largest outlet for Westerns has always been the juvenile market, which of course knows no boundary lines and is spread evenly over the nation. Since the advent of television, with a surfeit of its own Westerns, and its new crop of non-Western heroes with a marked science-fiction flavor (Superman, Captain Video, etc.), juvenile interest has been split. Saturday morning children's shows now very rarely present Westerns, although once they monopolized programming. The average Saturday morning show today tends to knockabout comedy of the Abbott and Costello sort and science-fiction fare, with an occasional Western thrown in. Possibly the biggest single market for Westerns, now that the juvenile market has so greatly declined, is the black market. In black areas in metropolitan centers like New York and Chicago, and, of course, in the South especially, the Western is still very much in demand. With so few new Westerns being produced, the older films are repeated frequently without complaint. The Negro audience for the Western has lately increased to a considerable extent, in the wake of the efforts of black cinema, from *Cotton Came to Harlem* (1970) to *Sweet Sweetback's Baadasss Song* (1971) and *Shaft* (1971), all extremely popular and financially successful non-Western pictures in which the Negro is at last portrayed as a hero. The emergence of the black cinema has of course opened the way to the Negro Western, with mixed results up to now, as stressed in the last chapter of this book.

Big cities like New York, Chicago, Los Angeles, San Francisco readily accept class "A" Westerns, but no real Western audience can be observed for the small Western. The theatrical circuits are so large that it is often not financially feasible even to try to show a small Western in a metropolitan center, since the cost, considering the number of prints involved, would be larger than any income the film could produce. In cities like New York, many of the smaller Westerns are not shown at all, or are merely shunted off to the few out-of-the-way theaters specializing in them. Rural areas around the country remain consistently good markets. The ranching territories, which are, of course, rural, particularly like Westerns; the cowboys are faithful fans who like to scoff at, and perhaps secretly believe, the films built around their trade as it *was*, if not as it is.

In England, Westerns are shown under much the same conditions as in the United States, with the same dependence on small towns rather than large cities. English youth retains more loyalty to the Western than does American. Perhaps due to England's smaller exposure to television, heroes from outer space have not yet come to dominate the screen. Because of the Western's foreign origin, it retains a kind of exotic appeal for the English child which it no longer has for the American.

Next to England, the European country that most welcomes Westerns is probably Germany, a country which has made many Westerns of its own. Because of the relatively few "B" Westerns shown there—it is single-feature territory—audiences do not make the same "A" and "B" distinctions we make. Other countries which have shown and continue to show major interest in American Westerns are France and Italy. Countries like Indonesia often regard the Western as potentially dangerous propaganda for their own minority groups, and Westerns dealing with mistreatment of Indians at the hands of the whites are not welcome. Australians proud of their own frontier days often condemn our frontier sagas with the phrase, "Western cliché"; but the French may praise the same film, calling it part of the "Western tradition."

In terms of criticism, we should state that since the Western is the most typically American of all films, it is often used as an excuse for an attack quite unwarranted by the quality of the film itself, an attack which may be actually political in nature. But for an example of the way American Westerns are thoroughly enjoyed—and taken far more seriously than they usually are in the land of their origin—we can do no better than to refer to a delightful article, "William Cowboy," written by Robert Dean Frisbie for the April, 1928, issue of *Photoplay,* dealing with the reaction of a South Sea audience to a William S. Hart Western. To the Polynesians, Hart was the supreme American, beside whom even Douglas Fairbanks paled into insignificance, and against whom Charlie Chaplin and Mary Pickford were no competition at all. Only one element in Hart's Westerns disturbed the literal-minded islanders. "Why do the white men so often leave their dead unburied?" they asked. Even the villain, thoroughly deserving of his fate when thrown from a cliff after a desperate encounter with the hero, should, they felt, have been given a decent burial, complete with weeping relatives and children with flowers! This very literal approach extended to other problems, as well: when Hart rode off with the heroine at the end, why was it never made clear whether he intended to make her his wife or his mistress? It was explained to the islanders that all these things could be taken for granted, that the villain was properly interred, and the heroine honorably married. But doubt remained. "If so," Polynesians reasoned, "why were they ashamed for us to know it?" The visiting European made a brave attempt to explain the theory of the movies, a theory that required the audience to imagine certain parts of the action. But even then the islanders had the last word. One of them commented, ingenuously, "But suppose we imagine the wrong thing, what then?"

A particularly defined *national*, let alone *international*, audience for the Western cannot easily be recognized in view of several factors, all of which rely on the wide diversity of taste and opinion among movie patrons. Women generally prefer love stories to Westerns, and yet in several cases such as *High Noon,* which presented an idealized woman's triumph in a man's world, and *Duel in the Sun*, which catered to the average woman's subconscious longing for exotic romance, women's interest and response has been very positive. On the whole, however, men are far more likely to be influenced by the Western than are women. Further, the recent trend of the psychological Western has tended to impress its views not only on the thinking adolescents and college students, but also on mature individuals in their forties and fifties. In spot interviews we have noted that there is no fundamental difference in the approach to the Western between people who live in cities and those who live in the country. While all welcome the tendency to greater authenticity and realism, less glamour and gloss, at the same time all audiences still want the factor which has always been the Western's stock-in-trade: action.

Since the *authentic* Western has always been popular among international audiences, it is not surprising that, on occasion, some countries have turned out their own "Westerns." The term "Western" is geographical rather than dramatically descriptive, referring to the locale of a story rather than to its content. But if *The Great Train Robbery,* made in Dover, New Jersey, in 1903 can be called a Western, then so can *The Hanging at Jefferson City*, an interesting little horse opera made in France not long afterwards. Ever since Broncho Billy and "Rio Jim" (as William S. Hart was known in France) earned the respect and admiration of European audiences, European film-makers have been producing Westerns, in small number only, but there have been interesting films among them. Inevitably, no single group of films has ever been more influenced by the traditions of the American Western than have these. The influence was especially strong in the pre-1913 period, when U. S. film-makers like Ince still treated the Indian as an individual, the equal of the white man. These little films, often imbued with a poetic sensitivity missing from the straightforward hero-versus-badman adventures, made their strongest mark on the French cinema, which duplicated their style quite creditably.

Germany, and to a lesser degree France and Italy, still make their small quota of Westerns "rip-snorting" adventures of the old school. As the titles almost never fail to designate, they are invariably set in Texas, Arizona, or New Mexico. Italy produced a wild and woolly group of Wild Bill Hickok adventures, which, if the stills are an accurate criterion, contained as much violent action as any American Western. Even the Czechs produced a deft double-edged satire in a pleasing puppet film, *Song of the Prairie* (1952). It is not only satirized Westerns *per se*, but it

The French conception of a frontier saloon: poker, liquor, a rodeo advertisement, and a bid for the cowboy tourist trade with a Spanish travel poster. A scene from Pendaison á Jefferson City (The Hanging at Jefferson City).

particularly singled out the Autry-Rogers type of Western already almost a parody of itself.

Unfortunately, relatively few of Europe's Westerns have been seen outside their native lands, presumably because they are not "prestige" or art-theater properties. Many European non-Western subjects that have been exported contain beautifully staged episodes of fast action in the Western mold, episodes that suggest that Westerns made with this kind of skill can be both vigorous and relatively authentic. Titles that come quickest to mind are Christian Jacque's *Carmen* (1942), with some particularly fine chases, the Swedish *Rain Follows the Dew* (like *Shane* and *Wagonmaster*, it utilized natural landscapes as an integral part of the film, not merely as scenic backdrops), and the grim *Ride Tonight* of 1942 (with a Hart-like austerity, and belief in the need for personal sacrifice extending even to death in the interests of law and order) and most especially perhaps, the Italian *In The Name of The Law* (1948), a film in many ways similar to *High Noon*, and about which more will be said later in the chapter.

Although England has yet to make an authentic Western, some films based upon British history drew heavily on American Westerns for basic patterns, for example, the early sound film, *Dick Turpin*, and *Lorna Doone* (1934).

In more recent years, the Western formula was used more ambitiously in several large-scale productions, the most notable of which was Harry Watt's *The Overlanders*, a worthy rival to America's *Red River*, Howard Hawks' 1947 study of a prolonged cattle drive with equally fine sweep in the spectacular stampede sequences, and the genuine feel of epic pioneering. Although a modern story, the urgency and sense of a group working for national, rather than individual ends, was brought back to the screen because of the really vital importance of the undertaking: herds of Australian cattle had to be driven overland to keep them out of the hands of the Japanese.

Perhaps the British film most influenced by Westerns was *Diamond City* (1950), a Rank production which, although laid in the diamond fields of Africa, might just as well have been set in the gold fields of California. The film abounded with saloon brawls, chases, stunts, and gun battles.

Very popular in Germany in the Twenties were semi-Westerns and backwoods adventures of the James Fenimore Cooper variety. Since there was no regular flow of this type of Western from the United States, the German film industry made its own—and highly efficiently, too. Undoubtedly behind this interest were the books of Karl Mai, an extremely popular writer whose tales of adventure often outsold Zane Grey and Fenimore Cooper. His astounding knowledge and the books' apparent authenticity (Mai claimed to have lived among the Indians, and to be writing of events of which he had heard firsthand accounts) became all the more amazing when he was finally forced to admit that he was a fraud. A fraud he was, but a brilliant and imaginative one, for his entire knowledge of the West had been gleaned from the writings of others, and from American motion pictures. Some of his stories were even written from a prison cell.

There has been a change in the style of the German Western since

Bela Lugosi (extreme right) as the Indian hero Uncas of the German-made The Last of the Mohicans.

the end of World War II. Before the war, they were often strongly nationalistic, sometimes built around obscure, or alleged, incidents in German and related history, sometimes, too, having more than just a little propaganda content. Such a film was Luis Trenker's *Kaiser of California*, a well-made but somewhat biased account of Sutter's spectacular rise and fall in California. At the same time, straightforward, non-propagandistic Westerns were also being made, such as *Gold in New Frisco*, released in Germany under that English title, an Otto Wernicke vehicle along the established lines of *The Spoilers*.

For all their careful staging and often brilliantly executed action, the German Westerns lacked the sustained speed and simplicity of the American originals. Development would be painstaking and plodding; the protagonists would spend far too much time discussing and contemplating before they acted. The elaborate production mountings, and the vigor and size of the action, when it came, certainly compensated for the long waits, but what truly exciting Westerns the Germans could have turned out had they only concentrated more on the plot essentials and movement, and less on sheer weight and padding!

Two of the best German Westerns starred Hans Albers, an enormously popular player who enjoyed the same sort of adulation as did

Clark Gable over an exactly corresponding period. He appeared in pictures which also stressed virile romance and action, but he got away with something that Gable could not: Albers delighted in outrageous sexual double-entendre dialogue and uninhibited swearing, usually quite off-the-cuff, to the despair of his producers, timorous of puritan protests, and to the delight of his audiences.

An interesting film with Albers, *Sergeant Berry* (1938) discloses some of the strengths and weaknesses of the German Westerns. It was a wildly

Hans Albers in Wasser für Canitoga.

extravagant adventure yarn with much of the flavor of such silent Douglas Fairbanks frolics as *His Majesty the American*. Obviously not meant to be taken seriously, at the same time it never descended to lampoon. Largely a vehicle for Albers, it cast him in a colorful Fairbanksian role with six or seven obvious, but enjoyably theatrical disguises and masquerades.

In it, Albers went out West to round up the badmen. What followed was a Western of the old "shoot-em-up" school, complete even to the heroine's runaway buggy. Apart from its vitality and good humor, much unexpected entertainment also resulted (to the non-German spectator) from the director's quite alarming enlargements and reshapings of stock Western clichés. There were sombreros and gaily colored shirts from South of every border in the Western Hemisphere. All the Mexicans were resolutely named Don Pedro, Don José, or Don Diego, regardless of the fact that the duplication of names among a large contingent of *Gauchos, bandidos,* and *rancheros* resulted in no little confusion. And since it would be false to do otherwise, the Mexicans, when excited, restricted their expletives to the time-honored "Caramba!" The heroine's father, who had just cause to be excited, rated just about one "Caramba!" to every three or four lines of dialogue.

These considerations apart, *Sergeant Berry* was a commendable effort. The sets were unusually lavish and the action scenes well staged, while the desert scenery—cactus included—looked authentic. The film did tend, however, to play for laughs as much as for melodrama and lacked the speed of good American Westerns. It also contained one very German ingredient: a decided touch of heavy vulgarity which would have been quite out of place in an American Western. This included some pointed sequences and "blue" dialogue involving Albers and the enterprising heroine, and an episode which featured Albers running around nude (discreetly photographed from the rear!) after he had lost his clothes while swimming.

The Horsemen (1952), a fine Russian film, beautifully photographed in color, with plenty of action, showed how carefully Soviet film-makers have studied the American Western and how readily, and efficiently, they can apply the *technique* of the Western to an essentially Russian theme, the resistance of the Russian peasantry to the Nazi occupation. In fact, the treatment smacked more of *Riders of Death Valley* with stampedes (creatively photographed from a helicopter), chases and fights climaxed by an admirably staged, photographed, and edited overland chase after a locomotive.

There is, of course, a difference between the outright *imitation* of the Western (as in the German films), the utilization of Western techniques (as in Russia's *The Horsemen*) and the *influence* of the Western upon films that do not necessarily rely on Western plot *or* technique.

Perhaps the most striking example of *influence* upon only casually related subjects is provided by some of the postwar Italian films, and most specifically by the work of director Pietro Germi. If Germi's first picture, *Lost Youth* (1947), was inspired by American treatment of gang-

Brazil's savage, realistic
Ô Cangaçeiro.

ster and juvenile delinquency themes, then his second film, *In the Name of the Law* (1948), was unmistakably stamped with the mark of the Western, although it was released in the United States under the title of *Mafia*. Critics of both countries have noted its close affinity to the Western.

Dealing with the conflict between the superior law of the state and local law based on—and provoking—murder and violence, the film's theme had obvious connections with the Western theme of vigilante law. As the Italian critic Renzo Renzi noted:

In this picture Germi borrows from the American formula a certain dramatic and narrative tranquillity, because it is a route which has already been tested . . . the imitation [of the Western] is furthered through details of action; the film begins with an ambush which reminds us of a stagecoach attack, and the backgrounds and landscape are alike. Massimo Girotti, alone against everyone (a hymn to the individual) finds his only true friend in a boy he meets in town. The boy's subsequent death serves as the emotional spring which convinces the hero that he should reconsider his decision to give up the fight. This is the resolving detail of the suspense element.

This latter plot detail has, of course, always been one of the fundamental motivating factors by which the Western transforms its hero from a man of peace to a man of justified violence. For example, Errol Flynn, in *Dodge City,* determinedly sets to work to clean up the town only *after* the death of a child, a death resulting directly from the hooliganism of the drunken heavies. Renzi goes on to point out that the conflict between Massimo Girotti and Charles Vanel in Germi's film is resolved in much the same manner as that between John Wayne and Montgomery Clift in *Red River,* made a year earlier.

In two other films, *The Road to Hope* (1951) and *The Outlaw of Tacca del Lupo* (1952), Germi continued to apply American, and specifically Western, formulas, but in both of them the American models were not in every case appropriate to Italian themes or, as in the case of *The Road to Hope,* a film very similar to the better-known Brazilian *Ô Cangaçeiro* (1950), to the purposes of the films themselves.

The experience of Germi in his enterprising, but unsuccessful, utilization of the Western model in Italian pictures is typical of similar experience by other Italian directors. In Germi's hands, the experiment came, however, nearest to a successful fruition.

But the list of nations and films influenced by the American Western is long. The Japanese, Indians, Mexicans, Brazilians, and many other peoples have all gone to the American Western at one time or another for inspiration, and therefore it is fair to say that the Western saga, historically as well as cinematically, has crossed the frontiers of nations, becoming truly international in its spirit.

Into the

"Films help change mass attitudes on condition that these attitudes have already begun to change."

SIEGFRIED KRACAUER

Sixties

18

Since 1945, the Western film has seen an astonishing array of new trends, cycles, and changes of format, many of which have been already discussed in earlier chapters; yet the number of really important Westerns to have emerged is surprisingly small. A number of ambitious productions, such as *Red River*, *The Big Sky*, and *Rio Bravo*, widely hailed as successors to *Stagecoach*, have subsequently been all but forgotten; it is perhaps no coincidence that all three were directed by Howard Hawks, an admirable director of melodramas with unusual depth and pace, but a man who has of late attempted to contrive inner layers of "meaning" where none are required, and who has also, like Henry King, demonstrated a liking for the spectacle for which he seems so ill suited. *Red River*, in particular, although ambitious in scope and impressive visually, appears quite pedestrian today; one must remember that this film probably received most of its critical acclaim on the basis of having arrived on the scene after a prolonged dearth of epic Westerns in the true sense of that term. However, it remains by far the best of this trio of Hawks Westerns. If overlong, at least its story line, spanning some twenty years and dealing predominantly with a long and arduous cattle drive, lent itself to protracted treatment, as the overly psychological and talkative *Rio Bravo* did not. Not only were its characters free of the neuroses that were to trouble so many later "epic" protagonists, but they were also very much

John Wayne and Mont-
gomery Clift in Howard
Hawks' Red River *(1947).*

characters of flesh and blood. John Wayne especially, as the bitter old
trail boss, was frequently shown in an unsympathetic light due to his
ruthless, if justified, handling of his men, handling that included bull-
whipping and other brutalities.

If other Hawks films were more overbearing in their pretentiousness,
Hawks, to be sure, had no copyright on the making of pretentious
Westerns: William Wyler's star-studded but dull *The Big Country* was
not nearly up to his simpler *Hell's Heroes* made a quarter of a century

John Wayne rose from a star of
"B" Westerns to a major star with
his own production company. Today
he is the logical successor to Gary
Cooper and one of the half-dozen
biggest "names" in the business.

earlier, and MGM's remake of *Cimarron* was a complete failure, squandering its inherent epic qualities to a soap opera theme that infuriated Edna Ferber, author of the novel.

The assembly-line look of many of the so-called super-Westerns made since 1950 may be attributed to a number of factors. For one thing, the disappearance of the "B" Western allowed plot clichés to creep back in, on some producers' theory that with fewer Westerns around, those that remained did not all have to aim diligently at originality. Thus the clichés persisted, although their presentation was better. The plot of *Duel in the Sun* spawned a number of outright imitations, such as *The Halliday Brand, The Violent Men,* and *Untamed Frontier.* Ford's *Fort Apache* was imitated in *Two Flags West* and other pictures showing martinet officers obsessed with hatred for the Indian. Ford's fine film, *The Searchers,* which dealt with the rescue of a white woman kidnapped and sexually possessed by Indians, was imitated in *Trooper Hook,* and by Ford himself, in *Two Rode Together.* Another contributing factor to the distressing uniformity of many of the bigger Westerns was the fact that Westerns, always reasonably safe commercial propositions, became vehicles for name stars, who were either slipping or working out the last few pictures of long-term contracts. Robert Taylor, Clark Gable, Stewart Granger, Gary Cooper, James Cagney, and Gregory Peck, at various periods in the Fifties, were shunted into large-scale but generally undistinguished motion pictures on the assumption that a top name plus a Western theme would guarantee box-office success. Gable's Westerns, *Lone Star* and *Across the Wide Missouri,* showed the production care and script values that a star of his caliber warranted, but many of the others were less notable, and some, like Peck's *The Bravados,* were without any redeeming factors whatsoever.

No new directorial talent of note emerged in the period, and most of the established Western directors either declined or at best held their own. John Ford, switching to more sustained concentration on Westerns after the success of *Fort Apache,* gradually lost vitality; but even the more conventional of his works that followed had enough of the old visual beauty and dramatic power to succeed while Westerns made by other directors failed both as films and as commercial ventures. In *The Horse Soldiers*, a Civil War epic, Ford took a known historical incident and fashioned a lively adventure around it. *Sergeant Rutledge,* less satisfying due to a preponderance of studio sets, was rather shrewdly conceived so that it could be sold on the basis of "sex and sensation" rather than on its Western values. It offered a Negro militia sergeant as chief protagonist, and displayed refreshing honesty at least in its discus-

sion of racial problems. *Two Rode Together,* on the other hand, was a casually directed Western, generally lacking in dramatic values or real action but it was interesting for its psychological studies, such as the superbly acted and directed scene in which Mae Marsh, a white prisioner of the Indian for years, explains why she does not wish to live again among whites.

Just as no new directors of stature emerged, no new Western stars were developed either. Audie Murphy, in his series at Universal, developed into a far better actor than his earlier films had promised. *Drums Across the River* was an expertly made action picture; *No Name on the Bullet* succeeded instead on exceptionally strong story value, while still others,

e.g., *Night Passage*, presented an unexpectedly authentic picture of some phase or other of Western history. The little known film, *Walk the Proud Land*, was a sincere and well-written account of the life of an Indian agent, based on the autobiography of one of those unsung but often maligned officials. It is most unfortunate that Murphy's plan to film the life of the Western painter Remington never materialized.

The most acclaimed and most influential Western of the decade, *High Noon*, offered a strong dramatic role to Gary Cooper and an appealing title song. The film was a smash success at the box-office. It has been, however, somewhat overrated, since its script was inauthentic, too "modern," displaying little knowledge of the real conditions of the old West. Its direction was over-studied, but a major cinematic asset was the creative editing of Elmo Williams. The film created the impression among public and critics that the "adult Western" had finally arrived, and it exerted considerable influence on a whole flock of talkative horse operas that followed. Some of these were *3:10 to Yuma, At Gunpoint!*, and *Star in the Dust*, all of which stressed the integrity of a fearless man who quietly goes about his dangerous job against the background of a community's hesitance to accept risk and danger on behalf of law and order.

Cooper, wearing unpicturesque garb and wrapped up in what seemed to be self-doubts, helped usher in the new breed of unglamorous and so-called "realistic" cowboys who were being introduced at the same time on television. This newest, and rather sudden, development found the lawman no longer only the instrument for the law's enforcement, but a man who had to mete out justice as well. A psychologist might with profit study the reasons why, in the Fifties, a rash of Westerns were made in which the hero had to lawfully execute the villain. In *Star in the Dust*, virtually the entire footage is spent outlining the problems facing a sheriff as he prepares to hang a killer. This morbid streak went one step further in the Robert Taylor vehicle, *The Hangman*, in which the lawman took on the fanatic, vengeful characteristics of a Mickey Spillane hero. And in *The Bravados*, we find Gregory Peck, *not a lawman*, taking the law into his own hands to track down and personally execute the members of a gang guilty of murder, robbery and rape. In the climax, with several deaths by now to the "hero's" credit, we suddenly find that those executed were actually innocent of the crimes for which they died; the fact that Peck had acted "in good faith," and that his victims were guilty of other crimes, seemed to make everything, if not quite right ethically, at least morally tolerable and legally acceptable!

The physical shape of the Western was altered with the coming of the first three-dimensional films, "three-dimension" being a remarkable device which was sadly underexploited by producers, ruined by the carelessness of the majority of projectionists, and doomed later by Cinemascope and other wide-screened processes. One of the best examples of three-dimensional photography was to be seen in *Hondo* (1953), which was also shown in a regular, non-stereoscopic vision. The Western was not harmed by technical innovations of this sort, and the broad expanses obtained a certain added majesty from the wider picture, while isolated action sequences—especially charges, chases, and other action designed for the horizontal frame—became somewhat more impressive. One of the best Westerns of the Fifties, Henry Hathaway's *From Hell to Texas,* made in Cinemascope, provided stunning color photography of chases, cattle stampedes, and gun duels in the deserted streets, the new technique providing freshness and vitality to familiar material. The production was glossy, but the script had honesty and intelligence, recalling at times the simplicity of William S. Hart. The hero, a sincerely religious cowhand reluctantly forced into becoming a killer, was a well-written character, and the little Western town, with its shabby, austere wooden shacks flung up in the middle of the plains, resembled the authenic small towns of the Ince days—missing perhaps the shaggy hogs invariably squatting in the mud of the street.

But if the wide screen helped make *From Hell to Texas* one of the two top Westerns of the Fifties, the other—George Stevens' *Shane*—was sadly hampered by it. *Shane* had been completed in leisurely, methodical fashion, just before the demand for the wide screen became irresistible. Paramount, later to develop the best of the wide-screen processes, VistaVision, decided to release the film as a wide-screen production, even though it meant a drastic shearing off of the tops and bottoms of the picture. This mutilation, hard to take even in a routine film—faces were cut off at the eyebrows and in the middle of the mouth—amounted to butchery on Stevens' film, in which every image had been carefully and lovingly composed. *Shane* was dramatically a good enough work to survive the pictorial loss, but even those audiences who endorsed the film wholeheartedly could not have imagined just how much of the real value they were losing.

A poetic and poignant Western, *Shane* was also an honestly violent one. The scene in which Elisha Cook, Jr., is knocked over backwards from the blast of a killer's six-shooter was quite a jolt after years of clichés in the presentation of gun fights. Such realism and *Shane's* basic plot, with its ending of sheer pathos, sent one's memories scurrying back to William Hart's *The Toll Gate.*

The wide screen was used really creatively in only a few Westerns. *The Charge at Feather River* and *White Feather* had exciting panoramic vistas. The rambling discussions of *At Gunpoint*, a film almost totally devoid of action, seemed absurdly overblown on the giant screen, while the atmosphere of impending doom was hard to accept amid so much cheerful color. *Wichita,* one of the simplest and best old-school Westerns made in the Fifties, would certainly have been more impressive had not everything looked so "big" and "epic" on the Cinemascope screen.

Soft politics

Politically there was a softening in Westerns throughout the Fifties. The anti-Russian propaganda, which had figured so heavily for a while in "B" Westerns, and even in such larger films as *The World in His Arms,* disappeared, probably because its limited possibilities had already been exhausted. And as long as there was no "hot war," audiences for Westerns could not really concern themselves with the Soviet menace on the frontier. The anti-Soviet "message" was instead diverted to espionage thrillers and science-fiction films. The characterization of a Nazi-stereotype leader, such as Widmark's wagon boss in *The Last Wagon,* also disappeared. The Mickey Spillane or "tyrant" hero of Gregory Peck in *The Bravados*, a man without responsibility to others, recognizing no law other than his own, performing heroically, usually for his own personal satisfaction, has become a recurring figure, but fortunately not a dominant one.

In other ways, the Western has been careful not to stick its political neck out. This is especially true in domestic politics, Hollywood paying particular attention to the South's delicate feelings. In Civil War films, and Westerns built around the subject, the South has emerged more sympathetically than ever before. A film like *Seven Angry Men,* a commendable attempt to make an off-beat historical Western, had to falsify and simplify certain aspects of the material in order to present abolitionist John Brown as a "nuisance" to both North and South, and really a man of no great importance!

Teen-age and adult markets

This pandering to audiences became noticeable in another, this time non-political way. Because of the increasing importance of the teen-age market in dramas, comedies, and musicals, there have been rather labored attempts to introduce juvenile delinquency into the Western, the classic example being *The Young Guns* with Russ Tamblyn, actually a rather interesting minor Western, spoiled only by being such an obvious attempt to transport *The Blackboard Jungle* to the West. In various films, Billy the Kid, the Daltons, and Jesse James became progressively younger in the persons of Audie Murphy, Tony Curtis, Jeffrey Hunter, and other teen-age idols. *The True Story of Jesse James* has the distinction of being the most historically distorted picture of this group. In a film made in 1940, *Jesse James,* Tyrone Power had played the outlaw as a somewhat whitewashed Robin Hood, but still and always a man; here,

Karl Malden and Marlon Brando in One Eyed Jacks *(1959).*

in the more up-to-date version, Jesse became a misunderstood, teen-age hero of Sherwood Forest.

But if Hollywood recognizes a teen-age market, it also recognizes an adult one, and since 1950 it has ostensibly been catering to that more mature public, while carefully insuring that the offerings appeal to the juvenile trade, as well. The term "adult," coined in television programming, was given the added connotation by Hollywood of "sexy and shocking," for obvious reasons. After having gone the limit within a traditional Western framework in pictures like *Johnny Concho* in which Sinatra played a despicable and cowardly "hero," Western producers looked further afield for their source material. Thus, *Last of the Comanches* was actually a remake of *Sahara*, a World War II story, which was in itself a remake of the old Russian classic, *The Thirteen*. In 1962, Frank Sinatra, Peter Lawford, and Sammy Davis, Jr., presented their cavalry-Indian opus, *Sergeants Three*, based on *Gunga Din*, while Lawford was preparing a remake of *The Great Train Robbery*, that one-reel "blueprint" for Westerns that had been remade by Republic once already in the Forties.

The modern West

If the old West did not come off well in the Fifties, there was a worthwhile emphasis on the modern West, and not in those "B" efforts in which uranium mining supplanted the old stories in which gold mines were claim-jumped. *Rodeo, Bronco Buster,* and especially Nicholas Ray's *The Lusty Men,* with its sad opening reminiscent of *The Grapes of Wrath,* dealt with the empty and unglamorous lives of touring professional rodeo riders. *Three Young Texans* by Delmer Daves and John Sturges' *Bad Day at Black Rock* dealt with problems in the contemporary West. John Huston's somewhat loose and ambiguous *The Misfits* often achieved real poignancy in its commentary on a disappearing way of life and on a fading breed of

How the West Was Won, *the first Cinerama Western.*

Wrath, dealt with the empty and unglamorous lives of touring professional rodeo riders. *Three Young Texans* by Delmar Daves and John Sturges' *Bad Day at Black Rock* dealt with problems in the contemporary West. John Huston's somewhat loose and ambiguous *The Misfits* often achieved real poignancy in its commentary on a disappearing way of life and on a fading breed of men. *Cowboy,* directed by Elmo Williams, was an excellent documentary on the cowboy's everyday life; Williams kept it generally realistic, but the use of ballads tended at times to romanticize the subject, and certain scenes appeared too patently staged.

The ultimate in the application of The Method to the West in performance, writing, and direction belongs to Paul Newman, the star, and to the writer and director of *The Left Handed Gun,* perhaps the most bizarre Western of them all, with The Method being employed at one point in a near-surrealist sequence that could have been borrowed bodily from Jean Vigo's *Zero de Conduite.* Another application of The Method, in a strikingly personal style, was the long and expensive *One Eyed Jacks,* directed and acted by Marlon Brando, a fascinatingly discontinuous film superbly photographed, in which the Western theme is implemented by a utilization of the sea as if it were the prairie of a more conventional horse opera. But let us not forget that Ince especially, and also George O'Brien, Roy Rogers, Gene Autry, and others had made use of these same seascapes. *One Eyed Jacks* is not to be considered merely a Western, since it contains so much of Brando's fiery desire to express his personal philosophy; the formula of the Western genre has served him only as a springboard for his own rendering of the West and the Western hero.

The enduring beauty of the West, free of restrictions and devoid of billboard advertising, will continue to appeal to a public that is increasingly hemmed in by the tensions and curtailments of modern living.

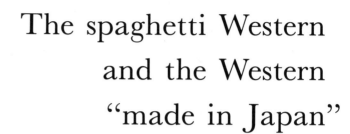

The spaghetti Western and the Western "made in Japan"

Jo Shishido in Mexico Mushuku (*1962*).

Remembering how popular Karl Mai's books about the American Far West had been in the Twenties, and the success of some of their film versions, West German producers in 1962 ventured an adaptation of Mai's old novel *The Treasure of Silver Lake*. Sure enough, their efforts were rewarded with a huge commercial success. In this rather pedestrian film, the roles of "Scout" Iron Hand and the phlegmatic "Apache" Winnetou were played, respectively, by the American Lex Barker—a former Tarzan—and the Frenchman Pierre Brice.

Until the extraordinary success of this film, the Italian producers had ignored the Western cinematic theme (except in a few isolated productions, such as an inept *Buffalo Bill á Roma* in 1949). Now at last they decided to join the bandwagon. This new experiment spread like a wildfire on the prairies: from 1963 to 1965 a total of about 130 westerns were produced in Europe by Italians with various Spanish, French, and West German companies, using Yugoslavian horses and natural scenery. In 1965 alone, out of a total of 144 Italian made and financed films, 24 were Westerns. For the next two years the "boom" continued, creating fortunes for some and dashing the hopes of less shrewd operators.

The "spaghetti Western" owes an everlasting debt for its existence to the famous *Per un pugno di dollari* (*For a Fistful of Dollars*), directed in 1964 by the Italian Sergio Leone under the American pseudonym of Bob Robertson. The producers, the technicians, and even some actors (Gian Maria Volonté was given the

19

"*On the Italian side, the commercial mortgage, with that certain amount of knavery which permeates the confection of low-grade products, blocks the potentialities of the Western as a gymnasium for new film makers: at best, it is a refuge of old and young sinners, a way to survive, a groceries' supply.*"

TULLIO KEZICH

"*The influence of the Western films upon Japanese cinema is very remarkable.*"

TADAO SATO

pseudonym of John Wells) were also camouflaged with American names. The story was freely adapted from Akira Kurosawa's Japanese Samurai film *Yojimbo* (1961). The film cost 120 million lire to produce and reaped billions of lire in profits, because of its complete saturation of all distribution outlets.

Despite its extraordinary display of violence and cruelty, *Per un pugno di dollari* was well received all over Italy, and then in Europe and America, because of its fresh, realistic approach. The film tried to dispose of many Hollywood stereotypes, introducing at the same time socio-psychological nuances that were easily understandable to the audience. It is important to remember that the foreign milieu of the American West was an easier vehicle for the Italian film makers to present political and social messages than was their own Italian background. Free from inhibitions, the film makers were able to express contemporary Italian problems with the rich symbolism of the Western saga.

Another important film of this type was *Minnesota Clay* (1965), directed by Sergio Corbucci. Like *Per un pugno di dollari,* it did not offer a spectacular cast, but based itself on the solid acting of the American Cameron Mitchell and the French actor George Rivière. It was the story of a *pistolero,* an outlaw, who, although he is unjustly accused of a crime and has a price on his head, brings peace and order to a town. This sort of anti-hero is meant to represent a man of our times, anguished and confused, without hope for the future, expressing through the action of the Western the bitterness and delusions of an individual crushed by the Establishment. And it was precisely because the moviegoers could identify themselves with Minnesota Clay that the film enjoyed its remarkable success.

Among other films of this period worth mentioning are *I Sette del Texas* (1964) by the Spaniard Joaquín Romero Marchent; *La battaglia di Fort Apache* by the Argentinian Hugo Fregonese and produced by German, Italian, French, and Yugoslav interests; *Per qualche dollaro in più (For a Few*

Dollars More) by Sergio Leone (1964); *Un dollaro bucato* (1965) by the Italian Giorgio Ferroni, who used the pseudonym of Kelvin Jackson Paget; and *Una pistola per Ringo* (1964) and *Il ritorno di Ringo* (1965), both written and directed by the Italian Duccio Tessari, who had ably assisted Sergio Leone in *Per un pugno di dollari*. The hero in *Un dollaro bucato* was played by Giuliano Gemma (presented as Montgomery Wood); he and the American actor Clint Eastwood of Leone's films became the top stars of the Italian Western. The golden age of the new trend lasted through 1967, and the Cinecittà Studios were kept busy going through the motions of the Prairie Drama, showing *urbi et orbi* how the West was won "where a man was a man."

There were of course some disappointments. In 1966–1967, for example, *Requiescant* by Carlo Lizzani and *Un fiume di dollari* by Lizzani as Lee Beaver, as well as *I lunghi giorni della vendetta* by Stan Vance (a pseudonym for the famed director Florestano Vancini), endeavored to capitalize on the successes of the genre, but audiences refused to accept their sickening excess of sado-masochistic exploits. A much more interesting film was *Yankee,* by the well-known Tinto Brass, which was an attempt at a "pop Western" influenced by the comic-strip style. The movie did not achieve the significance of American archetypes and was disowned by its director, who charged that manipulation by the producers distorted his intended meaning.

In *Sugar Colt* (1966), director Franco Giraldi (already known for his *Sette pistole per i MacGregor* (1965), an excellent realistic study of the West) looked back with nostalgia to the American Western of the Thirties, with the American actor Hunt Powers in a well-articulated role faithful to the spirit of that era. A year later he presented *Sette donne per i MacGregor,* a tongue-in-cheek treatment of the adventures of some Scottish brothers in the Old West. An excellent Italian Western of 1967 was *Se sei vivo spara,* directed by Giulio Questi. This film tried to branch out into an entirely new field, borrowing more from Edgar Allan Poe and Roger Corman than from Bret Harte and John Ford, as critic Tullio Kezich rightly pointed out. The

Enrico Maria Solerno in Bandidos.

no-holds-barred cruelty displayed by the anti-hero Tomas Milian was meant to be surrealistic rather than sado-masochistic, and Questi's stylistic approach to his character was thorough and interesting.

In that same year, Sergio Leone offered his *Il buono il brutto e il cattivo* (*The Good The Bad and The Ugly*), a rather dry and monotonous tale of Clint Eastwood, Eli Wallach, and Lee Van Cleef enmeshed in a gory kaleidoscope of battles, shoot-outs, and killings, accompanied by heavy use of bad language, against the background of the American Civil War. In this taut and bloody opus, Leone used all possible paraphernalia of the Western myth, showing Death in every form allowed on the screen. According to some cynical critics, *Per un pugno di dollari* was in comparison a rather bland exercise. By 1969 Leone was clearly weakening; his *C'era una volta il West* (*Once upon a Time in the West*), an ambitious attempt at a genuine American Western saga such as George Stevens' *Shane,* failed because of its ponderous rhythm and monotony.

By this time the genre of the spaghetti Western itself was in the pangs of crisis. The Cinecittà Studios were beginning to feel the pinch of unemployment. From 1967 on, the Western "made in Italy" declined; there had been too many films, and too many of them seemed the same. The boom seemed to have monopolized the energies of every Italian producer from the Alps to Sicily, mobilizing some of the best creative minds in the field.

Despite its present decline—as compared with its heyday in the Six-ties—the Italian Western keeps reappearing, adapting itself to a more efficient and articulate form of screenplay, direction, and camera work, often resulting in particularly sensitive films. One of the latest examples of the new trend is *Lo chiamavano Trinità . . .* (1971), produced and directed by Italo Zingarelli under the pseudonym of E. B. Clucher. A *pistolero* and his brother (a horse thief who likes to pass as a sheriff) fight for two Mormon sisters against a cynical major and his Mexican followers. The hero puts everything right and then goes back to his trampish life as a free and unfettered "hombre." This ironic twist, effectively presented in the film, introduces a new element in the treatment of the Code of the West. Even Sergio Leone is now experimenting with the Western spoof, in his *Duck, You Sucker* (*Giú la testa*) with Rod Steiger and James Coburn. The tradition of the Italian Western will not die as long as Italian pro-ducers retain their inventiveness.

A parody of the Western would be a most welcome innovation in style. As American director Anthony Mann said, after having seen *Per qualche dollaro in più:* "In that film the true spirit of the Western is lacking. We tell the story of simple men, not of professional assassins; simple men pushed to violence by circumstances. In a good Western the characters have a starting and a finish line; they follow a trajectory in the course of which they clash with life. The characters of *Per qualche dollaro in più* meet along their road only the 'black' of life. The bad ones. And the ugliness. My God, what faces! One or two is all right, but twenty-four no, it's too much!" And, furthermore: "The shoot-outs every five minutes reveal the director's fear that the audiences get bored because they do not have a character to follow. In a tale you may not put more than five or six minutes of 'suspense': the diagram of the emotions must be ascending, and not a kind of electrocardiogram for a clinic case."

Anita Ekberg and director Amerigo Anton during the film-ing of La Lunga cavalcata della vendetta.

And there is no doubt that the sado-masochism and intellectual perversions generously thrown to the worse instincts of the Sunday moviegoers, stupefied by Madison Avenue publicity campaigns, constitute the most negative aspects of the spaghetti Western. This phenomenon, already lamented by the Italian critics, has also been pitilessly condemned by their French colleagues. Gaston Haustrate, in an excellent essay devoted to the genre, states that the exasperated and exasperating overselling of themes in the Italian Western, its cynicism, gratuitous violence, the baroque construction that insists on the visible dynamism of shapes as a seal of vitality rather than on the complex rush which could present a multiplicity of phenomena and the flux of things in perpetual change—all this may probably one day see the "Roman Saga" die as it was born: in one blow.

As to what the genre will leave to posterity, Haustrate's theory is rather curious: the Italian Western, being the deliberate and destructive counter-mythology of the American Western, symbolizes the Latin jealousy for the splendid achievements overseas that the Old World had not been able to perform. In other words, the Italian Western could be construed as the Revenge of Europe against the colossus of the U. S. A. This is a highly intellectual approach and open to debate. In our opinion, the emergence and success of the Italian Western has mainly been due to the simple desire of Italian producers to exploit a new genre, to open new markets and reap richer profits. And since the American Western, a fundamental part of the history of the American nation, cannot easily be duplicated in genuine feeling, it was necessary to invent "original" aspects of treatment to make the moviegoers forget that the film was not American after all. The "baroque" character injected therefore into the Italian productions relied heavily on violence, sado-masochism and a display of horrors that echoed current events in Vietnam, the Middle East, Biafra, and so on. Considering this horrible background in its proper perspective, the Italian Western could have offered an extremely rich tapestry, interweaving beauty and ugliness, peace and war, goodness and cruelty, against a realistic background of the bygone days of the Far West, drawing the usual "lesson in morality" characteristic of the American Western. But this moral message, present in even the most modest American production, has been strangely missing from the Latin opuses. This lack detracts considerably from the texture and style of the Italian Western, branding these productions as mere fads, exercises in mercantile terms, like the infamous "Sandal and Spears" pseudo-historical films that the Italians literally threw on the market in the late Fifties and early Sixties.

There is no doubt that the Italian Western is much more meaningful than the "Sandal and Spears" epics. But it is a fact that a real opportunity was lost when the Italian cinema, which continues to offer us robust films with masterful perception of human problems, lamentably preferred to dismiss the fundamental lessons inherent in the American Western saga. This is not to imply, however, that the Italian Western has not exerted any influence over American film makers. For example, Sam Peckinpah's *The Wild Bunch* (1969) shows its debt by the bestial ignorance of the killers, who shoot everyone in sight just for kicks, and by the businesslike disposition of the criminals in the end of the film: four or five shots, and then the ironic, satisfied smile of Robert Ryan. *Le jeu est fait, rien va plus . . .* The "recovery" of actors Clint Eastwood and Lee Van Cleef, as well as some Hollywood contracts for Italian directors such as Sergio Leone, attest to the impact of Italian Westerns on American cinema.

Will the Italian Western survive as a viable cinematic form? Will it make any decisive contribution to the genre of the Frontier Saga? We believe that the spaghetti Western will continue. It is important to note that in the ocean of mediocre works there are still fine examples of cinematic style that cannot be underestimated, and that constant refinement and more audacious experimentation will bring about a breakthrough in the genre. The cooperation of young film makers will be essential for this purpose, because they speed the process of development, injecting new ideas and styles into the evaluation and description of a classic theme. New forces should enter the field, and old commercial practices should be totally revamped. Italy's rich history provides enough material that could be restaged in Western terms, to present universal human themes against a framework of specific geographic and historical conditions, conveying the moral lessons so easy to incorporate in the Western form. We need, in other words, a Western made with the same passion, understanding, and social analysis of the superb *Inchiesta su un cittadino al disopra di ogni sospetto* (*Investigation of a Citizen above Suspicion*) (1970), a film of today's world to be sure, but one whose thematic artistry is a magnificent example of what could be accomplished by a creative mind bent on depicting the Far West as it really was and not as the cinematic industry has so often presented it. The conflict between fact and fallacy, hope and despair, nobility and cruelty need not only be shown against the current Establishment. Perhaps a new school of Italian film makers will be able to achieve this miracle, to express the Frontier Saga in realistic human terms. This would be the best legacy that the American Western could make to the Italian cinema, which has already asserted its vitality in several other genres.

"Made in Japan"

To a superficial observer, anchored to the classic truism that "East is East, and West is West," the Japanese cinema might seem the least likely one to be swayed by the Western or, in turn, to influence it. Such an assumption is amply refuted by the analysis of Japanese cinematic history.

The first Japanese films were produced in Kyoto (subsequently in Tokyo, the new capital) in 1904–1905. They were directly inspired by the classic repertory of the Kabuki drama, often played in costume (Jidaigeki). In 1912, however, this source was relegated to limbo and replaced by popular legends, in which the hero saved the fairy princesses and administered stern justice to the villains. The exalted role of the hero was usually played by the actor Matsunosuke Onoe, who became the first "star" of the Japanese screen as the mythical symbol of chivalrous manhood.

After the First World War, the alliance between the militaristic government and the capitalistic motion picture industry stifled the majority of Japanese film makers, who had learned the cinematic lessons of D. W. Griffith and T. Ince quite well. They were forced to dish out an ever-increasing number of commercial pictures, including many "Westerns" in which the heroes were Japanese immigrants sent to farm the great plains in China and Manchuria. The so-called duel films (Kengeki), mostly directed by Daisuke Ito, were similar to this kind of production. The eternal *leitmotif* of the American Western, the struggle for justice carried on by a dedicated individual against apparently overwhelming and insurmountable odds, was interpreted by Denjiro Okoshi as the hero Sazen Tange.

Such Western-influenced activity prospered together with the famous school of contemporary realism (Gendaigeki), bent on describing the horrors of social and economic injustice. One of its finest and most striking examples is *Ningen Ku* (1923), directed by Kensaku Susuki. By 1932 the Japanese held the world record for film production (about 400 per year), and by the eve of the Second World War they had already produced a series of imposing pictures of remarkable artistry and social content. Among these were *Jinsei Geiko* (1936), *Hadaka no Machi* (1937), and *Tsuchi* (1939) by Tomu Uchida, *Gion no Shimai* (1936) by Kenji Mizoguchi, and particularly *Umarete wa Mita Keredo* (1932) by Yasujiro Ozu, whom Italian critic Roberto Paolella called the "most Japanese of the directors" because his world is always limited to the family, traditionally the center of Japanese civilization. And we cannot forget the admirable *Go-nin no Sekkohei* (1938) by Tomotaka Tasaka, which received a prize at the Sixth International Film Festival at Venice. At a time when the Japanese military had plunged into the "Chinese Incident" of 1937, with the rape of Nanking and the annihilation of thousands of Chinese, the extraordinarily vital appeal to peace and brotherhood presented in the film's tale of the odyssey of a five-man Japanese war patrol impressed critics and audiences.

After the Second World War and the American occupation, the Japanese cinema again exerted its resilience and vitality, capturing the Grand Prize at the 1951 Venice Film Festival for Akira Kurosawa's *Rashomon*. There was no doubt that the industry had reached its full maturity when in the Fifties the world witnessed a parade of masterpieces of the caliber of *Ugetsu Monogatari* (1953), *Gate of Hell* (1954), *The Golden Demon* (1955), and *Yang Kwei Fei* (1955). As for the Western, the most striking achievement is of course the famous *The Seven Samurai* (1954). Director Akira Kurosawa and

Toshiro Mifune in Seven Samurai *(1954).*

writer Shinobu Hashimoto took the Western theme of the local sheriff and his posse of farmers organized against attacking villains and added it to the world of the medieval Japanese peasantry, made familiar by many spectacle pictures dealing with medieval wars. These epics, however, had never included the idea of group fighting between peasants and bandits, and the resulting film was not merely an adaptation of the Western, but a meaningful and realistic historical inquiry on its own. The American version, *The Magnificent Seven* (1960), was satisfactory as a Western but lacked Kurosawa's lyricism.

Another Western-influenced film was *The Hidden Fortress* (1958), the story of men searching for gold in the wilds. This theme had never been exploited by the Japanese period drama, and for good reason, because, according to Japanese critic Tadao Sato, "there is hardly anything that can be called the wilds in the climate of Japan, and therefore such an image cannot be thought of, without imitating the Western." *Yojimbo* (1961) was not exactly an imitation of a Western, but it still contained enough elements of the genre to justify its adaptation into the Italian Western *Per un pugno di dollari* in 1964.

Between 1959 and 1961 the Nikkatsu Studios made a series of action films titled the "Birds of Passage Series," parodying the American Western. Their stories typically followed the travels of a righteous man (played by Akira Kobayashi) through the wilds on horseback, his arrival in a mining town, troubles with assorted ruffians, and gunfight with an outlaw (played by Jo Shishido). They are typical slapstick comedies, thoroughly enjoyed by Japanese audiences. A scene from the American film *Cry for Happy* (1961) shows such a Japanese "Western" and the reaction of American viewers to it.

Makoto Sato and Koji Tsuruta in Dokuritsu Gurentai (*1959*).

Makoto Sato in Dokuritsu
Gurentai (*1959*).

There was also the Japanese gangster film (Yazuka), a kind of sentimental action film portraying the professional gamblers of the Feudal Age
of Japan as its heroes. The Yazuka films came out of Japanese traditions,
but since the directors and script writers who created them were mostly
fans of the American Western of the Twenties and Thirties, it can be
assumed that they were consciously or unconsciously influenced by this
form. A very important picture in this field was *Dokuritsu Gurentai* (1959)
by Kihachi Okamoto. Technically it is a portrayal of the Northern front
of China in the last period of the Second World War, but upon closer
examination it clearly shows the format of a Western. The hero, played
by Makoto Sato, is a sergeant who has abandoned his outfit and is
wandering around on the front line, under the name of a news reporter.
He wants to avenge his brother, who was shot for having disclosed the
misdeeds of an officer. He finally achieves his aim in a small fort peopled
by soldiers, mostly rascals and gamblers, who have become demoralized
by the knowledge of the Japanese Army's defeat. The climax comes with

the approach of a large Chinese force, which engages the soldiers in battle. They die to the last man except for the hero, who survives the massacre and joins the Chinese, bidding farewell to military life. Director Okamoto, a fervent admirer of John Ford's *Stagecoach* (1939), staged the last battle scene as a fight between Indians and the U. S. Cavalry.

The "Samurai-sheriff" theme has been continued in the latest years by the Japanese cinema. *Samurai Banners,* directed by Hiroshi Inagaki and presented in the United States in 1971, has definitely Western-oriented music by Masaru Sato. Although based on the sixteenth-century exploits of a warlord of the Takeda clan, it clearly shows the *tour de force* of a brilliant military strategist, Samurai Kansuke Yamamoto (played with his usually remarkable personal style by Toshiro Mifune), who devotes his activities and, in sum, his whole existence and life to the ambitious lord of the Takeda, dying on the battlefield. Here we have the sacrifice of Roland at Roncesvalles, far from his King Arthur. Through the film's precious and polished visual depiction, the mythology of the hero, in the *Shane* tradition, shapes up at its best. Thus, the Japanese Western continues to move on, and to exert, in its own authoritative terms, the language of

Toshiro Mifune in Kakushitoride No San-akunin (*1958*).

Frontier Epic, with its counterpointing of Black and White, Good and Evil, Hope and Despair in a lucidity of thought and perfection of images that bring to mind the magnificent Haiku poem of Matsuo Basho, heir to Samurais, noblemen's teacher, Shintoist priest and Zen follower: "On a dried twig/ A crow has put/ Autumnal evening." The harsh realities of the American Western life, the hopes and the dreams, have been amply understood and expressed by a generous, sober, and profoundly devoted people that also believes in fighting for the final achievement of eternal values of peace and progress.

355

THE SPAGHETTI WESTERN
AND THE WESTERN
"MADE IN JAPAN"

After maturity: a projection into the future

"The demythologization of the Western Hero is an unstoppable and irreversible process in the American Cinema of the last decade."

ROBERTO CAMPARI

John Ford's The Man Who Shot Liberty Valance (*1962*). Copyright © *1962 by Paramount Pictures Corporation and John Ford Productions, Inc. All rights reserved.*

The Anti-hero

In 1973 the American Western reached its seventieth birthday, if we wish to identify its origin with Edwin S. Porter's *The Great Train Robbery* of 1903. Within these seven decades the genre has become fully grown, has even died and been resurrected from its ashes several times. Some may say that after such a long time almost everything has already been said, and therefore that the future is not likely to hold many more rejuvenations. And yet, the amazing vitality of the Western has always kept it springing back, more vigorous than ever, after periods of decadence. New trends and experimentation will continue to revive the genre, just as they have before.

The trend of the anti-hero could be detected in the beginning of the Sixties, as the Western was changed and "updated." It was beginning to reflect a mixture of nostalgia and a sort of desperation for the old West of yesteryear. John Ford's *The Man Who Shot Liberty Valance* (1962) was rather autumnal in tone. Tom Doniphon, the symbol of the old West, has shot a dreaded outlaw, but he dies forgotten and the glory of the deed goes to his friend Stoddard, who becomes a senator and witnesses the squalid last rites administered to the man who made him unjustly famous. In other films the brutality of the Western environment was shown together with the inability of man to cope with that environment, as the old-style West disappeared. The scenes of roping wild mustangs in Nevada shown in John Huston's

20

Camouflaged cameramen prepare to film the execution of diseased cattle in Hud (*1962*).

The *Misfits* (1961) actually spurred humane societies to try to save these horses from the rapacity of the horsemeat canners. *Hud* (1962), ably directed by Martin Ritt with the superb trio of Paul Newman, Melvyn Douglas, and Patricia Neal, has a stupendous sequence of the execution of diseased cattle that echoes Nazi horrors in Russia and Poland in the Second World War. It also shares with David Miller's *Lonely Are the Brave* (1962) the graphic imagery of death on a highway under the rain for their heroes who cannot adjust to the new West. The hero of *Lonely Are the Brave,* in Dalton Trumbo's excellent screenplay, is consigned to loneliness and spiritual death not because of Fate, but because he is unable to conform to the modern mechanized world.

Old and new West juxtaposed at the climax of Lonely Are the Brave (*1962*).

The anti-heroic theme was more broadly expressed in Sam Peckinpah's *Ride the High Country* (1961), the odyssey of two old *pistoleros* fighting their rheumatism and assorted enemies for an ore-filled mine. It finally plunged into comedy with *Cat Ballou* (1964) by Elliott Silverstein, the last word in the demythologization of the hero, who is a drunken gunfighter admirably played by Lee Marvin. The Western Superman was reduced to a bottle and his dirty red underwear.

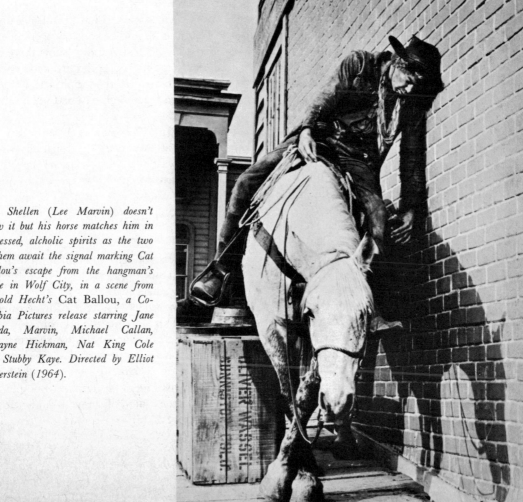

Kid Shellen (Lee Marvin) doesn't know it but his horse matches him in depressed, alcholic spirits as the two of them await the signal marking Cat Ballou's escape from the hangman's noose in Wolf City, in a scene from Harold Hecht's Cat Ballou, *a Columbia Pictures release starring Jane Fonda, Marvin, Michael Callan, Dwayne Hickman, Nat King Cole and Stubby Kaye. Directed by Elliot Silverstein (1964).*

In 1966 there was talk in the United States about the "decadence of the Western," exemplified by 1962's huge Cinerama monster *How the West Was Won* and the pitiful remake of *Stagecoach* (1966), directed by Gordon Douglas. But Western aficionados were able to point to several great films in reply, including *Duel at Diablo* (1966) by Ralph Nelson, previously noted for his extraordinarily moving *Requiem for a Heavyweight* and *Lilies of the Field.* The scenes of gory action in this movie, to a certain extent influenced by the Italian Western, were underlined by Neal Hefti's suspenseful musical score. The deadly staccato of drums carried tremendous force as human beings performed under genuine stress, not under conventional clichés. *Will Penny* (1968), directed by Tom Kries, presented Charlton Heston as a dried-up cowboy confronted by powerful passions. The movie became the subject of controversy, some defending the realistic portrayal of Montana cowboys and Charlton Heston's performance, others stressing the banalities in the man-woman-child relationship and the rather weak finale. The criticism is apt, but so is the praise. This "meditation on the old age of the cowboy," especially in the beginning, should be considered as an effort to depict the atmosphere of the West realistically and to show the misery of the life of a cowboy. Its message remains strong despite some stylistic shortcomings: *Will Penny* is another endeavor in the humanization of the hero, and as such belongs in the already rich vein exposed in the recent past by a number of astute directors.

Kries followed *Will Penny* in 1969 with *One Hundred Rifles,* a sardonic epic of Mexican revolutionaries using an American capitalist as "foreign exchange" between warring factions—vastly superior to *Villa Rides* (1968), by Buzz Kulik, in which the famed Mexican patriot was shown in typical Hollywood anti-historical perspective. Another action film of the period, which nevertheless shared in the movement towards cynical realism, was Andrew V. McLaglen's *Bandolero* (1968), with James Stewart as an aging former gunfighter trying to save his brother from the gallows. Veteran director Henry Hathaway joined the forces of demythologization with *Five Card Stud* (1968), in which Robert Mitchum gave a very successful performance as the cynical preacher-undertaker.

Finally there was *Hombre* (1967), by *Hud*'s talented team of director Martin Ritt and star Paul Newman. This was the uncompromising story of a cowboy raised by Apache Indians on the San Carlos Reservation who tries to make a life for himself in the society of the conquerors. Ritt and Newman conveyed all the heartbreaks of a person fighting against intolerance with a supreme indifference to his fate. The film was notable also for its crisp, realistic dialogue, as it might actually have sounded in the old West, and the efficient photography of James Wong Howe. American critic Rex Reed hoped that *Hombre* would start "a new trend towards humanizing the American Western", though it was not in itself a new trend, but rather an excellent example of the new vein of reality in the Western.

The humanization of the Western continued in 1969 and several remarkable films were produced. *Death of a Gunfighter,* directed by Allen Smithee (a pseudonym for the team of Robert Totten and Don Siegel), with a screenplay by Joseph Calvelli adapted from Lewis B. Pattern's novel, is the psychological study of a sheriff, played by the intelligent and sensitive actor Richard Widmark. The lawman is forced to kill a man in self-defense and then has to face the hostility of an entire town. The sordid secrets of the town's leading citizens are not explained clearly enough, but the film portrays the lonely fight of the old sheriff in a way that is reminiscent at times of *High Noon* in its depiction of the individual versus the hostile community. Lee Katzin's *Heaven with a Gun* used a religious theme to emphasize tolerance and coexistence, instead of individualism: a former outlaw who has renounced violence leads a "peace march" of women against feuding cattlemen and shepherds. A very interesting experimental Western was *Lonesome Cowboys,* written, photographed, directed, and produced by Andy Warhol. He had originally meant the film to be a Romeo and Juliet story set in a cowtown in the old West, but in the process of filming Warhol improvised more and more. The film is at times a disconcerting mixture of stark linear simplicity and far-out Pop Art imagery, but it does contain clever parodies of many classical Western situations.

Andy Warhol's Lonesome Cowboys.

Henry Hathaway contributed *True Grit*, a rather traditional plot enlivened by John Wayne's burlesque of the tough sheriff of horse operas in the Twenties, Thirties, and Forties. The John Wayne sheriff of 1969 lives with a Chinese and a cat; he exhibits vices in place of the virtues in films of thirty years earlier—he is sadistic instead of fair, too fond of the bottle, motivated by money instead of by a desire for justice. The unrealistic, romantic horse-opera sheriff has become something quite different.

History and Hollywood: Butch Cassidy's outlaw band in real life and in Butch Cassidy and the Sundance Kid (1969). (*Courtesy of Twentieth Century-Fox*)

One of the most successful films—and a complete revision of the classic Western—was George Roy Hill's *Butch Cassidy and the Sundance Kid*. It disposed of all the major myths of the genre: the two hero-bandits are not Robin Hoods representing the poor and oppressed, they have no moral code, nor do they suffer under a past trauma that allows the moviegoer to forgive them, as Italian critic Roberto Campari shrewdly notes. The adventures of the two boys assaulting trains are shown in such a matter-of-fact style that all the traditional values are thrown overboard, leaving only the deep humanity of the characters. The movie was made with magnificent cinematic technique: for example, the "bicycle dance" to the background of Burt Bacharach's song "Raindrops," a gem of freshness and simplicity; and the final scene of the two wounded friends coming out into the open and being "frozen" on the screen, as hundreds of South American soldiers shoot them down. Director Hill seems to have been influenced in this scene by Arthur Penn's *Bonnie and Clyde* (1967), with its final slow-motion massacre. *Butch Cassidy and the Sundance Kid* is undoubtedly one of the most articulate, original, and above all modern Westerns ever made, a work in which the humanization of the heroes is strikingly effective and which reveals how in most cases the "conquest of the West" was more of a game than a mission.

The year 1969 was also memorable for an extraordinary film by Sam Peckinpah, who had already won praise for *Ride the High Country* (1962) and *Major Dundee* (1965). *The Wild Bunch*, adapted from a novel by Walon Green, is the dramatic tale of a group of outlaws in 1913, when Pancho Villa was fighting in Mexico. Its violence echoes the influx of Italian Westerns and even surpasses *Bonnie and Clyde*. Critic William S. Pechter has asserted that in *Bonnie and Clyde* the use of slow motion in the final death scene has the effect of glamorizing not violence, but the film's title roles "as, in death, they attain their clichéd apotheosis as teenage rebels, struck down by that world they never made." In *The Wild Bunch,* on the other hand, the protraction of the moment of death impersonally forces the attention of the moviegoer to such a physical act as a "sensate experience in all its grotesque variations." It is, in sum, an appeal to the ambiguous feelings of the observer that accounts for the exceptional shock value of the film. To quote Pechter again: "We watch excitedly: the film remains morally neutral."

Ernest Borgnine (left) and William Holden. From the motion picture The Wild Bunch, *copyright © 1969 by Warner Bros.*

The Wild Bunch could be considered as an anti-Western, the total excoriation of the Western "Age of Innocence" represented in *Shane*. Between two massacres, one at the beginning, one at the end of the film, we witness the end of an era and the beginning of another. The change is symbolized by a phrase of the bandits' leader: "We gotta start thinking beyond our guns. Those days are closing fast." Mexico of 1913 was only two years away from the mechanized, mass-produced death of millions in the First World War. At the end of the movie's carnage, two survivors (saved only by the fact that they were not present at the carousel of death) go in search of an ambiguously stated "new cause," in which—it is hoped—children would never again torture a venomous scorpion or shoot men in the back. *The Wild Bunch*, despite its excessive violence, its rather conventional treatment of Mexicans, and the ambiguity of its conclusions, stands out as one of the finest Westerns ever made. The moral and sociological nihilism are very modern; they seem almost to be determined by the sorry state of the American image, with the nation divided and disillusioned. It is profoundly sad to observe that in the hopeless world that the film presents, the only note of hope is the selfless camaraderie of a wild bunch of outlaws.

Sam Peckinpah's gifts have been further exhibited in his following film, *The Ballad of Cable Hogue* (1970), an exuberant folk tale about a man (admirably played by Jason Robards) who made a pact with God and kept his obligation. In contrast to the "blood ballet" of *The Wild Bunch*, *The Ballad of Cable Hogue* is instead a delightful popular saga with excellent characterizations, rich in humor and tenderness, revealing the versatility of Peckinpah's talent.

The year 1970 also saw another fine treatment of the fading of the old West in *Monte Walsh*, directed by William A. Fraker (the cinematographer

Lee Marvin (left) and Jack Palance, cowboys with nothing to do, in Monte Walsh *(1970).*

of *Bullitt* and *Rosemary's Baby*) and based on the novel by Jack Shaefer. It was most effective describing the bleak expanses of the prairies and the men witnessing the end of an era: no more hunts, no more cattle drives, no more gunfights at the O.K. Corral. The West was settling down to barbed wire, telegraph, and Iron Horse, making the cowboys obsolescent. Monte Walsh (Lee Marvin), Chet Rollins (Jack Palance), and Shorty Austin (Mitch Ryan) face their new destinies in their own ways, in a twilight of the gods that climaxes in Monte's final realization of the total futility of trying to reverse a pitiless trend. Lee Marvin is an excellent anti-hero, grizzled and desperate; the dialogue is articulate; and in individual scenes the film reaches extremely high points.

There Was a Crooked Man (1970), on the other hand, is a rather discontinuous and self-defeating film. Joseph L. Mankiewicz's first Western, written by David Newman and Robert Benton of *Bonnie and Clyde* fame, is the tale of a charming outlaw (Kirk Douglas) and an honest, liberal-minded sheriff (Henry Fonda). The film was an attempt at satire, but it ended up in a morass of melodrama. However, it achieved some distinction in the orthodox Good-versus-Evil confrontation of Fonda and Douglas, although it certainly does not represent any notable contribution to a new interpretation of the Western.

A much more ambitious effort at parody is *Zachariah* (1971), directed by George Englund and presented as "the first electric Western." It is a very odd film, portraying homosexual love against a background of unending rocks and deserts. Young Zachariah is taught wisdom by an old man who hopes Zachariah will not become the fastest gun in the West. He is soon joined by Matthew, a gunslinger who has killed a character named Job Cain in a duel and is now spoiling for a fight. But in the final confrontation love prevails and the two boys literally ride into the sunset. The film is replete with symbolism, often in the Pop Art style of Andy Warhol's *Lonesome Cowboys*. It is an extremely interesting endeavor that proves that after seventy years the Western still has ample ground for experiment in practically every direction. With all its self-consciousness and its many defects, *Zachariah* nevertheless widened the horizons of the genre.

Along with experiments like *Zachariah,* we are still being saddled with conventional Western opuses, such as the inept *Rio Lobo* (1971). Veteran director Howard Hawks, the creator of some of the most distinguished Westerns in the past, put together a film using the most fundamental elements of the genre: the land and the guns, the conventional tragi-comic style, and the imperishable John Wayne. What makes this film so disappointing, despite Yakima Canutt's direction of the second unit, is that it is frozen in tradition and does not pretend to use any modern approach. We rather prefer films like *Valdez Is Coming* (1971), directed by Edwin Sharin, the stage director of *The Great White Hope*. He handles energetically the picturesque story of a Mexican lawman (played very convincingly by Burt Lancaster) who is brutalized by the white community because of his efforts on behalf of an innocent black man killed as a murder suspect. This tale of intolerance and racial hostility was brought to the screen in extremely vivid and honest terms, a most auspicious debut for Edwin Sharin, who joins the ranks of all those who have decided to use the medium of the Western to dramatize a message of peace and humanity.

Burt Lancaster as a Mexican-American constable, tied to a cross of mesquite poles to teach him "his place." From Valdez Is Coming (1971). © 1971 *by Norlan Productions, Inc. and Iris Steiner Productions, Inc. All rights reserved.*

Tolerance

The Mexicans are not the only beneficiaries of the contemporary Western's new emphasis on the brotherhood of man. The American Indian is finally being taken out of his stereotyped villainous role, and the historical realities of the Indian in the old West are being re-examined. Possibly the first film to be made in this new spirit was John Ford's splendid *Cheyenne Autumn* (1964), a lyrical poem about the exodus of a noble tribe, a hymn of love and esteem for a cruelly persecuted people. Four years later, in *Custer of the West* (1968), the veteran director Robert Siodmak tried to draw a parallel between the inhuman killer of Cheyennes and Nazism; young Robert Mulligan's *The Stalking Moon*, however, still failed to treat its Indians as human beings, showing a mawkish racial hostility. The Indian protagonist, trying to persuade a white woman to come back to him with their son, is portrayed as a beast to be shot by the first white man who comes along, in order to guarantee the "escape" of his two "victims."

Tell Them Willie Boy Is Here (1969) and *A Man Called Horse* (1970) were also disappointing in their portrayals of the Indian, updated but still intrinsically similar to the old Western stereotypes. A more distinctive film was Ralph Nelson's *Soldier Blue,* adapted from a novel by Theodore V. Olsen describing the massacre of Sand Creek on November 29, 1864. In retaliation for an attack on a stagecoach, the soldiers of the U. S. Cavalry, led by Colonel Chivington, massacred about 500 Cheyenne men, women, and children. With this episode Nelson wanted to depict on the screen the real story of the relationship between the whites and the Indians. Present-day events have made many Americans re-examine their past and discover that they, not the Indians, were the real villains of the West. As

Cavalry lining up in John Ford's motion picture Cheyenne Autumn, *copyright © 1965 by Warner Bros.*

director Nelson is quoted in the catalogue of the "International Cinema Meetings," Sorrento, Italy, in September, 1970: "Our official position is that we are in Vietnam to honor a commitment. But let us not forget that we have signed 400 treaties with the Indians, violating them all, one after the other."

Soldier Blue is the story of Honus Gant, a "blue soldier" (as the members of the U. S. Cavalry were then called), and a white woman, kidnapped by the Cheyenne, married to a chief, and later given back to the whites. They both witness the massacre of Sand Creek. Honus refuses to take part in it, is chained to a wagon, and will face a court-martial, while the woman, horrified by the carnage, repudiates her people and decides to share the squalid destiny of the surviving Cheyenne.

The massacre is the climax of the picture and its *raison d'être*. In its brutality and callous violence the film was clearly influenced, as was *The Wild Bunch,* by the Italian school. It must be considered one of the most impressive efforts towards a true historical perspective on the Western past. It is unfortunate, however, that Nelson did not complete his excellent essay on historical truth with a deeper, more realistic portrayal of the Indians themselves as well as the events in which they were involved.

This re-evaluation in depth was left to be done by Arthur Penn in his *Little Big Man* (1970), the best Western of the decade, based on the novel by Thomas Berger and adapted by Calder Willingham. The adventures of Jack Crabb, a one-hundred-twenty-year-old man who claims to be the sole white survivor of Custer's Last Stand, are an extraordinary testament to the American Dream of the West. At first, the witness is a ten-year-old boy, raised by the Cheyenne after his pioneer parents are killed by another Indian tribe. He is rescued by the whites five years later and forced into a multitude of new roles, including two marriages, bankruptcy, patent-medicine selling, and tar and feathers as a result, alcoholism, risking death at the hands of both whites and Indians, and finally facing Custer in his last hour against the braves of Red Cloud and Crazy Horse. It is a magnificent fresco, moving, funny, and bitter. As in *Soldier Blue,* one of the finest sequences in this film is also a massacre: the massacre of the Cheyennes on the Washita River in Oklahoma on November 27, 1868, by seven hundred men of the U. S. Cavalry led by George Armstrong Custer, then a colonel. In that horrible event, according to Custer's biographer Frederick van de Water, all one hundred fifty-three Cheyenne males were killed, and the fury of the whites consumed women and children as well—only fifty-three of them were taken prisoners to Fort Hays after the carnage. Moreover, upon specific orders from Custer, even the eight hundred seventy-five Indian ponies were shot down. Part of the power of Penn's story comes, of course, because his description of past horrors reminds us of present ones; a century after the Washita River massacre, one hundred forty-nine Vietnamese women and children were slaughtered at My Lai, in South Vietnam, by U. S. forces led by Lieutenant William Calley.

Dustin Hoffman in Little Big Man *(1970)*.

The real force in this film is not the star, Dustin Hoffman, although he is excellent. Rather it is Dan George, a Canadian Indian playing the Cheyenne chief Old Lodge Skins, who is the center of attention, embodying the dignity, pride, and resilience of a race that is still waiting for the redressing of uncounted wrongs. Penn uses the film to express his personal philosophy with vigor, saving his most passionate feeling for describing past horrors reminiscent of present ones. His excoriation of George Armstrong Custer is one of the most pitiless indictments of a pompous fool ever witnessed on the screen.

Several critics found *Little Big Man* too much a mixture of tragedy and comedy, a jarring juxtaposition of passion and amusing superficiality. It must be realized that Penn was obliged to telescope a large number of multifaceted historical events into 157 minutes, quite a feat considering that he did not spare any of the classical myths of the Western in the sweep of his iconoclastic vision. The deaths of Wild Bill Hickok and General Custer, for example, show how far the Western has progressed since the days of *The Plainsman* and *They Died with Their Boots On:* from romanticism to deliberate and didactic realism. *Little Big Man* is a milestone in the history of the Western, beyond any doubt the most advanced document in the process of re-evaluating its sacred myths, a work of art in the cause of peace and understanding.

Two other notable films have also dealt with the tragedy of the Indian in very different ways. *The Long Walk* (1970) by Phillip Greene is a documentary rather than an adventure story like *Little Big Man.* This excellent sixty-minute work describes the devastation of the Navajo nation between 1864 and 1865, two years in which they were subjected to every possible brutality by the whites in the notorious "concentration camp" of Bosque Redondo. A series of interviews with elder tribesmen provides detailed insight into the history and traditions of the Navajo and the current efforts to improve the lot of the descendants of these proud people, including the activity at the Indian-run Rough Rock School. It is a little gem, a sincere appeal for understanding the complex problems of the Indian within the white man's society, and it must not be missed in any honest evaluation of the Indian past and present.

Carol Reed's *Flap* (1970) is quite a different treatment of the modern Indians' plight, on both the tragic and the comic level. Clair Huffaker's excellent adaptation of his novel *Nobody Loves a Drunken Indian* is the story of Flapping Eagle, an Indian who fights desperately against the intolerance and indifference of the whites, finally paying for the awakening of his fellow citizens with his life. Anthony Quinn, himself of Mexican Indian descent, gives a magnificent portrayal of a decent tribesman who believes

Kirk Douglas (left) and Johnny Cash pose for a photographer before their gun battle in A Gunfight *(1971). Copyright © 1970 by Harvest and Thoroughbred Productions. All rights reserved.*

in human dignity and who wishes to find a "place in the sun" for his unhappy, dejected, castaway people. The film was shot in New Mexico; among the most splendid views are those of the plains and the city of Acoma, the oldest continuously inhabited town in the United States, in existence long before Columbus' discovery of the New World. Against this background *Flap* presents the contemporary second-class status of the Indian, in moving and often funny terms. The combination of Huffaker's taut and meaty story and Sir Carol Reed's sympathetic, profoundly human direction makes a powerful film.

The Indians have even financed their first film, very aptly a Western, and an interesting one at that. But *A Gunfight* (1971), directed by Lamont Johnson and backed by funds of the Jicarilla Apache Tribe, is surprisingly a Western without Indians; it concerns itself with a confrontation between Kirk Douglas and famed folk singer and balladeer Johnny Cash, in the respective roles of a once-famous Dodge City gunman who works now in a bar, attracting customers with tales of the old West, and a killer who failed to strike gold and is drifting along from town to town. The two protagonists organize a duel in an arena, for "good money," and carry their obligations to the last: one of them dies; the other, after having collected his share of the gates, rides out. It is an excellent "sleeper," a film in the class of *Lonely Are the Brave* and *Ride the High Country*.

Billy Jack (1971), directed by T. C. Frank, is an important Western in which the anti-war, anti-drug, anti-Establishment themes are expressed through the uncompromising fight carried on by a half-breed Indian, a Vietnam veteran, who leads his tribe to a decent existence in a white world, achieving peace by means of sacrifice. Young Tom Laughlin in the title role gives a lesson in humanity and highly articulate style to so many professional actors, without any trace of rhetorical overtones. The pioneer spirit, on the other hand, is entirely lost in the pretentious and boring *Man in the Wilderness* (1971), directed by Richard Sarafian, which starts with a jewel-like sequence showing a fur trapper (Richard Harris) being mauled by a grizzly and then slides down pitilessly towards limbo, while *Bless the Beasts and the Children* (1971) by Stanley Kramer picks up from Richard Brooks' *The Last Hunt* (1956) the theme of the American buffalo, through the crusade carried on by six rich misfit kids who try to avoid the annihilation of some "superfluous" quadrupeds in a corral. The message is clear: by saving the buffaloes, the children will save themselves; but the humanitarian punch which has characterized so many of Kramer's films up to now fails to materialize this time, although the photographic sequences of the roaming former King of the Plains are indeed remarkable.

In Bless the Beasts and Children (*1971*), *six campers crawl atop the fence as they prepare to free the captive buffalo. From left to right,* Teft (*Bill Mumy*), *Goodenow* (*Darel Glaser*), *Shecher* (*Miles Chapin*), *Lally 1* (*Bob Kramer*) *Cotton* (*Barry Robins*), *Lally 2* (*Marc Vahanian*).

A raw and glowing glimpse of a mining town beginning to emerge in the Northwest is the subject of an excellent film, *McCabe and Mrs. Miller* (1971), directed with vigor by Robert Altman. In a rather effective balance between comedy and satire, the director portrays the adventures of an ambitious promoter who attempts to bring "civilization" to the wilderness with a casino and a three-bed bordello, together with a very practical madam, and loses his free enterprise in a final duel with three hired gunmen. Photographed in Canada, the film offers some astonishingly beautiful sequences in which rain, sleet, snow, and wind counterpoint the natural adversities facing men and women of the old West, showing their bare instincts to the bone. Although weighted at times with metaphysical riddles, it represents a truly original and creative endeavor.

A highly personalized film, full of genuine conviction, is *The Last Movie* (1971), directed by Dennis Hopper in Peru. In it, the co-creator of *Easy Rider* bitterly denounces in satirical terms the American character obsessed by materialism and urged by the spirit of domination. It is a parable on the annihilation of innocence, in the violent clash between the greedy American culture and the primitive, equally violent Peruvian one. In the complexity of its many levels—Hopper making a film about making a film imitation of a Hollywood film, with him finally making faces at his own camera—*The Last Movie* stands out as a genial Western in American Gothic, the unique expression of Hopper's *film d'auteur*. *The Last Movie*, together with Alexandro Jodorowsky's *El Topo* (1971), the gory and symbolistic parody of Society in Western key, represent two strikingly effective exercises in intellectualism.

Tomas Milian (robed), Dennis Hopper (holding bottle), and a procession of Peruvian villagers acting out a Hollywood Western in The Last Movie (*1971*).

On the contrary, Peter Fonda's *The Hired Hand* (1971), in which he is the director and the star, represents undoubtedly a charming fable, an American pastoral lovingly dedicated to the open spaces, a sincere belief in the pristine purity of the old West and its denizens. The symbiosis between Man and Nature, counterpointed by the appealing music by Bruce Langhorne, enhances the value of the simple and human story of Collings, back home after seven years of wanderings, who must say farewell again to his wife and daughter in order to save a companion and meet his ultimate destiny. Thus, while Hopper stabs iconoclastically at everything, Fonda appeals to a return to the "good old times" as they should have been and must now be. A love for the old West is also reflected by Blake Edwards in *Wild Rovers* (1971), a story of the idealized comradeship of two men (Ryan O'Neal and William Holden) who rob a bank of $36.00 and travel towards Mexico, hoping to find a paradise lost but doomed instead in the majestic Monument Valley; for all its unevenness at times, this Western nonetheless carries the seeds of a fertile idea, that of a friendship enduring all evils, which was so frequent in the Wild West. Friendship and bank robbery are also the theme of *The Great Northfield, Minnesota, Raid* (1971), the first major feature directed by Philip Kaufman, who deliberately mixes symbolic imagery, crisp dialogue, and corny situations to invent a new style of storytelling in which fantasy and sardonic realism march hand in hand, with surprisingly valid results.

Severn Darden (left), Rita Rogers, and Peter Fonda in The Hired Hand (*1971*).

The theme of the rodeo has been lately emerging with great strength. *Junior Bonner* (1971), an elegiac opus by Sam Peckinpah, concocted in a definitely comic tone, describing with tongue-in-cheek irony the adventures of Robert Preston, Steve McQueen, and the admirable Ida Lupino (back to the screen after seventeen years), is without any doubt a definite contribution to the "motel cowboys." *J. W. Coop* (1972), written, directed, and produced by Cliff Robertson (who also stars in it), is the classic study of ten months in the life of a lonely rodeo circuit rider, a man who can make up to sixty thousand dollars a year, plus another sixty thousand for endorsing commercial products, unless a bad fall consigns him to a crippling physical and psychic obscurity overnight. A beautiful dialogue provides an effective track on which the rustic small-town Texas world slides firmly with all its foibles. *The Honkers* (1972), directed by Steve Ihnatz, is a sluggish description of three days in the life of another rodeo circuit rider (played by James Coburn). Oversentimental and rather self-centered (just like the rider himself), the film falls flat despite some skillful use of authentic rodeo characters.

Black Rodeo (1972), directed, edited, and produced by Jeff Kanew, a documentary on the black rodeo riders, is a rousing Western show implemented by apt comments by actor Woody Strode. It contains some amusing sequences rich in spontaneity, such as the one in which Muhammad Ali mingles with the rodeo denizens and rides a Brahma bull. It is indeed one of the very first examples of black presence in the Western, like the one, in the feature-film field, offered by *Man and Boy* (1972), directed by E. W. Swackhamer, describing the odyssey of a black man in the frontier West. Black actor Bill Cosby in the role of Caleb Revers, an ex-Union-soldier-turned-farmer, provides a very solid characterization of a black who adapts himself to a white society. In the recent emergence of black cinema, the role of the Negro in the Western Saga is still to be explored and fully projected to the screen. There is no doubt that, with the changing times, even this important gap will be filled when black directors, producers, and actors finally offer their contribution to the history of the old West, in which the Negro played a considerable role but which up to now has been ignored by Hollywood and the independents. The first black Westerns, such as *The Legend of Nigger Charley* (1971) and *Soul Soldiers* (1971), have been timid; but there is no doubt that the black director, writer, and producer will soon be able to give us their own *Little Big Man.*

In 1972, John Wayne appeared in another of his traditional "good and right" films, *The Cowboys*, directed by Mark Rydell; it is a glib tale of the recruitment of eleven young boys to get 1200 head of cattle from a ranch to a place 400 miles away, in a pyrotechnic display of "virtuosity" (as

Gary Grimes as Ben Mockridge, who completes his initiation into manhood by drawing his gun, in the climax of The Culpepper Cattle Co. (*1972*). (*Courtesy of Twentieth Century-Fox*)

blessed by the Establishment and the Parent-Teacher Association). The same year saw some deep-rooted anti-conformists, such as Dick Richards, whose *Culpepper Cattle Co.* is an extremely handsome Western, realistic and symbolic at the same time, describing the adventures of a young cook-helper learning the grim facts of life and, in a laconic, bloody finale, watching practically everybody belonging to his "old gang" get killed. It is a simple and devastating verdict on the "growing up" of a young fellow in the old West, and a film that makes one think about the old times without being swayed by subliminal, modern trends. To this same category belong *When Legends Die* (1972), directed by Stuart Millar and portraying the education of a fourteen-year-old orphaned Indian boy as a bronco rider, imparted by a tough, grizzled old hustler (played admirably by Richard Widmark); *Bad Company* (1972), Robert Benton's first film, devoted to adventures of an Ohio country boy who with the blessings of his parents eludes the draft in the War Between the States and travels towards Virginia City to make his fortune; *Hannie Caulder* (1972), a standard Western revenge drama directed by Burt Kennedy in which the eternal themes of friendship and the death of the young express the value of unexpected twists; and, finally, Robert Aldrich's *Ulzana's Raid* (1972), a first-rate Western that employs every cliché but with such a display of violence that in the long run the observer is bound to notice a self-parody injected for purely iconoclastic reasons. Aldrich does not leave room for sentiment, and the pursuit of a band of blood-thirsty Apaches by Burt Lancaster and Bruce Davison is in fact a sardonic comment on the time-honored cliché of crime and retribution which is literally exploded by the director in a series of savage sequences, thus confirming his absolute anti-conformism against the tenets of the classical Western.

Among the young screenwriters of value, recently emerging to the fore, who have dealt creatively with the Western theme is John Milius. His *Saga of Jeremiah Johnson* (1972), with Robert Redford, is a notable contribution to the Wild West myth. But in *The Life and Times of Judge Roy Bean* (1972),

Paul Newman as Judge Roy Bean, the Southwest's legendary "hanging judge" (*1972*).

A family portrait, on the occasion of a hanging, from The Life and Times of Judge Roy Bean (*1972*).

he achieves that rare balance between comedy and sardonic comment on the foibles of an era, by combining the story of an historical character, Judge Roy Bean, a self-appointed magistrate who hanged dozens of people, bringing the law west of the Pecos in Texas with a symbolic struggle carried on by the individual against the Establishment. Sporting the same derby hat that he wore in *Butch Cassidy and the Sundance Kid,* Paul Newman, under the taut direction of John Huston, provides the unforgettable portrayal of a fast-shooting and fast-talking denizen of the West who makes a business out of law and order and worships Miss Lily Langtry, an actress whom he will never meet in person (played by Ava Gardner).

Using the ironic text of Milius, Huston departs from the classical theme of racial prejudice narrated in *The Unforgiven* (1959), keeping in *The Life and Times of Judge Roy Bean* a fast tempo, anchored to fantasy and reality, which culminates in the spectacular destruction of the Texas town, wanting to remind us of an atomic holocaust. It is a jewel of a film, indeed, enhanced by the marvelous photography of Richard Moore, who has aptly used the savage nature around Tucson, Arizona, with remarkable results.

In the vein of the new comedy Western, furthermore, new incoming efforts are to be noted, such as those of Mel Brooks, who will direct *Black Bart,* the story of a black man who suddenly becomes sheriff in a Western town in the 1870s, a sweeping opus promising to be one of the most interesting undertakings in 1973. John Wayne continues to star in Westerns with methodical regularity, and will appear in another Western, *Wednesday Morning,* recruiting this time the services of Jackie Coogan ("The Kid") in the role of the town drunk.

Conclusion

Old aficionados of the Western may look upon the iconoclastic modernization of the genre with suspicion, but it is only the challenge of new ideas that save it from stagnation and eventual decline. It was about time that the Western took on a more human approach, since the genre has always been an attempt to explain human history—the urge to conquer the frontier and to found a new society. A few years ago the Western was still a sterile, detached document by a bygone era. Now it has become a tool for interpretation of that era in terms that we can understand, and hopefully a weapon against repetition in the future of the evils of the frontier mentality, its violence and intolerance. This is why the Western is now more "relevant" than ever. Spurred by the cinema's re-creation, past errors and injustices may be corrected and possibly even kept from being repeated.

There will always be an audience for the Western, for the Western represents romantic adventure and idealism, achievement, optimism for the future, justice, individualism, the beauty of the land, and the courage and independence of the individuals who won the land. It is in the Western that the American discovers himself again as one of the descendants of a people who knew how to work hard, who knew how to fight, who were prepared to die. This is all in contrast to the padded world in which the American so often finds himself today; the land is a little bit further away, and the day of the horse has passed.

The West stands out above all this, pristine and pure, strong and brave. How often we may let our thoughts drift to the Great Outdoors, wishing that we were once more there! And it is the peculiar function of the Western to provide the vehicle for our dreams, since in the general outline we have settled on our realities. Under such circumstances, there will surely always be a public to support the Western, and viewing our contemporary life, it is a public likely to increase rather than decrease with the passing of years.

Despite its indigenous American scenes, plots and characters, the Western is nevertheless a universal appeal to the universal imagination. It is the only aspect of the American cinema that is readily understood in Rome, Moscow, Tokyo, Bangkok, Sydney, Cairo, and Buenos Aires. It is an expression of the hopes and dreams of every man, as he struggles to assert his fundamental right to pursue peace and happiness, free from crooks on both sides of the law, and longing to look upon his fellow men as brothers. Someday, perhaps, that world will come.

The enduring beauty of the West, free of restrictions and devoid of billboard advertising, will continue to appeal to a public that is increasingly hemmed in by the tensions and curtailments of modern living.

INDEX

395